PRENTICE HALL LITERATURE

Reader's COMPANION

Copper Level

Upper Saddle River, New Jersey
Boston, Massachusetts

ISBN 0-13-180280-1
20 V011 11

Acknowledgments

Grateful acknowledgment is made to the following for copyrighted material:

Airmont Publishing Company, Inc.
"Water" from *The Story Of My Life* by Helen Keller. Copyright © 1965 by Airmont Publishing Company, Inc.

Ricardo E. Alegría
"The Three Wishes" from *The Three Wishes: A Collection Of Puerto Rican Folktales,* selected and adapted by Ricardo E. Alegria, translated by Elizabeth Culbert. Reprinted by permission.

Archaeology Magazine
"Human Footprints at Chauvet Cave," by Spencer P. M. Harrington, Volume 52, Number 5, p. 18, 1999. Reprinted with permission of *Archaeology Magazine*, Vol. 52, No. 5 (Copyright the Archaeological Institute of America, 1999).

Susan Bergholz Literary Services
"Names/Nombres," by Julia Alvarez. Copyright © 1985 by Julia Alvarez. First published in *Nuestro,* March, 1985. All rights reserved. "Eleven" from *Woman Hollering Creek* by Sandra Cisneros. Copyright © 1991 by Sandra Cisneros.

Georges Borchardt, Inc., for the Estate of John Gardner
"Dragon, Dragon" from *Dragon, Dragon And Other Tales* by John Gardner. Copyright © 1975 by Boskydell Artists Ltd.

Brandt & Hochman Literary Agents, Inc.
"Lob's Girl," from *A Whisper In The Night* by Joan Aiken, copyright © 1984 by Joan Aiken.

Boy Scouts of America
"Twist and Shout" by K. Wayne Wincey, from *Boys Life*, August 1999. Published by Boy Scouts of America.

Clarion Books, A division of Houghton Mifflin Company
"A Backwoods Boy" from *Lincoln: A Photobiography*. Copyright © 1987 by Russell Freedman. All rights reserved.

Cleveland.com
"An Astronaut's Answers" by John Glenn, from *Snappy*, published online on Cleveland Live. Copyright © 1998 by Cleveland Live. Reprint permission given by Cleveland.com, formerly Cleveland Live. All rights reserved.

Don Congdon Associates, Inc.
"The Sound of Summer Running" by Ray Bradbury. Published in *The Saturday Evening Post*, 2/18/56. Copyright © 1956 by the Curtis Publishing Co., renewed 1984 by Ray Bradbury. "Hard As Nails" from *The Good Times* by Russell Baker. Copyright © 1989 by Russell Baker. From *Bud, Not Buddy* by Christopher Paul Curtis. Copyright © 1999 by Christopher Paul Curtis. All rights reserved.

The Dallas Morning News
From "Chinese Immigrants Remember Detention at Angel Island" by Esther Wu, from *The Dallas Morning News*, May 19, 2000.

Dell Publishing, A division of Random House, Inc.
"Jeremiah's Song" by Walter Dean Myers, copyright © 1987 by Walter Dean Myers, from *Visions* by Doanld R. Gallo, Editor.

Doubleday, A division of Random House, Inc.
"The Fun They Had" from *Earth Is Room Enough* by Isaac Asimov, copyright © 1957 by Isaac Asimov.

The Field Museum
"Life and Times of Sue," from www.fieldmuseum.org. Copyright © 1999 by The Field Museum.

Samuel French, Inc.
The Phantom Tollbooth: A Children's Play In Two Acts by Susan Nanus and Norton Juster. Copyright © 1977 by Susan Nanus and Norton Juster. All rights reserved. CAUTION: Professionals and amateurs are hereby warned that "THE PHANTOM TOLLBOOTH," being fully protected under the copyright laws of the United States of America, the British Commonwealth countries, including Canada, and the other countries of the Copyright Union, is subject to royalty. All rights, including professional, amateur, motion picture, recitation, lecturing, public reading, radio, television and cable broadcasting, and the rights of translation into foreign languages, are strictly reserved. In its present form the play is dedicated to the reading public only. The amateur live performance rights are controlled exclusively by Samuel French, Inc. Any inquiry regarding the availability of performance rights, or the purchase of individual copies of the authorized acting edition, must be directed to Samuel French, Inc., 45 West 25th Street, NY, NY 10010 with other locations in Hollywood and Toronto, Canada.

(Acknowledgments continue on page 336)

Contents

Part 1: Selections With Interactive Support and Practice

Unit 6: Short Stories

Unit 7: Nonfiction

Unit 8: Drama

Unit 9: Poetry

Unit 10: The Oral Tradition

Part 2: Reading Informational Materials 263

Part 1

Selections With Interactive Reading Support and Practice

Part 1 is a companion for *Prentice Hall Literature: Timeless Voices, Timeless Themes.* It will guide and support you as you interact with the literature from *Prentice Hall Literature: Timeless Voices, Timeless Themes.*

- Start by looking at the **Prepare to Read** pages for the literature selection in *Prentice Hall Literature: Timeless Voices, Timeless Themes.*
- Review the **Literary Analysis** and **Reading Strategy** skills taught on those **Prepare to Read** pages. You will apply those skills as you use the *Reader's Companion.*
- Look at the art for the selection in *Prentice Hall Literature: Timeless Voices, Timeless Themes.*
- Now go to the **Preview** page in the *Reader's Companion.* Use the written and visual summaries of the selection to direct your reading.
- Then read the selection in the *Reader's Companion.*
- Respond to all the questions as you read. Write in the *Reader's Companion*—really! Circle things that interest you—underline things that puzzle you. Number ideas or events to help you keep track of them. Look for the **Mark the Text** logo for special help with active reading.
- Use the **Reader's Response** and **Thinking About the Skill** questions at the end of each selection to relate your reading to your own life.

Interacting With the Text

As you read, use the information and notes to guide you in interacting with the selection. The examples on these pages show you how to use the notes as a companion when you read. They will guide you in applying reading and literary skills and in thinking about the selection. When you read other texts, you can practice the thinking skills and strategies found here.

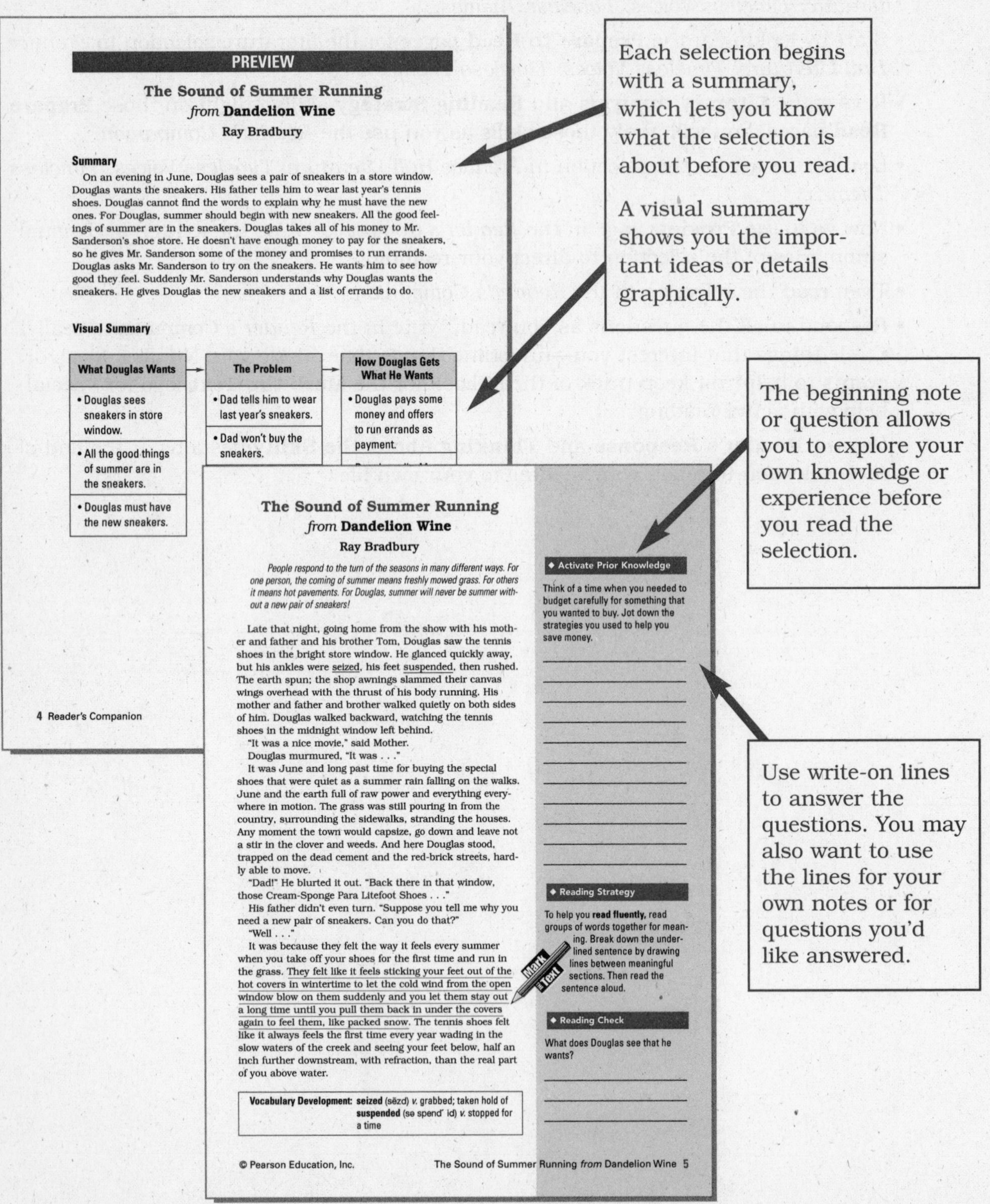

PREVIEW

The Sound of Summer Running
from **Dandelion Wine**
Ray Bradbury

Summary

On an evening in June, Douglas sees a pair of sneakers in a store window. Douglas wants the sneakers. His father tells him to wear last year's tennis shoes. Douglas cannot find the words to explain why he must have the new ones. For Douglas, summer should begin with new sneakers. All the good feelings of summer are in the sneakers. Douglas takes all of his money to Mr. Sanderson's shoe store. He doesn't have enough money to pay for the sneakers, so he gives Mr. Sanderson some of the money and promises to run errands. Douglas asks Mr. Sanderson to try on the sneakers. He wants him to see how good they feel. Suddenly Mr. Sanderson understands why Douglas wants the sneakers. He gives Douglas the new sneakers and a list of errands to do.

Visual Summary

What Douglas Wants	The Problem	How Douglas Gets What He Wants
• Douglas sees sneakers in store window.	• Dad tells him to wear last year's sneakers.	• Douglas pays some money and offers to run errands as payment.
• All the good things of summer are in the sneakers.	• Dad won't buy the sneakers.	
• Douglas must have the new sneakers.		

4 Reader's Companion

The Sound of Summer Running
from **Dandelion Wine**
Ray Bradbury

People respond to the turn of the seasons in many different ways. For one person, the coming of summer means freshly mowed grass. For others it means hot pavements. For Douglas, summer will never be summer without a new pair of sneakers!

Late that night, going home from the show with his mother and father and his brother Tom, Douglas saw the tennis shoes in the bright store window. He glanced quickly away, but his ankles were seized, his feet suspended, then rushed. The earth spun; the shop awnings slammed their canvas wings overhead with the thrust of his body running. His mother and father and brother walked quietly on both sides of him. Douglas walked backward, watching the tennis shoes in the midnight window left behind.

"It was a nice movie," said Mother.

Douglas murmured, "It was . . ."

It was June and long past time for buying the special shoes that were quiet as a summer rain falling on the walks. June and the earth full of raw power and everything everywhere in motion. The grass was still pouring in from the country, surrounding the sidewalks, stranding the houses. Any moment the town would capsize, go down and leave not a stir in the clover and weeds. And here Douglas stood, trapped on the dead cement and the red-brick streets, hardly able to move.

"Dad!" He blurted it out. "Back there in that window, those Cream-Sponge Para Litefoot Shoes . . ."

His father didn't even turn. "Suppose you tell me why you need a new pair of sneakers. Can you do that?"

"Well . . ."

It was because they felt the way it feels every summer when you take off your shoes for the first time and run in the grass. They felt like it feels sticking your feet out of the hot covers in wintertime to let the cold wind from the open window blow on them suddenly and you let them stay out a long time until you pull them back in under the covers again to feel them, like packed snow. The tennis shoes felt like it always feels the first time every year wading in the slow waters of the creek and seeing your feet below, half an inch further downstream, with refraction, than the real part of you above water.

Vocabulary Development: **seized** (sēzd) *v.* grabbed; taken hold of
suspended (sə spend´ id) *v.* stopped for a time

◆ Activate Prior Knowledge

Think of a time when you needed to budget carefully for something that you wanted to buy. Jot down the strategies you used to help you save money.

◆ Reading Strategy

To help you **read fluently,** read groups of words together for meaning. Break down the underlined sentence by drawing lines between meaningful sections. Then read the sentence aloud.

Mark the Text

◆ Reading Check

What does Douglas see that he wants?

© Pearson Education, Inc. The Sound of Summer Running *from* Dandelion Wine 5

Each selection begins with a summary, which lets you know what the selection is about before you read.

A visual summary shows you the important ideas or details graphically.

The beginning note or question allows you to explore your own knowledge or experience before you read the selection.

Use write-on lines to answer the questions. You may also want to use the lines for your own notes or for questions you'd like answered.

I'd be doing the things you'd rather not bother with? You stay in the nice cool store while I'm jumping all around town! But it's not me really, it's the shoes. They're going like mad down alleys, cutting corners, and back! There they go!"

Mr. Sanderson stood amazed with the rush of words. When the words got going the flow carried him; he began to sink deep in the shoes, to flex his toes, limber his arches, test his ankles. He rocked softly, secretly, back and forth in a small breeze from the open door. The tennis shoes silently hushed themselves deep in the carpet, sank as in a jungle grass, in loam and resilient clay. He gave one solemn bounce of his heels in the yeasty dough, in the yielding and welcoming earth. Emotions hurried over his face as if many colored lights had been switched on and off. His mouth hung slightly open. Slowly he gentled and rocked himself to a halt, and the boy's voice faded and they stood there looking at each other in a tremendous and natural silence.

A few people drifted by on the sidewalk outside, in the hot sun.

Still the man and boy stood there, the boy glowing, the man with revelation in his face.

"Boy," said the old man at last, "in five years, how would you like a job selling shoes in this emporium?"

"Gosh, thanks, Mr. Sanderson, but I don't know what I'm going to be yet."

"Anything you want to be, son," said the old man, "you'll be. No one will ever stop you."

The old man walked lightly across the store to the wall of ten thousand boxes, came back with some shoes for the boy, and wrote up a list on some paper while the boy was lacing the shoes on his feet and then standing there, waiting.

The old man held out his list. "A dozen things you got to do for me this afternoon. Finish them, we're even Stephen, and you're fired."

"Thanks, Mr. Sanderson!" Douglas bounded away.

"Stop!" cried the old man.

Douglas pulled up and turned.

Mr. Sanderson leaned forward. "How do they *feel*?"

The boy looked down at his feet deep in the rivers, in the fields of wheat, in the wind that already was rushing him out of the town. He looked up at the old man, his eyes burning, his mouth moving, but no sound came out.

"Antelopes?" said the old man, looking from the boy's face to his shoes. "Gazelles?"

The boy thought about it, hesitated, and nodded a quick

Vocabulary Development: **limber** (lim′ bər) *v.* loosen up (a muscle or limb); make easy to bend
revelation (rev′ ə lā′ shən) *n.* sudden rush of understanding

 The Sound of Summer Running *fro*

◆ **Literary Analysis**

Circle words in the bracketed text that show how Mr. Sanderson feels. What do you think Mr. Sanderson's feelings are as he bounces in the sneakers?

Mark the Text

◆ **Stop to Reflect**

Read the underlined sentence aloud. Why is this an important moment in the story?

◆ **Reading**

How does D Sanderson?

When you see this symbol, you should underline, circle, or mark the text as indicated.

nod. Almost immediately he vanished. He just spun about with a whisper and went off. The door stood empty. The sound of the tennis shoes faded in the jungle heat.

Mr. Sanderson stood in the sun-blazed door, listening. From a long time ago, when he dreamed as a boy, he remembered the sound. Beautiful creatures leaping under the sky, gone through brush, under trees, away, and only the soft echo their running left behind.

"Antelopes," said Mr. Sanderson. "Gazelles."

He bent to pick up the boy's abandoned winter shoes, heavy with forgotten rains and long-melted snows. Moving out of the blazing sun, walking softly, lightly, slowly, he headed back toward civilization. . . .

◆ **Reading Strategy**

Circle the words in the bracketed paragraph that describe what Mr. Sanderson is feeling. Then, read the paragraph aloud, with expression.

Mark the Text

Reader's Response: Do you think that most store owners would respond to Douglas's request in the way that Mr. Sanderson did? Why or why not?

Thinking About the Skill: How did using punctuation as a guide help you read aloud more fluently?

10 Reader's Companion

After reading, you can write your thoughts and reactions to the selection.

You can also comment on how certain skills and strategies were helpful to you. Thinking about a skill will help you apply it to other reading situations.

PREVIEW

The Sound of Summer Running
from Dandelion Wine
Ray Bradbury

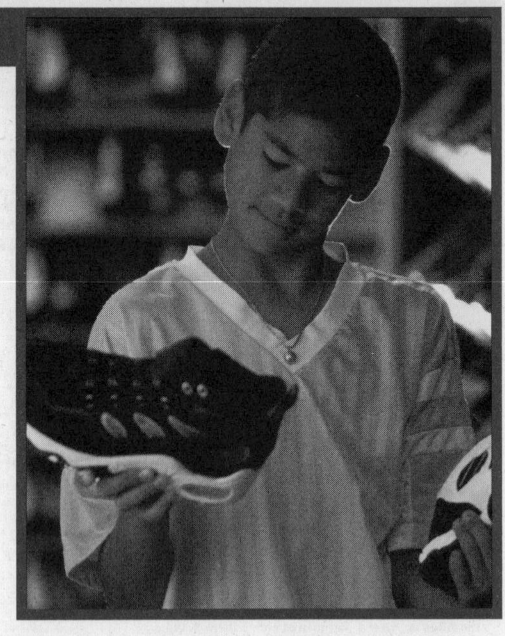

Summary

On an evening in June, Douglas sees a pair of sneakers in a store window. Douglas wants the sneakers. His father tells him to wear last year's tennis shoes. Douglas cannot find the words to explain why he must have the new ones. For Douglas, summer should begin with new sneakers. All the good feelings of summer are in the sneakers. Douglas takes all of his money to Mr. Sanderson's shoe store. He doesn't have enough money to pay for the sneakers, so he gives Mr. Sanderson some of the money and promises to run errands. Douglas asks Mr. Sanderson to try on the sneakers. He wants him to see how good they feel. Suddenly Mr. Sanderson understands why Douglas wants the sneakers. He gives Douglas the new sneakers and a list of errands to do.

Visual Summary

What Douglas Wants	The Problem	How Douglas Gets What He Wants
• Douglas sees sneakers in a store window.	• Dad tells him to wear last year's sneakers.	• Douglas pays some money and offers to run errands as payment.
• All the good things of summer are in the sneakers.	• Dad won't buy the sneakers.	• Douglas talks Mr. Sanderson into trying on sneakers.
• Douglas must have the new sneakers.	• Douglas does not have enough money to buy the sneakers.	• Mr. Sanderson gives Douglas the sneakers.

The Sound of Summer Running
from Dandelion Wine
Ray Bradbury

People respond to the turn of the seasons in many different ways. For one person, the coming of summer means freshly mowed grass. For others it means hot pavements. For Douglas, summer will never be summer without a new pair of sneakers!

Late that night, going home from the show with his mother and father and his brother Tom, Douglas saw the tennis shoes in the bright store window. He glanced quickly away, but his ankles were seized, his feet suspended, then rushed. The earth spun; the shop awnings slammed their canvas wings overhead with the thrust of his body running. His mother and father and brother walked quietly on both sides of him. Douglas walked backward, watching the tennis shoes in the midnight window left behind.

"It was a nice movie," said Mother.

Douglas murmured, "It was . . ."

It was June and long past time for buying the special shoes that were quiet as a summer rain falling on the walks. June and the earth full of raw power and everything everywhere in motion. The grass was still pouring in from the country, surrounding the sidewalks, stranding the houses. Any moment the town would capsize, go down and leave not a stir in the clover and weeds. And here Douglas stood, trapped on the dead cement and the red-brick streets, hardly able to move.

"Dad!" He blurted it out. "Back there in that window, those Cream-Sponge Para Litefoot Shoes . . ."

His father didn't even turn. "Suppose you tell me why you need a new pair of sneakers. Can you do that?"

"Well . . ."

It was because they felt the way it feels every summer when you take off your shoes for the first time and run in the grass. They felt like it feels sticking your feet out of the hot covers in wintertime to let the cold wind from the open window blow on them suddenly and you let them stay out a long time until you pull them back in under the covers again to feel them, like packed snow. The tennis shoes felt like it always feels the first time every year wading in the slow waters of the creek and seeing your feet below, half an inch further downstream, with refraction, than the real part of you above water.

Vocabulary Development: **seized** (sēzd) *v.* grabbed; taken hold of
suspended (sə spend′ id) *v.* stopped for a time

◆ Activate Prior Knowledge

Think of a time when you needed to budget carefully for something that you wanted to buy. Jot down the strategies you used to help you save money.

◆ Reading Strategy

Mark the Text

To help you **read fluently,** read groups of words together for meaning. Break down the underlined sentence by drawing lines between meaningful sections. Then read the sentence aloud.

◆ Reading Check

What does Douglas see that he wants?

◆ Literary Analysis

Character's motives are the emotions and desires that cause characters to act in a certain way. Why might Douglas's father be unwilling to buy him the tennis shoes? Make guesses about his father's **motives**.

____

____

____

____

____

"Dad," said Douglas, "it's hard to explain."

Somehow the people who made tennis shoes knew what boys needed and wanted. They put marshmallows and coiled springs in the soles and they wove the rest out of grasses bleached and fired in the wilderness. Somewhere deep in the soft loam of the shoes the thin hard sinews of the buck deer were hidden. The people that made the shoes must have watched a lot of winds blow the trees and a lot of rivers going down to the lakes. Whatever it was, it was in the shoes, and it was summer.

Douglas tried to get all this in words.

"Yes," said Father, "but what's wrong with last year's sneakers? Why can't you dig *them* out of the closet?"

Well, he felt sorry for boys who lived in California where they wore tennis shoes all year and never knew what it was to get winter off your feet, peel off the iron leather shoes all full of snow and rain and run barefoot for a day and then lace on the first new tennis shoes of the season, which was better than barefoot. The magic was always in the new pair of shoes. The magic might die by the first of September, but now in late June there was still plenty of magic, and shoes like these could jump you over trees and rivers and houses. And if you wanted, they could jump you over fences and sidewalks and dogs.

"Don't you see?" said Douglas. "I just *can't* use last year's pair."

For last year's pair were dead inside. They had been fine when he started them out, last year. But by the end of summer, every year, you always found out, you always knew, you couldn't really jump over rivers and trees and houses in them, and they were dead. But this was a new year, and he felt that this time, with this new pair of shoes, he could do anything, anything at all.

◆ Reading Strategy

In the underlined sentences, notice how the word *but* helps identify how the first sentence differs from the next sentence. Read the sentences aloud, emphasizing what has changed.

They walked up on the steps to their house. "Save your money," said Dad. "In five or six weeks—"

"Summer'll be over!"

Lights out, with Tom asleep, Douglas lay watching his feet, far away down there at the end of the bed in the moonlight, free of the heavy iron shoes, the big chunks of winter fallen away from them.

"Reason. I've got to think of reasons for the shoes."

Well, as anyone knew, the hills around town were wild with friends putting cows to riot, playing barometer to the

◆ Reading Check

Why does Douglas feel he needs these sneakers?

____

____

____

____

____

Vocabulary Development: **loam** (lōm) *n.* rich soil
barometer (bə räm′ ət ər) *n.* device for measuring air pressure; used to predict rain

atmospheric changes, taking sun, peeling like calendars each day to take more sun. To catch those friends, you must run much faster than foxes or squirrels. As for the town, it steamed with enemies grown irritable with heat, so remembering every winter argument and insult. *Find friends, ditch enemies!* That was the Cream-Sponge Para Litefoot motto. *Does the world run too fast? Want to catch up? Want to be alert, stay alert? Litefoot, then! Litefoot!*

He held his coin bank up and heard the faint small tinkling, the airy weight of money there.

Whatever you want, he thought, you got to make your own way. During the night now, let's find that path through the forest. . . .

Downtown, the store lights went out, one by one. A wind blew in the window. It was like a river going downstream and his feet wanting to go with it.

In his dreams he heard a rabbit running running running in the deep warm grass.

Old Mr. Sanderson moved through his shoe store as the proprietor of a pet shop must move through his shop where are kenneled animals from everywhere in the world, touching each one briefly along the way. Mr. Sanderson brushed his hands over the shoes in the window, and some of them were like cats to him and some were like dogs; he touched each pair with concern, adjusting laces, fixing tongues. Then he stood in the exact center of the carpet and looked around, nodding.

There was a sound of growing thunder.

One moment, the door to Sanderson's Shoe Emporium was empty. The next, Douglas Spaulding stood clumsily there, staring down at his leather shoes as if these heavy things could not be pulled up out of the cement. The thunder had stopped when his shoes stopped. Now, with painful slowness, daring to look only at the money in his cupped hand, Douglas moved out of the bright sunlight of Saturday noon. He made careful stacks of nickels, dimes, and quarters on the counter, like someone playing chess and worried if the next move carried him out into sun or deep into shadow.

"Don't say a word!" said Mr. Sanderson.

Douglas froze.

"First, I know just what you want to buy," said Mr. Sanderson. "Second, I see you every afternoon at my window; you think I don't see? You're wrong. Third, to give it its full name, you want the Royal Crown Cream-Sponge Para Litefoot Tennis Shoes: 'LIKE MENTHOL ON YOUR FEET!' Fourth, you want credit."

◆ Reading Strategy

Mark the Text Read the bracketed paragraph aloud, focusing on the meaning of the words. Circle the punctuation marks. Change the volume and tone of your voice when you read the sentences printed in italic type.

◆ Literary Analysis

What is Mr. Sanderson doing in the underlined text?

____

____

What do his actions tell you about Mr. Sanderson's **motives**?

____

____

____

____

◆ Reading Strategy

Words, such as *first* and *second* show order and relationships. Read aloud the bracketed text, emphasizing these signal words.

◆ **Reading Strategy**

Circle words in the bracketed text that give you clues about the voice of each speaker. **Read** the passage aloud **fluently**, using an appropriate voice for each speaker.

Mark the Text

◆ **Literary Analysis**

Think about **characters' motives,** and explain why Douglas wants Mr. Sanderson to try on a pair of the shoes.

____

____

____

____

◆ **Reading Check**

What does Douglas offer Mr. Sanderson in exchange for the sneakers?

____

____

____

◆ **Reading Strategy**

Read the underlined sentences aloud **fluently**. Focus on your expression as you read the words in italics and the ending questions.

"No!" cried Douglas, breathing hard, as if he'd run all night in his dreams. "I got something better than credit to offer!" he gasped. "Before I tell, Mr. Sanderson, you got to do me one small favor. Can you remember when was the last time you yourself wore a pair of Litefoot sneakers, sir?"

Mr. Sanderson's face darkened. "Oh, ten, twenty, say, thirty years ago. Why . . . ?"

"Mr. Sanderson, don't you think you owe it to your customers, sir, to at least try the tennis shoes you sell, for just one minute, so you know how they feel? People forget if they don't keep testing things. United Cigar Store man smokes cigars, don't he? Candy-store man samples his own stuff, I should think. So . . ."

"You may have noticed," said the old man, "I'm wearing shoes."

"But not sneakers, sir! How you going to sell sneakers unless you can rave about them and how you going to rave about them unless you know them?"

Mr. Sanderson backed off a little distance from the boy's fever, one hand to his chin. "Well . . ."

"Mr. Sanderson," said Douglas, "you sell me something and I'll sell you something just as valuable."

"Is it absolutely necessary to the sale that I put on a pair of the sneakers, boy?" said the old man.

"I sure wish you could, sir!"

The old man sighed. A minute later, seated panting quietly, he laced the tennis shoes to his long narrow feet. They looked detached and alien down there next to the dark cuffs of his business suit. Mr. Sanderson stood up.

"How do they *feel*?" asked the boy.

"How do they feel, he asks; they feel fine." He started to sit down.

"Please!" Douglas held out his hand. "Mr. Sanderson, now could you kind of rock back and forth a little, sponge around, bounce kind of, while I tell you the rest? It's this: I give you my money, you give me the shoes, I owe you a dollar. But, Mr. Sanderson, *but*—soon as I get those shoes on, you know what *happens*?"

"What?"

"Bang! I deliver your packages, pick up packages, bring you coffee, burn your trash, run to the post office, telegraph office, library! You'll see twelve of me in and out, in and out, every minute. Feel those shoes, Mr. Sanderson, *feel* how fast they'd take me? All those springs inside? Feel all the running inside? Feel how they kind of grab hold and can't let you alone and don't like you just *standing* there? Feel how quick

Vocabulary Development: alien (ā´ lē ən) *adj.* foreign; unfamiliar

I'd be doing the things you'd rather not bother with? You stay in the nice cool store while I'm jumping all around town! But it's not me really, it's the shoes. They're going like mad down alleys, cutting corners, and back! There they go!"

Mr. Sanderson stood amazed with the rush of words. When the words got going the flow carried him; he began to sink deep in the shoes, to flex his toes, limber his arches, test his ankles. He rocked softly, secretly, back and forth in a small breeze from the open door. The tennis shoes silently hushed themselves deep in the carpet, sank as in a jungle grass, in loam and resilient clay. He gave one solemn bounce of his heels in the yeasty dough, in the yielding and welcoming earth. Emotions hurried over his face as if many colored lights had been switched on and off. His mouth hung slightly open. Slowly he gentled and rocked himself to a halt, and the boy's voice faded and they stood there looking at each other in a tremendous and natural silence.

A few people drifted by on the sidewalk outside, in the hot sun.

Still the man and boy stood there, the boy glowing, the man with revelation in his face.

"Boy," said the old man at last, "in five years, how would you like a job selling shoes in this emporium?"

"Gosh, thanks, Mr. Sanderson, but I don't know what I'm going to be yet."

"Anything you want to be, son," said the old man, "you'll be. No one will ever stop you."

The old man walked lightly across the store to the wall of ten thousand boxes, came back with some shoes for the boy, and wrote up a list on some paper while the boy was lacing the shoes on his feet and then standing there, waiting.

The old man held out his list. "A dozen things you got to do for me this afternoon. Finish them, we're even Stephen, and you're fired."

"Thanks, Mr. Sanderson!" Douglas bounded away.

"Stop!" cried the old man.

Douglas pulled up and turned.

Mr. Sanderson leaned forward. "How do they *feel*?"

The boy looked down at his feet deep in the rivers, in the fields of wheat, in the wind that already was rushing him out of the town. He looked up at the old man, his eyes burning, his mouth moving, but no sound came out.

"Antelopes?" said the old man, looking from the boy's face to his shoes. "Gazelles?"

The boy thought about it, hesitated, and nodded a quick

Vocabulary Development: **limber** (lim´ bər) *v.* loosen up (a muscle or limb); make easy to bend
revelation (rev´ ə lā´ shən) *n.* sudden rush of understanding

◆ Literary Analysis

Mark the Text

Circle words in the bracketed text that show how Mr. Sanderson feels. What do you think Mr. Sanderson's **motives** are as he bounces in the sneakers?

◆ Stop to Reflect

Read the underlined sentence aloud. Why is this an important moment in the story?

◆ Reading Check

How does Douglas convince Mr. Sanderson?

◆ Reading Strategy

Circle the words in the bracketed paragraph that describe what Mr. Sanderson is feeling. Then, read the paragraph aloud, with expression.

Mark THE Text

nod. Almost immediately he vanished. He just spun about with a whisper and went off. The door stood empty. The sound of the tennis shoes faded in the jungle heat.

Mr. Sanderson stood in the sun-blazed door, listening. From a long time ago, when he dreamed as a boy, he remembered the sound. Beautiful creatures leaping under the sky, gone through brush, under trees, away, and only the soft echo their running left behind.

"Antelopes," said Mr. Sanderson. "Gazelles."

He bent to pick up the boy's abandoned winter shoes, heavy with forgotten rains and long-melted snows. Moving out of the blazing sun, walking softly, lightly, slowly, he headed back toward civilization. . . .

Reader's Response: Do you think that most store owners would respond to Douglas's request in the way that Mr. Sanderson did? Why or why not?

____

____

____

Thinking About the Skill: How did using punctuation as a guide help you read aloud more fluently?

____

____

____

PREVIEW

Jeremiah's Song

Walter Dean Myers

Summary

When Ellie returns after being away at college, she no longer wants to hear about the old ways of her people. She is more interested in what she can learn from books at school than in the stories her Grandpa Jeremiah tells. Grandpa says the stories are songs. They teach important lessons about Ellie's family history. The stories are a bridge between past and present and can help solve problems. When Grandpa has a stroke, their neighbor Macon comes over to help out. Macon often brings his guitar and plays softly while Grandpa tells his stories. The narrator is afraid to listen to the stories by himself. He feels braver when Macon is around. At first Ellie doesn't want Macon to spend so much time with Grandpa. She's afraid Grandpa won't get enough rest. After a while, Ellie changes her mind about Macon. She realizes that he makes Grandpa feel better. Grandpa tells the narrator that when he grows up he will tell stories to his own children and grandchildren. After Grandpa dies, the narrator and Ellie hear Macon play a new tune on his guitar. The narrator thinks that some day he might learn that tune.

Visual Summary

Main Characters	Other Characters
Narrator Ellie Grandpa Jeremiah Macon	Sister Todd Dr. Crawford

◆ Activate Prior Knowledge

Recall the last time that someone told you a family story. What was the story about?

◆ Literary Analysis

In **first-person point of view,** the narrator takes part in the action and tells the story. How do you know this story is written from the point of view of first person narrator? Who tells the story?

◆ Reading Check

What is the state of Grandpa Jeremiah's health when Ellie comes home from college?

Jeremiah's Song

Walter Dean Myers

The African people who arrived in America in the seventeenth century as slaves brought with them their heritage of storytelling. Since most were unable to read or write, telling stories became a way to keep their history and culture alive. Through storytelling they were able to pass their heritage along to their children. Eventually, local matters became part of the storytelling, too, as they do for Jeremiah.

I knowed my cousin Ellie was gonna be mad when Macon Smith come around to the house. She didn't have no use for Macon even when things was going right, and when Grandpa Jeremiah was fixing to die I just knowed she wasn't gonna be liking him hanging around. Grandpa Jeremiah raised Ellie after her folks died and they used to be real close. Then she got to go on to college and when she come back the first year she was different. She didn't want to hear all them stories he used to tell her anymore. Ellie said the stories wasn't true, and that's why she didn't want to hear them.

I didn't know if they was true or not. Tell the truth I didn't think much on it either way, but I liked to hear them stories. Grandpa Jeremiah said they wasn't stories anyway, they was songs.

"They the songs of my people," he used to say.

I didn't see how they was songs, not regular songs anyway. Every little thing we did down in Curry seemed to matter to Ellie that first summer she come home from college. You couldn't do nothin' that was gonna please her. She didn't even come to church much. 'Course she come on Sunday or everybody would have had a regular fit, but she didn't come on Thursday nights and she didn't come on Saturday even though she used to sing in the gospel choir.

"I guess they teachin' her somethin' worthwhile up there at Greensboro," Grandpa Jeremiah said to Sister Todd. "I sure don't see what it is, though."

"You ain't never had no book learning, Jeremiah," Sister Todd shot back. She wiped at where a trickle of sweat made a little path through the white dusting powder she put on her chest to keep cool. "Them old ways you got ain't got nothing for these young folks."

"I guess you right," Grandpa Jeremiah said.

He said it but I could see he didn't like it none. He was a big man with a big head and had most all his hair even if it was white. All that summer, instead of sitting on the porch telling stories like he used to when I was real little, he would sit out there by himself while Ellie stayed in the house and watched the television or read a book. Sometimes I would think about asking him to tell me one of them stories he used to tell but they was too scary now that I didn't have nobody to sleep with but myself. I asked Ellie to sleep with me but she wouldn't.

"You're nine years old," she said, sounding real proper. "You're old enough to sleep alone."

I *knew* that. I just wanted her to sleep with me because I liked sleeping with her. Before she went off to college she used to put cocoa butter on her arms and face and it would smell real nice. When she come back from college she put something else on, but that smelled nice too.

It was right after Ellie went back to school that Grandpa Jeremiah had him a stroke and Macon started coming around. I think his mama probably made him come at first, but you could see he liked it. Macon had always been around, sitting over near the stuck window at church or going on the blueberry truck when we went picking down at Mister Gregory's place. For a long time he was just another kid, even though he was older'n me, but then, all of a sudden, he growed something fierce. I used to be up to his shoulder one time and then, before I could turn around good, I was only up to his shirt pocket. He changed too. When he used to just hang around with the other boys and play ball or shoot at birds he would laugh a lot. He didn't laugh so much anymore and I figured he was just about grown. When Grandpa got sick he used to come around and help out with things around the house that was too hard for me to do. I mean, I could have done all the chores, but it would just take me longer.

When the work for the day was finished and the sows[1] fed, Grandpa would kind of ease into one of his stories and Macon, he would sit and listen to them and be real interested. I didn't mind listening to the stories when Grandpa told them to Macon because he would be telling them in the middle of the afternoon and they would be past my mind by the time I had to go to bed.

Macon had an old guitar he used to mess with, too. He wasn't too bad on it, and sometimes Grandpa would tell him to play us a tune. He could play something he called "the Delta Blues" real good, but when Sister Todd or somebody from the church come around he'd play "Precious Lord" or "Just a Closer Walk With Thee."

1. **sows** (souz) *n.* full-grown female pigs.

◆ **Reading Strategy**

Context clues are words and phrases that help you figure out unfamiliar words. Write the meaning of the compound word *cocoa butter* by using the underlined context clues.

◆ **Literary Analysis**

What do you find out about Grandpa's stories through the **first-person narrator**?

◆ **Reading Check**

What happened to Grandpa?

◆ Literary Analysis

What information, thoughts, and feelings does the narrator share in the bracketed passage?

◆ Reading Check

Why does Ellie ask people what they think about Dr. Crawford?

Grandpa Jeremiah had been feeling poorly from that stroke, and one of his legs got a little drag to it. Just about the time Ellie come from school the next summer he was real sick. He was breathing loud so you could hear it even in the next room and he would stay in bed a lot even when there was something that needed doing or fixing.

"I don't think he's going to make it much longer," Dr. Crawford said. "The only thing I can do is to give him something for the pain."

"Are you sure of your diagnosis?" Ellie asked. She was sitting around the table with Sister Todd, Deacon Turner, and his little skinny yellow wife.

Dr. Crawford looked at Ellie like he was surprised to hear her talking. "Yes, I'm sure," he said. "He had tests a few weeks ago and his condition was bad then."

"How much time he got?" Sister Todd asked.

"Maybe a week or two at best," Dr. Crawford said.

When he said that, Deacon Turner's wife started crying and goin' on and I give her a hard look but she just went on. I was the one who loved Grandpa Jeremiah the most and she didn't hardly even know him so I didn't see why she was crying.

Everybody started tiptoeing around the house after that. They would go in and ask Grandpa Jeremiah if he was comfortable and stuff like that or take him some food or a cold glass of lemonade. Sister Todd come over and stayed with us. Mostly what she did is make supper and do a lot of praying, which was good because I figured that maybe God would do something to make Grandpa Jeremiah well. When she wasn't doing that she was piecing on a fancy quilt she was making for some white people in Wilmington.

Ellie, she went around asking everybody how they felt about Dr. Crawford and then she went into town and asked about the tests and things. Sister Jenkins asked her if she thought she knowed more than Dr. Crawford, and Ellie rolled her eyes at her, but Sister Jenkins was reading out her Bible and didn't make no notice of it.

Then Macon come over.

He had been away on what he called "a little piece of a job" and hadn't heard how bad off Grandpa Jeremiah was. When he come over he talked to Ellie and she told him what was going on and then he got him a soft drink from the refrigerator and sat out on the porch and before you know it he was crying.

You could look at his face and tell the difference between

Vocabulary Development: **diagnosis** (dī´ əg nō´ sis) *n.* explanation of or prediction about a person's medical condition

him sweating and the tears. The sweat was close against his skin and shiny and the tears come down fatter and more sparkly.

Macon sat on the porch, without saying a word, until the sun went down and the crickets started chirping and carrying on. Then he went in to where Grandpa Jeremiah was and stayed in there for a long time.

Sister Todd was saying that Grandpa Jeremiah needed his rest and Ellie went in to see what Macon was doing. Then she come out real mad.

"He got Grandpa telling those old stories again," Ellie said. "I told him Grandpa needed his rest and for him not to be staying all night."

He did leave soon, but bright and early the next morning Macon was back again. This time he brought his guitar with him and he went on in to Grandpa Jeremiah's room. I went in, too.

Grandpa Jeremiah's room smelled terrible. It was all closed up so no drafts could get on him and the whole room was smelled down with disinfect and medicine. Grandpa Jeremiah lay propped up on the bed and he was so gray he looked scary. His hair wasn't combed down and his head on the pillow with his white hair sticking out was enough to send me flying if Macon hadn't been there. He was skinny, too. He looked like his skin got loose on his bones, and when he lifted his arms, it hung down like he was just wearing it instead of it being a part of him.

Macon sat slant-shouldered with his guitar across his lap. He was messin' with the guitar, not making any music, but just going over the strings as Grandpa talked.

"Old Carrie went around out back to where they kept the pigs penned up and she felt a cold wind across her face. . . ." Grandpa Jeremiah was telling the story about how a old woman out-tricked the Devil and got her son back. I had heard the story before, and I knew it was pretty scary. "When she felt the cold breeze she didn't blink nary an eye, but looked straight ahead. . . ."

All the time Grandpa Jeremiah was talking I could see Macon fingering his guitar. I tried to imagine what it would be like if he was actually plucking the strings. I tried to fix my mind on that because I didn't like the way the story went with the old woman wrestling with the Devil.

We sat there for nearly all the afternoon until Ellie and

Vocabulary Development: **disinfect** (dis′ in fekt′) *n.* dialect, or regional language, for disinfectant, a substance that kills germs

◆ **Reading Check**

How do you know that Macon is very upset?

◆ **Literary Analysis**

List three details the **first-person narrator** observes in the bracketed descriptive passage.

1.

2.

3.

◆ **Reading Strategy**

Mark the Text

Circle the **context clues** that help you figure out the meaning of the underlined word *fingering*. Then, define the word.

◆ **Reading Check**

What does Macon bring when he visits Grandpa?

◆ **Reading Strategy**

Use the underlined words as **context clues** to figure out the meaning of the word *setback.* Write the meaning.

◆ **Stop to Reflect**

What brings about the friendships between the narrator and Macon and between Ellie and Macon?

In what way do important events tend to bring people closer together?

◆ **Reading Check**

How has Grandpa Jeremiah's condition changed?

Sister Todd come in and said that supper was ready. Me and Macon went out and ate some collard greens, ham hocks,[2] and rice. Then Macon he went back in and listened to some more of Grandpa's stories until it was time for him to go home. I wasn't about to go in there and listen to no stories at night.

Dr. Crawford come around a few days later and said that Grandpa Jeremiah was doing a little better.

"You think the Good Lord gonna pull him through?" Sister Todd asked.

"I don't tell the Good Lord what He should or should not be doing," Dr. Crawford said, looking over at Sister Todd and at Ellie. "I just said that *my* patient seems to be doing okay for his condition."

"He been telling Macon all his stories," I said.

"Macon doesn't seem to understand that Grandpa Jeremiah needs his strength," Ellie said. "Now that he's improving, we don't want him to have a setback."

"No use in stopping him from telling his stories," Dr. Crawford said. "If it makes him feel good it's as good as any medicine I can give him."

I saw that this didn't set with Ellie, and when Dr. Crawford had left I asked her why.

"Dr. Crawford means well," she said, "but we have to get away from the kind of life that keeps us in the past."

She didn't say why we should be trying to get away from the stories and I really didn't care too much. All I knew was that when Macon was sitting in the room with Grandpa Jeremiah I wasn't nearly as scared as I used to be when it was just me and Ellie listening. I told that to Macon.

"You getting to be a big man, that's all," he said.

That was true. Me and Macon was getting to be good friends, too. I didn't even mind so much when he started being friends with Ellie later. It seemed kind of natural, almost like Macon was supposed to be there with us instead of just visiting.

Grandpa wasn't getting no better, but he wasn't getting no worse, either.

"You liking Macon now?" I asked Ellie when we got to the middle of July. She was dishing out a plate of smothered chops for him and I hadn't even heard him ask for anything to eat.

"Macon's funny," Ellie said, not answering my question. "He's in there listening to all of those old stories like he's really interested in them. It's almost as if he and Grandpa Jeremiah are talking about something more than the stories, a secret language."

2. **collard greens, ham hocks** leafy green vegetables and joints from a pig's leg; popular southern dishes.

I didn't think I was supposed to say anything about that to Macon, but once, when Ellie, Sister Todd, and Macon were out on the porch shelling butter beans after Grandpa got tired and was resting, I went into his room and told him what Ellie had said.

"She said that?" Grandpa Jeremiah's face was skinny and old looking but his eyes looked like a baby's, they was so bright.

"Right there in the kitchen is where she said it," I said. "And I don't know what it mean but I was wondering about it."

"I didn't think she had any feeling for them stories," Grandpa Jeremiah said. "If she think we talking secrets, maybe she don't."

"I think she getting a feeling for Macon," I said,

"That's okay, too," Grandpa Jeremiah said. "They both young."

"Yeah, but them stories you be telling, Grandpa, they about old people who lived a long time ago," I said.

"Well, those the folks you got to know about," Grandpa Jeremiah said. "You think on what those folks been through, and what they was feeling, and you add it up with what you been through and what you been feeling, then you got you something."

"What you got Grandpa?"

"You got you a bridge," Grandpa said. "And a meaning. Then when things get so hard you about to break, you can sneak across that bridge and see some folks who went before you and see how they didn't break. Some got bent and some got twisted and a few fell along the way, but they didn't break."

"Am I going to break, Grandpa?"

"You? As strong as you is?" Grandpa Jeremiah pushed himself up on his elbow and give me a look. "No way you going to break, boy. You gonna be strong as they come. One day you gonna tell all them stories I told you to your young'uns and they'll be as strong as you."

"Suppose I ain't got no stories, can I make some up?"

"Sure you can, boy. You make 'em up and twist 'em around. Don't make no mind. Long as you got 'em."

"Is that what Macon is doing?" I asked. "Making up stories to play on his guitar?"

"He'll do with 'em what he see fit, I suppose," Grandpa Jeremiah said. "Can't ask more than that from a man."

It rained the first three days of August. It wasn't a hard rain but it rained anyway. The mailman said it was good for the crops over East but I didn't care about that so I didn't pay him no mind. What I did mind was when it rain like that the field mice come in and get in things like the flour bin and I always got the blame for leaving it open.

◆ **Literary Analysis**

What information does the **first-person narrator** reveal about Ellie and Macon?

◆ **Reading Strategy**

Figure out the meaning of *break* in the bracketed text. Use the underlined context clues to determine the meaning.

◆ **Literary Analysis**

What personal feelings does the **first-person narrator** reveal in the bracketed text?

When the rain stopped I was pretty glad. Macon come over and sat with Grandpa and had something to eat with us. Sister Todd come over, too.

"How Grandpa doing?" Sister Todd asked. "They been asking about him in the church."

"He's doing all right," Ellie said.

"He's kind of quiet today," Macon said. "He was just talking about how the hogs needed breeding."

"He must have run out of stories to tell," Sister Todd said. "He'll be repeating on himself like my father used to do. That's the way I *hear* old folks get."

Everybody laughed at that because Sister Todd was pretty old, too. Maybe we was all happy because the sun was out after so much rain. When Sister Todd went in to take Grandpa Jeremiah a plate of potato salad with no mayonnaise like he liked it, she told him about how people was asking for him and he told her to tell them he was doing okay and to remember him in their prayers.

Sister Todd came over the next afternoon, too, with some rhubarb pie with cheese on it, which is my favorite pie. When she took a piece into Grandpa Jeremiah's room she come right out again and told Ellie to go fetch the Bible.

It was a hot day when they had the funeral. Mostly everybody was there. The church was hot as anything, even though they had the window open. Some yellowjacks flew in and buzzed around Sister Todd's niece and then around Deacon Turner's wife and settled right on her hat and stayed there until we all stood and sang "Soon-a Will Be Done."

At the graveyard Macon played "Precious Lord" and I cried hard even though I told myself that I wasn't going to cry the way Ellie and Sister Todd was, but it was such a sad thing when we left and Grandpa Jeremiah was still out to the grave that I couldn't help it.

During the funeral and all, Macon kind of told everybody where to go and where to sit and which of the three cars to ride in. After it was over he come by the house and sat on the front porch and played on his guitar. Ellie was standing leaning against the rail and she was crying but it wasn't a hard crying. It was a soft crying, the kind that last inside of you for a long time.

Macon was playing a tune I hadn't heard before. I thought it might have been what he was working at when Grandpa Jeremiah was telling him those stories and I watched his fingers but I couldn't tell if it was or not. It wasn't nothing special, that tune Macon was playing, maybe halfway between them Delta blues he would do when Sister Todd wasn't around and something you would play at church. It was

◆ Literary Analysis

In the underlined passage, what important fact has the **first-person narrator** left unmentioned?

____

____

◆ Reading Strategy

Circle the word *yellowjacks*. What **context clues** tell the reader that *yellowjacks* are a kind of insect?

Mark the Text

____

____

____

____

something different and something the same at the same time. I watched his fingers go over that guitar and figured I could learn that tune one day if I had a mind to.

Reader's Response: What would you say to the narrator to comfort him after his grandfather's death?

____

____

____

Thinking About the Skill: How did context clues help you figure out the meaning of unfamiliar words?

____

____

____

◆ Stop to Reflect

Why do you think the author ends the story with Macon's playing music?

____

____

____

PREVIEW

The King of Mazy May

Jack London

Summary

This story is set in the Klondike region of northwestern Canada. Walt is the fourteen-year-old son of a prospector. While his father is away on a trip, Walt watches as claim jumpers prepare to steal a neighbor's—Loren Hall's—claim. The boy quickly takes some of the claim jumpers' sled dogs. He races to catch up with Loren who is on his way to Dawson, where claims are officially recorded. The claim jumpers try to stop Walt. A wild dog-sled chase begins on the creek, known as the Mazy May. The chase continues at night along the frozen Yukon River. Walt outraces and outwits the thieves. He catches up with Loren and takes him to Dawson to record the claim.

Visual Summary

CONFLICT
• Walt wants to save Loren Hall's claim.
• Claim jumpers want to steal the claim.

CLIMAX
• Walt is chased by claim jumpers.
• Walt fights off claim jumpers and outruns them.

RESOLUTION
• Walt catches up with Loren Hall and takes him to Dawson, where Loren records the claim.

The King of Mazy May

Jack London

This story takes place more than a hundred years ago in northwestern Canada, but in some ways it is as up to date as a recent movie. The plot has a long chase scene, and the outcome is in doubt up to the very end.

Walt Masters is not a very large boy, but there is manliness in his make-up, and he himself, although he does not know a great deal that most boys know, knows much that other boys do not know. He has never seen a train of cars nor an elevator in his life, and for that matter he has never once looked upon a cornfield, a plow, a cow, or even a chicken. He has never had a pair of shoes on his feet, nor gone to a picnic or a party, nor talked to a girl. But he has seen the sun at midnight, watched the ice jams on one of the mightiest of rivers, and played beneath the northern lights,[1] the one white child in thousands of square miles of frozen wilderness.

Walt has walked all the fourteen years of his life in suntanned, moose-hide moccasins, and he can go to the Indian camps and "talk big" with the men, and trade calico and beads with them for their precious furs. He can make bread without baking powder, yeast, or hops, shoot a moose at three hundred yards, and drive the wild wolf dogs fifty miles a day on the packed trail.

Last of all, he has a good heart, and is not afraid of the darkness and loneliness, of man or beast or thing. His father is a good man, strong and brave, and Walt is growing up like him.

Walt was born a thousand miles or so down the Yukon,[2] in a trading post below the Ramparts. After his mother died, his father and he came up on the river, step by step, from camp to camp, till now they are settled down on the Mazy May Creek in the Klondike[3] country. Last year they and several others had spent much toil and time on the Mazy May, [and endured great hardships; the creek, in turn, was just beginning to show up its richness and to reward them for their heavy labor. But with the news of their discoveries, strange men began to come and go through the short days and long nights, and many unjust things they did to the men who had worked so long upon the creek.]

Vocabulary Development: **toil** (toil) *n.* hard work
endured (en do͝ord′) *v.* suffered through

1. **northern lights** glowing bands or streamers of light, sometimes appearing in the night sky of the Northern Hemisphere.
2. **Yukon** (yo͞o′ kän′) river flowing through the Yukon Territory of northwest Canada.
3. **Klondike** (klän′ dīk′): gold-mining region along a tributary of the Yukon River.

◆ **Active Prior Knowledge**

What do you already know about living conditions in regions with an extremely cold climate? Use this space to list anything you can remember.

____

____

____

____

____

____

____

____

◆ **Reading Strategy**

Signal words are words and phrases that indicate a change in the story's direction. *But, so, because* and *next* are signal words. In the bracketed passage, what change does the signal word *but* introduce?

____

____

____

____

◆ **Reading Check**

What three facts have you learned so far about Walt Masters?

1. ________________________________

____

2. ________________________________

____

3. ________________________________

____

◆ Reading Check

How did prospectors like Hartman and Lukens lose their claims?

Si Hartman had gone away on a moose hunt, to return and find new stakes driven and his claim jumped.[4] George Lukens and his brother had lost their claims in a like manner, having delayed too long on the way to Dawson to record them. In short, it was the old story, and quite a number of the earnest, industrious prospectors had suffered similar losses.

But Walt Masters's father had recorded his claim at the start, so Walt had nothing to fear now that his father had gone on a short trip up the White River prospecting for quartz. Walt was well able to stay by himself in the cabin, cook his three meals a day, and look after things. Not only did he look after his father's claim, but he had agreed to keep an eye on the adjoining one of Loren Hall, who had started for Dawson to record it.

Loren Hall was an old man, and he had no dogs, so he had to travel very slowly. After he had been gone some time, word came up the river that he had broken through the ice at Rosebud Creek and frozen his feet so badly that he would not be able to travel for a couple of weeks. Then Walt Masters received the news that old Loren was nearly all right again, and about to move on afoot for Dawson as fast as a weakened man could.

◆ Reading Strategy

Circle the two **signal words** *because* and *so* in the bracketed passage. How does each word change the direction of the story?

Mark THE Text

because:

so:

Walt was worried, however; the claim was liable to be jumped at any moment because of this delay, and a fresh stampede had started in on the Mazy May. He did not like the looks of the newcomers, and one day, when five of them came by with crack dog teams and the lightest of camping outfits, he could see that they were prepared to make speed, and resolved to keep an eye on them. So he locked up the cabin and followed them, being at the same time careful to remain hidden.

He had not watched them long before he was sure that they were professional stampeders, bent on jumping all the claims in sight. Walt crept along the snow at the rim of the creek and saw them change many stakes, destroy old ones, and set up new ones.

In the afternoon, with Walt always trailing on their heels, they came back down the creek, unharnessed their dogs, and went into camp within two claims of his cabin. When he

◆ Reading Check

What are Walt's responsibilities while his father is gone?

Vocabulary Development: prospectors (prä′ spekt′ erz) *n.* people who make their living searching for valuable ores, such as gold
liable (lī′ ə bəl) *adj.* likely (to do something or have something happen to one)

4. **claim jumped** A claim is a piece of land staked out by a miner (stakes are markers driven into the ground to show where the borders of the claim are). A claim that is jumped is stolen by someone.

saw them make preparations to cook, he hurried home to get something to eat himself, and then hurried back. He crept so close that he could hear them talking quite plainly, and by pushing the underbrush aside he could catch occasional glimpses of them. They had finished eating and were smoking around the fire.

"The creek is all right, boys," a large, black-bearded man, evidently the leader, said, "and I think the best thing we can do is to pull out tonight. The dogs can follow the trail; besides, it's going to be moonlight. What say you?"

"But it's going to be beastly cold," objected one of the party. "It's forty below zero now."

"An' sure, can't ye keep warm by jumpin' off the sleds an' runnin' after the dogs?" cried an Irishman. "An' who wouldn't? The creek's as rich as a United States mint! Faith, it's an ilegant chanst to be gettin' a run fer yer money! An' if ye don't run, it's mebbe you'll not get the money at all, at all."

"That's it," said the leader. "If we can get to Dawson and record, we're rich men; and there's no telling who's been sneaking along in our tracks, watching us, and perhaps now off to give the alarm. The thing for us to do is to rest the dogs a bit, and then hit the trail as hard as we can. What do you say?"

Evidently the men had agreed with their leader, for Walt Masters could hear nothing but the rattle of the tin dishes which were being washed. Peering out cautiously, he could see the leader studying a piece of paper. Walt knew what it was at a glance—a list of all the unrecorded claims on Mazy May. Any man could get these lists by applying to the gold commissioner at Dawson.

"Thirty-two," the leader said, lifting his face to the men. "Thirty-two isn't recorded, and this is thirty-three. Come on; let's take a look at it. I saw somebody had been working on it when we came up this morning."

Three of the men went with him, leaving one to remain in camp. Walt crept carefully after them till they came to Loren Hall's shaft. One of the men went down and built a fire on the bottom to thaw out the frozen gravel, while the others built another fire on the dump and melted water in a couple of gold pans. This they poured into a piece of canvas stretched between two logs, used by Loren Hall in which to wash his gold.

In a short time a couple of buckets of dirt were sent up by the man in the shaft, and Walt could see the others grouped anxiously about their leader as he proceeded to wash it. When this was finished, they stared at the broad streak of black sand and yellow gold grains on the bottom of the pan, and one of them called excitedly for the man who had remained in camp to come. Loren Hall had struck it rich and

◆ Literary Analysis

A **conflict** is a disagreement or struggle between characters in a story who have opposing goals. From what you know of Walt's character, what is his goal?

____

____

What is the goal of the men in the bracketed text?

____

____

What conflict is developing between Walt and the men?

____

____

____

____

◆ Reading Check

Why does Walt follow the stampeders?

____

____

____

____

____

◆ **Reading Strategy**

Look at the **signal word** *but.* How does the word signal a change in Walt's behavior?

What is the change?

◆ **Literary Analysis**

In the bracketed passage, the nature of the **conflict** between Walt and the stampeders undergoes a major change. What does Walt do to heighten the conflict between the characters?

◆ **Reading Check**

Why does the Irishman want to stop Walt?

his claim was not yet recorded. It was plain that they were going to jump it.

Walt lay in the snow, thinking rapidly. He was only a boy, but in the face of the threatened injustice to old lame Loren Hall he felt that he must do something. He waited and watched, with his mind made up, till he saw the men begin to square up new stakes. Then he crawled away till out of hearing, and broke into a run for the camp of the stampeders. Walt's father had taken their own dogs with him prospecting, and the boy knew how impossible it was for him to undertake the seventy miles to Dawson without the aid of dogs.

Gaining the camp, he picked out, with an experienced eye, the easiest running sled and started to harness up the stampeders' dogs. There were three teams of six each, and from these he chose ten of the best. Realizing how necessary it was to have a good head dog, he strove to discover a leader amongst them; but he had little time in which to do it, for he could hear the voices of the returning men. By the time the team was in shape and everything ready, the claim-jumpers came into sight in an open place not more than a hundred yards from the trail, which ran down the bed of the creek. They cried out to Walt, but instead of giving heed to them he grabbed up one of their fur sleeping robes, which lay loosely in the snow, and leaped upon the sled.

"Mush! Hi! Mush on!" he cried to the animals, snapping the keen-lashed whip among them.

The dogs sprang against the yoke straps, and the sled jerked under way so suddenly as to almost throw him off. Then it curved into the creek, poising perilously on the runner. He was almost breathless with suspense, when it finally righted with a bound and sprang ahead again. The creek bank was high and he could not see the men, although he could hear their cries and knew they were running to cut him off. He did not dare to think what would happen if they caught him; he just clung to the sled, his heart beating wildly, and watched the snow rim of the bank above him.

Suddenly, over this snow rim came the flying body of the Irishman, who had leaped straight for the sled in a desperate attempt to capture it; but he was an instant too late. Striking on the very rear of it, he was thrown from his feet, backward, into the snow. Yet, with the quickness of a cat, he had clutched the end of the sled with one hand, turned over, and was dragging behind on his breast, swearing at the boy and threatening all kinds of terrible things if he did not stop the dogs; but Walt cracked him sharply across the knuckles with the butt of the dog whip till he let go.

Vocabulary Development: poising (poiz′ iŋ) *adj.* balancing

It was eight miles from Walt's claim to the Yukon—eight very crooked miles, for the creek wound back and forth like a snake, "tying knots in itself," as George Lukens said. And because it was so crooked the dogs could not get up their best speed, while the sled ground heavily on its side against the curves, now to the right, now to the left.

Travelers who had come up and down the Mazy May on foot, with packs on their backs, had declined to go round all the bends, and instead had made shortcuts across the narrow necks of creek bottom. Two of his pursuers had gone back to harness the remaining dogs, but the others took advantage of these shortcuts, running on foot, and before he knew it they had almost overtaken him.

"Halt!" they cried after him. "Stop, or we'll shoot!"

But Walt only yelled the harder at the dogs, and dashed around the bend with a couple of revolver bullets singing after him. At the next bend they had drawn up closer still, and the bullets struck uncomfortably near him but at this point the Mazy May straightened out and ran for half a mile as the crow flies. Here the dogs stretched out in their long wolf swing, and the stampeders, quickly winded, slowed down and waited for their own sled to come up.

Looking over his shoulder, Walt reasoned that they had not given up the chase for good, and that they would soon be after him again. So he wrapped the fur robe about him to shut out the stinging air, and lay flat on the empty sled, encouraging the dogs, as he well knew how.

At last, twisting abruptly between two river islands, he came upon the mighty Yukon sweeping grandly to the north. He could not see from bank to bank, and in the quick-falling twilight it loomed a great white sea of frozen stillness. There was not a sound, save the breathing of the dogs, and the churn of the steel-shod sled.

No snow had fallen for several weeks, and the traffic had packed the main river trail till it was hard and glassy as glare ice. Over this the sled flew along, and the dogs kept the trail fairly well, although Walt quickly discovered that he had made a mistake in choosing the leader. As they were driven in single file, without reins, he had to guide them by his voice, and it was evident the head dog had never learned the meaning of "gee" and "haw."[5] He hugged the inside of the curves too closely, often forcing his comrades behind him into the soft snow, while several times he thus capsized[6] the sled.

Vocabulary Development: declined (di klīnd′) *v.* refused

5. **"gee" and "haw"** (jē) and (hô) commands used to tell an animal to turn to the right or the left.
6. **capsized** (kap′ sīzd′) *v.* overturned.

◆ Reading Check

How are the men, who are on foot, nearly able to catch up with the sled?

◆ Literary Analysis

In the bracketed passage, how do Walt's actions show that he is determined to beat the men to Dawson?

What actions show that the men are determined to get to Dawson first?

◆ Reading Check

What do the men do when Walt refuses to stop?

◆ Stop to Reflect

The low temperatures in the Klondike can be life threatening. How could getting off the sled and running save someone's life?

◆ Reading Strategy

Circle the **signal words** *on account of.* How does the phrase explain the relationship between the lead dog and the sled going off track?

Mark THE Text

◆ Reading Strategy

What change of tone does the word *now* signal?

There was no wind, but the speed at which he traveled created a bitter blast, and with the thermometer down to forty below, this bit through fur and flesh to the very bones. Aware that if he remained constantly upon the sled he would freeze to death, and knowing the practice of Arctic travelers, Walt shortened up one of the lashing thongs, and whenever he felt chilled, seized hold of it, jumped off, and ran behind till warmth was restored. Then he would climb on and rest till the process had to be repeated.

Looking back he could see the sled of his pursuers, drawn by eight dogs, rising and falling over the ice hummocks like a boat in a seaway. The Irishman and the black-bearded leader were with it, taking turns in running and riding.

Night fell, and in the blackness of the first hour or so Walt toiled desperately with his dogs. On account of the poor lead dog, they were continually floundering off the beaten track into the soft snow, and the sled was as often riding on its side or top as it was in the proper way. This work and strain tried his strength sorely. Had he not been in such haste he could have avoided much of it, but he feared the stampeders would creep up in the darkness and overtake him. However, he could hear them yelling to their dogs, and knew from the sounds they were coming up very slowly.

When the moon rose he was off Sixty Mile, and Dawson was only fifty miles away. He was almost exhausted, and breathed a sigh of relief as he climbed on the sled again. Looking back, he saw his enemies had crawled up within four hundred yards. At this space they remained, a black speck of motion on the white river breast. Strive as they would, they could not shorten this distance, and strive as he would, he could not increase it.

Walt had now discovered the proper lead dog, and he knew he could easily run away from them if he could only change the bad leader for the good one. But this was impossible, for a moment's delay, at the speed they were running, would bring the men behind upon him.

When he was off the mouth of Rosebud Creek, just as he was topping a rise, the report of a gun and the ping of a bullet on the ice beside him told him that they were this time shooting at him with a rifle. And from then on, as he cleared the summit of each ice jam, he stretched flat on the leaping sled till the rifle shot from the rear warned him that he was safe till the next ice jam was reached.

Now it is very hard to lie on a moving sled, jumping and plunging and yawing[7] like a boat before the wind, and to

Vocabulary Development: summit (sum´ it) *n.* highest part

7. **yawing** (yô´ iŋ) *adj.* swinging from side to side.

shoot through the deceiving moonlight at an object four hundred yards away on another moving sled performing equally wild antics. So it is not to be wondered at that the black-bearded leader did not hit him.

After several hours of this, during which, perhaps, a score of bullets had struck about him, their ammunition began to give out and their fire slackened. They took greater care, and shot at him at the most favorable opportunities. He was also leaving them behind, the distance slowly increasing to six hundred yards.

Lifting clear on the crest of a great jam off Indian River, Walt Masters met with his first accident. A bullet sang past his ears, and struck the bad lead dog.

The poor brute plunged in a heap, with the rest of the team on top of him.

Like a flash Walt was by the leader. Cutting the traces with his hunting knife, he dragged the dying animal to one side and straightened out the team.

He glanced back. The other sled was coming up like an express train. With half the dogs still over their traces, he cried "Mush on!" and leaped upon the sled just as the pursuers dashed abreast[8] of him.

The Irishman was preparing to spring for him—they were so sure they had him that they did not shoot—when Walt turned fiercely upon them with his whip.

He struck at their faces, and men must save their faces with their hands. So there was no shooting just then. Before they could recover from the hot rain of blows, Walt reached out from his sled, catching their wheel dog by the forelegs in midspring, and throwing him heavily. This snarled the team, capsizing the sled and tangling his enemies up beautifully.

Away Walt flew, the runners of his sled fairly screaming as they bounded over the frozen surface. And what had seemed an accident proved to be a blessing in disguise. The proper lead dog was now to the fore, and he stretched low and whined with joy as he jerked his comrades along.

By the time he reached Ainslie's Creek, seventeen miles from Dawson, Walt had left his pursuers, a tiny speck, far behind. At Monte Cristo Island he could no longer see them. And at Swede Creek, just as daylight was silvering the pines, he ran plump into the camp of old Loren Hall.

Almost as quick as it takes to tell it, Loren had his sleeping furs rolled up, and had joined Walt on the sled. They permitted the dogs to travel more slowly, as there was no sign of the chase in the rear, and just as they pulled up at the gold commissioner's office in Dawson, Walt, who had kept his eyes open to the last, fell asleep.

---

8. abreast (ə brest´) *adv.* alongside.

◆ Literary Analysis

Mark the Text

What event is the high point of the **conflict**? Underline the words that describe this event.

◆ Reading Check

How does Walt stop the men and get away?

◆ Stop to Reflect

Why would people call Walt "The King of Mazy May"?

____

____

List two of Walt's character qualities that help him beat the men.

1. _______________

____

____

2. _______________

____

____

And because of what Walt Masters did on this night, the men of the Yukon have become proud of him, and speak of him now as the King of Mazy May.

Reader's Response: Would you enjoy Walt's way of life? Why or why not?

____

____

____

Thinking About the Skill: How did recognizing signal words help you understand the story?

____

____

____

PREVIEW

The Circuit

Francisco Jiménez

Summary

In "The Circuit," Panchito and his family are migrant farm workers. They move from place to place to find a crop ready to pick. Panchito does not like the constant moving. He is sad to leave his old house behind. He is also sad to leave behind the friends he has made. Panchito hates picking grapes in Fresno. However, when grape-picking season is over, Panchito can go to school. His sixth-grade teacher helps him to learn difficult English words and even offers to teach him to play the trumpet. Panchito is very excited. He rushes home to tell his family. But as soon as he gets home, he sees that his family is packed and ready to leave once again.

Visual Summary

Key Events

- Panchito's family packs up and moves to Fresno.
- Panchito picks grapes.
- Panchito enrolls at school.
- Mr. Lema teaches Panchito difficult words and offers to teach him to play trumpet.
- Panchito's family has to move again.

THEME

Title of Story

"The Circuit"

Character's Thoughts

- Panchito is sad to have to move again.
- He is nervous during the first day at his new school.
- He is excited at the chance to learn to play the trumpet.
- He is very sad to have to move again.

◆ Activate Prior Knowledge

Constant change makes life difficult for Panchito. Have you ever had to face an unexpected change? Jot down your thoughts.

◆ Literary Analysis

The **theme** of a story is its central idea. The bracketed passage gives clues to the theme of "The Circuit." Underline the words that might indicate this theme.

Mark the Text

◆ Reading Check

How does Panchito feel about moving again?

The Circuit

Francisco Jiménez

Children sometimes think they would rather be anywhere but in school. But Panchito does not share this opinion. For Panchito, school is a place where he wishes he could spend much more time.

It was that time of year again. Ito, the strawberry sharecropper,[1] did not smile. It was natural. The peak of the strawberry season was over and the last few days the workers, most of them *braceros*,[2] were not picking as many boxes as they had during the months of June and July.

As the last days of August disappeared, so did the number of *braceros*. Sunday, only one—the best picker—came to work. I liked him. Sometimes we talked during our half-hour lunch break. That is how I found out he was from Jalisco, the same state in Mexico my family was from. That Sunday was the last time I saw him.

When the sun had tired and sunk behind the mountains, Ito signaled us that it was time to go home. "*Ya esora*,"[3] he yelled in his broken Spanish. Those were the words I waited for twelve hours a day, every day, seven days a week, week after week. And the thought of not hearing them again saddened me.

As we drove home Papá did not say a word. With both hands on the wheel, he stared at the dirt road. My older brother, Roberto, was also silent. He leaned his head back and closed his eyes. Once in a while he cleared from his throat the dust that blew in from outside.

Yes, it was that time of year. When I opened the front door to the shack, I stopped. Everything we owned was neatly packed in cardboard boxes. Suddenly I felt even more the weight of hours, days, weeks, and months of work. I sat down on a box. The thought of having to move to Fresno[4] and knowing what was in store for me there brought tears to my eyes.

That night I could not sleep. I lay in bed thinking about how much I hated this move.

A little before five o'clock in the morning, Papá woke everyone up. A few minutes later, the yelling and screaming of my little brothers and sisters, for whom the move was a great adventure, broke the silence of dawn. Shortly, the barking of the dogs accompanied them.

While we packed the breakfast dishes, Papá went outside

1. **sharecropper** (sher′ kräp′ ər) *n.* one who works for a share of a crop; tenant farmer.
2. **braceros** (brä ser′ os) *n.* migrant Mexican farm laborers who harvest crops.
3. **Ya esora** (yä es ô rä) Spanish for "It's time" (Ya es hora).
4. **Fresno** (frez′ nō) *n.* city in central California.

to start the "Carcanchita."[5] That was the name Papá gave his old '38 black Plymouth. He bought it in a used-car lot in Santa Rosa in the winter of 1949. Papá was very proud of his little jalopy. He had a right to be proud of it. He spent a lot of time looking at other cars before buying this one. When he finally chose the "Carcanchita," he checked it thoroughly before driving it out of the car lot. He examined every inch of the car. He listened to the motor, tilting his head from side to side like a parrot, trying to detect any noises that spelled car trouble. After being satisfied with the looks and sounds of the car, Papá then insisted on knowing who the original owner was. He never did find out from the car salesman, but he bought the car anyway. Papá figured the original owner must have been an important man because behind the rear seat of the car he found a blue necktie.

Papá parked the car out in front and left the motor running. "*Listo*,"[6] he yelled. Without saying a word, Roberto and I began to carry the boxes out to the car. Roberto carried the two big boxes and I carried the two smaller ones. Papá then threw the mattress on top of the car roof and tied it with ropes to the front and rear bumpers.

Everything was packed except Mamá's pot. It was an old large galvanized[7] pot she had picked up at an army surplus store in Santa María the year I was born. The pot had many dents and nicks, and the more dents and nicks it acquired the more Mamá liked it. "*Mi olla*,"[8] she used to say proudly.

I held the front door open as Mamá carefully carried out her pot by both handles, making sure not to spill the cooked beans. When she got to the car, Papá reached out to help her with it. Roberto opened the rear car door and Papá gently placed it on the floor behind the front seat. All of us then climbed in. Papá sighed, wiped the sweat off his forehead with his sleeve, and said wearily: "*Es todo*."[9]

As we drove away, I felt a lump in my throat. I turned around and looked at our little shack for the last time.

At sunset we drove into a labor camp near Fresno. Since Papá did not speak English, Mamá asked the camp foreman if he needed any more workers. "We don't need no more," said the foreman, scratching his head. "Check with Sullivan down the road. Can't miss him. He lives in a big white house with a fence around it."

When we got there, Mamá walked up to the house. She went through a white gate, past a row of rose bushes, up the stairs to the front door. She rang the doorbell. The porch light went on and a tall husky man came out. They exchanged a

---

5. **Carcanchita** (kär kän chē´ tä) affectionate name for the car.
6. **Listo** (lēs to) Spanish for "Ready."
7. **galvanized** (gal´ və nīzd´) *adj.* coated with zinc to prevent rusting.
8. **Mi olla** (mē ō´ yä) Spanish for "My pot."
9. **Es todo** (es tō´ thō) Spanish for "That's everything."

◆ Reading Strategy

To **read accurately,** break down long sentences into parts. Look for the subject of the sentence. In the underlined sentence, what is the subject?

____

What is the sentence about?

____
____
____
____
____
____

◆ Reading Check

Why are Papá, Mamá, and the family packing their few possessions and money?

____
____
____
____
____
____
____
____

◆ Reading Strategy

Break down the underlined sentence into parts that have meaning. What is the subject of the sentence?

Mark THE Text

What is the subject doing?

What else does the sentence tell you?

◆ Reading Check

Why is it important to the family that Roberto and Panchito do not go to school?

few words. After the man went in, Mamá clasped her hands and hurried back to the car. "We have work! Mr. Sullivan said we can stay there the whole season," she said, gasping and pointing to an old garage near the stables.

The garage was worn out by the years. It had no windows. The walls, eaten by termites, strained to support the roof full of holes. The dirt floor, populated by earthworms, looked like a gray road map.

That night, by the light of a kerosene lamp, we unpacked and cleaned our new home. Roberto swept away the loose dirt, leaving the hard ground. Papá plugged the holes in the walls with old newspapers and tin can tops. Mamá fed my little brothers and sisters. Papá and Roberto then brought in the mattress and placed it on the far corner of the garage. "Mamá, you and the little ones sleep on the mattress. Roberto, Panchito, and I will sleep outside under the trees," Papá said.

Early next morning Mr. Sullivan showed us where his crop was, and after breakfast, Papá, Roberto, and I headed for the vineyard to pick.

Around nine o'clock the temperature had risen to almost one hundred degrees. I was completely soaked in sweat and my mouth felt as if I had been chewing on a handkerchief. I walked over to the end of the row, picked up the jug of water we had brought, and began drinking. "Don't drink too much; you'll get sick," Roberto shouted. No sooner had he said that than I felt sick to my stomach. I dropped to my knees and let the jug roll off my hands. I remained motionless with my eyes glued on the hot sandy ground. All I could hear was the drone of insects. Slowly I began to recover. I poured water over my face and neck and watched the dirty water run down my arms to the ground.

I still felt a little dizzy when we took a break to eat lunch. It was past two o'clock and we sat underneath a large walnut tree that was on the side of the road. While we ate, Papá jotted down the number of boxes we had picked. Roberto drew designs on the ground with a stick. Suddenly I noticed Papá's face turn pale as he looked down the road. "Here comes the school bus," he whispered loudly in alarm.

Instinctively, Roberto and I ran and hid in the vineyards. We did not want to get in trouble for not going to school. The neatly dressed boys about my age got off. They carried books under their arms. After they crossed the street, the bus drove away. Roberto and I came out from hiding and joined

Vocabulary Development: **drone** (drōn) *n.* continuous humming sound
instinctively (in stiŋk´ tiv lē) *adv.* done by instinct, without thinking

Papá. "*Tienen que tener cuidado,*"[10] he warned us.

After lunch we went back to work. The sun kept beating down. The buzzing insects, the wet sweat, and the hot dry dust made the afternoon seem to last forever. Finally the mountains around the valley reached out and swallowed the sun. Within an hour it was too dark to continue picking. The vines blanketed the grapes, making it difficult to see the bunches. "*Vámonos,*"[11] said Papá, signaling to us that it was time to quit work. Papá then took out a pencil and began to figure out how much we had earned our first day. He wrote down numbers, crossed some out, wrote down some more. "*Quince,*"[12] he murmured.

When we arrived home, we took a cold shower underneath a waterhose. We then sat down to eat dinner around some wooden crates that served as a table. Mamá had cooked a special meal for us. We had rice and tortillas with "*carne con chile,*"[13] my favorite dish.

The next morning I could hardly move. My body ached all over. I felt little control over my arms and legs. This feeling went on every morning for days until my muscles finally got used to the work.

It was Monday, the first week of November. The grape season was over and I could now go to school. I woke up early that morning and lay in bed, looking at the stars and savoring the thought of not going to work and of starting sixth grade for the first time that year. Since I could not sleep, I decided to get up and join Papá and Roberto at breakfast. I sat at the table across from Roberto, but I kept my head down. I did not want to look up and face him. I knew he was sad. He was not going to school today. He was not going tomorrow, or next week, or next month. He would not go until the cotton season was over, and that was sometime in February. I rubbed my hands together and watched the dry, acid stained skin fall to the floor in little rolls.

When Papá and Roberto left for work, I felt relief. I walked to the top of a small grade next to the shack and watched the "Carcanchita" disappear in the distance in a cloud of dust.

Two hours later, around eight o'clock, I stood by the side of the road waiting for school bus number twenty. When it

Vocabulary Development: savoring (sā´ vər iŋ) *v.* enjoying with appreciation; tasting; relishing

10. **Tienen que tener cuidado** (tē en´ en kā ten er´ kwē thä´ thō) Spanish for "You have to be careful."
11. **Vámonos** (vä´ mō nōs) Spanish for "Let's go."
12. **Quince** (kēn´ sā) Spanish for "fifteen."
13. **"carne con chile"** (kär´ nā kən chil´ ā) dish of ground meat, hot peppers, beans, and tomatoes.

◆ Literary Analysis

A circuit is an unbroken path, like a circle—something that goes around and around without ever changing. How does the bracketed passage connect with this **theme**?

◆ Stop to Reflect

In the bracketed text, what is unusual about Panchito's just starting the sixth grade "for the first time that year"?

◆ Reading Check

Why is Panchito finally able to go to school?

◆ Literary Analysis

In the bracketed text, Panchito seems to know exactly what he must do to enroll in school, as if he has done it many times before. How does this fact relate to the circle **theme** of the story?

◆ Reading Strategy

Break up the underlined sentences into meaningful parts by making lines on the page. Use this strategy to help you **read accurately.** Who is the subject in sentences one and two?

Mark THE Text

What are the sentences about?

arrived I climbed in. Everyone was busy either talking or yelling. I sat in an empty seat in the back.

When the bus stopped in front of the school, I felt very nervous. I looked out the bus window and saw boys and girls carrying books under their arms. I put my hands in my pant pockets and walked to the principal's office. When I entered I heard a woman's voice say: "May I help you?" I was startled. I had not heard English for months. For a few seconds I remained speechless. I looked at the lady who waited for my answer. My first instinct was to answer her in Spanish, but I held back. Finally, after struggling for English words, I managed to tell her that I wanted to enroll in the sixth grade. After answering many questions, I was led to the classroom.

Mr. Lema, the sixth-grade teacher, greeted me and assigned me a desk. He then introduced me to the class. I was so nervous and scared at that moment when everyone's eyes were on me that I wished I were with Papá and Roberto picking cotton. After taking roll, Mr. Lema gave the class the assignment for the first hour. "The first thing we have to do this morning is finish reading the story we began yesterday," he said enthusiastically. He walked up to me, handed me an English book, and asked me to read. "We are on page 125," he said politely. When I heard this, I felt my blood rush to my head; I felt dizzy. "Would you like to read?" he asked hesitantly. I opened the book to page 125. My mouth was dry. My eyes began to water. I could not begin. "You can read later," Mr. Lema said understandingly.

For the rest of the reading period I kept getting angrier and angrier at myself. I should have read, I thought to myself.

During recess I went into the restroom and opened my English book to page 125. I began to read in a low voice, pretending I was in class. There were many words I did not know. I closed the book and headed back to the classroom.

Mr. Lema was sitting at his desk correcting papers. When I entered he looked up at me and smiled. I felt better. I walked up to him and asked if he could help me with the new words. "Gladly," he said.

The rest of the month I spent my lunch hours working on English with Mr. Lema, my best friend at school.

One Friday during lunch hour Mr. Lema asked me to take a walk with him to the music room. "Do you like music?" he asked me as we entered the building.

"Yes, I like corridos,"[14] I answered. He then picked up a trumpet, blew on it and handed it to me. The sound gave me goose bumps. I knew that sound. I had heard it in many corridos. "How would you like to learn how to play it?" he

14. **corridos** (kō rē′ thōs) *n.* ballads.

asked. He must have read my face because before I could answer, he added: "I'll teach you how to play it during our lunch hours."

That day I could hardly wait to get home to tell Papá and Mamá the great news. As I got off the bus, my little brothers and sisters ran up to meet me. They were yelling and screaming. I thought they were happy to see me, but when I opened the door to our shack, I saw that everything we owned was neatly packed in cardboard boxes.

Reader's Response: How do you think Panchito felt when he came back to the shack and found the packed boxes? Explain.

Thinking About the Skill: When you broke up a sentence into meaningful parts, how did it help you read more accurately?

◆ **Reading Check**

What happens in school that makes Panchito excited?

◆ **Literary Analysis**

The theme of this story is a circuit or circle. How does Panchito's experience at the end of the story support the story's theme?

Hard as Nails

Russell Baker

Summary

In his essay "Hard as Nails," Russell Baker describes his first job—delivering newspapers in Baltimore. He is hired on his twelfth birthday by Mr. Deems, a supervisor who works him hard. One evening, Deems gives the newsboys a tour of the newsroom of the *Baltimore News-Post*. Deems says that the newsboys might have important jobs at the newspaper someday. In a special paper for carriers, William Randolph Hearst, the publisher, writes that delivering newspapers is a great life. Young Russell agrees. When Deems quits his job, Russell thinks of him as "hard as nails," just like the newspaper business.

Visual Summary

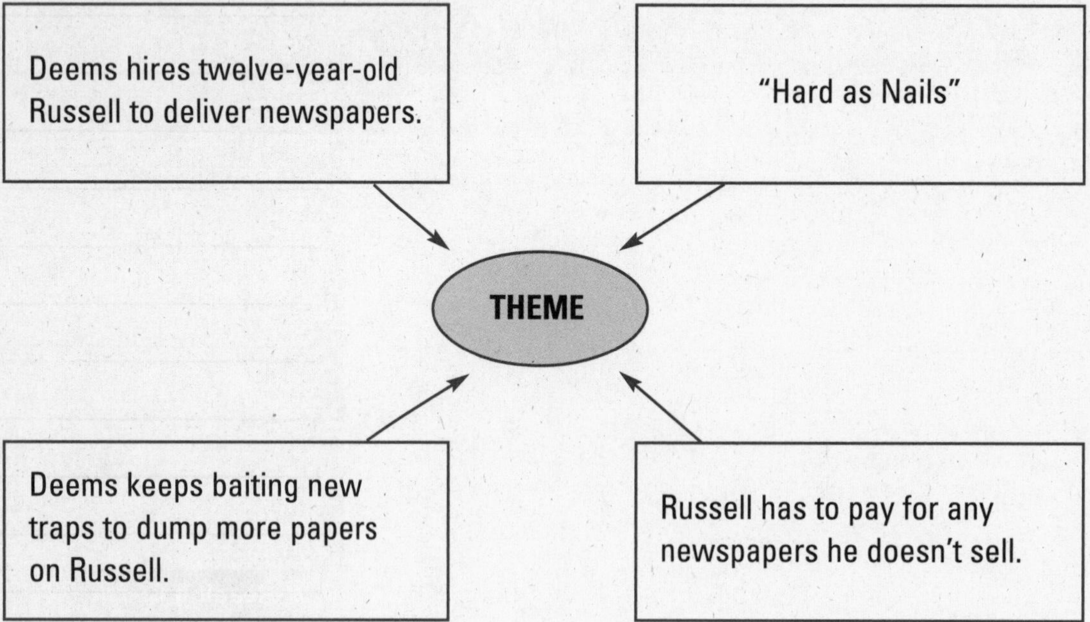
Deems hires twelve-year-old Russell to deliver newspapers.
"Hard as Nails"
THEME
Deems keeps baiting new traps to dump more papers on Russell.
Russell has to pay for any newspapers he doesn't sell.

Hard as Nails

Russell Baker

During the 1930s, one out of every four workers in the United States was unemployed. Russell Baker's father died in 1930, leaving his family with relatives.

My mother started me in newspaper work in 1937 right after my twelfth birthday. She would have started me younger, but there was a law against working before age twelve. She thought it was a silly law, and said so to Deems.

Deems was boss of a group of boys who worked home delivery routes for the *Baltimore News-Post.* She found out about him a few weeks after we got to Baltimore. She just went out on the street, stopped a paperboy, and asked how he'd got his job.

"There's this man Deems . . ."

Deems was short and plump and had curly brown hair. He owned a car and a light gray suit and always wore a necktie and white shirt. A real businessman, I thought the first time I saw him. My mother was talking to him on the sidewalk in front of the Union Square Methodist Church and I was standing as tall as I could, just out of earshot.

"Now, Buddy, when we get down there keep your shoulders back and stand up real straight," she had cautioned me after making sure my necktie was all right and my shirt clean.

[Watching the two of them in conversation, with Deems glancing at me now and then, I kept my shoulders drawn back in the painful military style I'd seen in movies, trying to look a foot taller than I really was.]

"Come over here, Russ, and meet Mister Deems," she finally said, and I did, managing to answer his greeting by saying, "The pleasure's all mine," which I'd heard people say in the movies. I probably blushed while saying it, because meeting strangers was painfully embarrassing to me.

"If that's the rule, it's the rule," my mother was telling Deems, "and we'll just have to put up with it, but it still doesn't make any sense to me."

As we walked back to the house she said I couldn't have a paper route until I was twelve. And all because of some foolish rule they had down here in Baltimore. You'd think if a boy wanted to work they would encourage him instead of making him stay idle so long that laziness got <u>embedded</u> in his bones.

That was April. We had barely finished the birthday cake

Vocabulary Development: embedded (em bed′ əd) *adj.* firmly fixed in a surrounding material

◆ Activate Prior Knowledge

Write about a time when you felt good because you were able to help your family or someone else. Describe the time below.

◆ Literary Strategy

Mark the Text

To help you **read accurately,** break down the bracketed passage into meaningful parts by marking lines. What is the subject of the sentence?

What is the subject doing?

What else is the sentence about?

◆ Reading Check

Why does the narrator want a paper route?

in August before Deems came by the apartment and gave me the tools of the newspaper trade: an account book for keeping track of the customers' bills and a long, brown web belt. Slung around one shoulder and across the chest, the belt made it easy to balance fifteen or twenty pounds of papers against the hip. I had to buy my own wire cutters for opening the newspaper bundles the trucks dropped at Wisengoff's store on the corner of Stricker and West Lombard streets.

In February my mother had moved us down from New Jersey, where we had been living with her brother Allen ever since my father died in 1930. This move of hers to Baltimore was a step toward fulfilling a dream. More than almost anything else in the world, she wanted "a home of our own." I'd heard her talk of that "home of our own" all through those endless Depression years when we lived as poor relatives dependent on Uncle Allen's goodness. "A home of our own. One of these days, Buddy, we'll have a home of our own."

That winter she had finally saved just enough to make her move, and she came to Baltimore. There were several reasons for Baltimore. For one, there were people she knew in Baltimore, people she could go to if things got desperate. And desperation was possible, because the moving would exhaust her savings, and the apartment rent was twenty-four dollars a month. She would have to find a job quickly. My sister Doris was only nine, but I was old enough for an after-school job that could bring home a few dollars a week. So as soon as it was legal I went into newspaper work.

The romance of it was almost unbearable on my first day as I trudged west along Lombard Street, then south along Gilmor, and east down Pratt Street with the bundle of newspapers strapped to my hip. I imagined people pausing to admire me as I performed this important work, spreading the news of the world, the city, and the racetracks onto doorsteps, through mail slots, and under door jambs. I had often gazed with envy at paperboys; to be one of them at last was happiness sublime.

Very soon, though, I discovered drawbacks. The worst of these was Deems. Though I had only forty customers, Deems sent papers for forty-five. Since I was billed for every paper left on Wisengoff's corner, I had to pay for the five extra copies out of income or try to hustle them on the street. I hated standing at streetcar stops yelling, "Paper! Paper!" at

Vocabulary Development: **exhaust** (ig zôst′) v. use up
sublime (sə blīm′) adj. majestic; causing awe
drawbacks (drô′ baks′) *n.* disadvantages

◆ Literary Analysis

The **theme,** or cental point, of this essay is that the newspaper business is really difficult or "hard as nails." What details in the bracketed text support the theme?

◆ Stop to Reflect

Why do you think a "home of our own" is so important to the narrator's mother?

◆ Reading Check

What is one good thing and one bad thing about being a newsboy, according to Baker?

Good:

Bad:

people getting off trolleys.[1] Usually, if my mother wasn't around to catch me, I stuck the extras in a dark closet and took the loss.

Deems was constantly baiting new traps to dump more papers on me. When I solved the problem of the five extras by getting five new subscribers for home delivery, Deems announced a competition with mouth-watering prizes for the newsboys who got the most new subscribers. Too innocent to cope with this sly master of private enterprise,[2] I took the bait.

"Look at these prizes I can get for signing up new customers," I told my mother. "A balloon-tire bicycle. A free pass to the movies for a whole year."

The temptation was too much. I reported my five new subscribers to help me in the competition.

Whereupon Deems promptly raised my order from forty-five to fifty papers, leaving me again with the choice of hustling to unload the five extras or losing money.

I won a free pass to the movies, though. It was good for a whole year. And to the magnificent Loew's Century located downtown on Lexington Street. The passes were good only for nights in the middle of the week when I usually had too much homework to allow for movies. Still, in the summer with school out, it was thrilling to go all the way downtown at night to sit in the Century's damask[3] and velvet splendor and see MGM's glamorous stars in their latest movies.

To collect my prize I had to go to a banquet the paper gave for its "honor carriers" at the Emerson Hotel. <u>There were fifty of us, and I was sure the other forty-nine would all turn out to be slicksters wised up to the ways of the world, who would laugh at my doltish ignorance of how to eat at a great hotel banquet</u>. My fear of looking foolish at the banquet made me lie awake nights dreading it and imagining all the humiliating mistakes I could make.

I had seen banquets in movies. Every plate was surrounded by a baffling array of knives, forks, and spoons. I knew it would be the same at the Emerson Hotel. The Emerson was one of the swankiest hotels in Baltimore. It was not likely to hold down on the silverware. I talked to my mother.

"How will I know what to eat what with?"

The question did not interest her.

"Just watch what everybody else does, and enjoy yourself," she said.

I came back to the problem again and again.

"Do you use the same spoon for your coffee as you do for dessert?"

---

1. **trolleys** (träl′ ēz) *n.* electric passenger trains, also called streetcars, running on rails in the city streets; discontinued in many American cities after the mid-1900s.
2. **private enterprise** business run for profit.
3. **damask** (dam′ əsk) *adj.* decorated with the shiny cloth called damask.

◆ Literary Analysis

Mark the Text

How does Deems get the newsboys to sell more newspapers? Underline the ideas he comes up with. How do these projects relate to the **theme** of the essay?

____

____

____

____

____

____

◆ Reading Strategy

Mark the Text

To help you **read accurately,** mark the underlined sentence with lines, dividing it into meaningful groups of words. Then, read the sentence aloud, pausing for punctuation. What is the subject?

____

____

What does the subject do?

____

____

____

____

____

____

____

◆ Reading Check

Why is Baker so nervous about going to the banquet?

◆ Reading Strategy

Read the underlined sentence aloud, pausing after the punctuation. Stress the subject, which falls at the end of the sentence. Circle the subject. What is the sentence about?

Mark THE Text

◆ Reading Check

Where does Deems take the newsboys?

"Don't worry about it. Everybody isn't going to be staring at you."

"Is it all right to butter your bread with the same knife you use to cut the meat?"

"Just go and have a good time."

Close to panic, I showed up at the Emerson, found my way to the banquet, and was horrified to find that I had to sit beside Deems throughout the meal. We probably talked about something, but I was so busy sweating with terror and rolling my eyeballs sidewise to see what silverware Deems was using to eat with that I didn't hear a word all night. The following week, Deems started sending me another five extras.

Now and then he also provided a treat. One day in 1938 he asked if I would like to join a small group of boys he was taking to visit the *News-Post* newsroom. My mother, in spite of believing that nothing came before homework at night, wasn't coldhearted enough to deny me a chance to see the city room[4] of a great metropolitan newspaper. I had seen plenty of city rooms in the movies. They were glamorous places full of exciting people like Lee Tracey, Edmund Lowe, and Adolphe Menjou[5] trading wisecracks and making mayors and cops look like saps. To see such a place, to stand, actually stand, in the city room of a great newspaper and look at reporters who were in touch every day with killers and professional baseball players—that was a thrilling prospect.

Because the *News-Post* was an afternoon paper, almost everybody had left for the day when we got there that night. The building, located downtown near the harbor, was disappointing. It looked like a factory, and not a very big factory either. Inside there was a smell compounded of ink, pulp, chemicals, paste, oil, gasoline, greasy rags, and hot metal. We took an elevator up and came into a long room filled with dilapidated[6] desks, battered telephones, and big blocky typewriters. Almost nobody there, just two or three men in shirtsleeves. It was the first time I'd ever seen Deems look awed.

"Boys, this is the nerve center of the newspaper," he said, his voice heavy and solemn like the voice of Westbrook Van Voorhis, the *March of Time*[7] man, when he said, "Time marches on."

I was confused. I had expected the newsroom to have glamour, but this place had nothing but squalor. The walls hadn't been painted for years. The windows were filthy.

4. **city room** the office at a newspaper used by those who report on city events.
5. **Lee Tracey, Edmund Lowe, and Adolphe Menjou** actors in movies of the period.
6. **dilapidated** (də lap′ ə dāt′ əd) *adj.* run-down; in bad condition.
7. ***March of Time*** *March of Time* was a newsreel series that ran from 1935 to 1951, showing current news events along with interviews and dramatizations. Newsreels were shown between feature films at movie theaters.

Desks were heaped with mounds of crumpled paper, torn sheets of newspaper, overturned paste pots, dog-eared telephone directories. The floor was ankle deep in newsprint, carbon paper, and crushed cigarette packages. Waist-high cans overflowed with trash. Ashtrays were buried under cigarette ashes and butts. Ugly old wooden chairs looked ready for the junk shop.

It looked to me like a place that probably had more cockroaches than we had back home on Lombard Street, but Deems was seeing it through rose-colored glasses.[8] As we stood looking around at the ruins, he started telling us how lucky we were to be newsboys. Lucky to have a foot on the upward ladder so early in life. If we worked hard and kept expanding our paper routes we could make the men who ran this paper sit up and notice us. And when men like that noticed you, great things could happen, because they were important men, the most important of all being the man who owned our paper: Mr. Hearst Himself, William Randolph Hearst, founder of the greatest newspaper organization in America. A great man, Mr. Hearst, but not so great that he didn't appreciate his newsboys, who were the backbone of the business. Many of whom would someday grow up and work at big jobs on this paper. Did we realize that any of us, maybe all of us, could end up one of these days sitting right here in this vitally important room, the newsroom, the nerve center of the newspaper?

Yes, Deems was right. Riding home on the streetcar that night, I realized I was a lucky boy to be getting such an early start up the ladder of journalism. It was childish to feel let down because the city room looked like such a dump instead of like city rooms in the movies. Deems might be a slave driver, but he was doing it for my own good, and I ought to be grateful. In *News Selling*, the four-page special paper Mr. Hearst published just for his newsboys, they'd run a piece that put it almost as beautifully as Deems had.

YOU'RE A MEMBER OF THE FOURTH ESTATE was the headline on it. I was so impressed that I put the paper away in a safe place and often took it out to read when I needed inspiration. It told how "a great English orator" named Edmund Burke "started a new name for a new profession—the Fourth Estate . . . the press . . . NEWSPAPER MEN."[9]

And it went on to say:

"The Fourth Estate was then . . . and IS now . . . a great estate for HE-men . . . workers . . . those who are proud of the business they're in!"

---

8. **seeing it through rose-colored glasses** ignoring its unappealing features or drawbacks.
9. **Edmund Burke . . . Fourth Estate** Edmund Burke (1729–1797) was an English political figure famous for his speeches and essays. He called the press the "Fourth Estate."

◆ **Reading Check**

What is Baker's first impression of the newsroom?

What is Deems's view of the newspaper business?

◆ **Reading Strategy**

Read the underlined passage aloud. What was Deems right about?

What is the subject of the second sentence?

◆ **Reading Check**

Why is Baker impressed by Hearst's special paper?

◆ **Stop to Reflect**

How might Baker's experience as a newsboy have prepared him for his job as a news reporter?

◆ **Reading Check**

How does Baker react to Deems's quitting?

(Mr. Hearst always liked plenty of exclamation marks, dots, and capital letters.)

"Get that kick of pride that comes from knowing you are a newspaper man. That means something!

"A newspaper man never ducks a dare. YOU are a newspaper man. A salesman of newspapers . . . the final cog[10] in the immense machine of newspaper production—a SERVICE for any man to be proud of.

"So throw back the chest. Hit the route hard each day. Deliver fast and properly. Sell every day. Add to your route because you add to the NEWSPAPER field when you do. And YOU MAKE MONEY DOING IT. It is a great life—a grand opportunity. Don't boot it—build it up. Leave it better than when you came into it."

"It is a great life." I kept coming back to that sentence as I read and reread the thing. No matter how awful it got, and it sometimes got terrible, I never quit believing it was a great life. I kept at it until I was almost sixteen, chest thrown back, delivering fast and properly, selling every day and adding to my route. At the end I'd doubled its size and was making as much as four dollars a week from it.

A few months after he took us down to see the city room, Deems quit. My mother said he'd found a better job. Later, when I thought about him, I wondered if maybe it wasn't because he hated himself for having to make life tough for boys. I hoped that wasn't the reason because he was the first newspaperman I ever knew, and I wanted him to be the real thing. Hard as nails.

Vocabulary Development: immense (i mens′) *adj.* huge

10. **cog** (cäg) *n.* gear.

Reader's Response: Would you like to work for Deems? Why or why not?

Thinking About the Skill: How did breaking down long sentences into parts help you understand this essay?

PREVIEW

How to Write a Letter

Garrison Keillor

Summary

In his informal essay "How to Write a Letter," Garrison Keillor offers amusing but practical advice to letter writers. He claims that letters are better than phone calls because they can be enjoyed over and over. People should write, he says, so that news of their lives will be known. He advises writers to forget the guilt of not having written for a long time. He suggests that they simply plunge into the task and not worry about grammar or style. If no ideas come, he advises writers to start by describing the present moment—where they are and what it's like. Keillor ends by saying that a writer's letters might be reread and enjoyed years later, even by the recipient's grandchildren.

Visual Summary

STEPS IN WRITING A LETTER

- Don't feel guilty for not writing.
- Keep writing stuff in one place.
- Think about person you will write to.
- Write the salutation and plunge in.
- Don't think about grammar or style. Don't try to impress.
- Don't worry about mistakes or form.

How to Write a Letter

Garrison Keillor

Historians have discovered many things about daily life in the past from letters people wrote each other. In this amusing essay, Garrison Keillor encourages you not to deprive future historians of this wonderful resource.

We shy persons need to write a letter now and then, or else we'll dry up and blow away. It's true. And I speak as one who loves to reach for the phone, dial the number, and talk. I say, "Big Bopper here—what's shakin', babes?" The telephone is to shyness what Hawaii is to February, it's a way out of the woods, *and yet*: a letter is better.

Such a sweet gift—a piece of handmade writing, in an envelope that is not a bill, sitting in our friend's path when she trudges home from a long day spent among wahoos and savages, a day our words will help repair. They don't need to be immortal, just sincere. She can read them twice and again tomorrow: *You're someone I care about, Corinne, and think of often and every time I do you make me smile.*

We need to write, otherwise nobody will know who we are. They will have only a vague impression of us as A Nice Person, because, frankly, we don't shine at conversation, we lack the confidence to thrust our faces forward and say, "Hi, I'm Heather Hooten; let me tell you about my week." Mostly we say "Uh-huh" and "Oh, really." People smile and look over our shoulder, looking for someone else to meet.

So a shy person sits down and writes a letter. To be known by another person—to meet and talk freely on the page—to be close despite distance. To escape from anonymity and be our own sweet selves and express the music of our souls.

Same thing that moves a giant rock star to sing his heart out in front of 123,000 people moves us to take ballpoint in hand and write a few lines to our dear Aunt Eleanor. *We want to be known.* We want her to know that we have fallen in love, that we quit our job, that we're moving to New York, and we want to say a few things that might not get said in casual conversation: *Thank you for what you've meant to me, I am very happy right now.*

The first step in writing letters is to get over the guilt of *not* writing. You don't "owe" anybody a letter. Letters are a gift. The burning shame you feel when you see unanswered mail makes it harder to pick up a pen and makes for a

Vocabulary Development: confidence (kän′ fi dəns′) *n.* belief in one's own abilities
anonymity (an′ ə nim′ ə tē) *n.* the condition of being unknown

◆ Activate Prior Knowledge

Jot down two helpful hints for someone who is about to write a letter to a friend.

1. ____________________

2. ____________________

____

◆ Literary Analysis

An **informal essay** is a brief nonfiction work. It is written in a conversational style. It may be humorous. Circle three details in the text that identify this as an informal essay.

Mark THE Text

◆ Reading Strategy

Let your voice reflect the meaning of words when you **read aloud.** In the bracketed paragraph, circle the author's main point. Underline a short sentence. Then read the paragraph aloud, slowing down for the main point, and pausing before the short sentence.

Mark THE Text

◆ Reading Check

What kind of person benefits most from writing a letter now and then?

____

____

____

____

cheerless letter when you finally do. *I feel bad about not writing, but I've been so busy,* etc. Skip this. Few letters are obligatory, and they are *Thanks for the wonderful gift* and *I am terribly sorry to hear about George's death* and *Yes, you're welcome to stay with us next month,* and not many more than that. Write those promptly if you want to keep your friends. Don't worry about the others, except love letters, of course. When your true love writes, *Dear Light of My Life, Joy of My Heart, O Lovely Pulsating Core of My Sensate*[1] *Life,* some response is called for.

Some of the best letters are tossed off in a burst of inspiration, so keep your writing stuff in one place where you can sit down for a few minutes and (*Dear Roy, I am in the middle of a book entitled* We Are Still Married *but thought I'd drop you a line. Hi to your sweetie, too*) dash off a note to a pal. Envelopes, stamps, address book, everything in a drawer so you can write fast when the pen is hot.

A blank white eight-by-eleven sheet can look as big as Montana if the pen's not so hot—try a smaller page and write boldly. Or use a note card with a piece of fine art on the front; if your letter ain't good, at least they get the Matisse.[2] Get a pen that makes a sensuous[3] line, get a comfortable typewriter, a friendly word processor—whichever feels easy to the hand.

Sit for a few minutes with the blank sheet in front of you, and meditate on the person you will write to, let your friend come to mind until you can almost see her or him in the room with you. Remember the last time you saw each other and how your friend looked and what you said and what perhaps was unsaid between you, and when your friend becomes real to you, start to write.

Write the salutation—*Dear You*—and take a deep breath and plunge in. A simple declarative sentence will do, followed by another and another and another. Tell us what you're doing and tell it like you were talking to us. Don't think about grammar, don't think about lit'ry style, don't try to write dramatically, just give us your news. Where did you go, who did you see, what did they say, what do you think?

If you don't know where to begin, start with the present moment: *I'm sitting at the kitchen table on a rainy Saturday morning. Everyone is gone and the house is quiet.* Let your simple description of the present moment lead to something else, let the letter drift gently along.

Vocabulary Development: obligatory (əb ligʹ ə torʹ ē) *adj.* required

1. **sensate** (senʹ sāt) *adj.* having the power of sensory perception.
2. **Matisse** Henri Matisse (än rē mə tēsʹ) (1869–1954), a French painter.
3. **sensuous** (senʹ sho͞o əs) *adj.* readily grasped by the senses.

◆ Stop to Reflect

Why do you think that the letters the writer describes are obligatory, or required?

____

____

____

____

____

◆ Literary Analysis

Mark the Text

Circle three words or word groups in the bracketed paragraph that show that Keillor is writing an **informal essay.**

◆ Reading Check

Mark the Text

Circle the sentence that tells what to do just before you start writing.

◆ Reading Strategy

Look closely at the underlined sentences and then **read** them **aloud.** Use the tone of your voice to distinguish the sentences in the italic type from the other sentence.

◆ Literary Analysis

If this were a formal rather than an **informal essay**, a few comical things in the bracketed paragraph might not be included. Circle two groups of words that make this paragraph seem informal.

Mark THE Text

◆ Stop to Reflect

Keillor says, "Writing is a means of discovery." What do you think you might discover from writing a letter?

The toughest letter to crank out is one that is meant to impress, as we all know from writing job applications; if it's hard work to slip off a letter to a friend, maybe you're trying too hard to be terrific. A letter is only a report to someone who already likes you for reasons other than your brilliance. Take it easy.

Don't worry about form. It's not a term paper. When you come to the end of one episode, just start a new paragraph. You can go from a few lines about the sad state of pro football to the fight with your mother to your fond memories of Mexico to your cat's urinary-tract infection to a few thoughts on personal indebtedness and on to the kitchen sink and what's in it. The more you write, the easier it gets, and when you have a True True Friend to write to, a *compadre*,[4] a soul sibling, then it's like driving a car down a country road, you just get behind the keyboard and press on the gas.

Don't tear up the page and start over when you write a bad line—try to write your way out of it. Make mistakes and plunge on. Let the letter cook along and let yourself be bold. Outrage, confusion, love—whatever is in your mind, let it find a way to the page. Writing is a means of discovery, always, and when you come to the end and write *Yours ever* or *Hugs and kisses*, you'll know something you didn't when you wrote *Dear Pal*.

Probably your friend will put your letter away, and it'll be read again a few years from now—and it will improve with age. And forty years from now, your friend's grandkids will dig it out of the attic and read it, a sweet and precious relic of the ancient eighties that gives them a sudden clear glimpse of you and her and the world we old-timers knew. You will then have created an object of art. Your simple lines about where you went, who you saw, what they said, will speak to those children and they will feel in their hearts the humanity of our times.

You can't pick up a phone and call the future and tell them about our times. You have to pick up a piece of paper.

Vocabulary Development: episode (ep′ ə sōd′) *n.* one in a series of related events
sibling (sib′ liŋ) *n.* brother or sister

4. **compadre** (kəm päd′ rā) *n.* Spanish for buddy; close friend.

Reader's Response: Did reading this essay make you feel that you wanted to write a letter to someone? Why, and to whom?

PREVIEW

Aaron's Gift

Myron Levoy

Summary

In "Aaron's Gift," ten-year-old Aaron Kandel finds an injured pigeon while he is skating in the park. He captures the pigeon and brings it home. There he sets the bird's broken wing. Aaron plans to give the pigeon to his grandmother as a birthday present. Unfortunately, a gang of neighborhood boys invites Aaron to join their club. Aaron discovers that the boys plan to burn the pigeon. He is beaten up rescuing the bird, which flies away. Aaron's grandmother is grateful for the gift of the bird's freedom.

Visual Summary

EVENT
Aaron finds injured pigeon.

↓

EVENT
Aaron fixes pigeon's broken wing and decides to give bird to his grandmother.

↓

EVENT
Boys invite Aaron to join their club and tell him to bring pigeon.

↓

CLIMAX
Aaron is beaten up rescuing the pigeon.

↓

CONCLUSION
Pigeon flies away and grandmother is grateful for gift of bird's freedom.

◆ **Activate Prior Knowledge**

Think of a time when you planned to give someone a special gift. What made this gift so special? Describe the situation below.

____

____

____

____

____

____

____

____

____

____

____

____

____

____

____

____

____

Aaron's Gift

Myron Levoy

Pigeons are a very common sight in every city, including New York City, where Aaron Kandel lives. Many people think of them as a nuisance. Aaron, though, is a good-hearted boy who tries to do something kind for his grandmother and ends up helping a defenseless bird as well.

Aaron Kandel had come to Tompkins Square Park to roller-skate, for the streets near Second Avenue were always too crowded with children and peddlers and old ladies and baby buggies. Though few children had bicycles in those days, almost every child owned a pair of roller skates. And Aaron was, it must be said, a Class A, triple-fantastic roller skater.

Aaron skated back and forth on the wide walkway of the park, pretending he was an aviator in an air race zooming around pylons, which were actually two lampposts. During his third lap around the racecourse, he noticed a pigeon on the grass, behaving very strangely. Aaron skated to the line of benches, then climbed over onto the lawn.

The pigeon was trying to fly, but all it could manage was to flutter and turn round and round in a large circle, as if it were performing a frenzied dance. The left wing was only half open and was beating in a clumsy, jerking fashion; it was clearly broken.

Luckily, Aaron hadn't eaten the cookies he'd stuffed into his pocket before he'd gone clacking down the three flights of stairs from his apartment, his skates already on. He broke a cookie into small crumbs and tossed some toward the pigeon. "Here pidge, here pidge," he called. The pigeon spotted the cookie crumbs and, after a moment, stopped thrashing about. It folded its wings as best it could, but the broken wing still stuck half out. Then it strutted over to the crumbs, its head bobbing forth-back, forth-back, as if it were marching a little in front of the rest of the body—perfectly normal, except for that half-open wing which seemed to make the bird stagger sideways every so often.

The pigeon began eating the crumbs as Aaron quickly unbuttoned his shirt and pulled it off. Very slowly, he edged toward the bird, making little kissing sounds like the ones he heard his grandmother make when she fed the sparrows on the back fire escape.

Then suddenly Aaron plunged. The shirt, in both hands, came down like a torn parachute. The pigeon beat its wings, but Aaron held the shirt to the ground, and the bird couldn't

◆ **Reading Check**

How is Aaron able to coax the pigeon to him?

____

____

____

____

____

Vocabulary Development: frenzied (fren′ zēd) *adj.* wild; frantic

escape. Aaron felt under the shirt, gently, and gently took hold of the wounded pigeon.

"Yes, yes, pidge," he said, very softly. "There's a good boy. Good pigeon, good."

The pigeon struggled in his hands, but little by little Aaron managed to soothe it. "Good boy, pidge. That's your new name. Pidge. I'm gonna take you home, Pidge. Yes, yes, *ssh.* Good boy. I'm gonna fix you up. Easy, Pidge, easy does it. Easy, boy."

Aaron squeezed through an opening between the row of benches and skated slowly out of the park, while holding the pigeon carefully with both hands as if it were one of his mother's rare, precious cups from the old country. How fast the pigeon's heart was beating! Was he afraid? Or did all pigeons' hearts beat fast?

It was fortunate that Aaron was an excellent skater, for he had to skate six blocks to his apartment, over broken pavement and sudden gratings and curbs and cobblestones. But when he reached home, he asked Noreen Callahan, who was playing on the stoop, to take off his skates for him. He would not chance going up three flights on roller skates this time.

"Is he sick?" asked Noreen.

"Broken wing," said Aaron. "I'm gonna fix him up and make him into a carrier pigeon or something."

"Can I watch?" asked Noreen.

"Watch what?"

"The operation. I'm gonna be a nurse when I grow up."

"OK," said Aaron. "You can even help. You can help hold him while I fix him up."

Aaron wasn't quite certain what his mother would say about his new-found pet, but he was pretty sure he knew what his grandmother would think. His grandmother had lived with them ever since his grandfather had died three years ago. And she fed the sparrows and jays and crows and robins on the back fire escape with every spare crumb she could find. In fact, Aaron noticed that she sometimes created crumbs where they didn't exist, by squeezing and tearing pieces of her breakfast roll when his mother wasn't looking.

Aaron didn't really understand his grandmother, for he often saw her by the window having long conversations with the birds, telling them about her days as a little girl in the Ukraine.[1] And once he saw her take her mirror from her handbag and hold it out toward the birds. She told Aaron that she wanted them to see how beautiful they were. Very strange. But Aaron did know that she would love Pidge, because she loved everything.

1. **Ukraine** (yo͞o krān´) country located in Eastern Europe. From 1924 to 1991, Ukraine was part of the Soviet Union.

◆ **Literary Analysis**

The plot of a story builds from event to event until it reaches the **climax**, or turning point. Do you think the pigeon's injury will be important to the plot and will help lead to the story's climax? Why?

____

____

____

____

____

____

____

____

◆ **Stop to Reflect**

Why does Aaron agree that Noreen can watch him fix Pidge?

____

____

____

____

◆ **Reading Check**

Mark the Text

Underline two sentences in the bracketed passage that clarify why Aaron thinks that his grandmother will love Pidge.

◆ **Stop to Reflect**

Why is the word *temporarily* repeated and set in italic type?

◆ **Reading Check**

How did Pidge react while having his wing fixed?

◆ **Reading Strategy**

A familiar word will sometimes be used in a new way. The word *longed* in the underlined sentence does not have anything to do with length. It means "wanted." Circle the words that help you understand its meaning.

Mark THE Text

To his surprise, his mother said he could keep the pigeon, temporarily, because it was sick, and we were all strangers in the land of Egypt,[2] and it might not be bad for Aaron to have a pet. *Temporarily.*

The wing was surprisingly easy to fix, for the break showed clearly and Pidge was remarkably patient and still, as if he knew he was being helped. Or perhaps he was just exhausted from all the thrashing about he had done. Two Popsicle sticks served as splints, and strips from an old undershirt were used to tie them in place. Another strip held the wing to the bird's body.

Aaron's father arrived home and stared at the pigeon. Aaron waited for the expected storm. But instead, Mr. Kandel asked, "Who *did* this?"

"Me," said Aaron. "And Noreen Callahan."

"Sophie!" he called to his wife. "Did you see this! Ten years old and it's better than Dr. Belasco could do. He's a genius!"

As the days passed, Aaron began training Pidge to be a carrier pigeon. He tied a little cardboard tube to Pidge's left leg and stuck tiny rolled-up sheets of paper with secret messages into it: THE ENEMY IS ATTACKING AT DAWN. Or: THE GUNS ARE HIDDEN IN THE TRUNK OF THE CAR. Or: VINCENT DEMARCO IS A BRITISH SPY. Then Aaron would set Pidge down at one end of the living room and put some popcorn at the other end. And Pidge would waddle slowly across the room, cooing softly, while the ends of his bandages trailed along the floor.

At the other end of the room, one of Aaron's friends would take out the message, stick a new one in, turn Pidge around, and aim him at the popcorn that Aaron put down on his side of the room.

And Pidge grew fat and contented on all the popcorn and crumbs and corn and crackers and Aaron's grandmother's breakfast rolls.

Aaron had told all the children about Pidge, but he only let his very best friends come up and play carrier-pigeon with him. But telling everyone had been a mistake. A group of older boys from down the block had a club—Aaron's mother called it a gang—and Aaron had longed to join as he had never longed for anything else. To be with them and share their secrets, the secrets of older boys. To be able to enter their clubhouse shack on the empty lot on the next street. To know the password and swear the secret oath. To belong.

2. **we were all . . . land of Egypt** a reference to the biblical story of the enslavement of the Hebrew people in Egypt.

About a month after Aaron had brought the pigeon home, Carl, the gang leader, walked over to Aaron in the street and told him he could be a member if he'd bring the pigeon down to be the club mascot. Aaron couldn't believe it; he immediately raced home to get Pidge. But his mother told Aaron to stay away from those boys, or else. And Aaron, miserable, argued with his mother and pleaded and cried and coaxed. It was no use. Not with those boys. No.

Aaron's mother tried to change the subject. She told him that it would soon be his grandmother's sixtieth birthday, a very special birthday indeed, and all the family from Brooklyn and the East Side would be coming to their apartment for a dinner and celebration. Would Aaron try to build something or make something for Grandma? A present made with his own hands would be nice. A decorated box for her hairpins or a crayon picture for her room or anything he liked.

In a flash Aaron knew what to give her: Pidge! Pidge would be her present! Pidge with his wing healed, who might be able to carry messages for her to the doctor or his Aunt Rachel or other people his grandmother seemed to go to a lot. It would be a surprise for everyone. And Pidge would make up for what had happened to Grandma when she'd been a little girl in the Ukraine, wherever that was.

Often, in the evening, Aaron's grandmother would talk about the old days long ago in the Ukraine, in the same way that she talked to the birds on the back fire escape. She had lived in a village near a place called Kishinev with hundreds of other poor peasant families like her own. Things hadn't been too bad under someone called Czar Alexander the Second,[3] whom Aaron always pictured as a tall handsome man in a gold uniform. But Alexander the Second was assassinated, and Alexander the Third, whom Aaron pictured as an ugly man in a black cape, became the Czar. And the Jewish people of the Ukraine had no peace anymore.

One day, a thundering of horses was heard coming toward the village from the direction of Kishinev. *The Cossacks! The Cossacks!* someone had shouted. The Czar's horsemen! Quickly, quickly, everyone in Aaron's grandmother's family had climbed down to the cellar through a little trapdoor hidden under a mat in the big central room of their shack. But

Vocabulary Development: **mascot** (mas´ kät) *n.* a person or animal adopted by a group
coaxed (kōkst) *v.* tried to persuade

3. **Czar Alexander the Second** leader of Russia from 1855 to 1881.

◆ **Literary Analysis**

How do the events in the bracketed paragraph help to increase tension as the story moves toward the **climax**?

◆ **Stop to Reflect**

Why might Aaron want to do something for his grandmother that would "make up" for what happened to her when she was a little girl?

◆ **Reading Check**

Now that his pigeon is getting well, what has Aaron decided to do with it?

his grandmother's pet goat, whom she'd loved as much as Aaron loved Pidge and more, had to be left above, because if it had made a sound in the cellar, they would never have lived to see the next morning. They all hid under the wood in the woodbin and waited, hardly breathing.

Suddenly, from above, they heard shouts and calls and screams at a distance. And then the noise was in their house. Boots pounding on the floor, and everything breaking and crashing overhead. The smell of smoke and the shouts of a dozen men.

The terror went on for an hour and then the sound of horses' hooves faded into the distance. They waited another hour to make sure, and then the father went up out of the cellar and the rest of the family followed. The door to the house had been torn from its hinges and every piece of furniture was broken. Every window, every dish, every stitch of clothing was totally destroyed, and one wall had been completely bashed in. And on the floor was the goat, lying quietly. Aaron's grandmother, who was just a little girl of eight at the time, had wept over the goat all day and all night and could not be consoled.

But they had been lucky. For other houses had been burned to the ground. And everywhere, not goats alone, nor sheep, but men and women and children lay quietly on the ground. The word for this sort of massacre, Aaron had learned, was *pogrom.* It had been a pogrom. And the men on the horses were Cossacks. Hated word. Cossacks.

And so Pidge would replace that goat of long ago. A pigeon on Second Avenue where no one needed trapdoors or secret escape passages or woodpiles to hide under. A pigeon for his grandmother's sixtieth birthday. *Oh wing, heal quickly so my grandmother can send you flying to everywhere she wants!*

But a few days later, Aaron met Carl in the street again. And Carl told Aaron that there was going to be a meeting that afternoon in which a map was going to be drawn up to show where a secret treasure lay buried on the empty lot. "Bring the pigeon and you can come into the shack. We got a badge for you. A new kinda membership badge with a secret code on the back."

Aaron ran home, his heart pounding almost as fast as the pigeon's. He took Pidge in his hands and carried him out the door while his mother was busy in the kitchen making stuffed cabbage, his father's favorite dish. And by the time he reached the street, Aaron had decided to take the bandages off. Pidge would look like a real pigeon again, and none of the older boys would laugh or call him a bundle of rags.

Vocabulary Development: consoled (kän sōld′) *v.* comforted

◆ Reading Check

What is a pogrom?

◆ Literary Analysis

Aaron's meeting with Carl adds tension to the story. What is troubling about their meeting?

Gently, gently he removed the bandages and the splints and put them in his pocket in case he should need them again. But Pidge seemed to hold his wing properly in place.

When he reached the empty lot, Aaron walked up to the shack, then hesitated. Four bigger boys were there. After a moment, Carl came out and commanded Aaron to hand Pidge over.

"Be careful," said Aaron. "I just took the bandages off."

"Oh sure, don't worry," said Carl. By now Pidge was used to people holding him, and he remained calm in Carl's hands.

"OK," said Carl. "Give him the badge." And one of the older boys handed Aaron his badge with the code on the back. "Now light the fire," said Carl.

"What . . . what fire?" asked Aaron.

"The fire. You'll see," Carl answered.

"You didn't say nothing about a fire," said Aaron. "You didn't say nothing to—"

"Hey!" said Carl. "I'm the leader here. And you don't talk unless I tell you that you have p'mission. Light the fire, Al."

The boy named Al went out to the side of the shack, where some wood and cardboard and old newspapers had been piled into a huge mound. He struck a match and held it to the newspapers.

"OK," said Carl. "Let's get 'er good and hot. Blow on it. Everybody blow."

Aaron's eyes stung from the smoke, but he blew alongside the others, going from side to side as the smoke shifted toward them and away.

"Let's fan it," said Al.

In a few minutes, the fire was crackling and glowing with a bright yellow-orange flame.

"Get me the rope," said Carl.

One of the boys brought Carl some cord and Carl, without a word, wound it twice around the pigeon, so that its wings were tight against its body.

"What . . . what are you *doing!*" shouted Aaron. "You're hurting his wing!"

"Don't worry about his wing," said Carl. "We're gonna throw him into the fire. And when we do, we're gonna swear an oath of loyalty to—"

"No! *No!*" shouted Aaron, moving toward Carl.

"Grab him!" called Carl. "Don't let him get the pigeon!"

But Aaron had leaped right across the fire at Carl, taking him completely by surprise. He threw Carl back against the shack and hit out at his face with both fists. Carl slid down to the ground and the pigeon rolled out of his hands. Aaron

◆ **Literary Analysis**

Mark the Text

The lighting of the fire raises the level of tension in the story. Circle the words that show Aaron is starting to worry.

◆ **Reading Check**

What do the boys plan to do with the pigeon?

____

____

____

scooped up the pigeon and ran, pretending he was on roller skates so that he would go faster and faster. And as he ran across the lot he pulled the cord off Pidge and tried to find a place, *any* place, to hide him. But the boys were on top of him, and the pigeon slipped from Aaron's hands.

"Get him!" shouted Carl.

Aaron thought of the worst, the most horrible thing he could shout at the boys. "Cossacks!" he screamed. "You're all Cossacks!"

Two boys held Aaron back while the others tried to catch the pigeon. Pidge fluttered along the ground just out of reach, skittering one way and then the other. Then the boys came at him from two directions. But suddenly Pidge beat his wings in rhythm, and rose up, up over the roof of the nearest tenement, up over Second Avenue toward the park.

With the pigeon gone, the boys turned toward Aaron and tackled him to the ground and punched him and tore his clothes and punched him some more. Aaron twisted and turned and kicked and punched back, shouting "Cossacks! Cossacks!" And somehow the word gave him the strength to tear away from them.

When Aaron reached home, he tried to go past the kitchen quickly so his mother wouldn't see his bloody face and torn clothing. But it was no use; his father was home from work early that night and was seated in the living room. In a moment Aaron was surrounded by his mother, father, and grandmother, and in another moment he had told them everything that had happened, the words tumbling out between his broken sobs. Told them of the present he had planned, of the pigeon for a goat, of the gang, of the badge with the secret code on the back, of the shack, and the fire, and the pigeon's flight over the tenement roof.

And Aaron's grandmother kissed him and thanked him for his present which was even better than the pigeon.

"What present?" asked Aaron, trying to stop the series of sobs.

And his grandmother opened her pocketbook and handed Aaron her mirror and asked him to look. But all Aaron saw was his dirty, bruised face and his torn shirt.

Aaron thought he understood and then, again, he thought he didn't. How could she be so happy when there really was no present? And why pretend that there was?

Later that night, just before he fell asleep, Aaron tried to imagine what his grandmother might have done with the pigeon. She would have fed it, and she certainly would have talked to it, as she did to all the birds, and . . . and then she

◆ Literary Analysis

The **climax** of the story occurs in the bracketed passage. Circle the sentence that you think is the most important. Then write why you think so.

Mark THE Text

____

____

____

____

____

____

◆ Stop to Reflect

Why do you think Aaron's grandmother is happy?

____

____

____

____

____

____

would have let it go free. Yes, of course. Pidge's flight to freedom must have been the gift that had made his grandmother so happy. Her goat has escaped from the Cossacks at last, Aaron thought, half dreaming. And he fell asleep with a smile.

Reader's Response: What would you have done if Carl had asked you to join his club? Explain.

____

____

____

Thinking About the Skill: How did clues you found in the context, or nearby text, help you understand the story?

____

____

◆ Stop to Reflect

In the underlined passage, why does Aaron think his grandmother's goat has escaped from the Cossacks?

____

____

____

____

____

____

PREVIEW

Water

Helen Keller

Summary

In "Water," six-year-old Helen Keller, who became blind and deaf at an early age, is extremely frustrated because she cannot understand the world around her. Her new teacher, Miss Sullivan, tries to teach Helen how to spell. Helen learns to hand-spell certain words by imitating her teacher. But she does not understand what the words mean. Helen grows impatient and acts in a destructive way. One day, Miss Sullivan runs water over one of Helen's hands and spells "w-a-t-e-r" in the other. For the first time, Helen makes a connection between a word and a thing she feels. Helen becomes eager to learn more.

Visual Summary

EVENT
Helen learns to spell d-o-l-l with her fingers by imitating Miss Sullivan, but doesn't know what it means.

EVENT
Helen grows impatient at Miss Sullivan's efforts to teach her and smashes her new doll on the floor.

CLIMAX
Helen makes the connection between w-a-t-e-r and water.

CONCLUSION
Helen becomes eager to learn more.

Water

Helen Keller

Everyone knows what water feels like. But not everyone experiences water as a doorway to understanding how words and things are connected, as Helen Keller did.

The morning after my teacher came she led me into her room and gave me a doll. The little blind children at the Perkins Institution had sent it and Laura Bridgman had dressed it; but I did not know this until afterward. When I had played with it a little while, Miss Sullivan slowly spelled into my hand the word "d-o-l-l." I was at once interested in this finger play and tried to imitate it. When I finally succeeded in making the letters correctly I was flushed with childish pleasure and pride. Running downstairs to my mother I held up my hand and made the letters for doll. I did not know that I was spelling a word or even that words existed; I was simply making my fingers go in monkey-like imitation. In the days that followed I learned to spell in this uncomprehending way a great many words, among them *pin, hat, cup* and a few verbs like *sit, stand* and *walk*. But my teacher had been with me several weeks before I understood that everything has a name.

One day, while I was playing with my new doll, Miss Sullivan put my big rag doll into my lap also, spelled "d-o-l-l" and tried to make me understand that "d-o-l-l" applied to both. Earlier in the day we had had a tussle over the words "m-u-g" and "w-a-t-e-r." Miss Sullivan had tried to impress it upon me that "m-u-g" is *mug* and that "w-a-t-e-r" is *water*, but I persisted in confounding the two. In despair she had dropped the subject for the time, only to renew it at the first opportunity. I became impatient at her repeated attempts and, seizing the new doll, I dashed it upon the floor. I was keenly delighted when I felt the fragments of the broken doll at my feet. Neither sorrow nor regret followed my passionate outburst. I had not loved the doll. In the still, dark world in which I lived there was no strong sentiment or tenderness. I felt my teacher sweep the fragments to one side of the hearth,[1] and I had a sense of satisfaction that the cause of my discomfort was removed. She brought me my hat, and I knew I was going out into the warm sunshine. This thought, if a wordless sensation may be called a thought, made me hop and skip with pleasure.

We walked down the path to the well-house, attracted by the fragrance of the honeysuckle with which it was covered.

1. **hearth** (härth) *n.* stone or brick floor of a fireplace, sometimes stretching out into the room.

◆ Activate Prior Knowledge

Think of a time when you felt frustrated because you could not understand something. Describe how you felt when you finally understood it.

____

____

____

____

____

____

____

____

◆ Reading Strategy

Sometimes a familiar word is used in a novel or new way. **Use context to clarify the meaning** of a difficult word by looking at the surrounding words. What is the meaning of *dashed* in the underlined passage?

____

____

What clues helped you figure it out?

____

____

____

◆ Reading Check

What skill is Miss Sullivan trying to teach Helen?

____

____

____

Some one was drawing water and my teacher placed my hand under the spout. As the cool stream gushed over one hand she spelled into the other the word *water*, first slowly, then rapidly. I stood still, my whole attention fixed upon the motions of her fingers. Suddenly I felt a misty consciousness as of something forgotten—a thrill of returning thought; and somehow the mystery of language was revealed to me. I knew then that "w-a-t-e-r" meant the wonderful cool something that was flowing over my hand. That living word awakened my soul, gave it light, hope, joy, set it free! There were barriers still, it is true, but barriers that could in time be swept away.

I left the well-house eager to learn. Everything had a name, and each name gave birth to a new thought. As we returned to the house every object which I touched seemed to quiver with life. That was because I saw everything with the strange, new sight that had come to me. On entering the door I remembered the doll I had broken. I felt my way to the hearth and picked up the pieces. I tried vainly to put them together. Then my eyes filled with tears; for I realized what I had done, and for the first time I felt repentance and sorrow.

I learned a great many new words that day. I do not remember what they all were; but I do know that *mother, father, sister, teacher* were among them—words that were to make the world blossom for me, "like Aaron's rod, with flowers." It would have been difficult to find a happier child than I was as I lay in my crib at the close of that eventful day and lived over the joys it had brought me, and for the first time longed for a new day to come.

Vocabulary Development: drawing (drô′ iŋ) *v.* bringing forth; making flow

◆ Literary Analysis

The climax of the story happens in the bracketed passage. Underline the sentences that describe it. Write a description of the moment of climax.

MARK THE TEXT

____

____

____

____

____

____

◆ Stop to Reflect

Why does Helen's discovery of words change her attitude about everything?

____

____

____

____

How could this discovery give her "new sight"?

____

____

____

____

____

____

____

____

____

Reader's Response: Do you think Helen should be excused for her behavior before she learned to communicate? Explain.

____

____

____

Thinking About the Skill: How does using the context help you understand the meaning of difficult words?

____

____

PREVIEW

Zlateh the Goat

Isaac Bashevis Singer

Summary

When Reuven the furrier has a bad year, he decides to sell Zlateh, the family's goat, to the town butcher. He sends his twelve-year-old son Aaron to take Zlateh to town. On the way, they are caught in a blizzard. The boy and the goat take shelter in a haystack. There they keep each other warm. Aaron depends on Zlateh to feed him with her milk and to keep him company. Zlateh needs Aaron to keep an air passage clear so they can breathe. As they keep each other alive, they come to love each other deeply. When the storm is over, Aaron brings Zlateh home. Neither he nor his family will ever again consider selling Zlateh. Now that the weather has turned cold, Reuven's fur business is doing well. Zlateh is like one of the family. She and Aaron remain loving friends.

Visual Summary

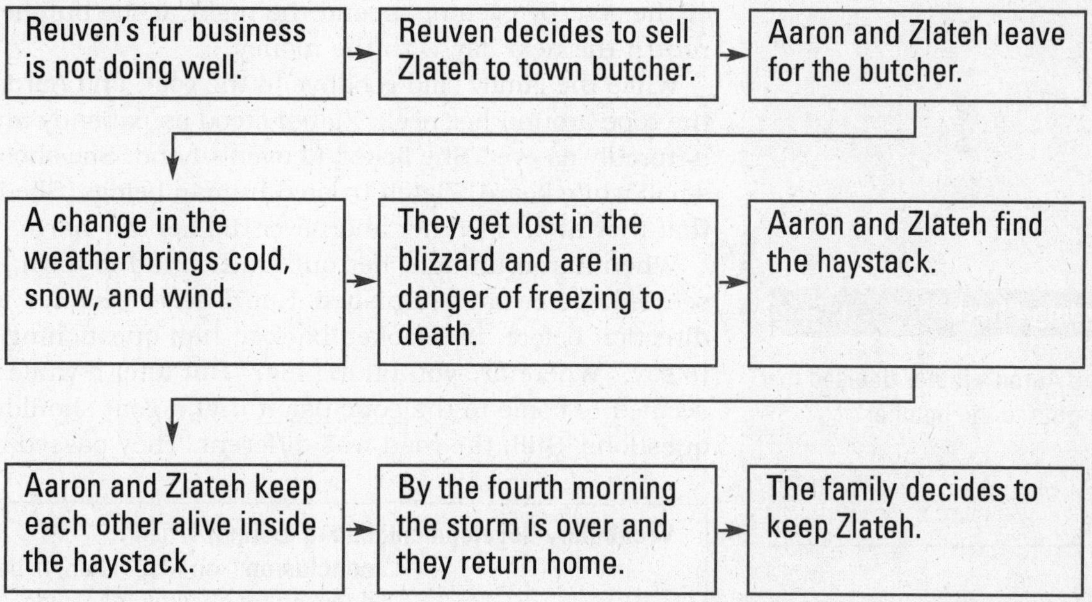

Reuven's fur business is not doing well.
Reuven decides to sell Zlateh to town butcher.
Aaron and Zlateh leave for the butcher.
A change in the weather brings cold, snow, and wind.
They get lost in the blizzard and are in danger of freezing to death.
Aaron and Zlateh find the haystack.
Aaron and Zlateh keep each other alive inside the haystack.
By the fourth morning the storm is over and they return home.
The family decides to keep Zlateh.

◆ Activate Prior Knowledge

Think of times when you have been outdoors and a change in the weather has surprised you. Jot down some notes describing how you felt and what you did.

◆ Literary Analysis

Mark the Text

What kind of **setting** does this story take place in? That is, what details of time and place do you notice? Circle words or sentences in the text that tell about the setting.

◆ Reading Check

Why has Aaron's father decided to sell the goat to the butcher?

Zlateh the Goat

Isaac Bashevis Singer

Farm animals eat hay, and a haystack is a place that can be a kind of playground for children on a farm. Aaron and Zlateh discover, however, that a haystack can be a lifesaver, too.

At Hanukkah[1] time the road from the village to the town is usually covered with snow, but this year the winter had been a mild one. Hanukkah had almost come, yet little snow had fallen. The sun shone most of the time. The peasants complained that because of the dry weather there would be a poor harvest of winter grain. New grass sprouted, and the peasants sent their cattle out to pasture.

For Reuven the furrier it was a bad year, and after long hesitation he decided to sell Zlateh the goat. She was old and gave little milk. Feivel the town butcher had offered eight gulden[2] for her. Such a sum would buy Hanukkah candles, potatoes and oil for pancakes, gifts for the children, and other holiday necessaries for the house. Reuven told his oldest boy Aaron to take the goat to town.

Aaron understood what taking the goat to Feivel meant, but had to obey his father. Leah, his mother, wiped the tears from her eyes when she heard the news. Aaron's younger sisters, Anna and Miriam, cried loudly. Aaron put on his quilted jacket and a cap with earmuffs, bound a rope around Zlateh's neck, and took along two slices of bread with cheese to eat on the road. Aaron was supposed to deliver the goat by evening, spend the night at the butcher's, and return the next day with the money.

While the family said goodbye to the goat, and Aaron placed the rope around her neck, Zlateh stood as patiently and good-naturedly as ever. She licked Reuven's hand. She shook her small white beard. Zlateh trusted human beings. She knew that they always fed her and never did her any harm.

When Aaron brought her out on the road to town, she seemed somewhat astonished. She'd never been led in that direction before. She looked back at him questioningly, as if to say, "Where are you taking me?" But after a while she seemed to come to the conclusion that a goat shouldn't ask questions. Still, the road was different. They passed new

Vocabulary Development: bound (bound) *v.* tied
conclusion (kən klo͞o′ zhən) *n.* belief or decision reached by reasoning

1. **Hanukkah** (khä′ no͞o kä) Jewish festival celebrated for eight days in early winter. Hanukkah is also called the "festival of lights" because a candle is lit on each of the eight days.
2. **gulden** (go͞ol′ dən) *n.* unit of money.

fields, pastures, and huts with thatched roofs. Here and there a dog barked and came running after them, but Aaron chased it away with his stick.

The sun was shining when Aaron left the village. Suddenly the weather changed. A large black cloud with a bluish center appeared in the east and spread itself rapidly over the sky. A cold wind blew in with it. The crows flew low, croaking. At first it looked as if it would rain, but instead it began to hail as in summer. It was early in the day, but it became dark as dusk. After a while the hail turned to snow.

In his twelve years Aaron had seen all kinds of weather, but he had never experienced a snow like this one. It was so dense it shut out the light of the day. In a short time their path was completely covered. The wind became as cold as ice. The road to town was narrow and winding. Aaron no longer knew where he was. He could not see through the snow. The cold soon penetrated his quilted jacket.

At first Zlateh didn't seem to mind the change in weather. She, too, was twelve years old and knew what winter meant. But when her legs sank deeper and deeper into the snow, she began to turn her head and look at Aaron in wonderment. Her mild eyes seemed to ask, "Why are we out in such a storm?" Aaron hoped that a peasant would come along with his cart, but no one passed by.

The snow grew thicker, falling to the ground in large, whirling flakes. Beneath it Aaron's boots touched the softness of a plowed field. He realized that he was no longer on the road. He had gone astray. He could no longer figure out which was east or west, which way was the village, the town. The wind whistled, howled, whirled the snow about in eddies.[3] It looked as if white imps were playing tag on the fields. A white dust rose above the ground. Zlateh stopped. She could walk no longer. Stubbornly she anchored her cleft hooves in the earth and bleated as if pleading to be taken home. Icicles hung from her white beard, and her horns were glazed with frost.

Aaron did not want to admit the danger, but he knew just the same that if they did not find shelter they would freeze to death. This was no ordinary storm. It was a mighty blizzard. The snow had reached his knees. His hands were numb, and he could no longer feel his toes. He choked when he breathed. His nose felt like wood, and he rubbed it with snow. Zlateh's bleating began to sound like crying. Those

Vocabulary Development: rapidly (rap′ id lē) *adv.* quickly

3. **eddies** (ed′ ēz) *n.* currents of air moving in circular motions; little whirlwinds.

◆ Reading Strategy

You begin to **summarize** a story by identifying the main events. List the most important story events so far, in the order in which they have occurred.

◆ Literary Analysis

All stories involve **conflict,** or a struggle between opposing forces. This story deals with **conflict with nature.** Underline sentences in the bracketed passage that show how Aaron and Zlateh are struggling with the weather.

Mark the Text

◆ Reading Check

What will happen if Aaron and Zlateh don't find shelter?

◆ Stop to Reflect

The bracketed passage gives very important information for the story. Circle the sentence that tells what Aaron found. On the lines below, explain why this find is so important.

Mark THE Text

◆ Reading Strategy

Summarize what has happened since your last summary by listing the most important events that have taken place since then.

◆ Reading Check

Why have Aaron and Zlateh climbed inside the haystack?

humans in whom she had so much confidence had dragged her into a trap. Aaron began to pray to God for himself and for the innocent animal.

Suddenly he made out the shape of a hill. He wondered what it could be. Who had piled snow into such a huge heap? He moved toward it, dragging Zlateh after him. When he came near it, he realized that it was a large haystack which the snow had blanketed.

Aaron realized immediately that they were saved. With great effort he dug his way through the snow. He was a village boy and knew what to do. When he reached the hay, he hollowed out a nest for himself and the goat. No matter how cold it may be outside, in the hay it is always warm. And hay was food for Zlateh. The moment she smelled it she became contented and began to eat. Outside, the snow continued to fall. It quickly covered the passageway Aaron had dug. But a boy and an animal need to breathe, and there was hardly any air in their hideout. Aaron bored a kind of a window through the hay and snow and carefully kept the passage clear.

Zlateh, having eaten her fill, sat down on her hind legs and seemed to have regained her confidence in man. Aaron ate his two slices of bread and cheese, but after the difficult journey he was still hungry. He looked at Zlateh and noticed her udders were full. He lay down next to her, placing himself so that when he milked her he could squirt the milk into his mouth. It was rich and sweet. Zlateh was not accustomed to being milked that way, but she did not resist. On the contrary, she seemed eager to reward Aaron for bringing her to a shelter whose very walls, floor, and ceiling were made of food.

Through the window Aaron could catch a glimpse of the chaos outside. The wind carried before it whole drifts of snow. It was completely dark, and he did not know whether night had already come or whether it was the darkness of the storm. Thank God that in the hay it was not cold. The dried hay, grass, and field flowers exuded the warmth of the summer sun. Zlateh ate frequently; she nibbled from above, below, from the left and right. Her body gave forth an animal warmth, and Aaron cuddled up to her. He had always loved Zlateh, but now she was like a sister. He was alone, cut off from his family, and wanted to talk. He began to talk to Zlateh. "Zlateh, what do you think about what has happened to us?" he asked.

"Maaaa," Zlateh answered.

Vocabulary Development: exuded (eg zyo͞od′ əd) *v.* gave off; oozed; radiated

"If we hadn't found this stack of hay, we would both be frozen stiff by now," Aaron said.

"Maaaa," was the goat's reply.

"If the snow keeps on falling like this, we may have to stay here for days," Aaron explained.

"Maaaa," Zlateh bleated.

"What does 'maaaa' mean?" Aaron asked. "You'd better speak up clearly."

"Maaaa, maaaa," Zlateh tried.

"Well, let it be 'maaaa' then," Aaron said patiently. "You can't speak, but I know you understand. I need you and you need me. Isn't that right?"

"Maaaa."

Aaron became sleepy. He made a pillow out of some hay, leaned his head on it, and dozed off. Zlateh, too, fell asleep.

When Aaron opened his eyes, he didn't know whether it was morning or night. The snow had blocked up his window. He tried to clear it, but when he had bored through to the length of his arm, he still hadn't reached the outside. Luckily he had his stick with him and was able to break through to the open air. It was still dark outside. The snow continued to fall and the wind wailed, first with one voice and then with many. Sometimes it had the sound of devilish laughter. Zlateh, too, awoke, and when Aaron greeted her, she answered, "Maaa." Yes, Zlateh's language consisted of only one word, but it meant many things. Now she was saying, "We must accept all that God gives us—heat, cold, hunger, satisfaction, light, and darkness."

Aaron had awakened hungry. He had eaten up his food, but Zlateh had plenty of milk.

For three days Aaron and Zlateh stayed in the haystack. Aaron had always loved Zlateh, but in these three days he loved her more and more. She fed him with her milk and helped him keep warm. She comforted him with her patience. He told her many stories, and she always cocked her ears and listened. When he patted her, she licked his hand and his face. Then she said, "Maaaa," and he knew it meant, I love you, too.

The snow fell for three days, though after the first day it was not as thick and the wind quieted down. Sometimes Aaron felt that there could never have been a summer, that the snow had always fallen, ever since he could remember. He, Aaron, never had a father or mother or sisters. He was a snow child, born of the snow, and so was Zlateh. It was so quiet in the hay that his ears rang in the stillness. Aaron and Zlateh slept all night and a good part of the day. As for Aaron's dreams, they were all about warm weather. He dreamed of green fields, trees covered with blossoms, clear brooks, and singing birds. By the third night the snow had stopped, but Aaron did not dare to find his way home in the

◆ **Literary Analysis**

Has the **conflict with nature** changed because Aaron and Zlateh have moved from the road to the haystack? Explain your answer.

____

____

____

____

____

____

◆ **Reading Strategy**

Mark the Text

Underline the passage in which Aaron seems to **summarize** Zlateh's point of view.

◆ **Reading Check**

How long does the blizzard last?

____

____

____

____

____

____

◆ **Reading Strategy**

This is the fourth day since Aaron and Zlateh left home. **Summarize** briefly what happened in the first three days.

____

____

____

____

____

____

____

◆ **Stop to Reflect**

Do you think the author wants you to learn something from Aaron's experience with Zlateh? What do you think he wants you to learn?

____

____

____

____

____

____

darkness. The sky became clear and the moon shone, casting silvery nets on the snow. Aaron dug his way out and looked at the world. It was all white, quiet, dreaming dreams of heavenly splendor. The stars were large and close. The moon swam in the sky as in a sea.

On the morning of the fourth day Aaron heard the ringing of sleigh bells. The haystack was not far from the road. The peasant who drove the sleigh pointed out the way to him—not to the town and Feivel the butcher, but home to the village. Aaron had decided in the haystack that he would never part with Zlateh.

Aaron's family and their neighbors had searched for the boy and the goat but had found no trace of them during the storm. They feared they were lost. Aaron's mother and sisters cried for him; his father remained silent and gloomy. Suddenly one of the neighbors came running to their house with the news that Aaron and Zlateh were coming up the road.

There was great joy in the family. Aaron told them how he had found the stack of hay and how Zlateh had fed him with her milk. Aaron's sisters kissed and hugged Zlateh and gave her a special treat of chopped carrots and potato peels, which Zlateh gobbled up hungrily.

Nobody ever again thought of selling Zlateh, and now that the cold weather had finally set in, the villagers needed the services of Reuven the furrier once more. When Hanukkah came, Aaron's mother was able to fry pancakes every evening, and Zlateh got her portion, too. Even though Zlateh had her own pen, she often came to the kitchen, knocking on the door with her horns to indicate that she was ready to visit, and she was always admitted. In the evening Aaron, Miriam, and Anna played dreidel.[4] Zlateh sat near the stove watching the children and the flickering of the Hanukkah candles.

Once in a while Aaron would ask her, "Zlateh, do you remember the three days we spent together?"

And Zlateh would scratch her neck with a horn, shake her white bearded head, and come out with the single sound which expressed all her thoughts, and all her love.

Vocabulary Development: trace (trās) *n.* mark left behind by something

4. **dreidel** (drā´ dəl) *n.* small top with Hebrew letters on each of four sides, spun in a game played by children.

Reader's Response: What do you think is the most frightening part of Aaron's experience?

____

____

PREVIEW

from The Pigman & Me

Paul Zindel

Summary

In "The Pigman & Me," Paul Zindel tells about his first days at a new school. He gets into trouble because he doesn't know the rules and doesn't bother to ask. While he is using the paddle-ball paddle, John Quinn asks to use it. Because Paul doesn't know about a fifteen-minute limit on use of the paddle, he assumes John is a bully who is trying to take advantage of him. Instead of giving the paddle to John, Paul strikes him with the paddle and gives him a black eye. John wants revenge, and he tells the other kids he is going to beat Paul up. Paul doesn't know how to fight and is afraid to face John. But he is ashamed not to fight. Nonno Frankie prepares Paul for the fight by showing him the Sicilian method of fighting. During the fight, Paul tries to follow Nonno Frankie's advice, but he trips himself and falls down. He then lets everyone think that John has knocked him down and gotten his revenge.

Visual Summary

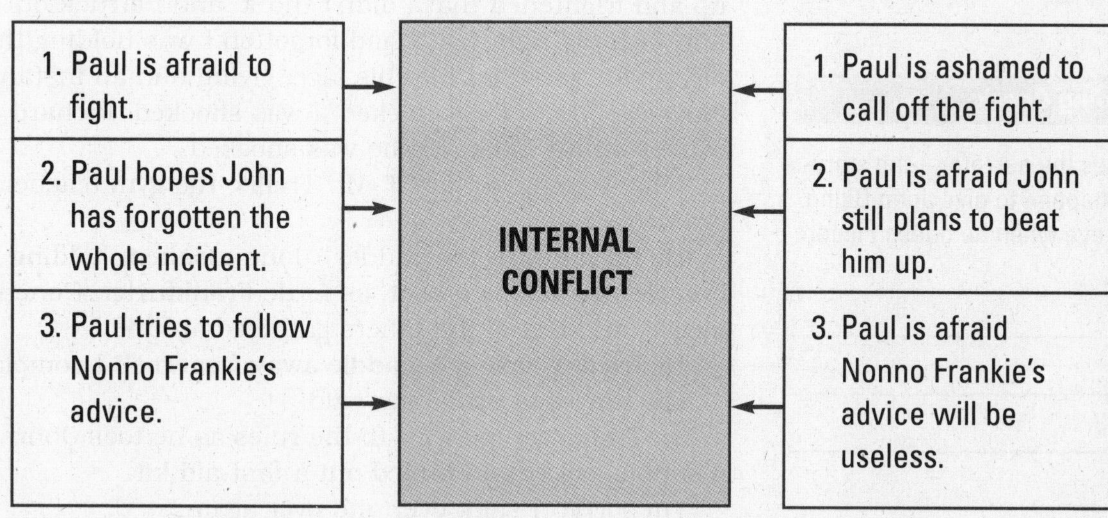

1. Paul is afraid to fight.
2. Paul hopes John has forgotten the whole incident.
3. Paul tries to follow Nonno Frankie's advice.
INTERNAL CONFLICT
1. Paul is ashamed to call off the fight.
2. Paul is afraid John still plans to beat him up.
3. Paul is afraid Nonno Frankie's advice will be useless.

from The Pigman & Me

Paul Zindel

Different places have different rules. Sometimes the rules are written out for you on signs or as instructions. At other times, rules are unwritten, such as not cutting in front of people in line. Unwritten rules can be as important as written rules, as the narrator Paul Zindel finds out.

When trouble came to me, it didn't involve anybody I thought it would. It involved the nice, normal, smart boy by the name of John Quinn. Life does that to us a lot. Just when we think something awful's going to happen one way, it throws you a curve and the something awful happens another way. This happened on the first Friday, during gym period, when we were allowed to play games in the school yard. A boy by the name of Richard Cahill, who lived near an old linoleum factory, asked me if I'd like to play paddle ball with him, and I said, "Yes." Some of the kids played softball, some played warball, and there were a few other games where you could sign out equipment and do what you wanted. What I didn't know was that you were allowed to sign out the paddles for only fifteen minutes per period so more kids could get a chance to use them. I just didn't happen to know that little rule, and Richard Cahill didn't think to tell me about it. Richard was getting a drink from the water fountain when John Quinn came up to me and told me I had to give him my paddle.

"No," I said, being a little paranoid about being the new kid and thinking everyone was going to try to take advantage of me.

"Look, you have to give it to me," John Quinn insisted.

That was when I did something berserk. I was so wound up and frightened that I didn't think, and I struck out at him with my right fist. I had forgotten I was holding the paddle, and it smacked into his face, giving him an instant black eye. John was shocked. I was shocked. Richard Cahill came running back and he was shocked.

"What's going on here?" Mr. Trellis, the gym teacher, growled.

"He hit me with the paddle," John moaned, holding his eye. He was red as a beet, as Little Frankfurter, Conehead, Moose, and lots of the others gathered around.

"He tried to take the paddle away from me!" I complained.

"His time was up," John said.

Mr. Trellis set me wise to the rules as he took John over to a supply locker and pulled out a first-aid kit.

"I'm sorry," I said, over and over again.

◆ Activate Prior Knowledge

Describe a time when you were in a new situation and worried about how to act or what to do.

◆ Reading Check

What was the paddle ball rule?

◆ Reading Check

How does the narrator—the storyteller—happen to give John Quinn a black eye when he doesn't mean to?

Then the bell rang, and all John Quinn whispered to me was that he was going to get even. He didn't say it like a nasty rotten kid, just more like an all-American boy who knew he'd have to regain his dignity about having to walk around school with a black eye. Before the end of school, Jennifer came running up to me in the halls and told me John Quinn had announced to everyone he was going to exact revenge on me after school on Monday. That was the note of disaster my first week at school ended on, and I was terrified because I didn't know how to fight. I had never even been in a fight. What had happened was all an accident. It really was.

When Nonno Frankie arrived on Saturday morning, he found me sitting in the apple tree alone. Mom had told him it was O.K. to walk around the whole yard now, as long as he didn't do any diggings or mutilations other than weed-pulling on her side. I was expecting him to notice right off the bat that I was white with fear, but instead he stood looking at the carvings Jennifer and I had made in the trunk of the tree. I thought he was just intensely curious about what "ESCAPE! PAUL & JENNIFER!" meant. Of course, the twins, being such copycats, had already added their names so the full carving away of the bark now read, "ESCAPE! PAUL & JENNIFER! & NICKY & JOEY!" And the letters circled halfway around the tree.

"You're killing it," Nonno Frankie said sadly.

"What?" I jumped down to his side.

"The tree will die if you cut any more."

I thought he was kidding, because all we had done was carve off the outer pieces of bark. We hadn't carved deep into the tree, not into the *heart* of the tree. The tree was too important to us. It was the most crucial place to me and Jennifer, and the last thing we'd want to do was hurt it.

"The heart of a tree isn't deep inside of it. Its heart and blood are on the *outside*, just under the bark," Nonno Frankie explained. "That's the living part of a tree. If you carve in a circle all around the trunk, it's like slitting its throat. The water and juices and life of the tree can't move up from the roots!" I knew about the living layer of a tree, but I didn't know exposing it would kill the whole tree. I just never thought about it, or I figured trees patched themselves up.

"Now it can feed itself from only half its trunk," Nonno Frankie explained. "You must not cut any more."

"I won't," I promised. Then I felt worse than ever. Not only was I scheduled to get beat up by John Quinn after school

Vocabulary Development: exact (eg zakt′) *v.* take using force or authority

◆ **Literary Analysis**

The narrator is experiencing an **internal conflict**—a struggle with different feelings. List two emotions that he is feeling in the bracketed paragraph.

1. ______________________________

____

2. ______________________________

____

◆ **Reading Strategy**

Mark the Text

Word origins tell you where words come from. Circle the word *nonno* in the text. It is an Italian word meaning "grandfather." The Italian word *nonna* means "grandmother." What English word sounds like *nonna* and means "grandmother"?

____

____

◆ **Reading Check**

Why does Paul say that he feels even worse now than he did before talking to his grandfather?

____

____

____

____

____

◆ **Stop to Reflect**

Think of a time when you talked to a friend about something that really worried you. How do you think Paul feels as he talks to Nonno Frankie?

◆ **Reading Strategy**

Circle the Italian word *pizza* in the text and write its meaning.

Mark the Text

◆ **Reading Check**

Why does Nonno Frankie want to give Paul a haircut?

on Monday, I was also a near tree-killer. Nonno Frankie finally looked closely at me.

"Your first week at school wasn't all juicy meatballs?" he asked.

That was all he had to say, and I spilled out each and every horrifying detail. Nonno Frankie let me babble on and on. He looked as if he understood exactly how I felt and wasn't going to call me stupid or demented or a big yellow coward. When I didn't have another word left in me, I just shut up and stared down at the ground.

"Stab nail at ill Italian bats!" Nonno Frankie finally said.

"What?"

He repeated the weird sentence and asked me what was special about it. I guessed, "It reads the same backward as forward?"

"Right! Ho! Ho! Ho! See, you learn! You remember things I teach you. So today I will teach you how to fight, and you will smack this John Quinn around like floured pizza dough."

"But I can't fight."

"I'll show you Sicilian combat tactics."

"Like what?"

"Everything about Italian fighting. It has to do with your mind and body. Things you have to know so you don't have to be afraid of bullies. Street smarts my father taught me. Like 'Never miss a good chance to shut up!'"

VAROOOOOOOOOOM!

A plane took off over our heads. We walked out beyond the yard to the great field overlooking the airport.

Nonno Frankie suddenly let out a yell. "*Aaeeeeeyaaaayeeeeeh*!" It was so bloodcurdlingly weird, I decided to wait until he felt like explaining it.

"*Aaeeeeeyaaaayeeeeeh*!" he bellowed again. "It's good to be able to yell like Tarzan!" he said. "This confuses your enemy, and you can also yell it if you have to retreat. You run away roaring and everyone thinks you at least have guts! It confuses everybody!"

"Is that all I need to know?" I asked, now more afraid than ever of facing John Quinn in front of all the kids.

"No. Tonight I will cut your hair."

"Cut it?"

"Yes. It's too long!"

"It is?"

"Ah," Nonno Frankie said, "you'd be surprised how many kids lose fights because of their hair. Alexander the Great always ordered his entire army to shave their heads. Long

Vocabulary Development: tactics (tak´ tiks) *n.* methods used for a particular purpose; tricks

hair makes it easy for an enemy to grab it and cut off your head."

"John Quinn just wants to beat me up!"

"You can never be too sure. This boy might have the spirit of Genghis Khan!"

"Who was Genghis Khan?"

"Who? He once killed two million enemies in one hour. Some of them he killed with yo-yos."

"Yo-yos?"

"See, these are the things you need to know. The yo-yo was first invented as a weapon. Of course, they were as heavy as steel pipes and had long rope cords, but they were still yo-yos!"

"I didn't know that," I admitted.

"That's why I'm telling you. You should always ask about the rules when you go to a new place."

"I didn't think there'd be a time limit on handball paddles."

"That's why you must ask."

"I can't ask everything," I complained.

"Then you *read*. You need to know all the rules wherever you go. Did you know it's illegal to hunt camels in Arizona?"

"No."

"See? These are little facts you pick up from books and teachers and parents as you grow older. Some facts and rules come in handy, some don't. You've got to be observant. Did you know that Mickey Mouse has only *four fingers* on each hand?"

"No."

"All you have to do is look. And rules change! You've got to remember that. In ancient Rome, my ancestors worshipped a god who ruled over mildew. Nobody does anymore, but it's an interesting thing to know. You have to be connected to the past and present and future. At NBC, when they put in a new cookie-cutting machine, I had to have an open mind. I had to prepare and draw upon everything I knew so that I didn't get hurt."

Nonno Frankie must have seen my mouth was open so wide a baseball could have flown into my throat and choked me to death. He stopped at the highest point in the rise of land above the airport. "I can see you want some meat and potatoes. You want to know exactly how to beat this vicious John Quinn."

"He's not vicious."

"Make believe he is. It'll give you more energy for the fight. When he comes at you, don't underestimate the power of negative thinking! You must have only positive thoughts in your heart that you're going to cripple this monster. Stick a piece of garlic in your pocket for good luck. A woman my

◆ **Reading Strategy**

Mark THE Text

Circle the word *yo-yos.* The invention of this toy dates back to 500 B.C. in Greece or even earlier in China. The **word origin** of *yo-yo* is from the language of the Philippines where it means "come-come," "come back," or "return." Write the meaning of *yo-yo.*

____

____

____

____

◆ **Stop to Reflect**

Think about the advice Nonno Frankie gives Paul about rules. How does this relate to Paul's problem?

____

____

____

____

____

____

◆ **Reading Check**

What is Nonno Frankie trying to teach Paul?

____

____

____

____

____

mother knew in Palermo did this, and she was able to fight off a dozen three-foot-tall muscular Greeks who landed and tried to eat her. You think this is not true, but half her town saw it. The Greeks all had rough skin and wore backpacks and one-piece clothes. You have to go with what you feel in your heart. One of my teachers in Sicily believed the Portuguese man-of-war jellyfish originally came from England. He felt that in his heart, and he eventually proved it. He later went on to be awarded a government grant to study tourist swooning sickness in Florence."

"But how do I hold my hands to fight? How do I hold my fists?" I wanted to know.

"Like *this*!" Nonno Frankie demonstrated, taking a boxing stance with his left foot and fist forward.

"And then I just swing my right fist forward as hard as I can?"

"No. First you curse him."

"*Curse* him?"

"Yes, you curse this John Quinn. You tell him, 'May your left ear wither and fall into your right pocket!' And you tell him he looks like a fugitive from a brain gang! And tell him he has a face like a mattress! And that an espresso coffee cup would fit on his head like a sombrero. And then you just give him the big Sicilian surprise!"

"What?"

"You kick him in the shins!"

By the time Monday morning came, I was a nervous wreck. Nonno Frankie had gone back to New York the night before, but had left me a special bowl of pasta and steamed octopus that he said I should eat for breakfast so I'd have "gusto" for combat. I had asked him not to discuss my upcoming bout with my mother or sister, and Betty didn't say anything so I assumed she hadn't heard about it.

Jennifer had offered to get one of her older brothers to protect me, and, if I wanted, she was willing to tell Miss Haines so she could stop anything from happening. I told her, "No." I thought there was a chance John Quinn would have even forgotten the whole incident and wouldn't make good on his revenge threat. Nevertheless, my mind was numb with fear all day at school. In every class I went to, it seemed there were a dozen different kids coming over to me and telling me they heard John Quinn was going to beat me up after school.

At 3 p.m. sharp, the bell rang.

All the kids started to leave school.

I dawdled.

I cleaned my desk and took time packing up my books. Jennifer was at my side as we left the main exit of the building. There, across the street in a field behind Ronkewitz's Candy Store, was a crowd of about 300 kids standing

◆ Reading Strategy

Circle the Italian word *espresso* and the Spanish word *sombrero*, and explain the meaning of each.

Mark THE Text

espresso: ____________________

____

____

sombrero: ____________________

____

____

◆ Literary Analysis

In the bracketed text, what **internal conflict** does Paul experience when Jennifer offers to help?

____

____

____

____

◆ Reading Check

Why does Paul spend time cleaning his desk and packing his books?

____

____

____

around like a big, undulating horseshoe, with John Quinn standing at the center bend glaring at me.

"You could *run*," Jennifer suggested, tossing her hair all to the left side of her face. She looked much more than pretty now. She looked loyal to the bone.

"No," I said. I just walked forward toward my fate, with the blood in my temples pounding so hard I thought I was going to pass out. Moose and Leon and Mike and Conehead and Little Frankfurter were sprinkled out in front of me, goading me forward. I didn't even hear what they said. I saw only their faces distorted in ecstasy and expectation. They looked like the mob I had seen in a sixteenth-century etching where folks in London had bought tickets to watch bulldogs attack water buffalo.

John stood with his black eye, and his fists up.

I stopped a few feet from him and put my fists up. A lot of kids in the crowd started to shout, "Kill him, Johnny!" but I may have imagined that part.

John came closer. He started to dance on his feet like all father-trained fighters do. I danced, too, as best I could. The crowd began to scream for blood. Jennifer kept shouting, "Hey, there's no need to fight! You don't have to fight, guys!"

But John came in for the kill. He was close enough now so any punch he threw could hit me. All I thought of was Nonno Frankie, but I couldn't remember half of what he told me and I didn't think any of it would work anyway.

"*Aaeeeeyaaaayeeeeh*!" I suddenly screamed at John. He stopped in his tracks and the crowd froze in amazed silence. Instantly, I brought back my right foot, and shot it forward to kick John in his left shin. The crowd was shocked, and booed me with mass condemnation for my Sicilian fighting technique. I missed John's shin, and kicked vainly again. He threw a punch at me. It barely touched me, but I was so busy kicking, I tripped myself and fell down. The crowd cheered. I realized everyone including John thought his punch had floored me. I decided to go along with it. I groveled in the dirt for a few moments, and then stood up slowly holding my head as though I'd received a death blow.

Vocabulary Development:

undulating (un´ dyo͞o lā´ tiŋ) *adj.* moving in waves, like a snake

goading (gō´ diŋ) *v.* pushing a person into acting, especially by using pain or insults

distorted (di stôr´ tid) *adj.* twisted out of the normal shape

condemnation (kän´ dem nā´ shən) *n.* extreme disapproval; harsh judgment

groveled (grä´ vəld) *v.* lay or crawled about before someone in hope of mercy

◆ Reading Check

What is the reaction of the other students to the developing fight?

Circle the phrases in the bracketed text that show the crowd's reaction. Then write your answer.

◆ Reading Check

What makes Paul fall during the fight? Circle the words in the bracketed passage that explain.

Why does Paul stay down on the ground when he is not hurt?

John put his fists down. He was satisfied justice had been done and his black eye had been avenged. He turned to leave, but Moose wasn't happy.

"Hey, ya didn't punch him enough," Moose complained to John.

"It's over," John said, like the decent kid he was.

"No, it's not," Moose yelled, and the crowd began to call for more blood. Now it was Moose coming toward me, and I figured I was dead meat. He came closer and closer. Jennifer shouted for him to stop and threatened to pull his eyeballs out, but he kept coming. And that was when something amazing happened. I was aware of a figure taller than me, running, charging. The figure had long blond hair, and it struck Moose from behind. I could see it was a girl and she had her hands right around Moose's neck, choking him. When she let him go, she threw him about ten feet, accidentally tearing off a religious medal from around his neck. Everyone stopped dead in their tracks, and I could see my savior was my sister.

"If any of you tries to hurt my brother again, I'll rip your guts out," she announced.

Moose was not happy. Conehead and Little Frankfurter were not happy. But the crowd broke up fast and everyone headed home. I guess that was the first day everybody learned that if nothing else, the Zindel kids stick together. As for Nonno Frankie's Sicilian fighting technique, I came to realize he was ahead of his time. In fact, these days it's called karate.

◆ Literary Analysis

Who suddenly appears? Circle the words that tell you in the bracketed text.

Mark THE Text

What happens?

Explain how Paul's **internal conflict** is resolved.

Reader's Response: If you had been in Paul's situation, would you have gone ahead with the fight or not? Explain.

Thinking About the Skill: How does knowing Paul's internal conflict help you to understand the story?

Thunder Butte

Virginia Driving Hawk Sneve

Summary

Native American traditions clash with current lifestyles in "Thunder Butte." Norman, a young Native American, accepts his grandfather Matt Two Bull's command to climb Thunder Butte. Norman's father agrees with the command but his mother disagrees. She thinks climbing the butte is a useless tradition based on old superstition. The butte is steep, and the climb is difficult. Norman bravely struggles to the top. He encounters a rattlesnake along the way. On the way down, Norman tumbles and happens to uncover an old stick covered with leather strips. Norman brings the stick to his grandfather who explains it is a *coup* stick which belonged to his ancestors. He tells Norman the *coup* stick should be hung in the house. Norman's mother disagrees. She doesn't want the stick indoors because she says it's a meaningless piece of the past. However, Norman's father hangs up the stick. He explains that the *coup* stick is a symbol of the Indians' past glory. The parents argue, upsetting and confusing Norman.

Visual Summary

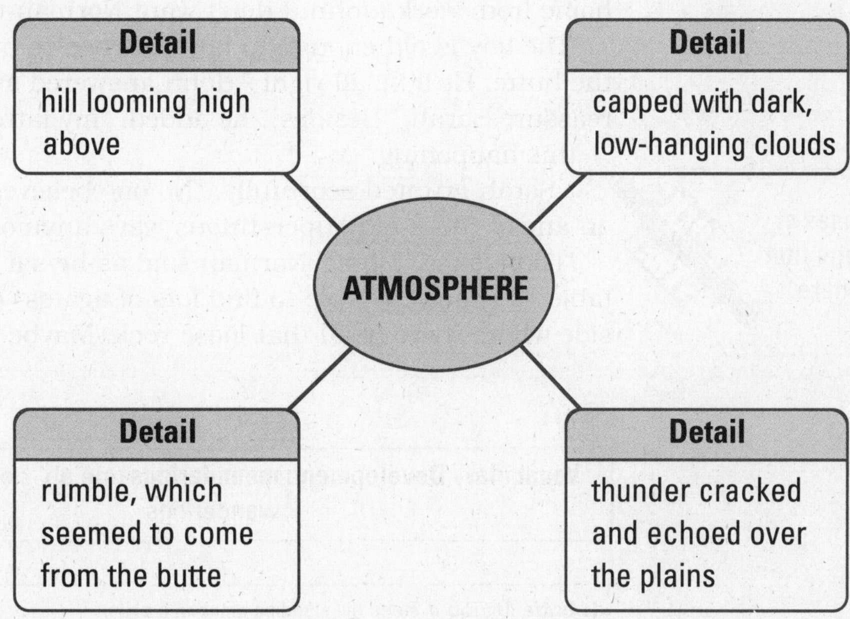

◆ Activate Prior Knowledge

Think of an item in your home that has special meaning for you. Jot down the memory, tradition, and association that you have with it.

◆ Literary Analysis

Atmosphere is the mood or feeling of a place. What is the atmosphere in the room as the family members voice their views on Norman's climbing the butte?

Circle words or phrases in the bracketed passage that suggest this atmosphere.

Mark the Text

Thunder Butte

Virginia Driving Hawk Sneve

The Sioux once lived throughout the northern plains of Minnesota, the Dakotas, and Nebraska. In these wide flat plains, steep flat-topped hills appear to rise out of nowhere. These land formations are called buttes. In the past, Native Americans climbed these buttes to look for enemies and animals and to view other activities on the plain.

The sun was just beginning to rise when John woke Norman the next morning.

"You must get an early start if you are going to go to the west side of the butte[1] and return by supper," John said to the sleepy boy. "If you are not home by the time I get back from work, I'll come looking for you."

Norman reluctantly rose. Last night he had accepted his grandfather's command to go to the Thunder Butte without too many doubts. Yet now in the morning's chill light the boy wondered if his grandfather's dreams were the meaningless meanderings of an old mind, or if his grandfather was really worthy of the tribe's respect as one of the few remaining wise elders who understood the ancient ways.

Norman dressed in his oldest clothes and pulled on worn and scuffed boots to protect his feet from the rocks and snakes of the butte. He heard his parents talking in the other room and knew his father was telling his mother where Norman was going.

As the boy entered the room, which was kitchen and living room as well as his parents' bedroom, he heard his mother say, "What if there is a rock slide and Norman is hurt or buried on the butte? We won't know anything until you get home from work, John. I don't want Norman to go."

"The boy is old enough to have learned to be careful on the butte. He'll be all right," John answered as he tried to reassure Sarah. "Besides," he added, "my father dreamed of this happening."

Sarah grunted scornfully, "No one believes in dreams or in any of those old superstitious ways anymore."

"I'll be okay, Mom," Norman said as he sat down at the table. "I should be able to find lots of agates[2] on the west side where there is all that loose rock. Maybe I can talk the

Vocabulary Development: meanderings (mē an´ dər iŋz) *n.* aimless wanderings

1. **butte** (byo͞ot) *n.* steep hill standing alone in a plain.
2. **agates** (ag´ its) *n.* hard, semiprecious stones with striped or clouded coloring.

trader into giving me money for them after all." He spoke bravely despite his own inner misgivings about going to the butte.

Sarah protested no more. Norman looked at her, but she lowered her head as she set a plate of pancakes in front of him. He knew she was hiding the worry she felt for him.

John put on his hat and went to the door. "Don't forget to take the willow branch with you," he said to Norman, "and be careful."

Norman nodded and ate his breakfast. When he was finished he stood up. "Guess I'll go," he said to his mother, who was pouring hot water from the tea kettle into her dish pan. When she didn't speak Norman took the willow cane from where he had propped it by the door and his hat from the nail above it.

"Wait," Sarah called and handed him a paper bag. "Here is a lunch for you. You'll need something to eat since you'll be gone all day." She gave him an affectionate shove. "Oh, go on. I know you'll be all right. Like your dad said, you're old enough to be careful."

Norman smiled at his mother. "Thanks," he said as he tucked the lunch into his shirt. He checked his back pocket to see if he'd remembered the salt bag to put the agates in.

He walked briskly across the open prairie and turned to wave at his mother, who had come outside to watch him leave. She waved back and Norman quickened his pace. He whistled, trying to echo the meadowlarks who were greeting the day with their happy song. He swiped the willow cane at the bushy sage and practiced spearing the pear cactus that dotted his path. The early morning air was cool, but the sun soon warmed the back of his neck and he knew it would be a hot day.

He crossed the creek south of where Matt Two Bull's tent was pitched and then he was climbing the gentle beginning slope of the butte. He stopped and studied the way before him and wondered if it wouldn't be easier to reach the west side by walking around the base of the butte even though it would be longer. Then Norman smiled as he remembered his grandfather's command to climb the south trail that wound to the top. He decided to do what the old man wanted.

The ascent sharply steepened and the sun rose with him as Norman climbed. What looked like a smooth path from the prairie floor was rough rocky terrain. The trail spiraled up a sharp incline and Norman had to detour around fallen rocks. He paused to rest about half way up and then saw how sharply the overhanging ledge of the butte protruded. Getting to the top of it was going to be a difficult struggle. He climbed on. His foot slipped and his ankle twisted painfully. Small pebbles bounced down the slope and he saw a rattlesnake slither out of the way. He tightly clutched the

◆ Reading Strategy

Words that are similar in meaning can have different **shades of meaning**—different feelings and associations, such as the words *ancient* and *old.* Looking at the surrounding text will help make the meaning of the word clear. Write the shades of meaning in the underlined word *misgivings* and the word *doubts.* The words "spoke bravely" will give you a clue to *misgivings.*

misgivings: ______________________

____

doubts: ______________________

____

◆ Literary Analysis

What **atmosphere** is created in the bracketed passage by descriptions of meadowlarks singing and Norman's whistling?

____

____

◆ Reading Check

Why does Norman decide to climb the South side of the butte?

____

____

____

◆ Reading Check

List two things that make climbing the butte dangerous.

1. ______________________

____

2. ______________________

____

◆ Reading Check

Why does Norman continue to hang on to the willow cane he is carrying?

◆ Stop to Reflect

What kind of physical strength would you need to climb Thunder Butte?

What character traits would you need to make it to the top?

Describe Norman's physical and mental characteristics.

What kind of **atmosphere** is created in the bracketed text?

Mark the Text

Underline the details that help create this atmosphere.

willow branch and leaned panting against the butte. He sighed with relief as the snake crawled out of sight. He wiggled his foot until the pain left his ankle. Then he started to trudge up the incline again.

At last only the ledge of the butte loomed over him. There appeared to be no way up. Disgusted that his laborious climb seemed dead-ended he stubbornly tried to reach the top. Remembering the courage of the ancient young men who had struggled in this same place to gain the summit and seek their visions, he was determined not to go back. His fingers found tiny cracks to hold on to. The cane was cumbersome and in the way. He was tempted to drop it, but he thought of the snake he'd seen and struggled on with it awkwardly under his arm.

Finally Norman spied a narrow opening in the ledge which tapered down to only a few feet from where he clung. He inched his way up until he reached the base of the opening and then he found a use for the cane. He jammed the stout branch high into the boulders above him. Cautiously he pulled to see if it would hold his weight. It held. Using the cane as a lever he pulled himself to the top.

This final exertion winded the boy and he lay exhausted on the summit, boots hanging over the edge. Cautiously he pulled his feet under him, stood and looked around.

He gazed at a new world. The sun bathed the eastern valley in pale yellow which was spotted with dark clumps of sage. The creek was a green and silver serpent winding its way to the southeast. His grandfather's tent was a white shoe box in its clearing, and beside it stood a diminutive form waving a red flag. It was Matt Two Bull signaling with his shirt, and Norman knew that his grandfather had been watching him climb. He waved his hat in reply and then walked to the outer edge of the butte.

The summit was not as smoothly flat as it looked from below. Norman stepped warily over the many cracks and holes that pitted the surface. He was elated that he had successfully made the difficult ascent, but now as he surveyed the butte top he had a sense of discomfort.

There were burn scars on the rough summit, and Norman wondered if these spots were where the lightning had struck, or were they evidence of ancient man-made fires? He remembered that this was a sacred place to the old ones and his uneasiness increased. He longed to be back on the secure level of the plains.

On the west edge he saw that the butte cast a sharp shadow below because the rim protruded as sharply as it had on

Vocabulary Development: diminutive (də min´ yo͞o tiv) *adj.* very small

the slope he'd climbed. Two flat rocks jutted up on either side of a narrow opening, and Norman saw shallow steps hewn into the space between. This must be the trail of which his grandfather had spoken.

Norman stepped down and then quickly turned to hug the butte face as the steps ended abruptly in space. The rest of the rocky staircase lay broken and crumbled below. The only way down was to jump.

He cautiously let go of the willow branch and watched how it landed and bounced against the rocks. He took a deep breath as if to draw courage from the air. He lowered himself so that he was hanging by his fingertips to the last rough step, closed his eyes and dropped.

The impact of his landing stung the soles of his feet. He stumbled and felt the cut of the sharp rocks against one knee as he struggled to retain his balance. He did not fall and finally stood upright breathing deeply until the wild pounding of his heart slowed. "Wow," he said softly as he looked back up at the ledge, "that must have been at least a twenty foot drop."

He picked up the willow branch and started walking slowly down the steep slope. The trail Matt Two Bull had told him about had been obliterated by years of falling rock. Loose shale and gravel shifted under Norman's feet, and he probed cautiously ahead with the cane to test the firmness of each step.

He soon found stones which he thought were agates. He identified them by spitting on each rock and rubbing the wet spot with his finger. The dull rock seemed to come alive! Variegated hues of brown and gray glowed as if polished. They were agates all right. Quickly he had his salt bag half full.

It was almost noon and his stomach growled. He stopped to rest against a large boulder and pulled out his lunch from his shirt. But his mouth was too dry to chew the cheese sandwich. He couldn't swallow without water.

Thirsty and hungry, Norman decided to go straight down the butte and head for home.

Walking more confidently as the slope leveled out he thrust the pointed cane carelessly into the ground. He suddenly fell as the cane went deep into the soft shale.

Norman slid several feet. Loose rocks rolled around him as he came to rest against a boulder. He lay still for a long time fearing that his tumble might cause a rock fall. But no thundering slide came, so he cautiously climbed back to where

Vocabulary Development: **variegated** (ver′ ē ə gāt′ id) *adj.* marked with different colors in spots or streaks

◆ Reading Strategy

Look at the underlined words *broken* and *crumbled* in the text. Although the words are similar in meaning, what is the difference in the **shades of meaning** of these two words?

broken: ______

crumbled: ______

◆ Stop to Reflect

Think about the steps Norman saw on the butte. Why would Native Americans have carved steps into this opening?

______

◆ Reading Check

What difficulties does Norman face in getting down from the top of the butte?

______

◆ **Reading Check**

What does Norman uncover in the hole?

Why does Norman's heart pound when he sees what he has found?

◆ **Literary Analysis**

In what way does Norman's discovery add to the **atmosphere** of suspense of the story?

◆ **Reading Check**

Why are Norman and his grandfather concerned about finding bones at the site of the *coup* stick?

the tip of the willow branch protruded from the ground.

He was afraid that the cane may have plunged into a rattlesnake den. Carefully he pulled at the stout branch, wiggling it this way and that with one hand while he dug with the other. It came loose, sending a shower of rocks down the hill, and Norman saw that something else was sticking up in the hole he had uncovered.

Curious, and seeing no sign of snakes, he kept digging and soon found the tip of a leather-covered stick. Bits of leather and wood fell off in his hand as he gently pulled. The stick, almost as long as he was tall and curved on one end, emerged as he tugged. Holding it before him, his heart pounding with excitement, he realized that he had found a thing that once belonged to the old ones.

Norman shivered at the thought that he may have disturbed a grave, which was tehinda (tā khin´ dä), forbidden. He cleared more dirt away but saw no bones nor other sign that this was a burial place. Quickly he picked up the stick and his willow cane and hurried down the hill. When he reached the bottom he discovered that in his fall the salt bag of agates had pulled loose from his belt. But he did not return to search for it. It would take most of the afternoon to travel around the base of the butte to the east side.

The creek was in the deep shade of the butte when he reached it and thirstily flopped down and drank. He crossed the shallow stream and walked to his grandfather's tent.

"You have been gone a long time," Matt Two Bull greeted as Norman walked into the clearing where the old man was seated.

"I have come from the west side of the butte, Grandpa," Norman said wearily. He sat down on the ground and examined a tear in his jeans and the bruise on his knee.

"Was it difficult?" the old man asked.

"Yes," Norman nodded. He told of the rough climb up the south slope, the jump down and finally of his fall which led him to discover the long leather-covered stick. He held the stick out to his grandfather who took it and examined it carefully.

"Are you sure there was no body in the place where you found this?"

Norman shook his head. "No, I found nothing else but the stick. Do you know what it is, Grandpa?"

"You have found a *coup* (ko͞o) stick which belonged to the old ones."

"I know that it is old because the wood is brittle and the leather is peeling, but what is—was a *coup* stick?" Norman asked.

"In the days when the old ones roamed all of the plains," the old man swept his hand in a circle, "a courageous act of valor was thought to be more important than killing an enemy. When a warrior rode or ran up to his enemy, close enough to touch the man with a stick, without killing or being killed, the action was called *coup.*

"The French, the first white men in this part of the land, named this brave deed *coup.* In their language the word meant 'hit' or 'strike.' The special stick which was used to strike with came to be known as a *coup* stick.

"Some sticks were long like this one," Matt Two Bull held the stick upright. "Some were straight, and others had a curve on the end like the sheep herder's crook," he pointed to the curving end of the stick.

"The sticks were decorated with fur or painted leather strips. A warrior kept count of his *coups* by tying an eagle feather to the crook for each brave deed. See," he pointed to the staff end, "here is a remnant of a tie thong which must have once held a feather."

The old man and boy closely examined the *coup* stick. Matt Two Bull traced with his finger the faint zig zag design painted on the stick. "See," he said, "it is the thunderbolt."

"What does that mean?" Norman asked.

"The Thunders favored a certain few of the young men who sought their vision on the butte. The thunderbolt may have been part of a sacred dream sent as a token of the Thunders' favor. If this was so, the young man could use the thunderbolt symbol on his possessions."

"How do you suppose the stick came to be on the butte?" Norman asked.

His grandfather shook his head. "No one can say. Usually such a thing was buried with a dead warrior as were his weapons and other prized belongings."

"Is the *coup* stick what you dreamed about, Grandpa?"

"No. In my dream I only knew that you were to find a *Wakan* (wä kän), a holy thing. But I did not know what it would be."

Norman laughed nervously. "What do you mean, *Wakan*? Is this stick haunted?"

Matt Two Bull smiled, "No, not like you mean in a fearful way. But in a sacred manner because it once had great meaning to the old ones."

"But why should I have been the one to find it?" Norman questioned.

His grandfather shrugged, "Perhaps to help you understand the ways—the values of the old ones."

"But nobody believes in that kind of thing anymore," Norman scoffed. "And even if people did, I couldn't run out and hit my enemy with the stick and get away with it." He smiled thinking of Mr. Brannon. "No one would think I was brave. I'd probably just get thrown in jail."

◆ Reading Check

Describe the *coup* stick.

______

______

Mark the Text

In ancient times, what did a warrior do with a *coup* stick? Circle the sentence that explains the action.

What did the stick say about the warrior?

______

______

______

◆ Reading Check

According to the bracketed text, why did young men go to Thunder Butte in ancient times?

______

______

Why was Thunder Butte a sacred place?

______

______

______

◆ Stop to Reflect

Why is Matt Two Bull so respectful of the stick Norman has found?

______

______

______

______

______

◆ Literary Analysis

What **atmosphere** does the distant thunder and lightning create?

Circle the details in the bracketed text that contribute to the atmosphere.

Mark the Text

◆ Reading Check

Why does Norman back away from the *coup* stick?

Why does Norman offer to give his grandfather the *coup* stick?

◆ Reading Check

According to Matt Two Bull, what is the importance of the *coup* stick?

Suddenly Norman felt compelled to stop talking. In the distance he heard a gentle rumble which seemed to come from the butte. He glanced up at the hill looming high above and saw that it was capped with dark, low-hanging clouds.

Matt Two Bull looked too and smiled. "The Thunders are displeased with your thoughts," he said to Norman. "Listen to their message."

A sharp streak of lightning split the clouds and the thunder cracked and echoed over the plains.

Norman was frightened but he answered with bravado, "The message I get is that a storm is coming," but his voice betrayed him by quavering. "Maybe you'd better come home with me, Grandpa. Your tent will get soaked through if it rains hard."

"No," murmured Matt Two Bull, "no rain will come. It is just the Thunders speaking." There was another spark of lightning, and an explosive reverberation sounded as if in agreement with the old man.

Norman jumped to his feet. "Well, I'm going home. Mom will be worried because I'm late now." He turned to leave.

"Wait!" Matt Two Bull commanded. "Take the *coup* stick with you."

Norman backed away, "No, I don't want it. You can have it."

The old man rose swiftly despite the stiffness of his years and sternly held out the stick to the boy. "You found it. It belongs to you. Take it!"

Norman slowly reached out his hands and took the stick.

"Even if you think the old ways are only superstition and the stick no longer has meaning, it is all that remains of an old life and must be treated with respect." Matt Two Bull smiled at the boy. "Take it," he repeated gently, "and hang it in the house where it will not be handled."

Norman hurried home as fast as he could carrying the long stick in one hand and the willow cane in the other. He felt vaguely uneasy and somehow a little frightened. It was only when he reached the security of his home that he realized the thunder had stopped and there had been no storm.

"Mom," he called as he went into the house, "I'm home."

His mother was standing at the stove. "Oh, Norman," she greeted him smiling. "I'm glad you're back. I was beginning to worry." Her welcoming smile turned to a frown as she saw the *coup* stick in Norman's hand. "What is that?"

"Grandpa says it's a *coup* stick. Here," Norman handed it to her, "take a look at it. It's interesting the way it is made and decor—"

"No," Sarah interrupted and backed away from him. "I won't touch that heathen thing no matter what it is! Get it out of the house!"

"What?" Norman asked, surprised and puzzled. "There is nothing wrong with it. It's just an old stick I found up on the butte."

"I don't care," Sarah insisted. "I won't have such a thing in the house!"

"But, Mom," Norman protested, "it's not like we believe in those old ways the way Grandpa does."

But Sarah was adamant. "Take it out of the house!" she ordered, pointing to the door. "We'll talk about it when your dad gets home."

Reluctantly Norman took the *coup* stick outside and gently propped it against the house and sat on the steps to wait for his father. He was confused. First by his grandfather's reverent treatment of the *coup* stick as if it were a sacred object and then by Sarah's rejection of it as a heathen symbol.

He looked at the stick where it leaned against the wall and shook his head. So much fuss over a brittle, rotten length of wood. Even though he had gone through a lot of hard, even dangerous, effort to get it he was now tempted to heave it out on the trash pile.

Norman wearily leaned his head against the house. He suddenly felt tired and his knee ached. As he sat wearily rubbing the bruise John Two Bull rode the old mare into the yard. Norman got up and walked back to the shed to help unsaddle the horse.

John climbed stiffly out of the saddle. His faded blue work shirt and jeans were stained with perspiration and dirt. His boots were worn and scuffed.

"Hard day, Dad?" Norman asked.

"Yeah," John answered, slipping the bridle over the mare's head. "Rustlers got away with twenty steers last night. I spent the day counting head and mending fences. Whoever the thief was cut the fence, drove a truck right onto the range and loaded the cattle without being seen." He began rubbing the mare down as she munched the hay in her manger.

"How did your day on the butte go?" John asked.

"Rough," Norman answered. "I'm beat too. The climb up the butte was tough and coming down was bad too." He told his father all that had happened on the butte, winding up with the climax of his falling and finding the old *coup* stick.

Vocabulary Development: **heathen** (hē´ *th*ən) *adj.* uncivilized
adamant (ad´ ə mənt´) *adj.* not flexible; not willing to give in

◆ **Reading Check**

How does Norman's mother react when she sees the *coup* stick?

◆ **Stop to Reflect**

Norman's grandfather and his mother have different reactions to the *coup* stick. In what way does Norman's grandfather represent the views of the past?

In what way does Norman's mother represent views in the present?

◆ **Reading Check**

What does John Two Bull do for a living?

What happened to him at work today?

◆ **Reading Check**

How does Norman's father react when Norman makes fun of his grandfather's beliefs? Underline the sentence that tells you.

Mark the Text

◆ **Literary Analysis**

What does Sarah say about the *coup* stick?

____

____

____

What does John say about the *coup* stick?

____

____

____

What **atmosphere** does this conversation between John and Sarah create?

____

____

____

◆ **Reading Check**

Why is Norman's father so angry with his wife?

____

____

____

____

John listened attentively and did not interrupt until Norman told of Matt Two Bull's reaction to the stick. "I think Grandpa's mind has gotten weak," Norman said. "He really believes that the *coup* stick has some sort of mysterious power and that the Thunders were talking."

"Don't make fun of your grandfather," John reprimanded, "or of the old ways he believes in."

"Okay, okay," Norman said quickly, not wanting another scolding. "But Mom is just the opposite from Grandpa," he went on. "She doesn't want the *coup* stick in the house. Says it's heathen."

He walked to the house and handed the stick to his father. John examined it and then carried it into the house.

"John!" Sarah exclaimed as she saw her husband bring the stick into the room. "I told Norman, and I tell you, that I won't have that heathenish thing in the house!"

But John ignored her and propped the stick against the door while he pulled his tool box out from under the washstand to look for a hammer and nails.

"John," Sarah persisted, "did you hear me?"

"I heard," John answered quietly, but Norman knew his father was angry. "And I don't want to hear anymore."

Norman was surprised to hear his father speak in such a fashion. John was slow to anger, usually spoke quietly and tried to avoid conflict of any kind, but now he went on.

"This," he said holding the *coup* stick upright, "is a relic of our people's past glory when it was a good thing to be an Indian. It is a symbol of something that shall never be again."

Sarah gasped and stepped in front of her husband as he started to climb a chair to pound the nails in the wall above the window. "But that's what I mean," she said. "Those old ways were just superstition. They don't mean anything now—they can't because such a way of life can't be anymore. We don't need to have those old symbols of heathen ways hanging in the house!" She grabbed at the *coup* stick, but John jerked it out of her reach.

"Don't touch it!" he shouted and Sarah fell back against the table in shocked surprise. Norman took a step forward as if to protect his mother. The boy had never seen his father so angry.

John shook his head as if to clear it. "Sarah, I'm sorry. I didn't mean to yell. It's just that the old ones would not permit a woman to touch such a thing as this." He handed Norman the stick to hold while he hammered the nails in the wall. Then he hung the stick above the window.

"Sarah," he said as he put the tools away, "think of the stick as an object that could be in a museum, a part of history. It's not like we were going to fall down on our knees and pray to it." His voice was light and teasing as he tried to make peace.

But Sarah stood stiffly at the stove preparing supper and would not answer. Norman felt sick. His appetite was gone. When his mother set a plate of food before him he excused himself saying, "I guess I'm too tired to eat," and went to his room.

But after he had undressed and crawled into bed he couldn't sleep. His mind whirled with the angry words his parents had spoken. They had never argued in such a way before. "I wish I had never brought that old stick home," he whispered and then pulled the pillow over his head to shut out the sound of the low rumble of thunder that came from the west.

Reader's Response: Norman is caught in the conflict between the old beliefs of his father and the new beliefs of his mother. With whom would you agree? Explain.

____

____

____

Thinking About the Skill: In what way did identifying the details that create atmosphere help you better understand the story?

____

____

____

◆ Reading Check

How does Norman feel at the end of the day?

____

____

____

____

____

____

PREVIEW

Mowgli's Brothers

Rudyard Kipling

Summary

One evening in the jungle, Father Wolf discovers a small child near his cave. He brings the boy into the cave and gently places him among the wolf cubs. Mother Wolf is taken with the child and names him Mowgli. Shere Khan the tiger comes to the wolves' cave. He tells Father and Mother Wolf that Mowgli is his prey, and demands that they hand him over. They refuse. Mother Wolf is determined to keep Mowgli as her own. Before she can keep Mowgli, the wolf Pack, led by Akela, must give its approval at the Pack Council. According to the Law of the Jungle, two members must speak in Mowgli's favor. Baloo the bear and Bagheera the panther help win the Council's acceptance of Mowgli into the Pack. Now Mowgli is ready to begin a new life among the animals of the jungle.

Visual Summary

PREDICTION	PREDICTION
The wolf pack won't accept Mowgli.	The wolf pack will accept Mowgli.

REASONS	REASONS
• Mowgli is a man's cub. • Akela, the leader of the wolf pack, has had bad experiences with men. • Shere Khan wants Mowgli.	• Mother Wolf treats Mowgli as one of her own cubs. • Baloo the bear and Bagheera the panther speak in favor of Mowgli. • The wolves accept Bagheera's bargain.

WHAT HAPPENS
Mowgli is accepted into the wolf pack.

Mowgli's Brothers
Rudyard Kipling

The behavior of the animals in this story is based on the real habits of animals in the jungle. Wolves live in packs or groups with a leader. Although they don't have "council" meetings as described in the story, they do cooperate and work as a group. Tigers, on the other hand, like to work and hunt alone.

Now Chil the Kite[1] brings home the night
That Mang the Bat sets free—
The herds are shut in byre[2] and hut
For loosed till dawn are we.
This is the hour of pride and power,
Talon and tush[3] and claw.
Oh hear the call!—Good hunting all
That keep the Jungle Law!
Night-Song in the Jungle

It was seven o'clock of a very warm evening in the Seeonee hills[4] when Father Wolf woke up from his day's rest, scratched himself, yawned, and spread out his paws one after the other to get rid of the sleepy feeling in their tips. Mother Wolf lay with her big gray nose dropped across her four tumbling, squealing cubs, and the moon shone into the mouth of the cave where they all lived. "Augrh!" said Father Wolf, "it is time to hunt again"; and he was going to spring downhill when a little shadow with a bushy tail crossed the threshold and whined: "Good luck go with you, O Chief of the Wolves; and good luck and strong white teeth go with the noble children, that they may never forget the hungry in this world."

It was the jackal[5]—Tabaqui the Dishlicker—and the wolves of India despise Tabaqui because he runs about making mischief, and telling tales, and eating rags and pieces of leather from the village rubbish-heaps. But they are afraid of him too, because Tabaqui, more than anyone else in the jungle, is apt to go mad, and then he forgets that he was ever afraid of anyone, and runs through the forest biting everything in his way. Even the tiger runs and hides when little Tabaqui goes mad, for madness is the most disgraceful thing that can overtake a wild creature. We call it hydrophobia, but they call it *dewanee*—the madness—and run.

"Enter, then, and look," said Father Wolf, stiffly; "but there is no food here."

---

1. **Kite** (kīt) *n.* bird of the hawk family.
2. **byre** (bīr) *n.* cow barn.
3. **tush** (tush) *n.* tusk.
4. **Seeonee** (sē ō´ nē) **hills** hills in central India.
5. **jackal** (jak´ əl) *n.* wild dog, smaller than a wolf, found in Asia and northern Africa.

◆ Activate Prior Knowledge

The boy in this story faces a life and death choice—but others make the choice for him. Which choices in your life do you make yourself and which choices are made for you by others?

◆ Literary Analysis

The characters in this story are **animal characters,** and they act according to their animal characteristics. What are the animal characteristics of the jackal?

In what way does the jackal act like a human character?

◆ Reading Strategy

When you **predict,** you make a logical guess about what will happen. Based on what you know about the jackal's character, predict what kind of trouble he might cause for the other characters in the story.

◆ **Reading Check**

What mischief does the jackal cause when he compliments the wolf children?

____

____

____

Underline the sentence that explains the mischief.

◆ **Literary Analysis**

What can you learn about the **character** of Father Wolf from the conversation in the bracketed text?

____

____

____

____

What can you learn about Shere Khan's character?

____

____

____

____

"For a wolf, no," said Tabaqui; "but for so mean a person as myself a dry bone is a good feast. Who are we, the Gidur-log [the jackal-people], to pick and choose?" He scuttled to the back of the cave, where he found the bone of a buck with some meat on it, and sat cracking the end merrily.

"All thanks for this good meal," he said, licking his lips. "How beautiful are the noble children! How large are their eyes! And so young too! Indeed, indeed, I might have remembered that the children of Kings are men from the beginning."

Now, Tabaqui knew as well as anyone else that there is nothing so unlucky as to compliment children to their faces; and it pleases him to see Mother and Father Wolf look uncomfortable.

Tabaqui sat still, rejoicing in the mischief that he had made: then he said spitefully:

"Shere Khan, the Big One, has shifted his hunting-grounds. He will hunt among these hills for the next moon, so he has told me."

Shere Khan was the tiger who lived near the Waingunga River, twenty miles away.

"He has no right!" Father Wolf began angrily— "By the Law of the Jungle he has no right to change his quarters without due warning. He will frighten every head of game within ten miles, and I—I have to kill for two, these days."

"His mother did not call him Lungri [the Lame One] for nothing," said Mother Wolf, quietly. "He has been lame in one foot from his birth. That is why he has only killed cattle. Now the villagers of the Waingunga are angry with him, and he has come here to make our villagers angry. They will scour the Jungle for him when he is far away, and we and our children must run when the grass is set alight. Indeed, we are very grateful to Shere Khan!"

"Shall I tell him of your gratitude?" said Tabaqui.

"Out!" snapped Father Wolf. "Out and hunt with thy master. Thou hast done harm enough for one night."

"I go," said Tabaqui, quietly. "Ye can hear Shere Khan below in the thickets. I might have saved myself the message."

Father Wolf listened, and below in the valley that ran down to a little river, he heard the dry, angry, snarly, singsong whine of a tiger who has caught nothing and does not care if all the Jungle knows it.

"The fool!" said Father Wolf. "To begin a night's work with that noise! Does he think that our buck are like his fat Waingunga bullocks?"[6]

Vocabulary Development: scuttled (skut′ əld) *v.* scurried; scampered

6. **bullocks** (bool′ əks) *n.* steers.

"H'sh! It is neither bullock nor buck he hunts tonight," said Mother Wolf. "It is Man." The whine had changed to a sort of humming purr that seemed to come from every quarter of the compass. It was the noise that bewilders woodcutters and gypsies sleeping in the open, and makes them run sometimes into the very mouth of the tiger.

"Man!" said Father Wolf, showing all his white teeth. "Faugh! Are there not enough beetles and frogs in the tanks that he must eat Man and on our ground too!"

The Law of the Jungle, which never orders anything without a reason, forbids every beast to eat Man except when he is killing to show his children how to kill, and then he must hunt outside the hunting-grounds of his pack or tribe. The real reason for this is that man-killing means, sooner or later, the arrival of white men on elephants, with guns, and hundreds of brown men with gongs and rockets and torches. Then everybody in the jungle suffers. The reason the beasts give among themselves is that Man is the weakest and most defenseless of all living things, and it is unsportsmanlike to touch him. They say too—and it is true—that man-eaters become mangy,[7] and lose their teeth.

The purr grew louder, and ended in the full-throated "Aaarh!" of the tiger's charge.

Then there was a howl—an untigerish howl—from Shere Khan. "He has missed," said Mother Wolf. "What is it?"

Father Wolf ran out a few paces and heard Shere Khan muttering and mumbling savagely, as he tumbled about in the scrub.

"The fool has had no more sense than to jump at a woodcutter's campfire, and has burned his feet," said Father Wolf, with a grunt. "Tabaqui is with him."

"Something is coming up hill," said Mother Wolf, twitching one ear. "Get ready."

The bushes rustled a little in the thicket, and Father Wolf dropped with his haunches under him, ready for his leap. Then, if you had been watching, you would have seen the most wonderful thing in the world—the wolf checked in midspring. He made his bound before he saw what it was he was jumping at, and then he tried to stop himself. The result was that he shot up straight into the air for four or five feet, landing almost where he left ground.

"Man!" he snapped. "A man's cub. Look!"

Directly in front of him, holding on by a low branch, stood a naked brown baby who could just walk—as soft and as dimpled a little atom[8] as ever came to a wolf's cave at night. He looked up into Father Wolf's face, and laughed.

---

7. **mangy** (mān′ jē) *adj.* having the mange, a skin disease of mammals that causes sores and loss of hair.

8. **atom** (at′ əm) *n.* tiny piece of matter.

◆ **Reading Check**

Circle the sentence in the first paragraph that explains how Mother Wolf knows that Shere Khan is hunting a human.

Mark the Text

◆ **Reading Check**

Find two reasons in the bracketed text explaining why the beasts of the jungle are forbidden to eat Man.

1. ____________________

2. ____________________

◆ **Literary Analysis**

Circle the human behavior that the **animal character** Shere Kahn shows in the underlined sentence.

Mark the Text

◆ **Reading Check**

What makes Father Wolf try to stop in midair?

____

◆ Stop to Reflect

The story events so far have happened in the jungle setting. Why might a baby be in the jungle?

______

______

______

◆ Reading Strategy

What character traits do Father Wolf and Mother Wolf show?

______

______

Predict what will happen to Man's cub.

______

______

◆ Reading Check

Why does Father Wolf refuse to give Man's cub to Shere Khan? Circle the paragraph that explains the reason.

Mark THE Text

◆ Literary Analysis

What human qualities does the **animal character** Mother Wolf show in this passage?

______

______

______

______

"Is that a man's cub?" said Mother Wolf. "I have never seen one. Bring it here."

A wolf accustomed to moving his own cubs can, if necessary, mouth an egg without breaking it, and though Father Wolf's jaws closed right on the child's back not a tooth even scratched the skin, as he laid it down among the cubs.

"How little! How naked, and—how bold!" said Mother Wolf, softly. The baby was pushing his way between the cubs to get close to the warm hide. "Ahai! He is taking his meal with the others. And so this is a man's cub. Now, was there ever a wolf that could boast of a man's cub among her children?"

"I have heard now and again of such a thing, but never in our Pack or in my time," said Father Wolf. "He is altogether without hair, and I could kill him with a touch of my foot. But see, he looks up and is not afraid."

The moonlight was blocked out of the mouth of the cave, for Shere Khan's great square head and shoulders were thrust into the entrance. Tabaqui, behind him, was squeaking: "My lord, my lord, it went in here!"

"Shere Khan does us great honor," said Father Wolf, but his eyes were very angry. "What does Shere Khan need?"

"My quarry. A man's cub went this way," said Shere Khan. "Its parents have run off. Give it to me."

Shere Khan had jumped at a woodcutter's campfire, as Father Wolf had said, and was furious from the pain of his burned feet. But Father Wolf knew that the mouth of the cave was too narrow for a tiger to come in by. Even where he was, Shere Khan's shoulders and forepaws were cramped for want of room, as a man's would be if he tried to fight in a barrel.

"The Wolves are a free people," said Father Wolf. "They take orders from the Head of the Pack, and not from any striped cattle-killer. The man's cub is ours—to kill if we choose."

"Ye choose and ye do not choose! What talk is this of choosing? By the bull that I killed, am I to stand nosing into your dog's den for my fair dues? It is I, Shere Khan, who speak!"

The tiger's roar filled the cave with thunder. Mother Wolf shook herself clear of the cubs and sprang forward, her eyes, like two green moons in the darkness, facing the blazing eyes of Shere Khan.

"And it is I, Raksha [The Demon], who answer. The man's cub is mine, Lungri—mine to me! He shall not be killed. He shall live to run with the Pack and to hunt with the Pack; and in the end, look you, hunter of little naked cubs—frog-

Vocabulary Development: quarry (kwôr´ ē) *n.* prey; anything being hunted or pursued

eater—fish-killer—he shall hunt *thee*! Now get hence, or by the Sambhur that I killed (I eat no starved cattle), back thou goest to thy mother, burned beast of the Jungle, lamer than ever thou camest into the world! Go!"

Father Wolf looked on amazed. He had almost forgotten the days when he won Mother Wolf in fair fight from five other wolves, when she ran in the Pack and was not called The Demon for compliment's sake. Shere Khan might have faced Father Wolf, but he could not stand up against Mother Wolf, for he knew that where he was she had all the advantage of the ground, and would fight to the death. So he backed out of the cave-mouth growling, and when he was clear he shouted:

"Each dog barks in his own yard! We will see what the Pack will say to this fostering of man-cubs. The cub is mine, and to my teeth he will come in the end, O bush-tailed thieves!"

Mother Wolf threw herself down panting among the cubs, and Father Wolf said to her gravely:

"Shere Khan speaks this much truth. The cub must be shown to the Pack. Wilt thou still keep him, Mother?"

"Keep him!" she gasped. "He came naked, by night, alone and very hungry; yet he was not afraid! Look, he has pushed one of my babies to one side already. And that lame butcher would have killed him and would have run off to the Waingunga while the villagers here hunted through all our lairs in revenge! Keep him? Assuredly I will keep him. Lie still, little frog. O thou Mowgli—for Mowgli the Frog I will call thee—the time will come when thou wilt hunt Shere Khan as he has hunted thee."

"But what will our Pack say?" said Father Wolf. The Law of the Jungle lays down very clearly that any wolf may, when he marries, withdraw from the Pack he belongs to; but as soon as his cubs are old enough to stand on their feet he must bring them to the Pack Council, which is generally held once a month at full moon, in order that the other wolves may identify them. After that inspection the cubs are free to run where they please, and until they have killed their first buck no excuse is accepted if a grown wolf of the Pack kills one of them. The punishment is death where the murderer can be found; and if you think for a minute you will see that this must be so.

Father Wolf waited till his cubs could run a little, and then on the night of the Pack Meeting took them and Mowgli and Mother Wolf to the Council Rock—a hilltop covered with stones and boulders where a hundred wolves could hide.

Vocabulary Development: fostering (fös´ tər iŋ) *n.* taking care of

◆ Reading Check

Mark the Text

Why does Shere Khan back down in the confrontation with Mother Wolf? Underline the sentence that tells you why. Then, write your answer.

◆ Literary Analysis

In what way is the behavior of the **animal character** Mother Wolf similar to that of a human mother?

◆ Reading Check

Mark the Text

Why is it necessary for Father Wolf to bring the cubs and Mowgli to the Pack Council? Circle the phrases in the bracketed passage that tell why.

◆ Reading Strategy

According to the bracketed text, what have Akela's past experiences been with humans?

Based on what you know, **predict** how Akela will feel about letting Mowgli join the pack.

◆ Stop to Reflect

Why do you think Akela acts as he does toward Mowgli?

◆ Reading Check

If there is a disagreement in the pack about whether or not to accept a cub, what rules do the wolves follow? Underline the answer.

Mark the Text

Akela, the great gray Lone Wolf, who led all the Pack by strength and cunning, lay out at full length on his rock, and below him sat forty or more wolves of every size and color, from badger-colored veterans who could handle a buck alone, to young black three-year-olds who thought they could. The Lone Wolf had led them for a year now. He had fallen twice into a wolf-trap in his youth, and once he had been beaten and left for dead; so he knew the manners and customs of men. There was very little talking at the Rock. The cubs tumbled over each other in the center of the circle where their mothers and fathers sat, and now and again a senior wolf would go quietly up to a cub, look at him carefully, and return to his place on noiseless feet. Sometimes a mother would push her cub far out into the moonlight, to be sure that he had not been overlooked. Akela from his rock would cry: "Ye know the Law—ye know the Law. Look well, O Wolves!" and the anxious mothers would take up the call: "Look—look well, O Wolves!"

At last—and Mother Wolf's neck-bristles lifted as the time came—Father Wolf pushed "Mowgli the Frog," as they called him, into the center, where he sat laughing and playing with some pebbles that glistened in the moonlight.

Akela never raised his head from his paws, but went on with the monotonous cry: "Look well!" A muffled roar came up from behind the rocks—the voice of Shere Khan crying: "The cub is mine. Give him to me. What have the Free People to do with a man's cub?" Akela never even twitched his ears: all he said was: "Look well, O Wolves! What have the Free People to do with the orders of any save the Free People? Look well!"

There was a chorus of deep growls, and a young wolf in his fourth year flung back Shere Khan's question to Akela: "What have the Free People to do with the man's cub?" Now the Law of the Jungle lays down that if there is any dispute as to the right of a cub to be accepted by the Pack, he must be spoken for by at least two members of the Pack who are not his father and mother.

"Who speaks for this cub?" said Akela. "Among the Free People who speaks?" There was no answer, and Mother Wolf got ready for what she knew would be her last fight, if things came to fighting.

Vocabulary Development: **veterans** (vet´ ər enz´) *n.* those having experience
monotonous (mə nät´ ən əs´) *adj.* tiresome because it does not vary
dispute (di spyo͞ot´) *n.* argument; debate; quarrel

Then the only other creature who is allowed at the Pack Council—Baloo, the sleepy brown bear who teaches the wolf cubs the Law of the Jungle: old Baloo, who can come and go where he pleases because he eats only nuts and roots and honey—rose up on his hind quarters and grunted.

"The man's cub—the man's cub?" he said. "*I* speak for the man's cub. There is no harm in a man's cub. I have no gift of words, but I speak the truth. Let him run with the Pack, and be entered with the others. I myself will teach him."

"We need yet another," said Akela. "Baloo has spoken, and he is our teacher for the young cubs. Who speaks besides Baloo?"

A black shadow dropped down into the circle. It was Bagheera the Black Panther, inky black all over, but with the panther marking showing up in certain lights like the pattern of watered silk. Everybody knew Bagheera, and nobody cared to cross his path; for he was as cunning as Tabaqui, as bold as the wild buffalo, and as reckless as the wounded elephant. But he had a voice as soft as wild honey dripping from a tree, and a skin softer than down.

"O Akela, and ye the Free People," he purred, "I have no right in your assembly; but the Law of the Jungle says that if there is a doubt which is not a killing matter in regard to a new cub, the life of that cub may be bought at a price. And the Law does not say who may or may not pay that price. Am I right?"

"Good! good!" said the young wolves, who are always hungry. "Listen to Bagheera. The cub can be bought for a price. It is the Law."

"Knowing that I have no right to speak here, I ask your leave."

"Speak then," cried twenty voices.

"To kill a naked cub is shame. Besides, he may make better sport for you when he is grown. Baloo has spoken in his behalf. Now to Baloo's word I will add one bull, and a fat one, newly killed, not half a mile from here, if ye will accept the man's cub according to the Law. Is it difficult?"

There was a clamor of scores of voices, saying: "What matter? He will die in the winter rains. He will scorch in the sun. What harm can a naked frog do us? Let him run with the Pack. Where is the bull, Bagheera? Let him be accepted." And then came Akela's deep bay, crying: "Look well—look well, O Wolves!"

Mowgli was still deeply interested in the pebbles, and he did not notice when the wolves came and looked at him one by one. At last they all went down the hill for the dead bull,

Vocabulary Development: clamor (klam´ ər) *n.* loud demand or complaint

◆ Stop to Reflect

What does Baloo eat?

______

Why would Baloo be allowed to come and go as he pleases?

______

◆ Literary Analysis

What kind of **animal character** is Bagheera?

______

______

______

Mark the Text

Circle any human qualities that Kipling gives to Bagheera in the underlined paragraph.

◆ Stop to Reflect

What bargain does Bagheera offer the wolves in the bracketed text?

______

______

Consider what you know of Bagheera's character. **Predict** whether Bagheera is making this offer for good or bad reasons. Write your prediction.

______

______

______

______

______

◆ **Reading Check**

What decision do the wolves make about Bagheera's offer?

◆ **Literary Analysis**

What human qualities does the **animal character** Akela show in his thoughts?

and only Akela, Bagheera, Baloo, and Mowgli's own wolves were left. Shere Khan roared still in the night, for he was very angry that Mowgli had not been handed over to him.

"Ay, roar well," said Bagheera, under his whiskers; "for the time comes when this naked thing will make thee roar to another tune, or I know nothing of man."

"It was well done," said Akela. "Men and their cubs are very wise. He may be a help in time."

"Truly, a help in time of need; for none can hope to lead the Pack forever," said Bagheera.

Akela said nothing. He was thinking of the time that comes to every leader of every pack when his strength goes from him and he gets feebler and feebler till at last he is killed by the wolves and a new leader comes up—to be killed in his turn.

"Take him away," he said to Father Wolf, "and train him as befits one of the Free People."

And that is how Mowgli was entered into the Seeonee wolf-pack at the price of a bull and on Baloo's good word.

Reader's Response: Would you have voted in favor of having Mowgli join the Pack? Explain why or why not?

Thinking About the Skill: How does understanding the human qualities of these animal characters help you better understand the story?

Names/Nombres

Julia Alvarez

Summary

In "Names/Nombres," Julia Alvarez recalls her family's early years as immigrants to the United States from the Dominican Republic. She describes how the family adjusts to the continual mispronunciation of their names. Julia is eager to fit in at school, so she allows herself to be called various names—Judy, Juliet, even Alcatraz. Julia struggles not to appear different. She does not like being asked where she is from or how to say her name in Spanish. Julia dreams of becoming a writer. When she graduates from high school, she wonders which name she will use as an author.

Visual Summary

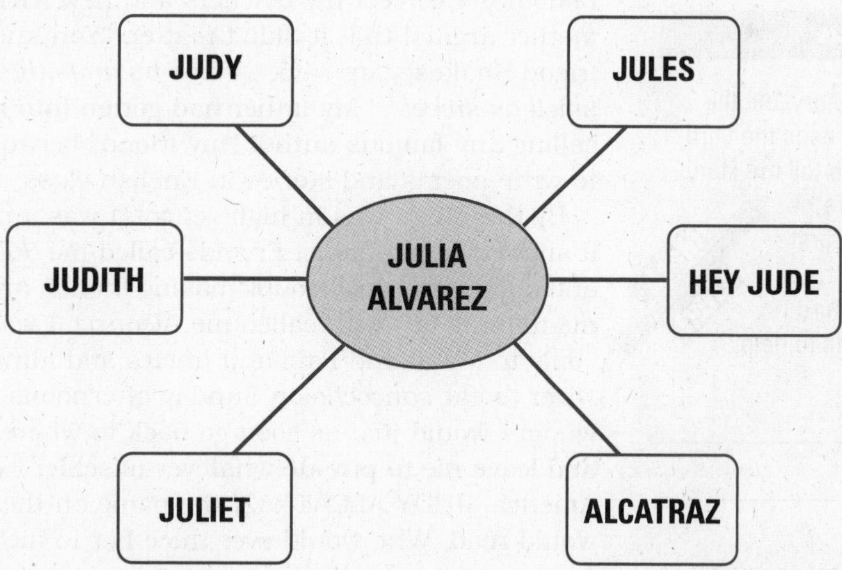

◆ **Activate Prior Knowledge**

Think of a time when you moved to a new neighborhood, changed schools, or joined a team. What did you do to fit in?

____

____

◆ **Reading Strategy**

To help focus your reading, you should **set a purpose for reading.** You might read to be entertained, to be informed, or to make a decision. Read the opening paragraph of this story. What did the immigration officer call the author's father?

____

Based on what you have read so far, set a purpose for reading.

____

____

____

◆ **Literary Analysis**

An author writes a story, but the **narrator** or **speaker** uses the third person (*he* or *she*) to tell the story. Sometimes, the narrator or speaker uses the first person (*I*). Is the narrator speaking in first or third person? Circle words to help with your answer.

Mark THE Text

____

____

How do you know that the writer is the same person as the speaker?

____

____

Names/Nombres

Julia Alvarez

Since the 1820s, millions of immigrants have come to the United States. Some came here to earn a better living. Others moved to escape political or religious persecution. Between the 1820s and the 1920s most immigrants came from Europe. More recently, many immigrants have arrived from Mexico, the Caribbean, Asia, India and the Philippines. Julia Alvarez's family came from the Caribbean.

When we arrived in New York City, our names changed almost immediately. At Immigration,[1] the officer asked my father, *Mister Elbures*, if he had anything to declare. My father shook his head, "No," and we were waved through. I was too afraid we wouldn't be let in if I corrected the man's pronunciation, but I said our name to myself, opening my mouth wide for the organ blast of the *a*, trilling my tongue for the drum-roll of the *r*, *All-vah-rrr-es*! How could anyone get *Elbures* out of that orchestra of sound?

At the hotel my mother was *Missus Alburest*, and I was *little girl*, as in, "Hey, little girl, stop riding the elevator up and down. It's *not* a toy."

When we moved into our new apartment building, the super[2] called my father *Mister Alberase*, and the neighbors who became mother's friends pronounced her name *Jew-lee-ah* instead of *Hoo-lee-ah*. I, her namesake, was known as *Hoo-lee-tah* at home. But at school, I was *Judy* or *Judith*, and once an English teacher mistook me for *Juliet*.

It took awhile to get used to my new names. I wondered if I shouldn't correct my teachers and new friends. But my mother argued that it didn't matter. "You know what your friend Shakespeare said, '*A rose by any other name would smell as sweet*.' " My father had gotten into the habit of calling any famous author "my friend" because I had begun to write poems and stories in English class.

By the time I was in high school, I was a popular kid, and it showed in my name. Friends called me *Jules* or *Hey Jude*, and once a group of troublemaking friends my mother forbade me to hang out with called me *Alcatraz*. I was *Hoo-lee-tah* only to Mami and Papi and uncles and aunts who came over to eat *sancocho* on Sunday afternoons—old world folk whom I would just as soon go back to where they came from and leave me to pursue whatever mischief I wanted to in America. JUDY ALCATRAZ: the name on the Wanted Poster would read. Who would ever trace her to me?

---

1. **Immigration** government agency that processes immigrants.
2. **super** superintendent; the person who manages an apartment building.

My older sister had the hardest time getting an American name for herself because *Mauricia* did not translate into English. Ironically, although she had the most foreign-sounding name, she and I were the Americans in the family. We had been born in New York City when our parents had first tried immigration and then gone back "home," too homesick to stay. My mother often told the story of how she had almost changed my sister's name in the hospital.

After the delivery, Mami and some other new mothers were cooing over their new baby sons and daughters and exchanging names and weights and delivery stories. My mother was embarrassed among the Sallys and Janes and Georges and Johns to reveal the rich, noisy name of *Mauricia*, so when her turn came to brag, she gave her baby's name as *Maureen*.

"Why'd ya give her an Irish name with so many pretty Spanish names to choose from?" one of the women asked.

My mother blushed and admitted her baby's real name to the group. Her mother-in-law had recently died, she apologized, and her husband had insisted that the first daughter be named after his mother, *Mauran*. My mother thought it the ugliest name she had ever heard, and she talked my father into what she believed was an improvement, a combination of *Mauran* and her own mother's name, *Felicia*.

"Her name is *Mao-ree-shee-ah*," my mother said to the group of women.

"Why that's a beautiful name," the new mothers cried. "*Moor-ee-sha, Moor-ee-sha*," they cooed into the pink blanket. *Moor-ee-sha* it was when we returned to the States eleven years later. Sometimes, American tongues found even that mispronunciation tough to say and called her *Maria* or *Marsha* or *Maudy* from her nickname *Maury*. I pitied her. What an awful name to have to transport across borders!

My little sister, Ana, had the easiest time of all. She was plain *Anne*—that is, only her name was plain, for she turned out to be the pale, blond "American beauty" in the family. The only Hispanic thing about her was the affectionate nicknames her boyfriends sometimes gave her. *Anita*, or as one goofy guy used to sing to her to the tune of the banana advertisement, *Anita Banana*.[3]

Later, during her college years in the late '60s, there was a push to pronounce Third World names correctly. I remember calling her long distance at her group house and a roommate answering.

Vocabulary Development: transport (trans pôrt′) *v.* carry from one place to another

3. ***Anita Banana*** a play on the Chiquita Banana name.

◆ **Reading Check**

What is Julia's sister's name?

____

Why does Julia's mother not want to tell the women the real name of her baby?

____

____

____

____

____

____

◆ **Literary Analysis**

The **narrator** or **speaker** of a story tells the events as he or she sees them. What sentences in the underlined passage tell you how the narrator feels? Circle the sentences.

Mark the Text

◆ **Literary Analysis**

Review your **purpose for reading** this selection. Does it still make sense as your purpose for reading?

____

____

If not, revise your purpose.

____

____

____

____

◆ **Reading Check**

Why does the narrator want to be known by an American name?

____

____

____

◆ **Stop to Reflect**

Why does the narrator not want to tell her classmates where she comes from?

____

____

Circle a phrase in the bracketed text that describes how the narrator feels when asked where she comes from.

Mark THE Text

Why do you think the narrator has such a strong reaction?

____

____

____

____

"Can I speak to Ana?" I asked, pronouncing her name the American way.

"Ana?" The man's voice hesitated. "Oh! you must mean *Ah-nah*!"

Our first few years in the States, though, ethnicity was not yet "in." Those were the blond, blue-eyed, bobby sock years of junior high and high school before the '60s ushered in peasant blouses, hoop earrings, serapes.[4] My initial desire to be known by my correct Dominican name faded. I just wanted to be Judy and merge with the Sallys and Janes in my class. But inevitably, my accent and coloring gave me away. "So where are you from, Judy?"

"New York," I told my classmates. After all, I had been born blocks away at Columbia Presbyterian Hospital.

"I mean, *originally*."

"From the Caribbean," I answered vaguely, for if I specified, no one was quite sure on what continent our island was located.

"Really? I've been to Bermuda. We went last April for spring vacation. I got the worst sunburn! So, are you from Portoriko?"

"No," I sighed. "From the Dominican Republic."

"Where's that?"

"South of Bermuda."

They were just being curious, I knew, but I burned with shame whenever they singled me out as a "foreigner," a rare, exotic friend.

"Say your name in Spanish, oh please say it!" I had made mouths drop one day by rattling off my full name, which according to Dominican custom, included my middle names, Mother's and Father's surnames for four generations back.

"Julia Altagracia María Teresa Álvarez Tavares Perello Espaillat Julia Pérez Rochet González," I pronounced it slowly, a name as chaotic with sounds as a Middle Eastern bazaar[5] or market day in a South American village.

My Dominican heritage was never more apparent than when my extended family attended school occasions. For my graduation, they all came, the whole lot of aunts and uncles and the many little cousins who snuck in without tickets. They sat in the first row in order to better understand the Americans' fast-spoken English. But how could they listen

Vocabulary Development: initial (i nish´ əl) *adj.* original
inevitably (in ev´ i tə blē) *adv.* unavoidably
chaotic (kā ät´ ik) *adj.* completely confused

4. **serapes** (sə rä´ pēz) *n.* colorful shawls worn in Latin America.
5. **bazaar** (bə zär´) *n.* marketplace; frequently, one held outdoors.

when they were constantly speaking among themselves in florid-sounding phrases, rococo[6] consonants, rich, rhyming vowels?

Introducing them to my friends was a further trial to me. These relatives had such complicated names and there were so many of them, and their relationships to myself were so convoluted. There was my Tía Josefina, who was not really an aunt but a much older cousin. And her daughter, Aida Margarita, who was adopted, *una hija de crianza.* My uncle of affection, Tío José, brought my *madrina* Tía Amelia and her *comadre* Tía Pilar. My friends rarely had more than a "Mom and Dad" to introduce.

After the commencement ceremony my family waited outside in the parking lot while my friends and I signed yearbooks with nicknames which recalled our high school good times: "Beans" and "Pepperoni" and "Alcatraz." We hugged and cried and promised to keep in touch.

Our goodbyes went on too long. I heard my father's voice calling out across the parking lot, "*Hoo-lee-tah! Vamonos!*"

Back home, my *tíos* and *tías* and *primas*, Mami and Papi, and *mis hermanas* had a party for me with *sancocho* and a store-bought *pudín*, inscribed with *Happy Graduation, Julie.* There were many gifts—that was a plus to a large family! I got several wallets and a suitcase with my initials and a graduation charm from my godmother and money from my uncles. The biggest gift was a portable typewriter from my parents for writing my stories and poems.

Someday, the family predicted, my name would be well-known throughout the United States. I laughed to myself, wondering which one I would go by.

Vocabulary Development: inscribed (in skrībd′) *adj.* written on

6. **rococo** (rə kō′ kō) *adj.* fancy, having the style of art of the early eighteenth century.

Reader's Response: Do you think the name Julia fits the author? Why or why not?

Thinking About the Skill: Did setting a purpose for reading help keep you focused while you were reading?

Explain.

◆ **Reading Check**

How does the narrator feel about her relatives coming to school functions?

◆ **Literary Analysis**

How does Alvarez make the connection for you between the **narrator** and **speaker** in the story and herself as an author?

Mark the Text

Circle the sentence in the bracketed text that makes the connection.

PREVIEW

Lob's Girl

Joan Aiken

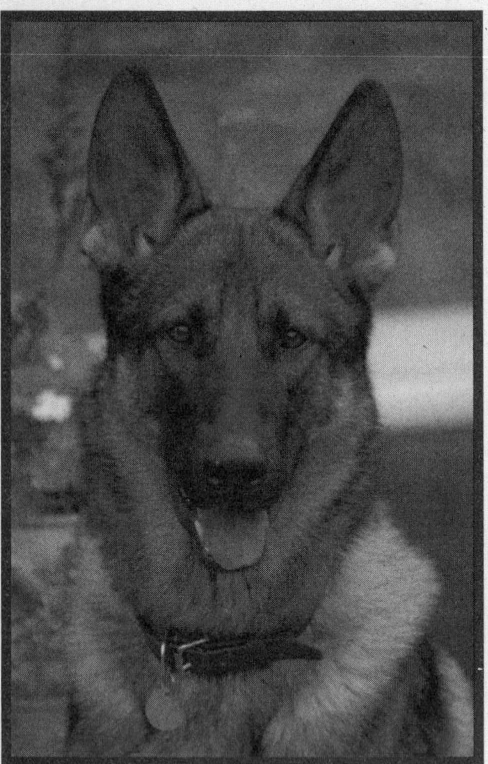

Summary

In "Lob's Girl," Joan Aiken writes about Lob, a young German shepherd who meets five-year-old Sandy on the beach one day. Lob becomes very attached to the girl. On two different occasions, he travels over four hundred miles to return to Sandy. Lob's owner finally agrees to let Lob live with Sandy and her family. Sandy and Lob become best friends and grow up together. Nine years later, a speeding truck hits Sandy and seriously injures her as she walks with Lob. Sandy is taken to the hospital. Not long after that, a guard at the entrance to the hospital notices a German shepherd trying to enter the hospital. Sandy's grandmother recognizes the dog as Lob, and she takes him to Sandy's room. Sandy responds to the dog's whine, and begins to recover from her coma. Then the dog disappears. Sandy's parents are puzzled by the appearance of Lob, because they know that Lob was killed by the speeding truck that injured Sandy.

Visual Summary

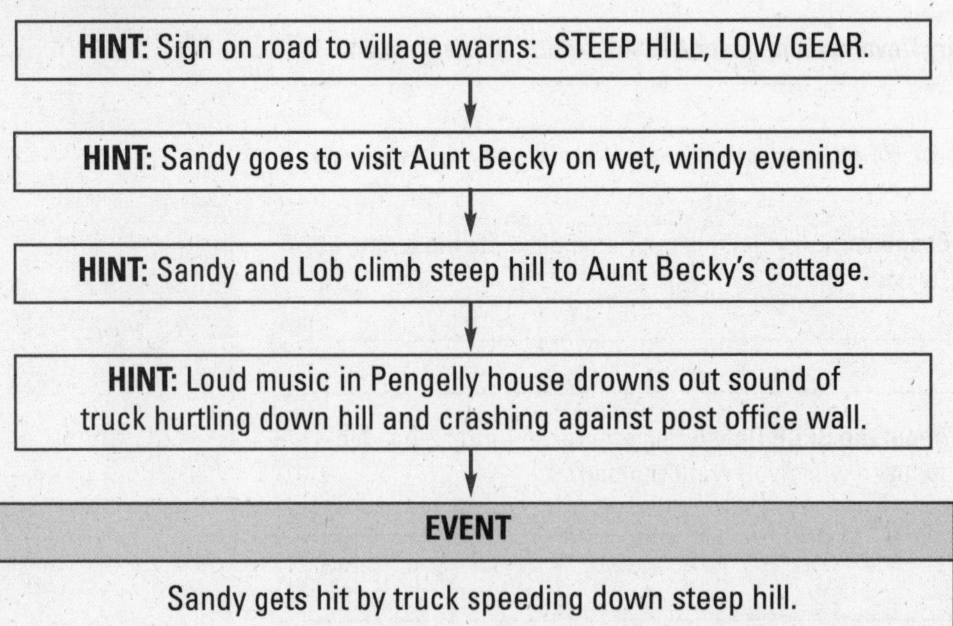

HINT: Sign on road to village warns: STEEP HILL, LOW GEAR.
HINT: Sandy goes to visit Aunt Becky on wet, windy evening.
HINT: Sandy and Lob climb steep hill to Aunt Becky's cottage.
HINT: Loud music in Pengelly house drowns out sound of truck hurtling down hill and crashing against post office wall.
EVENT
Sandy gets hit by truck speeding down steep hill.

Lob's Girl

Joan Aiken

If people are lucky, dogs give them loyalty and affection. When Lob and Sandy meet, a strong bond grows up between them. No distance or difficulty can keep Lob from Sandy's side. The strength of Lob's love and loyalty produce a strange and wonderful outcome to a story that could have ended very unhappily.

Some people choose their dogs, and some dogs choose their people. The Pengelly family had no say in the choosing of Lob; he came to them in the second way, and very decisively.

It began on the beach, the summer when Sandy was five, Don, her older brother, twelve, and the twins were three. Sandy was really Alexandra, because her grandmother had a beautiful picture of a queen in a diamond tiara and high collar of pearls. It hung by Granny Pearce's kitchen sink and was as familiar as the doormat. When Sandy was born everyone agreed that she was the living spit of the picture, and so she was called Alexandra and Sandy for short.

On this summer day she was lying peacefully reading a comic and not keeping an eye on the twins, who didn't need it because they were occupied in seeing which of them could wrap the most seaweed around the other one's legs. Father—Bert Pengelly—and Don were up on the Hard painting the bottom boards of the boat in which Father went fishing for pilchards. And Mother—Jean Pengelly—was getting ahead with making the Christmas puddings because she never felt easy in her mind if they weren't made and safely put away by the end of August. As usual, each member of the family was happily getting on with his or her own affairs. Little did they guess how soon this state of things would be changed by the large new member who was going to erupt into their midst.

Sandy rolled onto her back to make sure that the twins were not climbing on slippery rocks or getting cut off by the tide. At the same moment a large body struck her forcibly in the midriff and she was covered by flying sand. Instinctively she shut her eyes and felt the sand being wiped off her face by something that seemed like a warm, rough, damp flannel. She opened her eyes and looked. It was a tongue. Its owner was a large and bouncy young Alsatian, or German shepherd, with topaz eyes, black-tipped prick ears, a thick, soft coat, and a bushy black-tipped tail.

Vocabulary Development: decisively (di sīz´ siv lē´) *adv.* with determination

◆ Activate Prior Knowledge

What qualities do you associate with dogs? List them below.

◆ Reading Strategy

Mark the Text

When you **compare**, you look for similarities. When you **contrast**, you look for differences. Circle details about Sandy and the twins in the bracketed text. Then list what is similar and what is different about them.

◆ Reading Check

What happens when Sandy tries to check on the twins?

◆ Reading Strategy

Circle the words and phrases that show Sandy's reaction to Lob and Lob's reaction to Sandy. Are their reactions alike or different? Explain.

Mark THE Text

"*Lob*!" shouted a man farther up the beach. "Lob, come here!"

But Lob, as if trying to atone for the surprise he had given her, went on licking the sand off Sandy's face, wagging his tail so hard while he kept on knocking up more clouds of sand. His owner, a gray-haired man with a limp, walked over as quickly as he could and seized him by the collar.

"I hope he didn't give you a fright?" the man said to Sandy. "He meant it in play—he's only young."

"Oh, no, I think he's *beautiful*," said Sandy truly. She picked up a bit of driftwood and threw it. Lob, whisking easily out of his master's grip, was after it like a sand-colored bullet. He came back with the stick, beaming, and gave it to Sandy. At the same time he gave himself, though no one else was aware of this at the time. But with Sandy, too, it was love at first sight, and when, after a lot more stick-throwing, she and the twins joined Father and Don to go home for tea, they cast many a backward glance at Lob being led firmly away by his master.

"I wish we could play with him every day," Tess sighed.

"Why can't we?" said Tim.

Sandy explained. "Because Mr. Dodsworth, who owns him, is from Liverpool, and he is only staying at the Fisherman's Arms till Saturday."

"Is Liverpool a long way off?"

"Right at the other end of England from Cornwall, I'm afraid."

◆ Literary Analysis

When an author hints at things that have not yet happened, he or she is said to be **foreshadowing** events. What kind of event might the underlined sentence be foreshadowing?

It was a Cornish fishing village where the Pengelly family lived, with rocks and cliffs and a strip of beach and a little round harbor, and palm trees growing in the gardens of the little whitewashed stone houses. The village was approached by a narrow, steep, twisting hill-road, and guarded by a notice that said LOW GEAR FOR $1\frac{1}{2}$ MILES, DANGEROUS TO CYCLISTS.

The Pengelly children went home to scones with Cornish cream and jam, thinking they had seen the last of Lob. But they were much mistaken. The whole family was playing cards by the fire in the front room after supper when there was a loud thump and a crash of china in the kitchen.

"My Christmas puddings!" exclaimed Jean, and ran out.

"Did you put TNT in them, then?" her husband said.

◆ Reading Check

What part of England do the Pengellys live in?

But it was Lob, who, finding the front door shut, had gone around to the back and bounced in through the open kitchen window, where the puddings were cooling on the sill. Luckily only the smallest was knocked down and broken.

Lob stood on his hind legs and plastered Sandy's face with

Vocabulary Development: atone (a tōn´) *v.* make up for a wrong

licks. Then he did the same for the twins, who shrieked with joy.

"Where does this friend of yours come from?" inquired Mr. Pengelly.

"He's staying at the Fisherman's Arms—I mean his owner is."

"Then he must go back there. Find a bit of string, Sandy, to tie to his collar."

"I wonder how he found his way here," Mrs. Pengelly said, when the reluctant Lob had been led whining away and Sandy had explained about their afternoon's game on the beach. "Fisherman's Arms is right around the other side of the harbor."

Lob's owner scolded him and thanked Mr. Pengelly for bringing him back. Jean Pengelly warned the children that they had better not encourage Lob any more if they met him on the beach, or it would only lead to more trouble. So they dutifully took no notice of him the next day until he spoiled their good resolutions by dashing up to them with joyful barks, wagging his tail so hard that he winded Tess and knocked Tim's legs from under him.

They had a happy day, playing on the sand.

The next day was Saturday. Sandy had found out that Mr. Dodsworth was to catch the half-past-nine train. She went out secretly, down to the station, nodded to Mr. Hoskins, the stationmaster, who wouldn't dream of charging any local for a platform ticket, and climbed up on the footbridge that led over the tracks. She didn't want to be seen, but she did want to see. She saw Mr. Dodsworth get on the train, accompanied by an unhappy-looking Lob with drooping ears and tail. Then she saw the train slide away out of sight around the next headland, with a melancholy wail that sounded like Lob's last good-bye.

Sandy wished she hadn't had the idea of coming to the station. She walked home miserably, with her shoulders hunched and her hands in her pockets. For the rest of the day she was so cross and unlike herself that Tess and Tim were quite surprised, and her mother gave her a dose of senna.

A week passed. Then, one evening, Mrs. Pengelly and the younger children were in the front room playing snakes and ladders. Mr. Pengelly and Don had gone fishing on the evening tide. If your father is a fisherman, he will never be home at the same time from one week to the next.

Suddenly, history repeating itself, there was a crash from

Vocabulary Development: resolutions (rez′ ə lo͞o′ shənz) *n.* intentions; things decided
melancholy (mel′ ən käl′ ē) *adj.* sad; gloomy

◆ Literary Analysis

What event might Mrs. Pengelly's underlined statement **foreshadow**? Jot down your guess.

◆ Stop to Reflect

Mr. Dodsworth seems like a good man, but Lob would still rather be with Sandy. Briefly explain why you think Lob prefers Sandy's company.

◆ Reading Check

How does Sandy feel after she watches Lob and Mr. Dodsworth leave?

◆ **Stop to Reflect**

Why does Mrs. Pengelly cry, "My blackberry jelly!"?

◆ **Reading Check**

How does Lob get from Liverpool to the Pengellys' house?

◆ **Reading Strategy**

Compare and contrast the ways that Sandy, Don, and the twins react to parting with Lob. Circle in the bracketed paragraph the word groups that describe their reactions. Then, on the lines below, explain how the characters' reactions are similar and different.

Mark the Text

the kitchen. Jean Pengelly leaped up, crying, "My blackberry jelly!" She and the children had spent the morning picking and the afternoon boiling fruit.

But Sandy was ahead of her mother. With flushed cheeks and eyes like stars she had darted into the kitchen, where she and Lob were hugging one another in a frenzy of joy. About a yard of his tongue was out, and he was licking every part of her that he could reach.

"Good heavens!" exclaimed Jean. "How in the world did *he* get here?"

"He must have walked," said Sandy. "Look at his feet."

They were worn, dusty, and tarry. One had a cut on the pad.

"They ought to be bathed," said Jean Pengelly. "Sandy, run a bowl of warm water while I get disinfectant."

"What'll we do about him, Mother?" said Sandy anxiously.

Mrs. Pengelly looked at her daughter's pleading eyes and sighed.

"He must go back to his owner, of course," she said, making her voice firm. "Your dad can get the address from the Fisherman's tomorrow, and phone him or send a telegram. In the meantime he'd better have a long drink and a good meal."

Lob was very grateful for the drink and the meal, and made no objection to having his feet washed. Then he flopped down on the hearthrug and slept in front of the fire they had lit because it was a cold, wet evening, with his head on Sandy's feet. He was a very tired dog. He had walked all the way from Liverpool to Cornwall, which is more than four hundred miles.

The next day Mr. Pengelly phoned Lob's owner, and the following morning Mr. Dodsworth arrived off the night train, decidedly put out, to take his pet home. That parting was worse than the first. Lob whined, Don walked out of the house, the twins burst out crying, and Sandy crept up to her bedroom afterward and lay with her face pressed into the quilt, feeling as if she were bruised all over.

Jean Pengelly took them all into Plymouth to see the circus on the next day and the twins cheered up a little, but even the hour's ride in the train each way and the Liberty horses and performing seals could not cure Sandy's sore heart.

She need not have bothered, though. In ten days' time Lob was back—limping this time, with a torn ear and a patch missing out of his furry coat, as if he had met and tangled with an enemy or two in the course of his four-hundred-mile walk.

Bert Pengelly rang up Liverpool again. Mr. Dodsworth, when he answered, sounded weary. He said, "That dog has already cost me two days that I can't spare away from my work—plus endless time in police stations and drafting newspaper advertisements. I'm too old for these ups and downs. I think we'd better face the fact, Mr. Pengelly, that it's your family he wants to stay with—that is, if you want to have him."

Bert Pengelly gulped. He was not a rich man; and Lob was a pedigreed dog. He said cautiously, "How much would you be asking for him?"

"Good heavens, man, I'm not suggesting I'd sell him to you. You must have him as a gift. Think of the train fares I'll be saving. You'll be doing me a good turn."

"Is he a big eater?" Bert asked doubtfully.

By this time the children, breathless in the background listening to one side of this conversation, had realized what was in the wind and were dancing up and down with their hands clasped beseechingly.

"Oh, not for his size," Lob's owner assured Bert. "Two or three pounds of meat a day and some vegetables and gravy and biscuits—he does very well on that."

Alexandra's father looked over the telephone at his daughter's swimming eyes and trembling lips. He reached a decision. "Well, then, Mr. Dodsworth," he said briskly, "we'll accept your offer and thank you very much. The children will be overjoyed and you can be sure Lob has come to a good home. They'll look after him and see he gets enough exercise. But I can tell you," he ended firmly, "if he wants to settle in with us he'll have to learn to eat a lot of fish."

So that was how Lob came to live with the Pengelly family. Everybody loved him and he loved them all. But there was never any question who came first with him. He was Sandy's dog. He slept by her bed and followed her everywhere he was allowed.

[Nine years went by, and each summer Mr. Dodsworth came back to stay at the Fisherman's Arms and call on his erstwhile dog. Lob always met him with recognition and dignified pleasure, accompanied him for a walk or two—but showed no signs of wishing to return to Liverpool. His place, he <u>intimated</u>, was definitely with the Pengellys.]

In the course of nine years Lob changed less than Sandy. As she went into her teens he became a little slower, a little stiffer, there was a touch of gray on his nose, but he was still a handsome dog. He and Sandy still loved one another devotedly.

One evening in October all the summer visitors had left, and the little fishing town looked empty and secretive. It was a wet, windy dusk. When the children came home from

Vocabulary Development: intimated (in′ tə māt′ id) *v.* hinted; made known

◆ Reading Strategy

Mr. Dodsworth offers to give Lob to the Pengellys. Mr. Pengelly looks at Sandy and accepts the offer. What do the two men have in common?

◆ Stop to Reflect

Read the bracketed paragraph, and underline the words that suggest that Mr. Dodsworth had taken good care of Lob before Lob left him to live with Sandy.

Mark the Text

◆ Reading Check

How many years have passed since Lob became Sandy's dog?

◆ **Reading Strategy**

Circle the words that tell how Aunt Rebecca feels about dogs. Then **contrast** how Sandy and Aunt Rebecca feel about dogs.

Mark THE Text

◆ **Literary Analysis**

What do you think the truck crashing against the post office wall may **foreshadow** in the plot of the story?

◆ **Reading Check**

Who is the child Dr. and Mrs. Travers find?

school—even the twins were at high school now, and Don was a full-fledged fisherman—Jean Pengelly said, "Sandy, your Aunt Rebecca says she's lonesome because Uncle Will Hoskins has gone out trawling, and she wants one of you to go and spend the evening with her. You go, dear; you can take your homework with you."

Sandy looked far from enthusiastic.

"Can I take Lob with me?"

"You know Aunt Becky doesn't really like dogs—Oh, very well." Mrs. Pengelly sighed. "I suppose she'll have to put up with him as well as you."

Reluctantly Sandy tidied herself, took her schoolbag, put on the damp raincoat she had just taken off, fastened Lob's lead to his collar, and set off to walk through the dusk to Aunt Becky's cottage, which was five minutes' climb up the steep hill.

The wind was howling through the shrouds of boats drawn up on the Hard.

"Put some cheerful music on, do," said Jean Pengelly to the nearest twin. "Anything to drown that wretched sound while I make your dad's supper." So Don, who had just come in, put on some rock music, loud. Which was why the Pengellys did not hear the truck hurtle down the hill and crash against the post office wall a few minutes later.

Dr. Travers was driving through Cornwall with his wife, taking a late holiday before patients began coming down with winter colds and flu. He saw the sign that said STEEP HILL. LOW GEAR FOR 1½ MILES. Dutifully he changed into second gear.

"We must be nearly there," said his wife, looking out of her window. "I noticed a sign on the coast road that said the Fisherman's Arms was two miles. What a narrow, dangerous hill! But the cottages are very pretty—Oh, Frank, stop, *stop!* There's a child, I'm sure it's a child—by the wall over there!"

Dr. Travers jammed on his brakes and brought the car to a stop. A little stream ran down by the road in a shallow stone culvert, and half in the water lay something that looked, in the dusk, like a pile of clothes—or was it the body of the child? Mrs. Travers was out of the car in a flash, but her husband was quicker.

"Don't touch her, Emily!" he said sharply. "She's been hit. Can't be more than a few minutes. Remember that truck that overtook us half a mile back, speeding like the devil? Here, quick, go into that cottage and phone for an ambulance. The girl's in a bad way. I'll stay here and do what I can to stop the bleeding. Don't waste a minute."

Doctors are expert at stopping dangerous bleeding, for they know the right places to press. This Dr. Travers was able to do, but he didn't dare do more; the girl was lying in a queerly crumpled heap, and he guessed she had a number of bones broken and that it would be highly dangerous to move her. He watched her with great concentration, wondering where the truck had got to and what other damage it had done.

Mrs. Travers was very quick. She had seen plenty of accident cases and knew the importance of speed. The first cottage she tried had a phone; in four minutes she was back, and in six an ambulance was wailing down the hill.

Its attendants lifted the child onto a stretcher as carefully as if she were made of fine thistledown. The ambulance sped off to Plymouth—for the local cottage hospital did not take serious accident cases—and Dr. Travers went down to the police station to report what he had done.

He found that the police already knew about the speeding truck—which had suffered from loss of brakes and ended up with its radiator halfway through the post-office wall. The driver was concussed and shocked, but the police thought he was the only person injured—until Dr. Travers told his tale.

At half-past nine that night Aunt Rebecca Hoskins was sitting by her fire thinking aggrieved thoughts about the inconsiderateness of nieces who were asked to supper and never turned up, when she was startled by a neighbor, who burst in, exclaiming, "Have you heard about Sandy Pengelly, then, Mrs. Hoskins? Terrible thing, poor little soul, and they don't know if she's likely to live. Police have got the truck driver that hit her—ah, it didn't ought to be allowed, speeding through the place like that at umpty miles an hour, they ought to jail him for life—not that that'd be any comfort for poor Bert and Jean."

Horrified, Aunt Rebecca put on a coat and went down to her brother's house. She found the family with white shocked faces; Bert and Jean were about to drive off to the hospital where Sandy had been taken, and the twins were crying bitterly. Lob was nowhere to be seen. But Aunt Rebecca was not interested in dogs; she did not inquire about him.

"Thank the Lord you've come, Beck," said her brother. "Will you stay the night with Don and the twins? Don's out looking for Lob and heaven knows when we'll be back; we may get a bed with Jean's mother in Plymouth."

"Oh, if only I'd never invited the poor child," wailed Mrs. Hoskins. But Bert and Jean hardly heard her.

Vocabulary Development: aggrieved (ə grēvd′) *adj.* offended; wronged

◆ **Stop to Reflect**

Why was it very lucky for Sandy that Dr. and Mrs. Travers were the people who found her after the accident?

______

◆ **Reading Check**

Why are Father and Mother so glad to see Aunt Rebecca?

______

◆ Stop to Reflect

Don was out looking for Lob. What might the result of his search be, based on the details in the underlined sentence?

◆ Literary Analysis

What is **foreshadowed** by the statement, "worse still, there was no Lob"?

That night seemed to last forever. The twins cried themselves to sleep. Don came home very late and grim-faced. Bert and Jean sat in a waiting room of the Western Counties Hospital, but Sandy was unconscious, they were told, and she remained so. All that could be done for her was done. She was given transfusions to replace all the blood she had lost. The broken bones were set and put in slings and cradles.

"Is she a healthy girl? Has she a good constitution?" the emergency doctor asked.

"Aye, doctor, she is that," Bert said hoarsely. The lump in Jean's throat prevented her from answering; she merely nodded.

"Then she ought to have a chance. But I won't conceal from you that her condition is very serious, unless she shows signs of coming out from this coma."

But as hour succeeded hour, Sandy showed no signs of recovering consciousness. Her parents sat in the waiting room with haggard faces; sometimes one of them would go to telephone the family at home, or to try to get a little sleep at the home of Granny Pearce, not far away.

At noon next day Dr. and Mrs. Travers went to the Pengelly cottage to inquire how Sandy was doing, but the report was gloomy: "Still in a very serious condition." The twins were miserably unhappy. They forgot that they had sometimes called their elder sister bossy and only remembered how often she had shared her pocket money with them, how she read to them and took them for picnics and helped with their homework. Now there was no Sandy, no Mother and Dad, Don went around with a gray, shuttered face, and worse still, there was no Lob.

The Western Counties Hospital is a large one, with dozens of different departments and five or six connected buildings, each with three or four entrances. By that afternoon it became noticeable that a dog seemed to have taken up position outside the hospital, with the fixed intention of getting in. Patiently he would try first one entrance and then another, all the way around, and then begin again. Sometimes he would get a little way inside, following a visitor, but animals were, of course, forbidden, and he was always kindly but firmly turned out again. Sometimes the guard at the main entrance gave him a pat or offered him a bit of sandwich—he looked so wet and beseeching and desperate. But he never ate the sandwich. No one seemed to own him or to know where he came from; Plymouth is a large city and he might have belonged to anybody.

At tea time Granny Pearce came through the pouring rain to bring a flask of hot tea with brandy in it to her daughter and son-in-law. Just as she reached the main entrance the guard was gently but forcibly shoving out a large, agitated, soaking-wet Alsatian dog.

"No, old fellow, you can *not* come in. Hospitals are for people, not for dogs."

"Why, bless me," exclaimed old Mrs. Pearce. "That's Lob! Here, Lob, Lobby boy!"

Lob ran to her, whining. Mrs. Pearce walked up to the desk.

"I'm sorry, madam, you can't bring that dog in here," the guard said.

Mrs. Pearce was a very determined old lady. She looked the porter in the eye.

"Now, see here, young man. That dog has walked twenty miles from St. Killan to get to my granddaughter. Heaven knows how he knew she was here, but it's plain he knows. And he ought to have his rights! He ought to get to see her! Do you know," she went on, bristling, "that dog has walked the length of England—*twice*—to be with that girl? And you think you can keep him out with your fiddling rules and regulations?"

"I'll have to ask the medical officer," the guard said weakly.

"You do that, young man." Granny Pearce sat down in a determined manner, shutting her umbrella, and Lob sat patiently dripping at her feet. Every now and then he shook his head, as if to dislodge something heavy that was tied around his neck.

Presently a tired, thin, intelligent-looking man in a white coat came downstairs, with an impressive, silver-haired man in a dark suit, and there was a low-voiced discussion. Granny Pearce eyed them, biding her time.

"Frankly. . . not much to lose," said the older man. The man in the white coat approached Granny Pearce.

"It's strictly against every rule, but as it's such a serious case we are making an exception," he said to her quietly. "But only *outside* her bedroom door—and only for a moment or two."

Without a word, Granny Pearce rose and stumped upstairs. Lob followed close to her skirts, as if he knew his hope lay with her.

They waited in the green-floored corridor outside Sandy's room. The door was half shut. Bert and Jean were inside. Everything was terribly quiet. A nurse came out. The white-coated man asked her something and she shook her head.

◆ Stop to Reflect

Who is the dog that is trying to get into the hospital? Explain why you think so.

____

____

____

____

____

____

____

◆ Reading Strategy

Underline details in the bracketed text that show the **contrast** between how the guard and Granny Pearce view Lob's presence.

Mark the Text

◆ Reading Check

What is Lob trying to do?

____

____

____

____

◆ **Reading Check**

How does Sandy's grandmother get the dog into Sandy's hospital room?

◆ **Stop to Reflect**

Underline details in the bracketed text that give you clues to the seriousness of Sandy's condition.

Mark the Text

◆ **Reading Check**

How does Sandy react to Lob's presence?

She had left the door ajar and through it could now be seen a high, narrow bed with a lot of gadgets around it. Sandy lay there, very flat under the covers, very still. Her head was turned away. All Lob's attention was riveted on the bed. He strained toward it, but Granny Pearce clasped his collar firmly.

"I've done a lot for you, my boy, now you behave yourself," she whispered grimly. Lob let out a faint whine, anxious and pleading.

At the sound of that whine Sandy stirred just a little. She sighed and moved her head the least fraction. Lob whined again. And then Sandy turned her head right over. Her eyes opened, looking at the door.

"Lob?" she murmured—no more than a breath of sound. "Lobby, boy?"

The doctor by Granny Pearce drew a quick, sharp breath. Sandy moved her left arm—the one that was not broken—from below the covers and let her hand dangle down, feeling, as she always did in the mornings, for Lob's furry head. The doctor nodded slowly.

"All right," he whispered. "Let him go to the bedside. But keep a hold of him."

Granny Pearce and Lob moved to the bedside. Now she could see Bert and Jean, white-faced and shocked, on the far side of the bed. But she didn't look at them. She looked at the smile on her granddaughter's face as the groping fingers found Lob's wet ears and gently pulled them. "Good boy," whispered Sandy, and fell asleep again.

Granny Pearce led Lob out into the passage again. There she let go of him and he ran off swiftly down the stairs. She would have followed him, but Bert and Jean had come out into the passage, and she spoke to Bert fiercely.

"*I* don't know why you were so foolish as not to bring the dog before! Leaving him to find the way here himself—"

"But, Mother!" said Jean Pengelly. "That can't have been Lob. What a chance to take! Suppose Sandy hadn't—" She stopped, with her handkerchief pressed to her mouth.

"Not Lob? I've known that dog nine years! I suppose I ought to know my own granddaughter's dog?"

"Listen, Mother," said Bert. "Lob was killed by the same truck that hit Sandy. Don found him—when he went to look for Sandy's schoolbag. He was—he was dead. Ribs all smashed. No question of that. Don told me on the phone—he and Will Hoskins rowed a half mile out to sea and sank the dog with a lump of concrete tied to his collar. Poor old boy. Still—he was getting on. Couldn't have lasted forever."

"*Sank him at sea*? Then what—?"

Slowly old Mrs. Pearce, and then the other two, turned to look at the trail of dripping-wet footprints that led down the hospital stairs.

In the Pengellys' garden they have a stone, under the palm tree. It says: "Lob. Sandy's dog. Buried at sea."

Reader's Response: Did you like the way the story ended? Explain your answer.

____

____

Thinking About the Skill: How did comparing characters and their traits help you understand the story?

____

____

◆ Stop to Reflect

"Every now and then he shook his head, as if to dislodge something heavy that was tied around his neck." What do you now think the author was trying to suggest when she wrote that sentence?

____

____

____

____

____

____

____

____

____

Greyling

Jane Yolen

Summary

In "Greyling," a fisherman and his wife have everything they could want, except a child. One day the fisherman brings home a seal pup for his wife to love. The seal becomes a strange child with grey eyes and grey hair, and they name him Greyling. He is a selchie, a human on land and seal in the sea. Determined to keep him human, the fisherman's wife won't let Greyling go into the sea. When Greyling is fifteen, his father is caught at sea in a great storm. No one in the village will try to save him. Greyling dives into the sea and becomes a seal again. He saves his father and carries him back to shore. But Greyling decides to leave his home on land and live forever in the ocean, his real home.

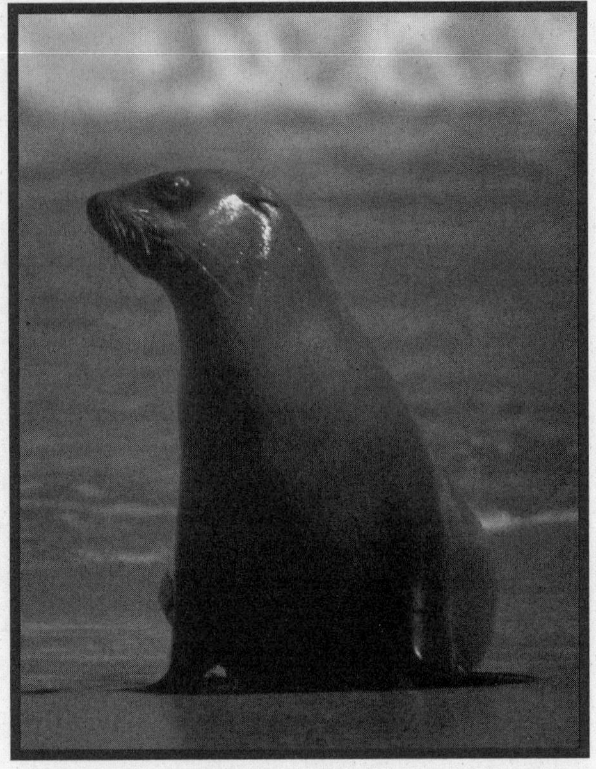

Visual Summary

STORY SITUATION

Greyling sees that his father's boat is in danger of sinking during the storm at sea, and his father may drown.

↓

PREDICTION

Greyling will jump into the water to try to save his father.

→ **REASONS**

- Nobody else is willing to risk his life.
- Greyling loves his father and doesn't want him to drown.

↓

WHAT ACTUALLY HAPPENS

Greyling jumps into the water and saves his father.

Greyling

Jane Yolen

People sometimes find themselves torn between the wishes of others and their own ideas. Deciding what to do can involve difficult choices, as this story suggests.

Once on a time when wishes were aplenty, a fisherman and his wife lived by the side of the sea. All that they ate came out of the sea. Their hut was covered with the finest mosses that kept them cool in the summer and warm in the winter. And there was nothing they needed or wanted except a child.

Each morning, when the moon touched down behind the water and the sun rose up behind the plains, the wife would say to the fisherman, "You have your boat and your nets and your lines. But I have no baby to hold in my arms." And again, in the evening, it was the same. She would weep and wail and rock the cradle that stood by the hearth. But year in and year out the cradle stayed empty.

Now the fisherman was also sad that they had no child. But he kept his sorrow to himself so that his wife would not know his grief and thus double her own. Indeed, he would leave the hut each morning with a breath of song and return each night with a whistle on his lips. His nets were full but his heart was empty, yet he never told his wife.

One sunny day, when the beach was a tan thread spun between sea and plain, the fisherman as usual went down to his boat. But this day he found a small grey seal stranded on the sandbar, crying for its own.

The fisherman looked up the beach and down. He looked in front of him and behind. And he looked to the town on the great grey cliffs that sheared off into the sea. But there were no other seals in sight.

So he shrugged his shoulders and took off his shirt. Then he dipped it into the water and wrapped the seal pup carefully in its folds.

"You have no father and you have no mother," he said. "And I have no child. So you shall come home with me."

And the fisherman did no fishing that day but brought the seal pup, wrapped in his shirt, straight home to his wife.

When she saw him coming home early with no shirt on, the fisherman's wife ran out of the hut, fear riding in her heart. Then she looked wonderingly at the bundle which he held in his arms.

Vocabulary Development: **grief** (grēf) *n.* deep sadness
sheared (shird) *v.* cut off sharply

◆ Activate Prior Knowledge

What do you know about seals? Jot down two facts about them.

1. ______________________

2. ______________________

◆ Reading Strategy

A **prediction** is a logical guess about something that has not yet happened. It is based on things you already know or details given in the story. Read the bracketed text and then predict whether the couple will get their wish for a child.

____

◆ Reading Check

Why are the fisherman and his wife sad?

____

◆ **Literary Analysis**

Stories involve some kind of **conflict**, or struggle between forces that oppose each other. Underline words in the bracketed passage that suggest the conflict the fisherman is feeling.

Mark THE Text

◆ **Stop to Reflect**

The underlined sentence indicates that Greyling wants something, but he doesn't know what he wants. Have you ever felt as he does?

____

____

____

____

____

◆ **Reading Strategy**

Will someone save the fisherman? If so, who?

____

____

____

____

"It's nothing," he said, "but a seal pup I found stranded in the shallows and longing for its own. I thought we could give it love and care until it is old enough to seek its kin."

The fisherman's wife nodded and took the bundle. Then she uncovered the wrapping and gave a loud cry. "Nothing!" she said. "You call this nothing?"

The fisherman looked. Instead of a seal lying in the folds, there was a strange child with great grey eyes and silvery grey hair, smiling up at him.

The fisherman wrung his hands. "It is a selchie," he cried. "I have heard of them. They are men upon the land and seals in the sea. I thought it was but a tale."

"Then he shall remain a man upon the land," said the fisherman's wife, clasping the child in her arms, "for I shall never let him return to the sea."

"Never," agreed the fisherman, for he knew how his wife had wanted a child. And in his secret heart, he wanted one, too. Yet he felt, somehow, it was wrong.

"We shall call him Greyling," said the fisherman's wife, "for his eyes and hair are the color of a storm-coming sky. Greyling, though he has brought sunlight into our home."

And though they still lived by the side of the water in a hut covered with mosses that kept them warm in the winter and cool in the summer, the boy Greyling was never allowed into the sea.

He grew from a child to a lad. He grew from a lad to a young man. He gathered driftwood for his mother's hearth and searched the tide pools for shells for her mantel. He mended his father's nets and tended his father's boat. But though he often stood by the shore or high in the town on the great grey cliffs, looking and longing and grieving his heart for what he did not really know, he never went into the sea.

Then one wind-wailing morning just fifteen years from the day that Greyling had been found, a great storm blew up suddenly in the North. It was such a storm as had never been seen before: the sky turned nearly black and even the fish had trouble swimming. The wind pushed huge waves onto the shore. The waters gobbled up the little hut on the beach. And Greyling and the fisherman's wife were forced to flee to the town high on the great grey cliffs. There they looked down at the roiling,[1] boiling, sea. Far from shore they spied the fisherman's boat, its sails flapping like the wings of a wounded gull. And clinging to the broken mast was the fisherman himself, sinking deeper with every wave.

The fisherman's wife gave a terrible cry. "Will no one save him?" she called to the people of the town who had gathered on the edge of the cliff. "Will no one save my own dear husband who is all of life to me?"

---

1. roiling (roil´ iŋ) *adj.* stirred up; angry.

But the townsmen looked away. There was no man there who dared risk his life in that sea, even to save a drowning soul.

"Will no one at all save him?" she cried out again.

"Let the boy go," said one old man, pointing at Greyling with his stick. "He looks strong enough."

But the fisherman's wife clasped Greyling in her arms and held his ears with her hands. She did not want him to go into the sea. She was afraid he would never return.

"Will no one save my own dear heart?" cried the fisherman's wife for a third and last time.

But shaking their heads, the people of the town edged to their houses and shut their doors and locked their windows and set their backs to the ocean and their faces to the fires that glowed in every hearth.

"I will save him, Mother," cried Greyling, "or die as I try."

And before she could tell him no, he broke from her grasp and dived from the top of the great cliffs, down, down, down into the tumbling sea.

"He will surely sink," whispered the women as they ran from their warm fires to watch.

"He will certainly drown," called the men as they took down their spyglasses from the shelves.

They gathered on the cliffs and watched the boy dive down into the sea.

As Greyling disappeared beneath the waves, little fingers of foam tore at his clothes. They snatched his shirt and his pants and his shoes and sent them bubbling away to the shore. And as Greyling went deeper beneath the waves, even his skin seemed to slough off till he swam, free at last, in the sleek grey coat of a great grey seal.

The selchie had returned to the sea.

But the people of the town did not see this. All they saw was the diving boy disappearing under the waves and then, farther out, a large seal swimming toward the boat that wallowed in the sea. The sleek grey seal, with no effort at all, eased the fisherman to the shore though the waves were wild and bright with foam. And then, with a final salute, it turned its back on the land and headed joyously out to sea.

The fisherman's wife hurried down to the sand. And behind her followed the people of the town. They searched up the beach and down, but they did not find the boy.

Vocabulary Development: slough (sluf) *v.* be shed; come off
wallowed (wäl′ ōd) *v.* rolled and tilted

◆ Literary Analysis

Mark the Text

Circle the sentences in the first bracketed paragraph that express the **conflict** the fisherman's wife is struggling with. Then describe the conflict in your own words.

◆ Reading Strategy

Read the second bracketed passage, and **predict** what will happen to Greyling.

◆ Reading Check

How was Greyling able to rescue the fisherman?

◆ **Stop to Reflect**

Do you think the fisherman's wife was right in trying to keep Greyling out of the sea? Explain.

___

___

___

___

___

___

___

___

___

___

___

___

"A brave son," said the men when they found his shirt, for they thought he was certainly drowned.

"A very brave son," said the women when they found his shoes, for they thought him lost for sure.

"Has he really gone?" asked the fisherman's wife of her husband when at last they were alone.

"Yes, quite gone," the fisherman said to her. "Gone where his heart calls, gone to the great wide sea. And though my heart grieves at his leaving, it tells me this way is best."

The fisherman's wife sighed. And then she cried. But at last she agreed that, perhaps, it was best. "For he is both man and seal," she said. "And though we cared for him for a while, now he must care for himself." And she never cried again. So once more they lived alone by the side of the sea in a new little hut which was covered with mosses to keep them warm in the winter and cool in the summer.

Yet, once a year, a great grey seal is seen at night near the fisherman's home. And the people in town talk of it, and wonder. But seals do come to the shore and men do go to the sea; and so the townfolk do not dwell upon it very long.

But it is no ordinary seal. It is Greyling himself come home—come to tell his parents tales of the lands that lie far beyond the waters, and to sing them songs of the wonders that lie far beneath the sea.

Reader's Response: Do you think that Greyling is better off living in the sea as a seal? Why?

___

___

___

Thinking About the Skill: Did predicting as you read help you understand the story? Why?

___

___

___

PREVIEW

A Backwoods Boy

Russell Freedman

Summary

"A Backwoods Boy" is a factual historical account of Abraham Lincoln's youth. It follows Lincoln's family as they move from home to home. It tells about Lincoln's lack of formal education. Poor but hardworking, Lincoln tries and fails at many different jobs before going into politics. He even loses his first election. Lincoln continues to better himself, always reading and teaching himself new skills. He teaches himself law so he will have a paying career once he does get elected to the Illinois legislature. By the end of this historical account, Lincoln has been elected to a second term in the legislature. He has also accepted a job as junior partner in a law office.

Visual Summary

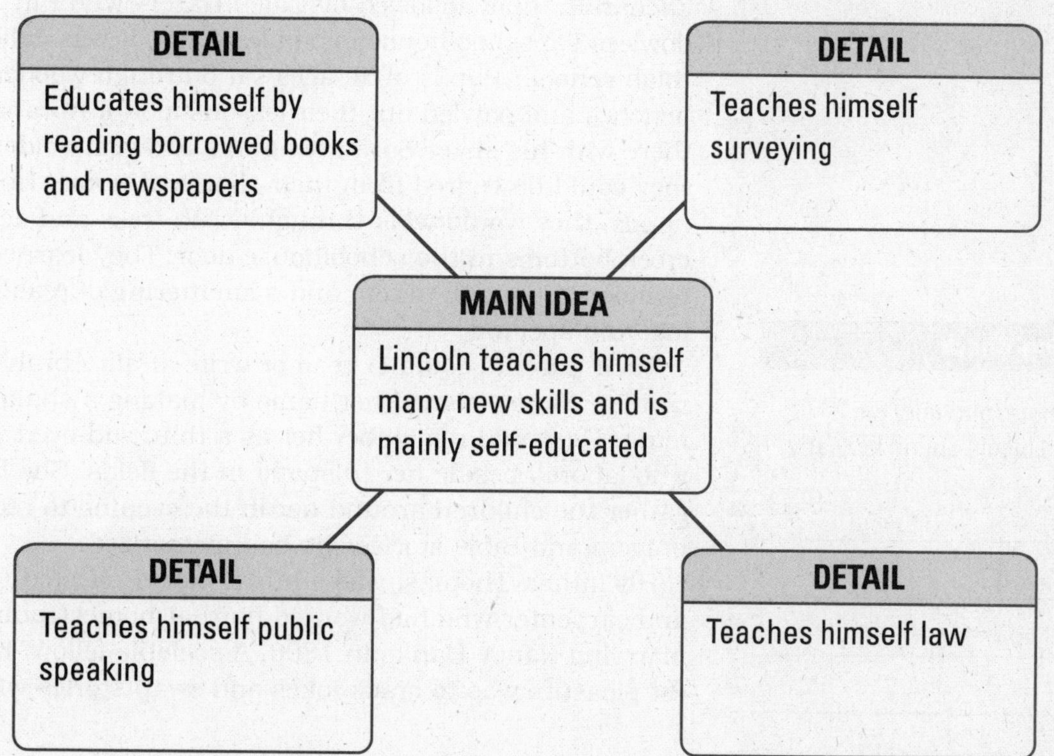

DETAIL
Educates himself by reading borrowed books and newspapers
DETAIL
Teaches himself surveying
MAIN IDEA
Lincoln teaches himself many new skills and is mainly self-educated
DETAIL
Teaches himself public speaking
DETAIL
Teaches himself law

A Backwoods Boy

Russell Freedman

When someone is determined to learn, he or she will use every free moment, no matter how brief it is. Abraham Lincoln's determination brought him all the way to the presidency.

◆ Activate Prior Knowledge

Think of someone you know or have read about who overcame an obstacle. List a few things that you admire about that person.

◆ Literary Analysis

A **historical account** is a story about real people and real events. In the bracketed paragraphs, underline three passages that state important facts about the young Lincoln.

Mark THE Text

◆ Reading Check

When, where, and how did Abraham Lincoln spend his early life?

Abraham Lincoln never liked to talk much about his early life. A poor backwoods farm boy, he grew up swinging an ax on frontier homesteads in Kentucky, Indiana, and Illinois.

He was born near Hodgenville, Kentucky, on February 12, 1809, in a log cabin with one window, one door, a chimney, and a hardpacked dirt floor. His parents named him after his pioneer grandfather. The first Abraham Lincoln had been shot dead by hostile Indians in 1786, while planting a field of corn in the Kentucky wilderness.

Young Abraham was still a toddler when his family packed their belongings and moved to another log-cabin farm a few miles north, on Knob Creek. That was the first home he could remember, the place where he ran and played as a barefoot boy.

He remembered the bright waters of Knob Creek as it tumbled past the Lincoln cabin and disappeared into the Kentucky hills. Once he fell into the rushing creek and almost drowned before he was pulled out by a neighbor boy. Another time he caught a fish and gave it to a passing soldier.

Lincoln never forgot the names of his first teachers—Zachariah Riney followed by Caleb Hazel—who ran a windowless log schoolhouse two miles away. It was called a "blab school." Pupils of all ages sat on rough wooden benches and bawled out their lessons aloud. Abraham went there with his sister Sarah, who was two years older, when they could be spared from their chores at home. Holding hands, they would walk through scrub trees and across creek bottoms to the schoolhouse door. They learned their numbers from one to ten, and a smattering of reading, writing, and spelling.

Their parents couldn't read or write at all. Abraham's mother, Nancy, signed her name by making a shakily drawn mark. He would remember her as a thin, sad-eyed woman who labored beside her husband in the fields. She liked to gather the children around her in the evening to recite prayers and Bible stories she had memorized.

His father, Thomas, was a burly, barrel-chested farmer and carpenter who had worked hard at homesteading since marrying Nancy Hanks in 1806. A sociable fellow, his greatest pleasure was to crack jokes and swap stories with his chums. With painful effort, Thomas Lincoln could scrawl his name. Like his wife, he had grown up without education, but that wasn't unusual in those days. He supported his family by living off his own land, and he watched for a chance to better himself.

In 1816, Thomas decided to pull up stakes again and move north to Indiana, which was about to join the Union as the nation's nineteenth state. Abraham was seven. He remembered the one-hundred-mile journey as the hardest experience of his life. The family set out on a cold morning in December, loading all their possessions on two horses. They crossed the Ohio River on a makeshift ferry, traveled through towering forests, then hacked a path through tangled underbrush until they reached their new homesite near the backwoods community of Little Pigeon Creek.

Thomas put up a temporary winter shelter—a crude, three-sided lean-to of logs and branches. At the open end, he kept a fire burning to take the edge off the cold and scare off the wild animals. At night, wrapped in bearskins and huddled by the fire, Abraham and Sarah listened to wolves howl and panthers scream.

Abraham passed his eighth birthday in the lean-to. He was big for his age, "a tall spider of a boy," and old enough to handle an ax. He helped his father clear the land. They planted corn and pumpkin seeds between the tree stumps. And they built a new log cabin, the biggest one yet, where Abraham climbed a ladder and slept in a loft beneath the roof.

Soon after the cabin was finished, some of Nancy's kinfolk arrived. Her aunt and uncle with their adopted son Dennis had decided to follow the Lincolns to Indiana. Dennis Hanks became an extra hand to Thomas and a big brother to Abraham, someone to run and wrestle with.

A year later, Nancy's aunt and uncle lay dead, victims of the dreaded "milk sickness" (now known to be caused by a poisonous plant called white snake root). An epidemic of the disease swept through the Indiana woods in the summer of 1818. Nancy had nursed her relatives until the end, and then she too came down with the disease. Abraham watched his mother toss in bed with chills, fever, and pain for seven days before she died at the age of thirty-four. "She knew she was going to die," Dennis Hanks recalled. "She called up the children to her dying side and told them to be good and kind to their father, to one another, and to the world."

Thomas built a coffin from black cherry wood, and nine-year-old Abraham whittled the pegs that held the wooden planks together. They buried Nancy on a windswept hill,

◆ Reading Strategy

What is the **main idea**, or most important point, of the story so far?

◆ Stop to Reflect

Read the first bracketed passage. How do you think Thomas Lincoln felt about moving his family from place to place?

◆ Literary Analysis

Mark the Text

In the second bracketed passage, underline two sentences that include facts that changed Lincoln's family life. Write the facts in your own words below.

next to her aunt and uncle. Sarah, now eleven, took her mother's place, cooking, cleaning, and mending clothes for her father, brother, and cousin Dennis in the forlorn and lonely cabin.

Thomas Lincoln waited for a year. Then he went back to Kentucky to find himself a new wife. He returned in a four-horse wagon with a widow named Sarah Bush Johnston, her three children, and all her household goods. Abraham and his sister were fortunate, for their stepmother was a warm and loving person. She took the motherless children to her heart and raised them as her own. She also spruced up the neglected Lincoln cabin, now shared by eight people who lived, ate, and slept in a single smoky room with a loft.

◆ **Reading Strategy**

The bracketed passage includes many facts about Lincoln's work and schooling. What is the **main idea** that connects these facts?

Abraham was growing fast, shooting up like a sunflower, a spindly youngster with big bony hands, unruly black hair, a dark complexion, and luminous gray eyes. He became an expert with the ax, working alongside his father, who also hired him out to work for others. For twenty-five cents a day, the boy dug wells, built pigpens, split fence rails, felled trees. "My how he could chop!" exclaimed a friend. "His ax would flash and bite into a sugar tree or a sycamore, and down it would come. If you heard him felling trees in a clearing, you would say there were three men at work, the way the trees fell."

Meanwhile, he went to school "by littles," a few weeks one winter, maybe a month the next. Lincoln said later that all his schooling together "did not amount to one year." Some fragments of his schoolwork still survive, including a verse that he wrote in his homemade arithmetic book: "Abraham Lincoln/his hand and pen/he will be good but/god knows When."

◆ **Reading Check**

How much formal education did Lincoln probably have as a boy?

Mostly, he educated himself by borrowing books and newspapers. There are many stories about Lincoln's efforts to find enough books to satisfy him in that backwoods country. Those he liked he read again and again, losing himself in the adventures of *Robinson Crusoe* or the magical tales of *The Arabian Nights*. He was thrilled by a biography of George Washington, with its stirring account of the Revolutionary War. And he came to love the rhyme and rhythm of poetry, reciting passages from Shakespeare or the Scottish poet Robert Burns at the drop of a hat. He would carry a book out to the field with him, so he could read at the end of each plow furrow, while the horse was getting its breath. When noon came, he would sit under a tree and read while he ate. "I never saw Abe after he was twelve that he didn't have a book in his hand or in his pocket," Dennis Hanks remembered. "It didn't seem natural to see a feller read like that."

By the time he was sixteen, Abraham was six feet tall—"the gangliest awkwardest feller . . . he appeared to be all joints," said a neighbor. He may have looked awkward, but hard physical labor had given him a tough, lean body with muscular arms like steel cables. He could grab a woodsman's ax by the handle and hold it straight out at arm's length. And he was one of the best wrestlers and runners around.

He also had a reputation as a comic and storyteller. Like his father, Abraham was fond of talking and listening to talk. About this time he had found a book called *Lessons in Elocution*, which offered advice on public speaking. He practiced before his friends, standing on a tree stump as he entertained them with fiery imitations of the roving preachers and politicians who often visited Little Pigeon Creek.

Folks liked young Lincoln. They regarded him as a good-humored, easy-going boy—a bookworm maybe, but smart and willing to oblige. Yet even then, people noticed that he could be moody and withdrawn. As a friend put it, he was "witty, sad, and reflective by turns. "

At the age of seventeen, Abraham left home for a few months to work as a ferryman's helper on the Ohio River. He was eighteen when his sister Sarah died early in 1828, while giving birth to her first child.

That spring, Abraham had a chance to get away from the backwoods and see something of the world. A local merchant named James Gentry hired Lincoln to accompany his son Allen on a twelve-hundred-mile flatboat voyage to New Orleans. With their cargo of country produce, the two boys floated down the Ohio River and into the Mississippi, maneuvering with long poles to avoid snags and sandbars, and to navigate in the busy river traffic.

New Orleans was the first real city they had ever seen. Their eyes must have popped as the great harbor came into view, jammed with the masts of sailing ships from distant ports all over the world. The city's cobblestone streets teemed with sailors, traders, and adventurers speaking strange languages. And there were gangs of slaves everywhere. Lincoln would never forget the sight of black men, women, and children being driven along in chains and auctioned off like cattle. In those days, New Orleans had more than two hundred slave dealers.

The boys sold their cargo and their flatboat and returned upriver by steamboat. Abraham earned twenty-four dollars—a good bit of money at the time—for the three-month trip. He handed the money over to his father, according to law and custom.

Thomas Lincoln was thinking about moving on again. Lately he had heard glowing reports about Illinois, where instead of forests there were endless prairies with plenty of

◆ **Reading Strategy**

Underline the words in the bracketed passage that express the **main idea** of the passage.

Mark the Text

◆ **Stop to Reflect**

Lincoln was president during the Civil War, which ended slavery in the United States. When he went to New Orleans, he saw "gangs of slaves everywhere." Do you think this sight affected his feelings about slavery? Explain your answer.

____

____

____

____

____

____

____

____

____

rich black soil. Early in 1830, Thomas sold his Indiana farm. The Lincolns piled everything they owned into two ox-drawn wagons and set out over muddy roads, with Abraham, just turned twenty-one, driving one of the wagons himself. They traveled west to their new homesite in central Illinois, not far from Decatur. Once again, Abraham helped his father build a cabin and start a new farm.

◆ Literary Analysis

In the first bracketed passage, underline the part of the **historical account** that explains to the reader why Lincoln could now leave home.

Mark THE Text

He stayed with his family through their first prairie winter, but he was getting restless. He had met an enterprising fellow named Denton Offutt, who wanted him to take another boatload of cargo down the river to New Orleans. Abraham agreed to make the trip with his stepbrother, John Johnston, and a cousin, John Hanks.

When he returned to Illinois three months later, he paid a quick farewell visit to his father and stepmother. Abraham was twenty-two now, of legal age, free to do what he wanted. His parents were settled and could get along without him. Denton Offutt was planning to open a general store in the flourishing village of New Salem, Illinois, and he had promised Lincoln a steady job.

Lincoln arrived in New Salem in July 1831 wearing a faded cotton shirt and blue jeans too short for his long legs—a "friendless, un-educated, penniless boy," as he later described himself. He tended the counter at Denton Offutt's store and slept in a room at the back.

The village stood in a wooded grove on a bluff above the Sangamon River. Founded just two years earlier, it had about one hundred people living in one- and two-room log houses. Cattle grazed behind split-rail fences, hogs snuffled along dusty lanes, and chickens and geese flapped about underfoot. New Salem was still a small place, but it was growing. The settlers expected it to become a frontier boom town.

◆ Reading Strategy

Underline parts of the second bracketed passage that give examples that support its **main idea**—that Lincoln had a talent for getting along with people.

Mark THE Text

With his gifts for swapping stories and making friends, Lincoln fit easily into the life of the village. He showed off his skill with an ax, competed in footraces, and got along with everyone from Mentor Graham, the schoolmaster, to Jack Armstrong, the leader of a rowdy gang called the Clary's Grove boys. Armstrong was the wrestling champion of New Salem. He quickly challenged Lincoln to a match.

On the appointed day, an excited crowd gathered down by the river, placing bets as the wrestlers stripped to the waist for combat. They circled each other, then came to grips, twisting and tugging until they crashed to the ground with Lincoln on top. As he pinned Armstrong's shoulders to the ground, the other Clary's Grove boys dived in to join the scuffle. Lincoln broke away, backed against a cliff, and defiantly offered to take them all on—one at a time. Impressed, Armstrong jumped to his feet and offered Lincoln his hand, declaring the match a draw. After that, they were fast friends.

Lincoln also found a place among the town's intellectuals. He joined the New Salem Debating Society, which met once a week in James Rutledge's tavern. The first time he debated, he seemed nervous. But as he began to speak in his high, reedy voice, he surprised everyone with the force and logic of his argument. "He was already a fine speaker," one debater recalled. "All he lacked was culture."

Lincoln was self-conscious about his meager education, and ambitious to improve himself. Mentor Graham, the schoolmaster and a fellow debater, took a liking to the young man, lent him books, and offered to coach him in the fine points of English grammar. Lincoln had plenty of time to study. There wasn't much business at Offutt's store, so he could spend long hours reading as he sat behind the counter.

When the store failed in 1832, Offutt moved on to other schemes. Lincoln had to find something else to do. At the age of twenty-three, he decided to run for the Illinois state legislature. Why not? He knew everyone in town, people liked him, and he was rapidly gaining confidence as a public speaker. His friends urged him to run, saying that a bright young man could go far in politics. So Lincoln announced his candidacy and his political platform. He was in favor of local improvements, like better roads and canals. He had made a study of the Sangamon River, and he proposed that it be dredged and cleared so steamboats could call at New Salem—insuring a glorious future for the town.

Before he could start his campaign, an Indian war flared up in northern Illinois. Chief Black Hawk of the Sauk and Fox tribes had crossed the Mississippi, intending, he said, to raise corn on land that had been taken from his people thirty years earlier. The white settlers were alarmed, and the governor called for volunteers to stop the invasion. Lincoln enlisted in a militia company made up of his friends and neighbors. He was surprised and pleased when the men elected him as their captain, with Jack Armstrong as first sergeant. His troops drilled and marched, but they never did sight any hostile Indians. Years later, Lincoln would joke about his three-month stint as a military man, telling how he survived "a good many bloody battles with mosquitoes."

By the time he returned to New Salem, election day was just two weeks off. He jumped into the campaign—pitching horseshoes with voters, speaking at barbecues, chatting with farmers in the fields, joking with customers at country stores. He lost, finishing eighth in a field of thirteen. But in his own precinct,[1] where folks knew him, he received 227 votes out of 300 cast.

1. **precinct** (prē′ siŋkt) *n.* election district.

◆ Reading Strategy

The underlined sentence connects the **main idea** of the paragraph it is part of with the main idea of the next paragraph. Rewrite those ideas in your own words.

1. ______________________________

____

____

2. ______________________________

____

____

◆ Literary Analysis

Lincoln "was in favor of local improvements." Underline the sentence in the bracketed paragraph that gives facts to support this statement.

Mark the Text

◆ Reading Check

What did Lincoln do in a single year that made people think he could be a politician?

____

____

____

____

____

____

____

____

____

◆ **Reading Strategy**

What is the **main idea** of the first bracketed paragraph, and how does the underlined sentence relate to that idea?

◆ **Reading Strategy**

How does the **main idea** of the second bracketed paragraph connect to ideas the author has already stated?

◆ **Reading Check**

What happened when Lincoln ran for the legislature a second time?

Defeated as a politician, he decided to try his luck as a frontier merchant. With a fellow named William Berry as his partner, Lincoln operated a general store that sold everything from axes to beeswax. But the two men showed little aptitude for business, and their store finally "winked out," as Lincoln put it. Then Berry died, leaving Lincoln saddled with a $1,100 debt—a gigantic amount for someone who had never earned more than a few dollars a month. Lincoln called it "the National Debt," but he vowed to repay every cent. He spent the next fifteen years doing so.

To support himself, he worked at all sorts of odd jobs. He split fence rails, hired himself out as a farmhand, helped at the local gristmill.[2] With the help of friends, he was appointed postmaster of New Salem, a part-time job that paid about fifty dollars a year. Then he was offered a chance to become deputy to the local surveyor.[3] He knew nothing about surveying, so he bought a compass, a chain, and a couple of textbooks on the subject. Within six weeks, he had taught himself enough to start work—laying out roads and townsites, and marking off property boundaries.

As he traveled about the county, making surveys and delivering mail to faraway farms, people came to know him as an honest and dependable fellow. Lincoln could be counted on to witness a contract, settle a boundary dispute, or compose a letter for folks who couldn't write much themselves. For the first time, his neighbors began to call him "Abe."

In 1834, Lincoln ran for the state legislature again. This time he placed second in a field of thirteen candidates, and was one of four men elected to the Illinois House of Representatives from Sangamon County. In November, wearing a sixty-dollar tailor-made suit he had bought on credit, the first suit he had ever owned, the twenty-five-year-old legislator climbed into a stagecoach and set out for the state capitol in Vandalia.

In those days, Illinois lawmakers were paid three dollars a day to cover their expenses, but only while the legislature was in session. Lincoln still had to earn a living. One of his fellow representatives, a rising young attorney named John Todd Stuart, urged Lincoln to take up the study of law. As Stuart pointed out, it was an ideal profession for anyone with political ambitions.

And in fact, Lincoln had been toying with the idea of becoming a lawyer. For years he had hung around frontier courthouses, watching country lawyers bluster and strut as

Vocabulary Development: aptitude (ap´ tə to͞od´) *n.* natural ability

2. **gristmill** (grist´ mil´) *n.* place where grain is ground into flour.
3. **surveyor** (sər vā´ ər) *n.* person who determines the boundaries of land.

they cross-examined witnesses and delivered impassioned speeches before juries. He had sat on juries himself, appeared as a witness, drawn up legal documents for his neighbors. He had even argued a few cases before the local justice of the peace.

Yes, the law intrigued him. It would give him a chance to rise in the world, to earn a respected place in the community, to live by his wits instead of by hard physical labor.

Yet Lincoln hesitated, unsure of himself because he had so little formal education. That was no great obstacle, his friend Stuart kept telling him. In the 1830's, few American lawyers had ever seen the inside of a law school. Instead, they "read law" in the office of a practicing attorney until they knew enough to pass their exams.

Lincoln decided to study entirely on his own. He borrowed some law books from Stuart, bought others at an auction, and began to read and memorize legal codes[4] and precedents.[5] Back in New Salem, folks would see him walking down the road, reciting aloud from one of his law books, or lying under a tree as he read, his long legs stretched up the trunk. He studied for nearly three years before passing his exams and being admitted to practice on March 1, 1837.

By then, the state legislature was planning to move from Vandalia to Springfield, which had been named the new capital of Illinois. Lincoln had been elected to a second term in the legislature. And he had accepted a job as junior partner in John Todd Stuart's Springfield law office.

In April, he went back to New Salem for the last time to pack his belongings and say goodbye to his friends. The little village was declining now. Its hopes for growth and prosperity had vanished when the Sangamon River proved too treacherous for steamboat travel. Settlers were moving away, seeking brighter prospects elsewhere.

By 1840, New Salem was a ghost town. It would have been forgotten completely if Abraham Lincoln hadn't gone there to live when he was young, penniless, and ambitious.

Vocabulary Development: intrigued (in trēgd′) *v.* fascinated
treacherous (trech′ ər əs) *adj.* dangerous

4. **legal codes** body of laws, as for a nation or a city, arranged systematically.
5. **precedents** (pres′ ə dənts) *n.* legal cases that may serve as a reference.

Reader's Response: What did you learn about Abraham Lincoln that most surprised you?

____

____

◆ Stop to Reflect

Lincoln hesitated before deciding to become a lawyer. Think about what you have read, and describe why he decided as he did.

____

Jackie Robinson: Justice at Last

Geoffrey C. Ward and Ken Burns

Dodgers
17

Summary

"Jackie Robinson: Justice at Last" is the story of two brave men who change the course of history in sports. Branch Rickey, the owner of the Brooklyn Dodgers, recognizes the importance of having players of all races on major league baseball teams. He asks Jackie Robinson to become the first African American player on his team. Rickey knows that the first black player might be attacked, even by his own teammates. He tells Robinson that he must never lose his temper. If he gets into just one fight, integration will not work. In spite of warnings that this new road will be difficult, Robinson signs on. By accepting this challenge with dignity and strength, Robinson becomes a role model for future generations.

Visual Summary

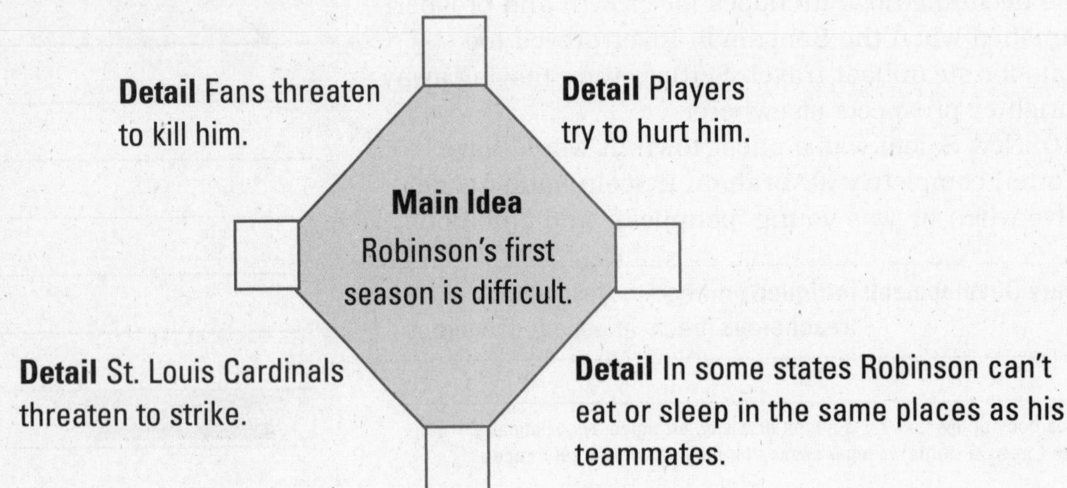
Detail Fans threaten to kill him.
Detail Players try to hurt him.
Main Idea Robinson's first season is difficult.
Detail St. Louis Cardinals threaten to strike.
Detail In some states Robinson can't eat or sleep in the same places as his teammates.

Jackie Robinson: Justice at Last

Geoffrey C. Ward and Ken Burns

It is natural to want to fight back against unfairness and injustice. Jackie Robinson showed that doing your very best and keeping your dignity can be the most effective weapons.

It was 1945, and World War II had ended. Americans of all races had died for their country. Yet black men were still not allowed in the major leagues. The national pastime was loved by all America, but the major leagues were for white men only.

Branch Rickey of the Brooklyn Dodgers thought that was wrong. He was the only team owner who believed blacks and whites should play together. Baseball, he felt, would become even more thrilling, and fans of all colors would swarm to his ballpark.

Rickey decided his team would be the first to integrate. There were plenty of brilliant Negro league players, but he knew the first black major leaguer would need much more than athletic ability.

Many fans and players were prejudiced—they didn't want the races to play together. Rickey knew the first black player would be cursed and booed. Pitchers would throw at him; runners would spike him. Even his own teammates might try to pick a fight.

But somehow this man had to rise above that. No matter what happened, he must never lose his temper. No matter what was said to him, he must never answer back. If he had even one fight, people might say integration wouldn't work.

When Rickey met Jackie Robinson, he thought he'd found the right man. Robinson was 28 years old, and a superb athlete. In his first season in the Negro leagues, he hit .387. But just as importantly, he had great intelligence and sensitivity. Robinson was college-educated, and knew what joining the majors would mean for blacks. The grandson of a slave, he was proud of his race and wanted others to feel the same.

In the past, Robinson had always stood up for his rights. But now Rickey told him he would have to stop. The Dodgers needed "a man that will take abuse."

At first Robinson thought Rickey wanted someone who was afraid to defend himself. But as they talked, he realized that in this case a truly brave man would have to avoid fighting. He thought for a while, then promised Rickey he would not fight back.

Vocabulary Development: integrate (in′ tə grāt′) *v.* remove barriers and allow access to all

◆ Activate Prior Knowledge

Think of a time when you were someplace where you were not sure whether people liked you. How did you feel?

◆ Literary Analysis

In a **historical account**, writers often explain why things are as they are. Underline the sentences in the bracketed paragraph that explain why Branch Rickey thought Robinson was the right man to integrate major-league baseball.

Mark the Text

◆ Reading Check

What baseball team were Robinson and Rickey associated with?

Robinson signed with the Dodgers and went to play in the minors in 1946. Rickey was right—fans insulted him, and so did players. But he performed brilliantly and avoided fights. Then, in 1947, he came to the majors.

Many Dodgers were angry. Some signed a petition demanding to be traded. But Robinson and Rickey were determined to make their experiment work.

On April 15—Opening Day—26,623 fans came out to Ebbets Field. More than half of them were black—Robinson was already their hero. Now he was making history just by being on the field.

The afternoon was cold and wet, but no one left the ballpark. The Dodgers beat the Boston Braves, 5–3. Robinson went hitless, but the hometown fans didn't seem to care—they cheered his every move.

Robinson's first season was difficult. Fans threatened to kill him; players tried to hurt him. The St. Louis Cardinals said they would strike if he took the field. And because of laws separating the races in certain states, he often couldn't eat or sleep in the same places as his teammates.

Yet through it all, he kept his promise to Rickey. No matter who insulted him, he never retaliated.

Robinson's dignity paid off. Thousands of fans jammed stadiums to see him play. The Dodgers set attendance records in a number of cities.

Slowly his teammates accepted him, realizing that he was the spark that made them a winning team. No one was more daring on the base paths or better with the glove. At the plate, he had great bat control—he could hit the ball anywhere. That season, he was named baseball's first Rookie of the Year.

Jackie Robinson went on to a glorious career. But he did more than play the game well—his bravery taught Americans a lesson. Branch Rickey opened a door, and Jackie Robinson stepped through it, making sure it could never be closed again. Something wonderful happened to baseball—and America—the day Jackie Robinson joined the Dodgers.

◆ Stop to Reflect

Jackie Robinson became both a great player and a popular one. Do you think his decision not to fight, no matter what, made him more popular? Why?

◆ Reading Strategy

Think about the story you have just finished reading. What is its **main idea**? Circle groups of words that support your opinion.

Mark the Text

Vocabulary Development: retaliated (ri tal′ ē at′ id) *v.* harmed or did wrong to someone in return for an injury or wrong that person has done

Reader's Response: Do you think it was difficult for Jackie Robinson to hold his temper? Explain.

The Fun They Had

Isaac Asimov

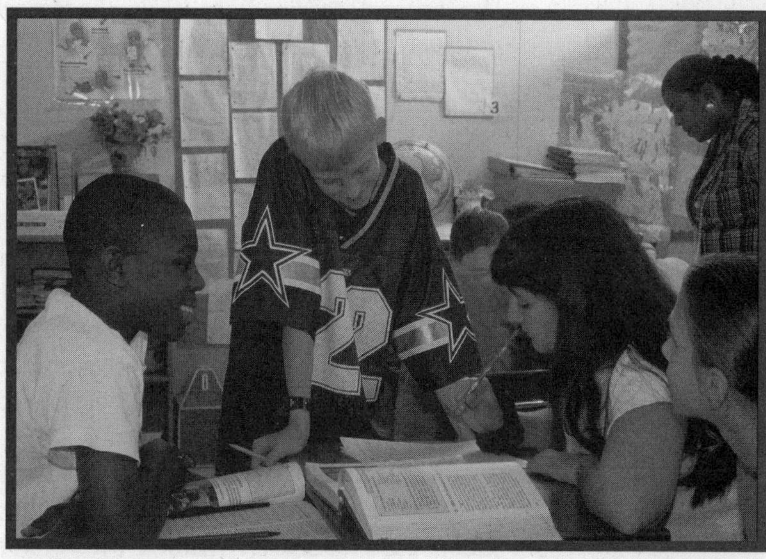

Summary

Margie, age eleven, and Tommy, age thirteen, are neighbors living in the year 2155. In their world, students do not go to school. Instead, they are taught lessons by a mechanical teacher on television. One day, Tommy finds a book in his attic and shares the book with Margie. The book is about school in the old days, about two hundred years in the past. Tommy explains that in the past there were no mechanical teachers. A real person taught lessons. Also, school was not held in a special room at home. Kids from all over the neighborhood attended school in a special building away from home. Kids of the same age learned the same things. Margie thinks about how much fun school must have been back then compared with how dull it is in her world.

Visual Summary

Comparing and Contrasting	
School in 2155	**School in the past**
Kids learn alone at home	Kids go to school
Mechanical teacher	Human teacher
Kids work at their own pace	Kids of the same age learn the same thing
Kids read a television screen	Kids read books

◆ Activate Prior Knowledge

Jot down objects that you would consider to be from the past, such as records, which have been replaced by CD's.

◆ Literary Analysis

This story is **science fiction**—writing that tells about imaginary events and involves science and technology. Science fiction is often set in the future. Circle the words in the bracketed text that tell you that this story is science fiction. Explain.

Mark THE Text

◆ Reading Check

What does Tommy find?

The Fun They Had

Isaac Asimov

In 1957, when this story was published, commercial TV had only been around for about twenty years, and most TV pictures were black and white. Personal computers were introduced in the 1970s, and the World Wide Web became available in the 1990s. The technology that you take for granted was only a scientific idea.

Margie even wrote about it that night in her diary. On the page headed May 17, 2155, she wrote, "Today Tommy found a real book."

It was a very old book. Margie's grandfather once said that when he was a little boy, his grandfather told him that there was a time when all stories were printed on paper.

They turned the pages, which were yellow and crinkly, and it was awfully funny to read words that stood still instead of moving the way they were supposed to—on a screen, you know. And then, when they turned back to the page before, it had the same words on it that it had had when they read it the first time.

"Gee," said Tommy, "what a waste. When you're through with the book, you just throw it away, I guess. Our television screen must have had a million books on it and it's good for plenty more. I wouldn't throw it away."

"Same with mine," said Margie. She was eleven and hadn't seen as many telebooks as Tommy had. He was thirteen.

She said, "Where did you find it?"

"In my house." He pointed without looking, because he was busy reading. "In the attic."

"What's it about?"

"School."

Margie was scornful. "School? What's there to write about school? I hate school." Margie always hated school, but now she hated it more than ever. The mechanical teacher had been giving her test after test in geography, and she had been doing worse and worse until her mother had shaken her head sorrowfully and sent for the county inspector.

He was a round little man with a red face and a whole box of tools with dials and wires. He smiled at her and gave her an apple, then took the teacher apart. Margie had hoped he wouldn't know how to put it together again, but he knew how all right, and after an hour or so, there it was again, large and ugly, with a big screen on which all the lessons where shown and the questions were asked. That wasn't so bad. The part she hated most was the slot where she had to put homework and test papers. She always had to write them out in a punch code they made her learn when she was six years old, and the mechanical teacher calculated the mark in no time.

The inspector had smiled after he was finished and patted her head. He said to her mother, "It's not the little girl's fault, Mrs. Jones. I think the geography sector was geared a little too quick. Those things happen sometimes. I've slowed it up to an average ten-year level. Actually, the overall pattern of her progress is quite satisfactory." And he patted Margie's head again.

Margie was disappointed. She had been hoping they would take the teacher away altogether. They had once taken Tommy's teacher away for nearly a month because the history sector had blanked out completely.

So she said to Tommy, "Why would anyone write about school?"

Tommy looked at her with very superior eyes. "Because it's not our kind of school, stupid. This is the old kind of school that they had hundreds and hundreds of year ago." He added loftily, pronouncing the word carefully, *"Centuries ago."*

Margie was hurt. "Well, I don't know what kind of school they had all that time ago." She read the book over his shoulder for a while, then said, "Anyway, they had a teacher."

"Sure they had a teacher, but it wasn't a regular teacher. It was a man."

"A man? How could a man be a teacher?"

"Well, he just told the boys and girls things and gave them homework and asked them questions."

"A man isn't smart enough."

"Sure he is. My father knows as much as my teacher."

"He can't. A man can't know as much as a teacher."

"He knows almost as much I betcha."

Margie wasn't prepared to dispute that. She said, "I wouldn't want a strange man in my house to teach me."

Tommy screamed with laughter. "You don't know much, Margie. The teachers didn't live in the house. They had a special building and all the kids went there."

"And all the kids learned the same thing?"

"Sure, if they were the same age."

"But my mother says a teacher has to be adjusted to fit the mind of each boy and girl it teaches and that each kid has to be taught differently."

"Just the same, they didn't do it that way then. If you don't like it, you don't have to read the book."

Vocabulary Development: calculated (kal′ kyo͞o lāt′ id) *v.* determined by using math
loftily (lof′ tə lē) *adv.* in a superior way
dispute (di spyo͞ot′) *v.* argue; debate

◆ Literary Analysis

What does the man do to fix the machine?

______

______

______

Circle the details in the bracketed text that tell you that this situation is **science fiction**.

◆ Reading Check

What is the difference between Margie's teacher and your teacher?

______

______

◆ Reading Strategy

When you **evaluate an author's message** you consider if the message makes sense. Then you decide whether you agree or disagree. Asimov's message is that learning in a group from a real teacher is better than learning from a computer. What is Margie's mother's idea of a good teacher?

______

______

______

Would Margie's mother agree or disagree with Asimov's message? Explain.

______

______

______

______

◆ **Stop to Reflect**

Consider your teacher and classroom. Then consider Tommy's and Margie's teacher and classroom. Compare school today with school in 2155.

What are some positive things about having a real teacher and going to school instead of having a mechanical teacher?

◆ **Reading Strategy**

How would Margie **evaluate the author's message?** Write whether or not Margie would agree or disagree with Asimov.

"I didn't say I didn't like it," Margie said quickly. She wanted to read about those funny schools.

They weren't even half finished when Margie's mother called, "Margie! School!"

Margie looked up. "Not yet, Mamma."

"Now," said Mrs. Jones. "And it's probably time for Tommy, too."

Margie said to Tommy, "Can I read the book some more with you after school?"

"Maybe," he said, nonchalantly. He walked away whistling, the dusty old book tucked beneath his arm.

Margie went into the schoolroom. It was right next to her bedroom, and the mechanical teacher was on and waiting for her. It was always on at the same time every day except Saturday and Sunday, because her mother said little girls learned better if they learned at regular hours.

The screen was lit up, and it said: "Today's arithmetic lesson is on the addition of proper fractions. Please insert yesterday's homework in the proper slot."

Margie did so with a sigh. She was thinking about the old schools they had when her grandfather's grandfather was a little boy. All the kids from the whole neighborhood came, laughing and shouting in the schoolyard, sitting together in the schoolroom, going home together at the end of the day. They learned the same things so they could help one another on the homework and talk about it.

And the teachers were people. . . .

The mechanical teacher was flashing on the screen: "When we add the fractions 1/2 and 1/4 . . ."

Margie was thinking about how the kids must have loved it in the old days. She was thinking about the fun they had.

Vocabulary Development: nonchalantly (nän′ shə lant′ lē) *adv.* without concern or interest

Reader's Response: Would you rather be in a school like Margie's and Tommy's or in your own school? Explain.

Thinking About the Skill: How did knowing that this is science fiction help you better understand the story?

from Exploring the *Titanic*

Robert D. Ballard

Summary

In April, 1912, the *Titanic* began its maiden voyage across the Atlantic Ocean. Moving out of port, it narrowly missed hitting another ship. Four days later, the radio operators received iceberg warnings. They notified Captain Smith, who seemed unconcerned. Seven iceberg warnings came in that day. The night was calm, clear, moonless, and cold. Suddenly, there was an iceberg ahead. The alarm was sounded, and the engines were reversed, but it was too late. Many people were asleep. Nearly all were sure that the ship was unsinkable. As the hull rapidly filled with water, the "CQD" distress call went out.

Visual Summary

Building Suspense

Shortly after beginning its maiden voyage, *Titanic* narrowly avoids collision with another ship.

↓

Titanic receives radio reports of icebergs ahead, but captain seems unconcerned.

↓

More warnings of icebergs are received. Moonless night makes it difficult to spot icebergs.

↓

Fred Fleet sees the huge iceberg directly ahead! He sounds the alarm bell. Orders are given to immediately turn the ship to try to avoid the ice.

from Exploring the *Titanic*

Robert D. Ballard

The Titanic *was the largest and most luxurious ocean liner of its time. Huge watertight doors between sections and a strong construction made the* Titanic *seem safer than other ships. According to the publicity, it was also "unsinkable." There were not enough lifeboats for all the passengers, perhaps because the owners were sure that lifeboats would never be needed. More than 1,500 people died when the ship sank in 1912.*

At noon on Wednesday, April 10, the *Titanic* cast off. The whistles on her huge funnels were the biggest ever made. As she began her journey to the sea, they were heard for miles around.

Moving majestically down the River Test, and watched by a crowd that had turned out for the occasion, the *Titanic* slowly passed two ships tied up to a dock. All of a sudden, the mooring ropes holding the passenger liner *New York* snapped with a series of sharp cracks like fireworks going off. The enormous pull created by the *Titanic* moving past her had broken the *New York's* ropes and was now drawing her stern toward the *Titanic.*

Jack Thayer watched in horror as the two ships came closer and closer. "It looked as though there surely would be a collision," he later wrote. "Her stern could not have been more than a yard or two from our side. It almost hit us." At the last moment, some quick action by Captain Smith and a tugboat captain nearby allowed the *Titanic* to slide past with only inches to spare.

It was not a good sign. Did it mean that the *Titanic* might be too big a ship to handle safely? Those who knew about the sea thought that such a close call at the beginning of a maiden voyage was a very bad omen.

Jack Phillips, the first wireless operator on the *Titanic,* quickly jotted down the message coming in over his headphones. "It's another iceberg warning," he said wearily to his young assistant, Harold Bride. "You'd better take it up to the bridge." Both men had been at work for hours in the *Titanic's* radio room trying to get caught up in sending out a large number of personal messages. In 1912, passengers on ocean liners thought it was a real novelty to send postcard-style messages to friends at home from the middle of the Atlantic.

Vocabulary Development: majestically (mə jes´ tik lē) *adv.* grandly
collision (kə lizh´ ən) *n.* coming together with a sudden violent force; a crash
novelty (näv´ əl tē) *n.* something new or unusual

◆ Activate Prior Knowledge

The sinking of the *Titanic* has been covered in movies, books, and documentaries. Write down what you already know about the *Titanic.*

◆ Reading Strategy

Nonfiction works often include **facts and opinions.** A fact is information that can be proven. An opinion is a belief that can be supported but not proven, such as a statement that *Titanic* owners were irresponsible. Circle one fact and underline one opinion in the bracketed text.

Mark the Text

◆ Reading Check

What happens to the *Titanic* at the beginning of the voyage out of the harbor?

Bride picked up the iceberg message and stepped out onto the boat deck. It was a sunny but cold Sunday morning, the fourth day of the *Titanic's* maiden voyage. The ship was steaming at full speed across a calm sea. Harold Bride was quite pleased with himself at having landed a job on such a magnificent new ship. After all, he was only twenty-two years old and had just nine months' experience at operating a "wireless set," as a ship's radio was then called. As he entered the bridge area, he could see one of the crewmen standing behind the ship's wheel steering her course toward New York.

Captain Smith was on duty in the bridge, so Bride handed the message to him. "It's from the *Caronia*, sir. She's reporting icebergs and pack ice ahead." The captain thanked him, read the message, and then posted it on the bulletin board for other officers on watch to read. On his way back to the radio room, Bride thought the captain had seemed quite unconcerned by the message. But then again, he had been told that it was not unusual to have ice floating in the sea lanes during an April crossing. Besides, what danger could a few pieces of ice present to an unsinkable ship?

Elsewhere on board, passengers relaxed on deck chairs, reading or taking naps. Some played cards, some wrote letters, while others chatted with friends. As it was Sunday, church services had been held in the morning, the first-class service led by Captain Smith. Jack Thayer spent most of the day walking about the decks getting some fresh air with his parents.

Two more ice warnings were received from nearby ships around lunch time. In the chaos of the radio room, Harold Bride only had time to take one of them to the bridge. The rest of the day passed quietly. Then, in the late afternoon, the temperature began to drop rapidly. Darkness approached as the bugle call announced dinner.

Jack Thayer's parents had been invited to a special dinner for Captain Smith, so Jack ate alone in the first-class dining room. After dinner, as he was having a cup of coffee, he was joined by Milton Long, another passenger going home to the States. Long was older than Jack, but in the easy-going atmosphere of shipboard travel, they struck up a conversation and talked together for an hour or so.

At 7:30 P.M., the radio room received three more warnings of ice about fifty miles ahead. One of them was from the steamer *Californian* reporting three large icebergs. Harold Bride took this message up to the bridge, and it was again politely received. Captain Smith was attending the dinner party being held for him when the warning was delivered. He never got to see it. Then, around 9:00 P.M., the captain excused himself and went up to the bridge. He and his officers talked about how difficult it was to spot icebergs on a

◆ Literary Analysis

The anticipation about the outcome of an event is called **suspense**. Sometimes, the outcome is uncertain. Other times, as in the sinking of the *Titanic*, you know the outcome, but you do not know *how* or *when* it will occur. Circle the sentence in the bracketed text that adds to the suspense.

Mark the Text

◆ Reading Check

How does Captain Smith react to the messages that there are icebergs ahead?

____

____

____

____

◆ Literary Analysis

Circle two sentences in the bracketed text that add to the suspense by indicating that something may happen soon.

Mark the Text

◆ **Stop to Reflect**

What are the weather conditions on this night?

____

____

Why is it so difficult to see the icebergs?

____

____

____

____

◆ **Reading Check**

Why don't the radio operators answer the final message from the *Californian*?

____

____

____

____

◆ **Literary Analysis**

What two details add to the suspense in the bracketed text? Write the details.

1. ______________________________

____

____

2. ______________________________

____

____

____

____

____

calm, clear, moonless night like this with no wind to kick up white surf around them. Before going to bed, the captain ordered the lookouts to keep a sharp watch for ice.

After trading travel stories with Milton Long, Jack Thayer put on his coat and walked around the deck. "It had become very much colder," he said later. "It was a brilliant, starry night. There was no moon, and I have never seen the stars shine brighter . . . sparkling like diamonds. . . . It was the kind of night that made one feel glad to be alive." At eleven o'clock, he went below to his cabin, put on his pajamas, and got ready for bed.

In the radio room, Harold Bride was exhausted. The two operators were expected to keep the radio working twenty-four hours a day, and Bride lay down to take a much-needed nap. Phillips was so busy with the passenger messages that he actually brushed off the final ice warning of the night. It was from the *Californian*. Trapped in a field of ice, she had stopped for the night about nineteen miles north of the *Titanic*. She was so close that the message literally blasted in Phillips's ears. Annoyed by the loud interruption, he cut off the *Californian's* radio operator with the words, "Shut up, shut up, I'm busy."

The radio room had received a total of seven ice warning messages in one day. It was quite clear that floating icebergs lay ahead of the *Titanic*. High up in the crow's nest on the forward mast, Fred Fleet had passed a quiet watch. It was now 11:40 P.M., and he and his fellow lookout were waiting to be relieved so they could head below, perhaps for a hot drink before hopping into their warm bunks. The sea was dead calm. The air bitterly cold.

Suddenly, Fleet saw something. A huge, dark shape loomed out of the night directly ahead of the *Titanic*. An iceberg! He quickly sounded the alarm bell three times and picked up the telephone.

"What did you see?" asked the duty officer.

"Iceberg right ahead," replied Fleet.

Immediately, the officer on the bridge ordered the wheel turned as far as it would go. The engine room was told to reverse the engines, while a button was pushed to close the doors to the watertight compartments in the bottom of the ship.

The lookouts in the crow's nest braced themselves for a collision. Slowly the ship started to turn. It looked as though they would miss it. But it was too late. They had avoided a head-on crash, but the iceberg had struck a glancing blow along the *Titanic's* starboard bow.[1] Several tons of ice fell on

Vocabulary Development: watertight *adv.* put together so that no water can get through

1. **starboard bow** right side of the front of the ship.

the ship's decks as the iceberg brushed along the side of the ship and passed into the night. A few minutes later, the *Titanic* came to a stop.

Many of the passengers didn't know the ship had hit anything. Because it was so cold, almost everyone was inside, and most people had already gone to bed. Ruth Becker and her mother were awakened by the dead silence. They could no longer hear the soothing hum of the vibrating engines from below. Jack Thayer was about to step into bed when he felt himself sway ever so slightly. The engines stopped. He was startled by the sudden quiet.

Sensing trouble, Ruth's mother looked out of the door of their second-class cabin and asked a steward[2] what had happened. He told her that nothing was the matter, so Mrs. Becker went back to bed. But as she lay there, she couldn't help feeling that something was very wrong.

Jack heard running feet and voices in the hallway outside his first-class cabin. "I hurried into my heavy overcoat and drew on my slippers. All excited, but not thinking anything serious had occurred, I called in to my father and mother that I was going up on deck to see the fun."

On deck, Jack watched some third-class passengers playing with the ice that had landed on the forward deck as the iceberg had brushed by. Some people were throwing chunks at each other, while a few skidded about playing football with pieces of ice.

Down in the very bottom of the ship, things were very different. When the iceberg had struck, there had been a noise like a big gun going off in one of the boiler rooms. A couple of stokers had been immediately hit by a jet of icy water. The noise and the shock of cold water had sent them running for safety.

Twenty minutes after the crash, things looked very bad indeed to Captain Smith. He and the ship's builder, Thomas Andrews, had made a rapid tour below decks to inspect the damage. The mail room was filling up with water, and sacks of mail were floating about. Water was also pouring into some of the forward holds and two of the boiler rooms.

Captain Smith knew that the *Titanic's* hull was divided into a number of watertight compartments. She had been designed so that she could still float if only the first four compartments were flooded, but not any more than that. But water was pouring into the first five compartments. And when the water filled them, it would spill over into the next compartment. One by one all the remaining compartments would flood, and the ship would eventually sink. Andrews told the captain that the ship could last an hour, an hour and a half at the most.

2. steward worker on a ship who attends to the needs of the passengers.

◆ **Reading Check**

What indication do the passengers have that there might be trouble?

____

____

____

____

____

____

◆ **Stop to Reflect**

Why do passengers and crew continue to believe that there is nothing seriously wrong?

____

____

____

◆ **Reading Strategy**

Circle two details that are facts and one statement that is an opinion in the bracketed text.

Mark the Text

◆ Reading Check

What call does Phillips send for assistance? Why does he think the call is unnecessary?

Harold Bride had just awakened in the radio room when Captain Smith stuck his head in the door. "Send the call for assistance," he ordered.

"What call should I send?" Phillips asked.

"The regulation international call for help. Just that." Then the captain was gone. Phillips began to send the Morse code "CQD" distress call, flashing away and joking as he did it. After all, they knew the ship was unsinkable.

Reader's Response: If you had the chance to interview someone on board the *Titanic*, who would it be and what one question would you ask that person?

Thinking About the Skill: How does knowing that the statement that the *Titanic* is unsinkable is an opinion, not a fact, help you understand the story.

Breaker's Bridge

Laurence Yep

Summary

Breaker is a clever bridge builder. The emperor orders Breaker to build a bridge over a river near his hunting palace. Breaker must succeed or be beheaded. The river's currents are fierce, destroying each pier Breaker builds. The river also breaks the dam Breaker constructs.

Breaker does not know what he will do. Then, he meets an old man who needs a new crutch. Breaker makes a crutch for the man. In return, the old man gives Breaker two magic pellets to create the bridge. When Breaker drops the first pellet in the river, the swirling waters build a pier out of stones from the bottom of the river. Breaker accidentally crushes the second pellet, so he and his men must build that pier to complete the bridge. Breaker's life is saved, thanks to the kindness and mysterious power of the old man.

Visual Summary

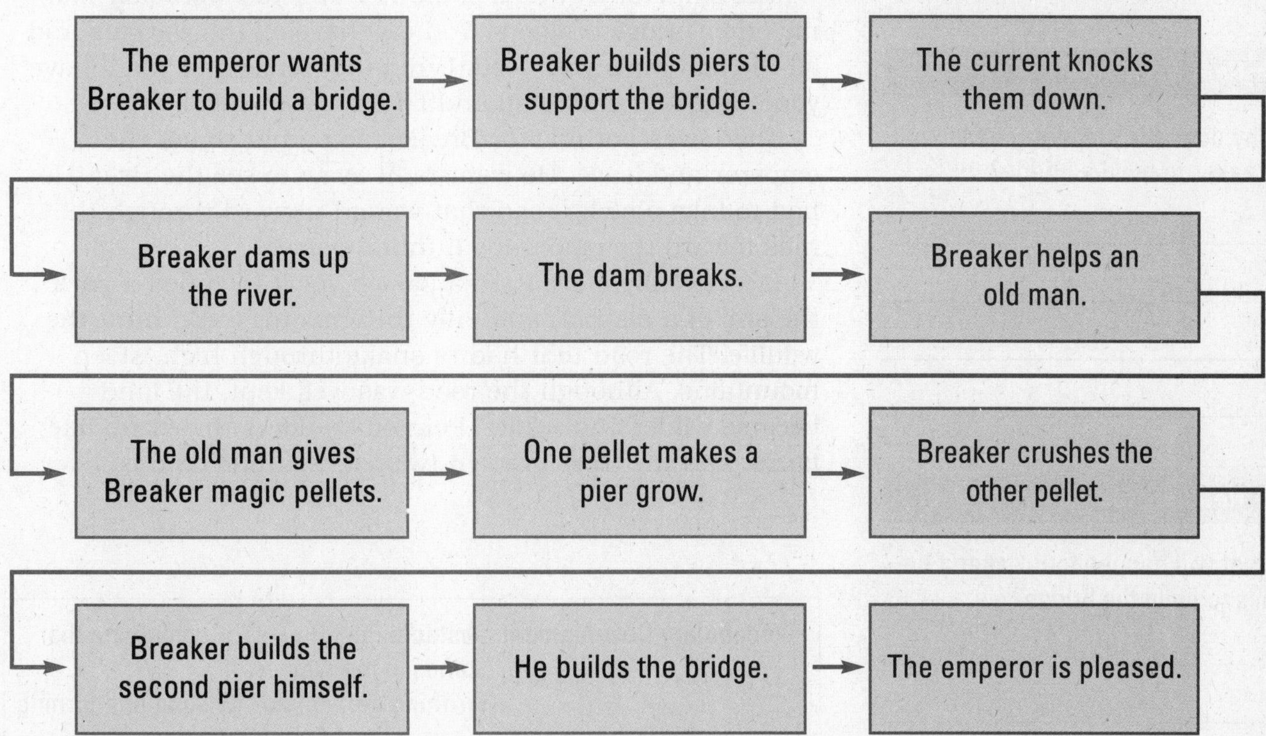

The emperor wants Breaker to build a bridge.
Breaker builds piers to support the bridge.
The current knocks them down.
Breaker dams up the river.
The dam breaks.
Breaker helps an old man.
The old man gives Breaker magic pellets.
One pellet makes a pier grow.
Breaker crushes the other pellet.
Breaker builds the second pier himself.
He builds the bridge.
The emperor is pleased.

◆ Activate Prior Knowledge

Have you ever faced a seemingly impossible job? Jot down how you accomplished your aim.

Breaker's Bridge

Laurence Yep

Most long bridges are built with piers—columns that support the weight of the bridge. Without piers, a bridge can cover only a short distance. Even with modern equipment and technology, building piers in deep water is difficult and expensive. For Breaker in ancient China, building piers in a deep, raging river seemed impossible.

There was once a boy who was always breaking things. He didn't do it on purpose. He just had very clumsy hands. No matter how careful he tried to be, he always dropped whatever he picked up. His family soon learned not to let him set the table or send him for eggs. Everyone in the village called him Breaker.

But Breaker was as clever as he was clumsy. When he grew up, he managed to outlive his nickname. He could design a bridge to cross any obstacle. No canyon was too wide. No river was too deep. Somehow the clever man always found a way to bridge them all.

Eventually the emperor heard about this clever builder and sent for him.

"There is a river in the hills," the emperor said to him. "Everyone tells me it is too swift and deep to span. So I have to go a long way around it to get to my hunting palace. But you're famous for doing the impossible."

The kneeling man bowed his head to the floor. "So far I have been lucky. But there is always a first time when you can't do something."

The emperor frowned. "I didn't think you were lazy like my other bridge builders. You can have all the workers and all the materials you need. Build the bridge and you'll have your weight in gold. Fail and I'll have your head."

There was nothing for Breaker to do but thank the emperor and leave. He went right away to see the river. He had to take a steep road that wound upward through the hills toward the emperor's hunting palace.

It was really more than a palace, for it included a park the size of a district, and only the emperor could hunt the wildlife. The road to it had to snake through high, steep mountains. Although the road was well kept, the land became wilder and wilder. Pointed boulders thrust up like fangs, and the trees grew in twisted, writhing clumps.

◆ Literary Analysis

Character traits are qualities that determine a person's or character's personality and actions. What character traits does Breaker have according to the bracketed text?

◆ Reading Check

Why does the emperor need Breaker to build a bridge?

◆ Reading Check

What will happen to Breaker if he fails to build the bridge?

Vocabulary Development: obstacle (äb′ stə kəl′) *n.* something that stands in the way

writhing (rīth′ iŋ) *adj.* twisting and turning

Breaker became uneasy. "This is a place that doesn't like people very much."

The road twisted suddenly to the left when it came to a deep river gorge. On the other side of the gorge, the many trees of the palace looked like a dark-green sea. The yellow-tiled roofs looked like golden rafts floating on its top. Dark mountains, their tops capped with snow all year round, loomed behind the palace like monstrous guards.

Breaker carefully sidled to the edge of the gorge and looked down. Far below, he saw the river. When the snow melted in the distant mountains, the water flowed together to form this river. It raced faster than a tiger and stronger than a thousand buffalo. When it splashed against a rock, it threw up sheets of white spray like an ocean wave.

Breaker shook his head in dismay. "The emperor might as well have commanded me to bridge the sea."

But his failure would mean the loss of his head, so the next day Breaker set to work. The river was too wide to span with a simple bridge. Breaker would have to construct two piers in the middle of the river. The piers would support the bridge like miniature stone islands.

From the forests of the south came huge logs that were as tough and heavy as iron. From the quarries of the west came large, heavy stones of granite. The workers braved the cold water to sink the logs in the muddy riverbed. Breaker had to change the teams of workers often. The cold numbed anyone who stayed too long in the river.

Once the logs had been pounded into the mud, he tried to set the stones on top of the logs. But the river did not want to be tamed. It bucked and fought like a herd of wild stallions. It crushed the piles of stones into pebbles. It dug up the logs and smashed them against the rocky sides until they were mounds of soggy toothpicks.

Over the next month, Breaker tried every trick he knew; and each time the river defeated him. With each new failure, Breaker suspected more and more that he had met his match. The river flowed hard and strong and fast like the lifeblood of the earth itself. Breaker might as well have tried to tame the mountains.

In desperation, he finally tried to build a dam to hold back the river while he constructed the biggest and strongest piers yet. As he was supervising the construction, an official came by from the emperor.

"This bridge has already cost a lot of money," he announced to the wrecker. "What do you have to show for it?"

Vocabulary Development: piers (pirz) *n.* heavy structures supporting the sections of a bridge

◆ Stop to Reflect

Mark the Text

What does Breaker see that makes him feel uneasy? Circle these details. What do you think will happen when Breaker builds the bridge?

◆ Reading Check

Why does the job of building the bridge fill Breaker with dismay and anxiety?

◆ Reading Strategy

Learn to identify **causes and effects**. A cause—the reason why something happens—brings about an effect—the result. For example, Breaker's clumsiness causes him to break things. The effect of his clumsiness is that he is called Breaker. What is the effect of the wild river on the bridge supports?

◆ Reading Strategy

What is the **cause** of the distant roar?

Breaker pointed to the two piers. They rose like twin towers toward the top of the gorge. "With a little luck, the emperor will have his bridge."

Suddenly, they heard a distant roar. The official looked up at the sky. "It sounds like thunder, but I don't see a cloud in the sky."

Breaker cupped his hands around his mouth to amplify his voice. "Get out," he shouted to his men. "Get out. The river must have broken our dam."

His men slipped and slid on the muddy riverbed, but they all managed to scramble out just as a wall of water rolled down the gorge. The river swept around the two piers, pulling and tugging at the stones.

Everyone held their breath. Slowly the two piers began to rock back and forth on their foundations until they toppled over with a crash into the river. Water splashed in huge sheets over everyone, and when the spray finally fell back into the river, not one sign of the piers remained.

"All this time and all this money, and you have nothing to show for it." The official took a soggy yellow envelope from his sleeve.

Breaker and the other workers recognized the imperial color of the emperor. They instantly dropped to their knees and bowed their heads.

◆ Literary Analysis

What **character trait** does the emperor display by threatening such a severe punishment?

Then, with difficulty, Breaker opened the damp envelope and unfolded the letter. "In one month," it said, "I will have a bridge or I will have your head." It was sealed in red ink with the official seal of the emperor.

Breaker returned the letter and bowed again. "I'll try," he promised.

"You will do more than try," the official snapped. "You will build that bridge for the emperor. Or the executioner will be sharpening his sword." And the official left.

Wet and cold and tired, Breaker made his way along a path toward the room he had taken in an inn. It was getting late, so the surrounding forest was black with shadows. As he walked, Breaker tried to come up with some kind of new scheme, but the dam had been his last resort. In a month's time, he would feel the "kiss" of the executioner's sword.

◆ Reading Check

What does the old man mean when he says that Breaker will have an excuse not to wear a hat?

"Hee, hee, hee," an old man laughed in a creaky voice that sounded like feet on old, worn steps. "You never liked hats anyway. Now you'll have an excuse not to wear them."

Breaker turned and saw a crooked old man sitting by the side of the road. He was dressed in rags, and a gourd hung from a strap against his hip. One leg was shorter than the other.

Vocabulary Development: executioner (ek´ si kyo͞o´ shən ər) *n.* one who carries out a death penalty imposed by the courts or a ruler

"How did you know that, old man?" Breaker wondered.

"Hee, hee, hee. I know a lot of things: the softness of clouds underneath my feet, the sounds of souls inside bodies." And he shook his gourd so that it rattled as if there were beans inside. "It is the law of the universe that all things must change; and yet Nature hates change the most of all."

"The river certainly fits that description." Although he was exhausted and worried, Breaker squatted down beside the funny old man. "But you better get inside, old man. Night's coming on and it gets cold up in these mountains."

"Can't." The old man nodded to his broken crutch.

Breaker looked all around. It was growing dark, and his stomach was aching with hunger. But he couldn't leave the old man stranded in the mountains, so Breaker took out his knife. "If I make you a new crutch, can you reach your home?"

"If you make me a crutch, we'll all have what we want." It was getting so dim that Breaker could not be sure if the old man smiled.

Although it was hard to see, Breaker found a tall, straight sapling and tried to trim the branches from its sides; but being Breaker, he dropped his knife several times and lost it twice among the old leaves on the forest floor. He also cut each of his fingers. By the time he was ready to cut down the sapling, he couldn't see it. Of course, he cut his fingers even more. And just as he was trimming the last branch from the sapling, he cut the sapling right in two.

He tried to carve another sapling and broke that one. It was so dark by now that he could not see at all. He had to find the next sapling by feel. This time he managed to cut it down and began to trim it. But halfway through he dropped his knife and broke it. "He'll just have to take it as it is," Breaker said.

When he finally emerged from the forest, the moon had come out. Sucking on his cut fingers, Breaker presented the new crutch to the funny old man.

The old man looked at the branches that grew from the sides of his new crutch. "A little splintery."

Breaker angrily took his cut finger from his mouth. "Don't insult someone who's doing you a favor."

The crooked old man lifted his right arm with difficulty and managed to bring it behind his neck. "Keep that in mind yourself." He began to rub the back of his neck.

Breaker thrust the crutch at the old man. "Here, old man. This is what you wanted. "

But the old man kept rubbing the back of his neck. "Rivers are like people: Every now and then, they have to be reminded that change is the law that binds us all."

◆ Stop to Reflect

From what you have learned about the old man, who do you think he might be?

______

______

______

______

◆ Literary Analysis

What **character trait** shows in Breaker's actions toward the old man?

______

______

______

______

◆ Reading Strategy

List at least three **effects caused** by Breaker's clumsiness in the bracketed passage. Circle the phrases in the text.

Mark the Text

1. ______

______

______

______

2. ______

______

______

______

3. ______

______

______

______

"It's late. I'm tired and hungry and I have to come up with a new plan. Here's your crutch." And Breaker laid the crutch down beside the old man.

But before Breaker could straighten, the old man's left hand shot out and caught hold of Breaker's wrist. The old man's grip was as strong as iron. "Even the least word from me will remind that river of the law."

Breaker tried to pull away, but as strong as he was, he could not break the old man's hold. "Let me go."

But the crooked old man lowered his right hand so that Breaker could see that he had rubbed some of the dirt and sweat from his skin. "We are all bound together," the old man murmured, "and by the same laws." He murmured that over and over until he was almost humming like a bee. At the same time, his fingers quickly rolled the dirt and sweat into two round little pellets.

Frightened, Breaker could only stare at the old man. "Ar-ar-are you some mountain spirit?" he stammered.

The old man turned Breaker's palm upward and deposited the two little pellets on it. Then he closed Breaker's fingers over them. "Leave one of these at each spot where you want a pier. Be sure not to lose them."

"Yes, all right, of course," Breaker promised quickly.

The old man picked up the crutch and thrust himself up from the ground. "Then you'll have what you want too." And he hobbled away quickly.

Breaker kept hold of the pellets until he reached the inn. Once he was among the inn's bright lights and could smell a hot meal, he began to laugh at himself. "You've let the emperor's letter upset you so much that you let a harmless old man scare you."

Even so, Breaker didn't throw away the pellets but put them in a little pouch. And the next morning when he returned to the gorge, he took along the pouch.

The canyon widened at one point so that there was a small beach. Breaker kept his supplies of stone and logs there. Figuring that he had nothing to lose, Breaker walked down the steep path. Then he took the boat and rowed out onto the river.

As he sat in the bobbing boat, he thought of the funny old man again. "You and I," he said to the river, "are both part of the same scheme of things. And it's time you faced up to it."

Although it was difficult to row at the same time, he got out the pouch with the two pellets. "I must be even crazier than that old man." He opened the pouch and shook one of the pellets into his hand.

◆ Reading Check

What does the old man want Breaker to do?

◆ Reading Check

Explain Breaker's statement, underlined here, in your own words.

When he was by the spot where the first pier should be, Breaker threw the pellet in. For a moment, nothing happened. There was only the sound of his oars slapping at the water.

And suddenly the surface began to boil. Frantically, he tried to row away, but the water began to whirl and whirl around in circles. Onshore, the workers shouted and ran to higher ground as waves splashed over the logs and stones.

From beneath the river came loud thumps and thuds and the grinding of stone on stone. A rock appeared above the surface. The water rose in another wave. On top of the wave another stone floated as if it were a block of wood. The river laid the first stone by the second.

Open-mouthed, Breaker watched the river lay stone after stone. The watery arms reached higher and higher until the first pier rose to the top of the gorge.

As the waters calmed, Breaker eagerly rowed the boat over to the second spot. At the same time that he tried to row enough to keep himself in the right place, Breaker reached for the pouch and opened it.

But in his hurry, his clumsy fingers crushed part of the pellet. He threw the remainder of the pellet into the water and then shook out the contents of the pouch. But this time, the river only swirled and rippled.

Breaker leaned over the side and peered below. He could just make out the pale, murky shape of a mound, but that was all. Even so, Breaker wasn't upset. His workers could easily build a second pier and meet the emperor's deadline.

So Breaker finished the bridge, and that summer the emperor reached his hunting palace with ease. When the emperor finished hunting and returned to his capital, he showered Breaker with gold and promised him all the work he could ever want.

However, winter brought deep snows once again to the mountains. That spring, when the snow thawed, the river grew strong and wild again. It roared down the gorge and smashed against the first pier. But the first pier was solid as a mountain.

However, the second pier had not been built with magic. The river swept away the second pier as if it were nothing but twigs.

The bridge was repaired before the summer hunting, but the emperor angrily summoned Breaker to his hunting palace. "You were supposed to build a bridge for me," the emperor declared.

"Hee, hee, hee," laughed a creaky old voice. "He did, but you didn't say how long it was supposed to stay up."

◆ **Reading Check**

What happens when Breaker throws the pellet into the water?

◆ **Literary Analysis**

Mark the Text

What **character trait** does Breaker display when the second pellet doesn't work? Underline the sentence that gives you the clue in the bracketed text.

◆ **Literary Analysis**

What **character trait** does the emperor demonstrate in the bracketed paragraph?

◆ Reading Strategy

What is the **effect caused** by the old man's appearance before the court?

____

____

____

◆ Reading Strategy

What **causes** part of the bridge to need rebuilding each year?

____

____

____

____

____

____

Breaker turned around and saw it was the crooked old man. He was leaning on the crutch that Breaker had made for him. "How did you get here?" he asked the old man. But from the corner of his eye, he could see all the court officials kneeling down. And when Breaker looked back at the throne, he saw even the emperor kneeling.

"How can we serve you and the other eight immortals?" the emperor asked the crooked old man.

"We are all bound by the same laws," the old man croaked again, and then vanished.

And then Breaker knew the old man for what he truly was—a saint and a powerful magician.

So the emperor spared Breaker and sent him to build other projects all over China. And the emperor never regretted that he had let Breaker keep his head. But every year, the river washed away part of the bridge and every year it was rebuilt. And so things change and yet do not change.

Vocabulary Development: immortals (im môrt′ əlz) *n.* beings who live forever

Reader's Response: Do you think that the emperor treated Breaker fairly? Explain.

____

____

____

Thinking About the Skill: How did identifying cause and effect help you understand this tale?

____

____

____

PREVIEW

Why the Tortoise's Shell Is Not Smooth

Chinua Achebe

Summary

All the birds are invited to a feast in the sky. Tortoise is very hungry and would like to go, too. He is a smooth talker and convinces each bird to give him a feather to make wings. He flies to the feast with them. Tortoise tells the birds that they all need to choose new names for the occasion. They follow his suggestion. Tortoise chooses "All of you" as his own name. When they arrive in the sky, Tortoise asks their host for whom the feast has been prepared. When the man says "for all of you," Tortoise tells the birds that they will be served after he has eaten. Tortoise then eats the best parts of all the foods. There is very little left for the birds. The birds get their revenge by taking back their feathers. Tortoise falls to the ground, shattering his shell in pieces. When the shell is glued back together, it is not smooth—that's why a tortoise's shell has patterns.

Visual Summary

Carrying on the Oral Tradition

- People are talking and singing.
- Okonkwo listens.
- Ekwefi tells a story.
- Ezinma asks a question.

A Story Within a Story

- Tortoise tricks the birds.
- The birds are angry.
- Tortoise falls.

◆ Activate Prior Knowledge

Stories grow and change as they are told over and over. Jot down ways you added to another person's story when you retold it.

◆ Literary Analysis

Oral tradition is the passing along of songs, stories, and poems by word of mouth. Stories told orally reflect the beliefs and traditions of a culture. Circle the details in the bracketed text that tell you that this is a story told in the oral tradition.

Mark the Text

◆ Reading Check

Why does Tortoise want to become a bird?

Why the Tortoise's Shell Is Not Smooth

Chinua Achebe

A tortoise is a turtle that lives only on land. In general, tortoises have high, domed shells. The shell is made of two layers. The inner layer is actually part of the skeleton. The outer layer consists of tough "scales." Because the shell is connected to the backbone, a broken or cracked shell usually means death for the tortoise. This tale offers an explanation of why a tortoise's shell has a pattern.

Low voices, broken now and again by singing, reached Okonkwo (ō kōn´ kwō) from his wives' huts as each woman and her children told folk stories. Ekwefi (e kwe´ fē) and her daughter, Ezinma, (e zēn´ mä) sat on a mat on the floor. It was Ekwefi's turn to tell a story.

"Once upon a time," she began, "all the birds were invited to a feast in the sky. They were very happy and began to prepare themselves for the great day. They painted their bodies with red cam wood[1] and drew beautiful patterns on them with dye.

"Tortoise saw all these preparations and soon discovered what it all meant. Nothing that happened in the world of the animals ever escaped his notice; he was full of cunning. As soon as he heard of the great feast in the sky his throat began to itch at the very thought. There was a famine in those days and Tortoise had not eaten a good meal for two moons. His body rattled like a piece of dry stick in his empty shell. So he began to plan how he would go to the sky."

"But he had no wings," said Ezinma.

"Be patient," replied her mother. "That is the story. Tortoise had no wings, but he went to the birds and asked to be allowed to go with them.

"'We know you too well,' said the birds when they had heard him. 'You are full of cunning and you are ungrateful. If we allow you to come with us you will soon begin your mischief.'

"'You do not know me,' said Tortoise. 'I am a changed man. I have learned that a man who makes trouble for others is also making it for himself.'

"Tortoise had a sweet tongue, and within a short time all the birds agreed that he was a changed man, and they each gave him a feather, with which he made two wings.

Vocabulary Development: famine (fa´ min) *n.* shortage of food

1. **red cam** (cam) **wood** hard West African wood that makes a red dye.

"At last the great day came and Tortoise was the first to arrive at the meeting place. When all the birds had gathered together, they set off in a body. Tortoise was very happy as he flew among the birds, and he was soon chosen as the man to speak for the party because he was a great orator.

"'There is one important thing which we must not forget,' he said as they flew on their way. 'When people are invited to a great feast like this, they take new names for the occasion. Our hosts in the sky will expect us to honor this age-old custom.'

"None of the birds had heard of this custom but they knew that Tortoise, in spite of his failings in other directions, was a widely traveled man who knew the customs of different peoples. And so they each took a new name. When they had all taken, Tortoise also took one. He was to be called *All of you.*

"At last the party arrived in the sky and their hosts were very happy to see them. Tortoise stood up in his many-colored plumage and thanked them for their invitation. His speech was so eloquent that all the birds were glad they had brought him, and nodded their heads in approval of all he said. Their hosts took him as the king of the birds, especially as he looked somewhat different from the others.

"After kola nuts[2] had been presented and eaten, the people of the sky set before their guests the most delectable dishes Tortoise had ever seen or dreamed of. The soup was brought out hot from the fire and in the very pot in which it had been cooked. It was full of meat and fish. Tortoise began to sniff aloud. There was pounded yam[3] and also yam pottage[4] cooked with palm oil and fresh fish. There were also pots of palm wine. When everything had been set before the guests, one of the people of the sky came forward and tasted a little from each pot. He then invited the birds to eat. But Tortoise jumped to his feet and asked: 'For whom have you prepared this feast?'

"'For all of you,' replied the man.

"Tortoise turned to the birds and said: 'You remember that my name is *All of you.* The custom here is to serve the spokesman first and the others later. They will serve you when I have eaten.'

Vocabulary Development: orator (ôr´ ə ter) *n.* speaker
eloquent (el´ ə kwint) *adj.* persuasive and expressive

2. **kola** (kō´ lə) **nuts** the seeds of the African cola tree. These seeds contain caffeine and are used to make soft drinks and medicines.
3. **yam** (yam) *n.* sweet potato.
4. **pottage** (pät´ ij) *n.* thick soup or stew.

◆ **Reading Strategy**

Mark the Text

Learn to **evaluate faulty reasoning.** Faulty reasoning is thinking that looks logical because it contains facts. Actually it is not logical because the facts are not supported. Here is an example of faulty reasoning: *Since many people own cats, cats are the best kind of pet.*

Read the bracketed text and determine what custom Tortoise tells the birds they must follow. Underline the sentence.

Why do the birds believe Tortoise? Circle the sentence that tells you.

In what way do these sentences show **faulty reasoning?**

______

______

______

◆ **Literary Analysis**

Why would mentioning specific foods, such as yams and kola nuts be appropriate in the **oral tradition** of storytelling?

______

______

______

______

◆ **Reading Check**

How does Tortoise's new name allow him to eat before the birds?

______

______

______

◆ **Stop to Reflect**

In what way do animals in this tale take on the character qualities and behavior of humans?

◆ **Literary Analysis**

How does the writer connect you to the **oral tradition** in the bracketed text?

"He began to eat and the birds grumbled angrily. The people of the sky thought it must be their custom to leave all the food for their king. And so Tortoise ate the best part of the food and then drank two pots of palm wine, so that he was full of food and drink and his body grew fat enough to fill out his shell.

"The birds gathered round to eat what was left and to peck at the bones he had thrown all about the floor. Some of them were too angry to eat. They chose to fly home on an empty stomach. But before they left, each took back the feather he had lent to Tortoise. And there he stood in his hard shell full of food and wine but without any wings to fly home. He asked the birds to take a message for his wife, but they all refused. In the end Parrot, who had felt more angry than the others, suddenly changed his mind and agreed to take the message.

"'Tell my wife,' said Tortoise, 'to bring out all the soft things in my house and cover the compound[5] with them so that I can jump down from the sky without very great danger.'

"Parrot promised to deliver the message, and then flew away. But when he reached Tortoise's house he told his wife to bring out all the hard things in the house. And so she brought out her husband's hoes, machetes,[6] spears, guns, and even his cannon. Tortoise looked down from the sky and saw his wife bringing things out, but it was too far to see what they were. When all seemed ready he let himself go. He fell and fell and fell until he began to fear that he would never stop falling. And then like the sound of his cannon he crashed on the compound."

"Did he die?" asked Ezinma.

"No," replied Ekwefi. "His shell broke into pieces. But there was a great medicine man in the neighborhood. Tortoise's wife sent for him and he gathered all the bits of shell and stuck them together. That is why Tortoise's shell is not smooth."

5. **compound** (käm′ pound) *n.* grounds surrounded by buildings.
6. **machetes** (mə shet′ ēz) *n.* large heavy-bladed knives.

Reader's Response: Do you think the tortoise got what he deserved? Why or why not?

PREVIEW

Dragon, Dragon

John Gardner

Summary

The youngest son of a wise old cobbler becomes a hero by listening to his father. A dragon is terrorizing an entire kingdom. The king offers half his kingdom and his daughter in marriage to the man who slays the beast. The cobbler's oldest son volunteers. Before he leaves, he asks his father for advice. His father gives him a poem to recite to the dragon. Unfortunately, the son ignores the advice, does not recite the poem, and gets eaten. The second son goes next. He also ignores his father's advice and is eaten. Finally, it is the youngest son's turn. He follows his father's advice and recites the poem. The poem makes the dragon laugh so hard that he falls on his back. The cobbler's son then cuts off the dragon's head and wins the princess plus half the kingdom.

Visual Summary

Problem	A fierce dragon is terrorizing the kingdom.
Goal	To stop the dragon
↓	**Event 1:** The king offers a reward to the man who slays the dragon. **Event 2:** The cobbler's oldest son tries, but he ignores his father's advice and the dragon eats him. **Event 3:** The middle son tries, but he ignores his father's advice and the dragon eats him. **Event 4:** The youngest son follows his father's advice. **Event 5:** The dragon laughs so hard he falls on his back.
Resolution	He slays the dragon, and everyone is happy.

◆ Activate Prior Knowledge

Have you ever had to complete a task that seemed impossible? How did you approach the problem?

◆ Literary Analysis

The **plot** of a story is the sequence of events arranged around a problem or conflict. What is the problem in the kingdom?

◆ Reading Check

Why does the king call a meeting?

Dragon, Dragon

John Gardner

Dragon stories have been told all over the world for centuries. Different cultures have different beliefs about these creatures. Asian dragons are believed to be wise and good; other dragons are greedy, evil creatures. In most Western folklore, a brave, strong warrior kills the dragon.

There was once a king whose kingdom was plagued by a dragon. The king did not know which way to turn. The king's knights were all cowards who hid under their beds whenever the dragon came in sight, so they were of no use to the king at all. And the king's wizard could not help either because, being old, he had forgotten his magic spells. Nor could the wizard look up the spells that had slipped his mind, for he had unfortunately misplaced his wizard's book many years before. The king was at his wit's end.

Every time there was a full moon the dragon came out of his lair and ravaged the countryside. He frightened maidens and stopped up chimneys and broke store windows and set people's clocks back and made dogs bark until no one could hear himself think.

He tipped over fences and robbed graves and put frogs in people's drinking water and tore the last chapters out of novels and changed house numbers around so that people crawled into bed with their neighbors.

He stole spark plugs out of people's cars and put firecrackers in people's cigars and stole the clappers from all the church bells and sprung every bear trap for miles around so the bears could wander wherever they pleased.

And to top it all off, he changed around all the roads in the kingdom so that people could not get anywhere except by starting out in the wrong direction.

"That," said the king in a fury, "is enough!" And he called a meeting of everyone in the kingdom.

Now it happened that there lived in the kingdom a wise old cobbler who had a wife and three sons. The cobbler and his family came to the king's meeting and stood way in back by the door, for the cobbler had a feeling that since he was nobody important there had probably been some mistake, and no doubt the king had intended the meeting for everyone in the kingdom except his family and him.

"Ladies and gentlemen," said the king when everyone was present, "I've put up with that dragon as long as I can. He has got to be stopped."

Vocabulary Development: **plagued** (plāgd) *v.* tormented
ravaged (rav′ ijd) *v.* violently destroyed; ruined

All the people whispered amongst themselves, and the king smiled, pleased with the impression he had made. But the wise cobbler said gloomily, "It's all very well to talk about it—but how are you going to do it?"

And now all the people smiled and winked as if to say, "Well, King, he's got you there!"

The king frowned.

"It's not that His Majesty hasn't tried," the queen spoke up loyally.

"Yes," said the king, "I've told my knights again and again that they ought to slay that dragon. But I can't *force* them to go. I'm not a tyrant."

"Why doesn't the wizard say a magic spell?" asked the cobbler.

"He's done the best he can," said the king.

The wizard blushed and everyone looked embarrassed. "I used to do all sorts of spells and chants when I was younger," the wizard explained. "But I've lost my spell book, and I begin to fear I'm losing my memory too. For instance, I've been trying for days to recall one spell I used to do. I forget, just now, what the deuce it was for. It went something like—

Bimble,
Wimble,
Cha, cha
CHOOMPF!

Suddenly, to everyone's surprise, the queen turned into a rosebush.

"Oh dear," said the wizard.

"Now you've done it," groaned the king.

"Poor Mother," said the princess.

"I don't know what can have happened," the wizard said nervously, "but don't worry, I'll have her changed back in a jiffy." He shut his eyes and racked his brain for a spell that would change her back.

But the king said quickly, "You'd better leave well enough alone. If you change her into a rattlesnake we'll have to chop off her head."

Meanwhile the cobbler stood with his hands in his pockets, sighing at the waste of time. "About the dragon . . ." he began.

"Oh yes," said the king. "I'll tell you what I'll do. I'll give the princess's hand in marriage to anyone who can make the dragon stop."

"It's not enough," said the cobbler. "She's a nice enough girl, you understand. But how would an ordinary person support her? Also, what about those of us that are already married?"

Vocabulary Development: tyrant (tī´ rənt) *n.* cruel, unjust ruler

◆ **Reading Check**

Name two reasons why the king has not been able to get rid of the dragon.

1. ______________________

2. ______________________

◆ **Reading Strategy**

When you **compare and contrast** characters, you look for similarities and differences. In the bracketed text, what is the difference between the character of the king and the character of the cobbler?

King's character: ______________________

Cobbler's character: ______________________

◆ Literary Analysis

What key event occurs in the story's **plot**? Underline the place in the bracketed passage where the action rises or picks up.

Mark THE Text

◆ Reading Strategy

Compare and contrast the behavior of the cobbler's eldest son with the behavior of the youngest son in the underlined text.

◆ Reading Check

What happens to the queen?

"In that case," said the king, "I'll offer the princess's hand or half the kingdom or both—whichever is most convenient." The cobbler scratched his chin and considered it. "It's not enough," he said at last. "It's a good enough kingdom, you understand, but it's too much responsibility."

"Take it or leave it," the king said.

"I'll leave it," said the cobbler. And he shrugged and went home.

But the cobbler's eldest son thought the bargain was a good one, for the princess was very beautiful and he liked the idea of having half the kingdom to run as he pleased. So he said to the king, "I'll accept those terms, Your Majesty. By tomorrow morning the dragon will be slain."

"Bless you!" cried the king.

"Hooray, hooray, hooray!" cried all the people, throwing their hats in the air.

The cobbler's eldest son beamed with pride, and the second eldest looked at him enviously. The youngest son said timidly, "Excuse me, Your Majesty, but don't you think the queen looks a little unwell? If I were you I think I'd water her."

"Good heavens," cried the king, glancing at the queen who had been changed into a rosebush, "I'm glad you mentioned it!"

Now the cobbler's eldest son was very clever and was known far and wide for how quickly he could multiply fractions in his head. He was perfectly sure he could slay the dragon by somehow or other playing a trick on him, and he didn't feel that he needed his wise old father's advice. But he thought it was only polite to ask, and so he went to his father, who was working as usual at his cobbler's bench, and said, "Well, Father, I'm off to slay the dragon. Have you any advice to give me?"

The cobbler thought a moment and replied, "When and if you come to the dragon's lair, recite the following poem:

Dragon, dragon, how do you do?
I've come from the king to murder you.

Say it very loudly and firmly and the dragon will fall, God willing, at your feet."

"How curious!" said the eldest son. And he thought to himself, "The old man is not as wise as I thought. If I say something like that to the dragon, he will eat me up in an instant. The way to kill a dragon is to out-fox him." And keeping his opinion to himself, the eldest son set forth on his quest.

When he came at last to the dragon's lair, which was a cave, the eldest son slyly disguised himself as a peddler and knocked on the door and called out, "Hello there!"

"There's nobody home!" roared a voice.

The voice was as loud as an earthquake, and the eldest

son's knees knocked together in terror.

"I don't come to trouble you," the eldest son said meekly. "I merely thought you might be interested in looking at some of our brushes. Or if you'd prefer," he added quickly, "I could leave our catalogue with you and I could drop by again, say, early next week."

"I don't want any brushes," the voice roared, "and I especially don't want any brushes next week."

"Oh," said the eldest son. By now his knees were knocking together so badly that he had to sit down.

Suddenly a great shadow fell over him, and the eldest son looked up. It was the dragon. The eldest son drew his sword, but the dragon lunged and swallowed him in a single gulp, sword and all, and the eldest son found himself in the dark of the dragon's belly. "What a fool I was not to listen to my wise old father!" thought the eldest son. And he began to weep bitterly.

"Well," sighed the king the next morning, "I see the dragon has not been slain yet."

"I'm just as glad, personally," said the princess, sprinkling the queen. "I would have had to marry that eldest son, and he had warts."

Now the cobbler's middle son decided it was his turn to try. The middle son was very strong and he was known far and wide for being able to lift up the corner of a church. He felt perfectly sure he could slay the dragon by simply laying into him, but he thought it would be only polite to ask his father's advice. So he went to his father and said to him, "Well, Father, I'm off to slay the dragon. Have you any advice for me?"

The cobbler told the middle son exactly what he'd told the eldest.

"When and if you come to the dragon's lair, recite the following poem:

Dragon, dragon, how do you do?
I've come from the king to murder you.

Say it very loudly and firmly, and the dragon will fall, God willing, at your feet."

"What an odd thing to say," thought the middle son. "The old man is not as wise as I thought. You have to take these dragons by surprise." But he kept his opinion to himself and set forth.

When he came in sight of the dragon's lair, the middle son spurred his horse to a gallop and thundered into the entrance swinging his sword with all his might.

But the dragon had seen him while he was still a long way off, and being very clever, the dragon had crawled up on top of the door so that when the son came charging in he went under the dragon and on to the back of the cave and slammed into the wall. Then the dragon chuckled and got

◆ **Literary Analysis**

What events in the **plot** have occurred so far? List at least 3.

1. ____________________

____

2. ____________________

____

3. ____________________

____

◆ **Stop to Reflect**

What lesson does the eldest son learn from his struggle with the dragon?

____

____

____

____

____

____

◆ **Reading Check**

What advice did the cobbler give his middle son?

____

____

____

____

____

◆ **Literary Analysis**

Compare the character and behavior of the eldest son and the middle son.

____

____

____

____

____

____

____

◆ **Reading Strategy**

Circle the words and phrases in the bracketed passage that **contrast** the character of the youngest son with those of his older brothers.

Mark the Text

◆ **Literary Analysis**

As the **plot** of a story develops, the problem or conflict increases in the rising action. How does the plot build in this scene in the underlined passage?

____

____

____

____

____

____

down off the door, taking his time, and strolled back to where the man and the horse lay unconscious from the terrific blow. Opening his mouth as if for a yawn, the dragon swallowed the middle son in a single gulp and put the horse in the freezer to eat another day.

"What a fool I was not to listen to my wise old father," thought the middle son when he came to in the dragon's belly. And he too began to weep bitterly.

That night there was a full moon, and the dragon ravaged the countryside so terribly that several families moved to another kingdom.

"Well," sighed the king in the morning, "still no luck in this dragon business, I see."

"I'm just as glad, myself," said the princess, moving her mother, pot and all, to the window where the sun could get at her. "The cobbler's middle son was a kind of humpback."

Now the cobbler's youngest son saw that his turn had come. He was very upset and nervous, and he wished he had never been born. He was not clever, like his eldest brother, and he was not strong, like his second-eldest brother. He was a decent, honest boy who always minded his elders.

He borrowed a suit of armor from a friend of his who was a knight, and when the youngest son put the armor on it was so heavy he could hardly walk. From another knight he borrowed a sword, and that was so heavy that the only way the youngest son could get it to the dragon's lair was to drag it along behind his horse like a plow.

When everything was in readiness, the youngest son went for a last conversation with his father.

"Father, have you any advice to give me?" he asked.

"Only this," said the cobbler. "When and if you come to the dragon's lair, recite the following poem:

Dragon, dragon, how do you do?
I've come from the king to murder you.

Say it very loudly and firmly, and the dragon will fall, God willing, at your feet."

"Are you certain?" asked the youngest son uneasily.

"As certain as one can ever be in these matters," said the wise old cobbler.

And so the youngest son set forth on his quest. He traveled over hill and dale and at last came to the dragon's cave.

The dragon, who had seen the cobbler's youngest son while he was still a long way off, was seated up above the door, inside the cave, waiting and smiling to himself. But minutes passed and no one came thundering in. The dragon frowned, puzzled, and was tempted to peek out. However, reflecting

Vocabulary Development: reflecting (ri flekt′ iŋ) *adj.* thinking seriously

that patience seldom goes unrewarded, the dragon kept his head up out of sight and went on waiting. At last, when he could stand it no longer, the dragon craned his neck and looked. There at the entrance of the cave stood a trembling young man in a suit of armor twice his size, struggling with a sword so heavy he could lift only one end of it at a time.

At sight of the dragon, the cobbler's youngest son began to tremble so violently that his armor rattled like a house caving in. He heaved with all his might at the sword and got the handle up level with his chest, but even now the point was down in the dirt. As loudly and firmly as he could manage, the youngest son cried—

Dragon, dragon, how do you do?
I've come from the king to murder you.

"What?" cried the dragon, flabbergasted. "You? *You?* Murder *Me*???" All at once he began to laugh, pointing at the little cobbler's son. "*He he he ho ha!*" he roared, shaking all over, and tears filled his eyes. "*He he he ho ho ho ha ha!*" laughed the dragon. He was laughing so hard he had to hang onto his sides, and he fell off the door and landed on his back, still laughing, kicking his legs helplessly, rolling from side to side, laughing and laughing and laughing.

The cobbler's son was annoyed, "I *do* come from the king to murder you," he said. "A person doesn't like to be laughed at for a thing like that."

"*He he he!*" wailed the dragon, almost sobbing, gasping for breath. "Of course not, poor dear boy! But really, *he he*, the *idea* of it, *ha, ha, ha!* And that simply ri*dic*ulous *poem!*" Tears streamed from the dragon's eyes and he lay on his back perfectly helpless with laughter.

"It's a good poem," said the cobbler's youngest son loyally. "My father made it up." And growing angrier he shouted, "I want you to stop that laughing, or I'll—I'll—" But the dragon could not stop for the life of him. And suddenly, in a terrific rage, the cobbler's son began flopping the sword end over end in the direction of the dragon. Sweat ran off the youngest son's forehead, but he labored on, blistering mad, and at last, with one supreme heave, he had the sword standing on its handle a foot from the dragon's throat. Of its own weight the sword fell, slicing the dragon's head off.

"*He he ho huk*," went the dragon—and then he lay dead.

The two older brothers crawled out and thanked their younger brother for saving their lives. "We have learned our lesson," they said.

Then the three brothers gathered all the treasures from the dragon's cave and tied them to the back end of the

Vocabulary Development: craned (krānd) *v.* stretched out (one's neck) for a better view

◆ Literary Anaylsis

In the **plot** of the story, the conflict increases until it reaches a climax or turning point. In the bracketed text, circle the climax of the action.

Mark the Text

◆ Stop to Reflect

What reaction do you think the youngest son expected from the dragon when he recited the poem?

___

___

___

___

___

___

◆ Literary Analysis

In the **plot,** how is the conflict or problem in the story resolved?

___

___

___

___

___

___

◆ **Stop to Reflect**

Do you think that the Cobbler knew all along how his advice would affect his three sons? Explain.

Do you think that the cobbler knew all along how the dragon would react to the poem? Explain.

◆ **Reading Check**

Why is the queen soaking wet?

◆ **Literary Anaylsis**

What is the conclusion of the **plot** of the story?

youngest brother's horse, and tied the dragon's head on behind the treasures, and started home. "I'm glad I listened to my father," the youngest son thought. "Now I'll be the richest man in the kingdom."

There were hand-carved picture frames and silver spoons and boxes of jewels and chests of money and silver compasses and maps telling where there were more treasures buried when these ran out. There was also a curious old book with a picture of an owl on the cover, and inside, poems and odd sentences and recipes that seemed to make no sense.

When they reached the king's castle the people all leaped for joy to see that the dragon was dead, and the princess ran out and kissed the youngest brother on the forehead, for secretly she had hoped it would be him.

"Well," said the king, "which half of the kingdom do you want?"

"My wizard's book!" exclaimed the wizard. "He's found my wizard's book!" He opened the book and ran his finger along under the words and then said in a loud voice, "Glmuzk, shkzmlp, blam!"

Instantly the queen stood before them in her natural shape, except she was soaking wet from being sprinkled too often. She glared at the king.

"Oh dear," said the king, hurrying toward the door.

Reader's Response: Would you have followed the cobbler's advice?

Thinking About the Skill: How did understanding the elements of the plot help you better understand the story?

PREVIEW

Becky and the Wheels-and-Brake Boys

James Berry

Summary

Becky wants a bike to ride through her village with the Wheels-and-Brake Boys. Unfortunately, being a girl, Becky has been raised to learn only sewing, cooking, and cleaning. Becky has other ideas and keeps asking for a bike. Her mother and Granny-Liz tell Becky she is foolish. Her mother also says she cannot afford a bike. Ever since Becky's dad died, Becky's mother has supported the family by sewing. Becky tries to sell something of her dad's to a fireman, thinking she will buy a bike with the money. Instead, the fireman takes Becky home and has a serious conversation with Becky's mother. Then, Becky's mother and the fireman take Becky to his house. He gives her a bike. The bike once belonged to his nephew who has moved to America. Becky gets her wish and rides her bike with the Wheels-and-Brake Boys. In addition, the fireman becomes a special friend to Becky and her mother.

Visual Summary

Characters:	Becky, Becky's mother, the Wheels-and-Brake Boys
Setting:	a small village in Jamaica
Conflict:	Becky wants a bike, but her family cannot afford one.
Events that contribute to the conflict:	• Becky watches the Wheels-and-Brake Boys with envy. • Becky asks over and over for a bike. • Becky sees how hard her mother works. • Becky tries to sell her father's hat to a fireman. • The fireman offers to sell Becky's mother a bike.
Resolution:	Becky's mother buys her the fireman's bike.

◆ Activate Prior Knowledge

Jot down how you feel when you use roller blades, a skateboard, or ride a bicycle.

____

____

____

____

____

◆ Literary Analysis

The **conflict** in a story is the struggle between opposing forces. The conflict moves the story action forward. What is the conflict in the bracketed text?

____

____

____

____

____

____

◆ Reading Check

Why can't Becky have a bike?

____

____

____

____

____

____

____

Becky and the Wheels-and-Brake Boys

James Berry

People who speak the same language may come from different countries or regions, have different accents, or use different words for the same thing. These different forms of a single language are called dialects. The characters in this story speak a West Indian dialect of English.

Even my own cousin Ben was there—riding away, in the ringing of bicycle bells down the road. Every time I came to watch them—see them riding round and round enjoying themselves—they scooted off like crazy on their bikes.

They can't keep doing that. They'll see!

I only want to be with Nat, Aldo, Jimmy, and Ben. It's no fair reason they don't want to be with me. Anybody could go off their head for that. Anybody! A girl can not, not, let boys get away with it all the time.

Bother! I have to walk back home, alone.

I know total-total that if I had my own bike, the Wheels-and-Brake Boys wouldn't treat me like that. I'd just ride away with them, wouldn't I?

Over and over I told my mum I wanted a bike. Over and over she looked at me as if I was crazy. "Becky, d'you think you're a boy? Eh? D'you think you're a boy? In any case, where's the money to come from? Eh?"

Of course I know I'm not a boy. Of course I know I'm not crazy. Of course I know all that's no reason why I can't have a bike. No reason! As soon as I get indoors I'll just have to ask again—ask Mum once more.

At home, indoors, I didn't ask my mum.

It was evening time, but sunshine was still big patches in yards and on housetops. My two younger brothers, Lenny and Vin, played marbles in the road. Mum was taking measurements of a boy I knew, for his new trousers and shirt. Mum made clothes for people. Meggie, my sister two years younger than me, was helping Mum on the veranda. Nobody would be pleased with me not helping. I began to help.

Granny-Liz would always stop fanning herself to drink up a glass of ice water. I gave my granny a glass of ice water, there in her rocking chair. I looked in the kitchen to find shelled coconut pieces to cut into small cubes for the fowls' morning feed. But Granny-Liz had done it. I came and

Vocabulary Development: **veranda** (və ran´ də) *n.* open porch, usually with a roof, along the outside of a building

started tidying up bits and pieces of cut-off material around my mum on the floor. My sister got nasty, saying she was already helping Mum. Not a single good thing was happening for me.

With me even being all so thoughtful of Granny's need of a cool drink, she started up some botheration[1] against me.

Listen to Granny-Liz: "Becky, with you moving about me here on the veranda, I hope you dohn have any centipedes or scorpions[2] in a jam jar in your pocket."

"No, mam," I said sighing, trying to be calm. "Granny-Liz," I went on, "you forgot. My centipede and scorpion died." All the same, storm broke against me.

"Becky," my mum said. "You know I don't like you wandering off after dinner. Haven't I told you I don't want you keeping company with those awful riding-about bicycle boys? Eh?"

"Yes, mam."

"Those boys are a menace. Riding bicycles on sidewalks and narrow paths together, ringing bicycle bells and braking at people's feet like wild bulls charging anybody, they're heading for trouble."

"They're the Wheels-and-Brake Boys, mam."

"The what?"

"The Wheels-and-Brake Boys."

"Oh! Given themselves a name as well, have they? Well, Becky, answer this. How d'you always manage to look like you just escaped from a hair-pulling battle? Eh? And don't I tell you not to break the backs down and wear your canvas shoes like slippers? Don't you ever hear what I say?"

"Yes, mam."

"D'you want to end up a field laborer? Like where your father used to be overseer?"[3]

"No, mam."

"Well, Becky, will you please go off and do your homework?"

Everybody did everything to stop me. I was allowed no chance whatsoever. No chance to talk to Mum about the bike I dream of day and night! And I knew exactly the bike I wanted. I wanted a bike like Ben's bike. Oh, I wished I still had even my scorpion on a string to run up and down somebody's back!

Vocabulary Development: menace (men′ əs) *n.* threat; a troublesome or annoying person

1. **botheration** (bäth′ ər ā′ shən) *n.* trouble.
2. **scorpions** (skôr′ pē ənz) *n.* close relatives of spiders, with a poisonous stinger at the end of their tails; found in warm regions.
3. **overseer** (ō′ vər sē′ ər) *n.* supervisor of laborers.

◆ **Literary Analysis**

Circle two sentences in the bracketed text that give details about the **conflict** between Becky and her mother.

Mark the Text

◆ **Reading Strategy**

Predicting is making a logical guess based on information in the story or past experience. Based on what you have read so far, predict whether or not Becky will give up the idea of getting a bike.

◆ **Reading Check**

What does Becky's mother want her to do instead of bicycle riding?

◆ Stop to Reflect

Why do you think getting a bicycle is so important to Becky?

◆ Reading Check

What is the fight about between Becky and Shirnette? Circle the sentences in the bracketed text that help explain the disagreement.

Mark THE Text

I answered my mum. "Yes, mam." I went off into Meg's and my bedroom.

I sat down at the little table, as well as I might. Could homework stay in anybody's head in broad daylight outside? No. Could I keep a bike like Ben's out of my head? Not one bit. That bike took me all over the place. My beautiful bike jumped every log, every rock, every fence. My beautiful bike did everything cleverer than a clever cowboy's horse, with me in the saddle. And the bell, the bell was such a glorious gong of a ring!

If Dad was alive, I could talk to him. If Dad was alive, he'd give me money for the bike like a shot.

I sighed. It was amazing what a sigh could do. I sighed and tumbled on a great idea. Tomorrow evening I'd get Shirnette to come with me. Both of us together would be sure to get the boys interested to teach us to ride. Wow! With Shirnette they can't just ride away!

Next day at school, everything went sour. For the first time, Shirnette and me had a real fight, because of what I hated most.

Shirnette brought a cockroach to school in a shoe-polish tin. At playtime she opened the tin and let the cockroach fly into my blouse. Pure panic and disgust nearly killed me. I crushed up the cockroach in my clothes and practically ripped my blouse off, there in open sunlight. Oh, the smell of a cockroach is the nastiest ever to block your nose! I started running with my blouse to go and wash it. Twice I had to stop and be sick.

I washed away the crushed cockroach stain from my blouse. Then the stupid Shirnette had to come into the toilet, falling about laughing. All right, I knew the cockroach treatment was for the time when I made my centipede on a string crawl up Shirnette's back. But you put fair-is-fair aside. I just barged into Shirnette.

When it was all over, I had on a wet blouse, but Shirnette had one on, too.

Then, going home with the noisy flock of children from school, I had such a new, new idea. If Mum thought I was scruffy, Nat, Aldo, Jimmy, and Ben might think so, too. I didn't like that.

After dinner I combed my hair in the bedroom. Mum did her machining[4] on the veranda. Meggie helped Mum. Granny sat there, wishing she could take on any job, as usual.

I told Mum I was going to make up a quarrel with Shirnette. I went, but my friend wouldn't speak to me, let alone come out to keep my company. I stood alone and watched the Wheels-and-Brake Boys again.

4. **machining** (mə shēn´ iŋ) *v.* sewing.

This time the boys didn't race away past me. I stood leaning against the tall coconut palm tree. People passed up and down. The nearby main road was busy with traffic. But I didn't mind. I watched the boys. Riding round and round the big flame tree, Nat, Aldo, Jimmy, and Ben looked marvelous.

At first each boy rode round the tree alone. Then each boy raced each other round the tree, going round three times. As he won, the winner rang his bell on and on, till he stopped panting and could laugh and talk properly. Next, most reckless and fierce, all the boys raced against each other. And, leaning against their bicycles, talking and joking, the boys popped soft drinks open, drank, and ate chipped bananas.

I walked up to Nat, Aldo, Jimmy, and Ben and said, "Can somebody teach me to ride?"

"Why don't you stay indoors and learn to cook and sew and wash clothes?" Jimmy said.

I grinned. "I know all that already," I said. "And one day perhaps I'll even be mum to a boy child, like all of you. Can you cook and sew and wash clothes, Jimmy? All I want is to learn to ride. I want you to teach me."

I didn't know why I said what I said. But everybody went silent and serious.

One after the other, Nat, Aldo, Jimmy, and Ben got on their bikes and rode off. I wasn't at all cross with them. I only wanted to be riding out of the playground with them. I knew they'd be heading into the town to have ice cream and things and talk and laugh.

Mum was sitting alone on the veranda. She sewed buttons onto a white shirt she'd made. I sat down next to Mum. Straightaway, "Mum," I said, "I still want to have a bike badly."

"Oh, Becky, you still have that foolishness in your head? What am I going to do?"

Mum talked with some sympathy. Mum knew I was honest. "I can't get rid of it, mam," I said.

Mum stopped sewing. "Becky," she said, staring in my face, "how many girls around here do you see with bicycles?"

"Janice Gordon has a bike," I reminded her.

"Janice Gordon's dad has acres and acres of coconuts and bananas, with a business in the town as well."

I knew Mum was just about to give in. Then my granny had to come out onto the veranda and interfere. Listen to that Granny-Liz. "Becky, I heard your mother tell you over

Vocabulary Development: reckless (rek′ lis) *adj.* not careful; taking chances

◆ Reading Strategy

Predict whether or not the boys will include Becky or ignore her.

◆ Literary Analysis

In the bracketed text, what is the change in the **conflict** between Becky and her mother? Underline the words that support your answer.

Mark the Text

◆ Reading Check

What does Becky ask the boys to do?

and over she cahn[5] afford to buy you a bike. Yet you keep on and on. Child, you're a girl."

"But I don't want a bike because I'm a girl."

"D'you want it because you feel like a bwoy?" Granny said.

"No. I only want a bike because I want it and want it and want it."

Granny just carried on. "A tomboy's like a whistling woman and a crowing hen, who can only come to a bad end. D'you understand?"

I didn't want to understand. I knew Granny's speech was an awful speech. I went and sat down with Lenny and Vin, who were making a kite.

By Saturday morning I felt real sorry for Mum. I could see Mum really had it hard for money. I had to try and help. I knew anything of Dad's—anything—would be worth a great mighty hundred dollars.

I found myself in the center of town, going through the busy Saturday crowd. I hoped Mum wouldn't be too cross. I went into the fire station. With lots of luck I came face to face with a round-faced man in uniform. He talked to me. "Little miss, can I help you?"

I told him I'd like to talk to the head man. He took me into the office and gave me a chair. I sat down. I opened out my brown paper parcel. I showed him my dad's sun helmet. I told him I thought it would make a good fireman's hat. I wanted to sell the helmet for some money toward a bike, I told him.

The fireman laughed a lot. I began to laugh, too. The fireman put me in a car and drove me back home.

Mum's eyes popped to see me bringing home the fireman. The round-faced fireman laughed at my adventure. Mum laughed, too, which was really good. The fireman gave Mum my dad's hat back. Then—mystery, mystery—Mum sent me outside while they talked.

My mum was only a little cross with me. Then—mystery and more mystery—my mum took me with the fireman in his car to his house.

The fireman brought out what? A bicycle! A beautiful, shining bicycle! His nephew's bike. His nephew had been taken away, all the way to America. The bike had been left with the fireman-uncle for him to sell it. And the good, kind fireman-uncle decided we could have the bike—on small payments. My mum looked uncertain. But in a big, big way, the fireman knew it was all right. And Mum smiled a little. My mum had good sense to know it was all right. My mum took the bike from the fireman Mr. Dean.

And guess what? Seeing my bike much, much newer than his, my cousin Ben's eyes popped with envy. But he took on

◆ Reading Strategy

Predict what you think will happen next. How do you think the conflict will be solved?

____

____

____

____

____

____

◆ Reading Check

What does Becky do to get money for her bicycle?

____

____

____

____

____

____

____

---

5. cahn can't.

the big job. He taught me to ride. Then he taught Shirnette.

I ride into town with the Wheels-and-Brake Boys now. When she can borrow a bike, Shirnette comes too. We all sit together. We have patties and ice cream and drink drinks together. We talk and joke. We ride about, all over the place.

And, again, guess what? Fireman Mr. Dean became our best friend, and Mum's especially. He started coming around almost every day.

Reader's Response: Would you like to have Becky as a friend? Why or why not?

Thinking About the Skill: How does making predictions as you read help you understand the story?

◆ **Literary Analysis**

How is the **conflict** between Becky and her mother over the bicycle solved?

Eleven

Sandra Cisneros

Summary

"Eleven" is about young Rachel, whose teacher finds an old, ugly sweater hanging in the classroom closet. Everyone else in the class says the sweater is not his or hers, so the teacher gives the sweater to Rachel. Rachel is too shy to say that the ugly-looking sweater is not hers either. Instead, she shoves the sweater to the edge of her desk. This causes the teacher to yell at her, and insist that she put the sweater on. Rachel pulls on the sweater, and begins to cry in front of everyone. Another student suddenly remembers that the sweater is hers. Rachel quickly gives it to her, but Rachel's teacher does not apologize for the mix-up. Rachel feels especially bad because the incident takes place on her eleventh birthday. It makes her feel much younger than eleven.

Visual Summary

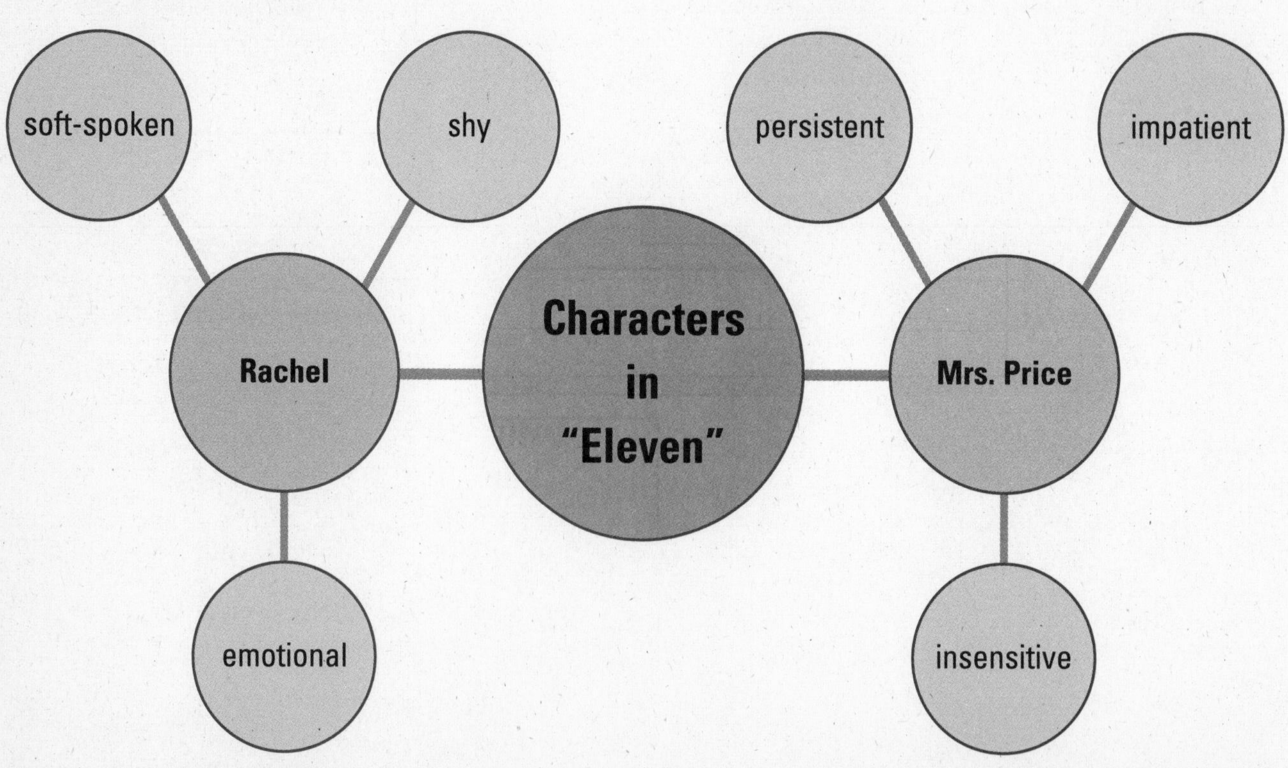

Eleven
Sandra Cisneros

Sometimes it seems that nothing goes well, and you just have to hope that tomorrow will be better.

What they don't understand about birthdays and what they never tell you is that when you're eleven, you're also ten, and nine, and eight, and seven, and six, and five, and four, and three, and two, and one. And when you wake up on your eleventh birthday you expect to feel eleven, but you don't. You open your eyes and everything's just like yesterday, only it's today. And you don't feel eleven at all. You feel like you're still ten. And you are—underneath the year that makes you eleven.

Like some days you might say something stupid, and that's the part of you that's still ten. Or maybe some days you might need to sit on your mama's lap because you're scared, and that's the part of you that's five. And one day when you're all grown up maybe you will need to cry like if you're three, and that's okay. That's what I tell Mama when she's sad and needs to cry. Maybe she's feeling three.

Because the way you grow old is kind of like an onion or like the rings inside a tree trunk or like my little wooden dolls that fit one inside the other, each year inside the next one. That's how being eleven years old is.

You don't feel eleven. Not right away. It takes a few days, weeks even, sometimes even months before you say eleven when they ask you. And you don't feel smart eleven, not until you're almost twelve. That's the way it is.

Only today I wish I didn't have just eleven years rattling inside me like pennies in a tin Band-Aid box. Today I wish I was one-hundred-and-two instead of eleven because if I was one-hundred-and-two I'd have known what to say when Mrs. Price put the red sweater on my desk. I would've known how to tell her it wasn't mine instead of just sitting there with that look on my face and nothing coming out of my mouth.

"Whose is this?" Mrs. Price says, and she holds the red sweater up in the air for all the class to see. "Whose? It's been sitting in the coatroom for a month."

"Not mine," says everybody. "Not me."

"It has to belong to somebody," Mrs. Price keeps saying, but nobody can remember. It's an ugly sweater with red plastic buttons and a collar and sleeves all stretched out like you could use it for a jump rope. It's maybe a thousand years old and even if it belonged to me I wouldn't say so.

Maybe because I'm skinny, maybe because she doesn't like me, that stupid Felice Garcia says, "I think it belongs to Rachel." An ugly sweater like that, all raggedy and old, but

◆ Activate Prior Knowledge

Has there ever been a time when someone didn't believe you, even though you were telling the truth? Describe the incident briefly.

◆ Stop to Reflect

Do you agree with the narrator that growing older is like adding layers? Explain.

◆ Reading Check

What does Mrs. Price ask the students about?

◆ Literary Analysis

Characterization is the art of developing a character. Authors reveal characters' traits, or qualities, through their words, thoughts, and actions. In the bracketed section, circle words and actions of Mrs. Price that show that she is not a patient or sympathetic character.

Mark the Text

◆ Stop to Reflect

Why do you think Rachel reminds herself about the birthday celebration to come?

____

____

____

____

____

◆ Reading Check

What does Rachel do after putting on the sweater?

____

____

____

____

____

Mrs. Price believes her. Mrs. Price takes the sweater and puts it right on my desk, but when I open my mouth nothing comes out.

"That's not, I don't, you're not . . . not mine," I finally say in a little voice that was maybe me when I was four.

"Of course it's yours," Mrs. Price says, "I remember you wearing it once." Because she's older and the teacher, she's right and I'm not.

Not mine, not mine, not mine, but Mrs. Price is already turning to page 32, and math problem number four. I don't know why but all of a sudden I'm feeling sick inside, like the part of me that's three wants to come out of my eyes, only I squeeze them shut tight and bite down on my teeth real hard and try to remember today I am eleven, eleven. Mama is making a cake for me for tonight, and when Papa comes home everybody will sing happy birthday, happy birthday to you.

But when the sick feeling goes away and I open my eyes, the red sweater's still sitting there like a big red mountain. I move the red sweater to the corner of my desk with my ruler. I move my pencil and books and eraser as far from it as possible. I even move my chair a little to the right. Not mine, not mine, not mine.

In my head I'm thinking how long till lunch time, how long till I can take the red sweater and throw it over the schoolyard fence, or leave it hanging on a parking meter, or bunch it up into a little ball and toss it in the alley. Except when math period ends Mrs. Price says loud and in front of everybody, "Now, Rachel, that's enough," because she sees I've shoved the red sweater to the tippy-tip corner of my desk and it's hanging all over the edge like a waterfall, but I don't care.

"Rachel," Mrs. Price says. She says it like she's getting mad. "You put that sweater on right now and no more nonsense."

"But it's not . . ."

"Now!" Mrs. Price says.

This is when I wish I wasn't eleven, because all the years inside of me—ten, nine, eight, seven, six, five, four, three, two, and one—are all pushing at the back of my eyes when I put one arm through one sleeve of the sweater that smells like cottage cheese, and then the other arm through the other and stand there with my arms apart as if the sweater hurts me and it does, all itchy and full of germs that aren't even mine.

That's when everything I've been holding in since this morning, since when Mrs. Price put the sweater on my desk, finally lets go, and all of a sudden I'm crying in front of everybody. I wish I was invisible but I'm not. I'm eleven and it's my birthday today and I'm crying like I'm three in front of everybody. I put my head down on the desk and bury my face in my stupid clown sweater arms. My face all hot and spit coming out of my mouth because I can't stop the little animal noises from coming out of me, until there aren't any more tears left in my eyes, and it's just my body shaking like when you have the hiccups, and my whole head hurts like when you drink milk too fast.

But the worst part is right before the bell rings for lunch. That stupid Phyllis Lopez, who is even dumber than Felice Garcia, says she remembers the red sweater is hers! I take it off right away and give it to her, only Mrs. Price pretends like everything's okay.

Today I'm eleven. There's a cake Mama's making for tonight, and when Papa comes home from work we'll eat it. There'll be candles and presents and everybody will sing happy birthday, happy birthday to you, Rachel, only it's too late.

I'm eleven today. I'm eleven, ten, nine, eight, seven, six, five, four, three, two, and one, but I wish I was one-hundred-and-two. I wish I was anything but eleven, because I want today to be far away already, far away like a tiny kite in the sky, so tiny-tiny you have to close your eyes to see it.

Reader's Response: What would you like to say to Rachel, or to Mrs. Price, or to Felice Garcia?

____

____

____

____

____

____

Thinking About the Skill: Do you think the author did a good job revealing the characters of Mrs. Price and Rachel? Why or why not?

____

____

____

◆ Literary Analysis

What does Rachel's crying tell you about how deeply she feels things?

____

____

____

____

____

◆ Stop to Reflect

What do you think Rachel means when she says "only it's too late" in the underlined sentence?

____

____

____

____

____

The Wounded Wolf

Jean Craighead George

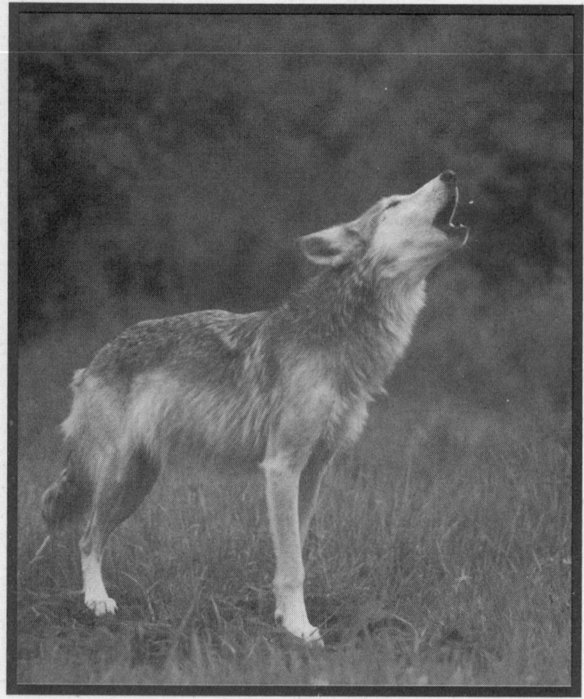

Summary

The setting for "The Wounded Wolf" is Toklat Ridge in the Arctic. The wolf Roko is badly hurt while fighting for food during the starvation season. He is followed closely by a number of other hungry animals, including ravens, an owl, a fox, and a grizzly bear. These animals prey on dead or dying animals, and they sense that Roko is near death. Desperate, the wounded wolf struggles to the safety of a sheltering rock. When Roko does not bark during roll call, his wolf pack knows he is hurt. A raven cries out that death is near. The raven's cries guide the leader of the wolf pack to Roko's location. The leader brings food to the wounded wolf. Roko begins to heal. Before long, Roko barks at roll call and the pack howls joyfully.

Visual Summary

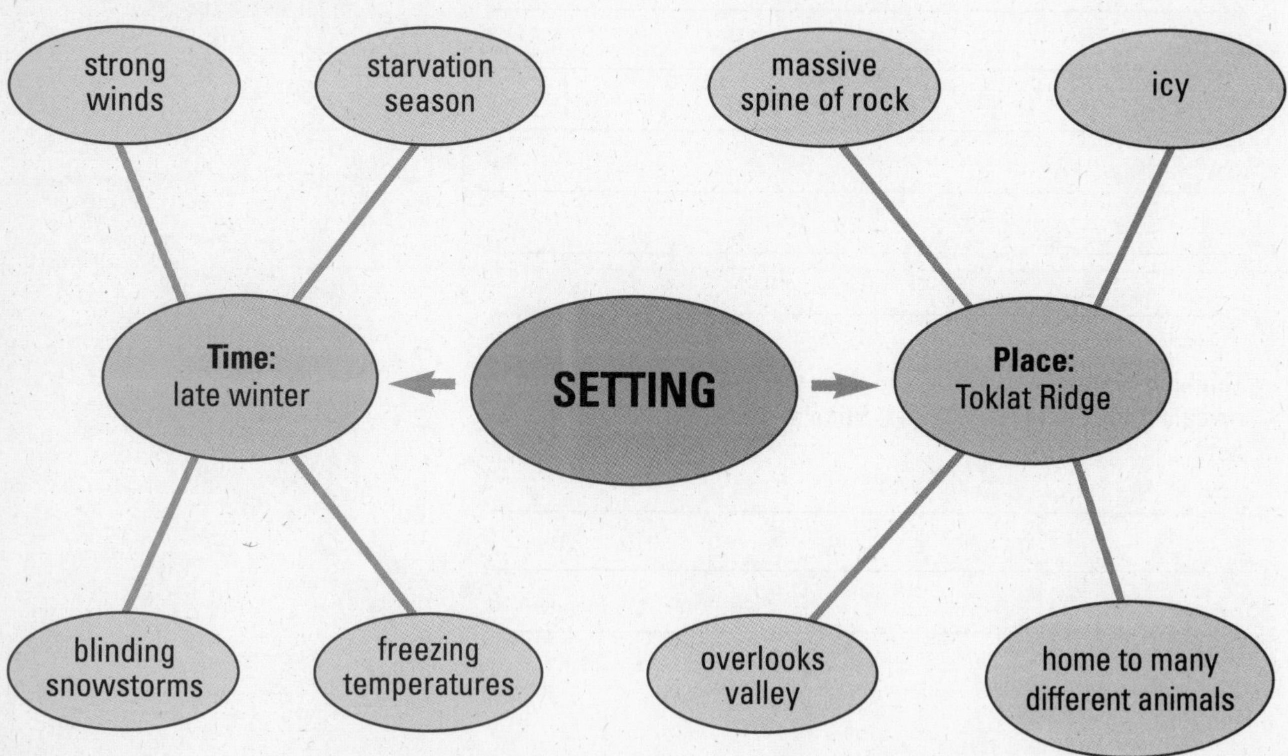

The Wounded Wolf

Jean Craighead George

This story is based on an incident the author heard from a scientist. In retelling it, she leaves out any trace of human observation.

A wounded wolf climbs Toklat Ridge, a massive spine of rock and ice. As he limps, dawn strikes the ridge and lights it up with sparks and stars. Roko, the wounded wolf, blinks in the ice fire, then stops to rest and watch his pack run the thawing Arctic valley.

They plunge and turn. They fight the mighty caribou that struck young Roko with his hoof and wounded him. He jumped between the beast and Kiglo, leader of the Toklat pack. Young Roko spun and fell. Hooves, paws, and teeth roared over him. And then his pack and the beast were gone.

Gravely injured, Roko pulls himself toward the shelter rock. Weakness overcomes him. He stops. He and his pack are thin and hungry. This is the season of starvation. The winter's harvest has been taken. The produce of spring has not begun.

Young Roko glances down the valley. He droops his head and stiffens his tail to signal to his pack that he is badly hurt. Winds wail. A frigid blast picks up long shawls of snow and drapes them between young Roko and his pack. And so his message is not read.

A raven scouting Toklat Ridge sees Roko's signal. "Kong, kong, kong," he bells—death is coming to the ridge; there will be flesh and bone for all. His voice rolls out across the valley. It penetrates the rocky cracks where the Toklat ravens rest. One by one they hear and spread their wings. They beat their way to Toklat Ridge. They alight upon the snow and walk behind the wounded wolf.

"Kong," they toll[1] with keen excitement, for the raven clan is hungry, too. "Kong, kong"—there will be flesh and bone for all.

Roko snarls and hurries toward the shelter rock. A cloud of snow envelops him. He limps in blinding whiteness now.

A ghostly presence flits around. "Hahahahahahaha," the white fox states—death is coming to the Ridge. Roko smells the fox tagging at his heels.

Vocabulary Development: massive (mass′ iv) *adj.* huge; large and impressive

1. **toll** (tōl) *v.* announce.

◆ Activate Prior Knowledge

What have you heard or read about wolves? Summarize it below.

◆ Literary Analysis

Mark the Text

The **setting** of a story is the time and location in which its events take place. The time might include the season, time of day, and historical era. The location may be general (outer space) or specific (a particular street). The weather is also part of a setting. Circle the words in the first paragraph of the story that tell you where the story takes place. Underline details that show that the wolf is in a mountain range.

◆ Reading Check

What has happened to Roko?

◆ Reading Strategy

When you **picture the setting,** you make a scene come alive in your mind, which can help you understand the action better. Use details in the bracketed section to describe the setting and the locations of the animals within the setting.

◆ Reading Check

What makes the animals run away from Roko?

◆ Stop to Reflect

What do you think the wolf's chances of survival are at this point? Explain.

The cloud whirls off. Two golden eyes look up at Roko. The snowy owl has heard the ravens and joined the deathwatch.

Roko limps along. The ravens walk. The white fox leaps. The snowy owl flies and hops along the rim of Toklat Ridge. Roko stops. Below the ledge out on the flats the musk-ox herd is circling. They form a ring and all face out, a fort of heads and horns and fur that sweeps down to their hooves. Their circle means to Roko that an enemy is present. He squints and smells the wind. It carries scents of thawing ice, broken grass—and earth. The grizzly bear is up! He has awakened from his winter's sleep. A craving need for flesh will drive him.

Roko sees the shelter rock. He strains to reach it. He stumbles. The ravens move in closer. The white fox boldly walks beside him. "Hahaha," he yaps. The snowy owl flies ahead, alights, and waits.

The grizzly hears the eager fox and rises on his flat hind feet. He twists his powerful neck and head. His great paws dangle at his chest. He sees the animal procession and hears the ravens' knell[2] of death. Dropping to all fours, he joins the march up Toklat Ridge.

Roko stops; his breath comes hard. A raven alights upon his back and picks the open wound. Roko snaps. The raven flies and circles back. The white fox nips at Roko's toes. The snowy owl inches closer. The grizzly bear, still dulled by sleep, stumbles onto Toklat Ridge.

Only yards from the shelter rock, Roko falls.

Instantly the ravens mob him. They scream and peck and stab at his eyes. The white fox leaps upon his wound. The snowy owl sits and waits.

Young Roko struggles to his feet. He bites the ravens. Snaps the fox. And lunges at the stoic owl. He turns and warns the grizzly bear. Then he bursts into a run and falls against the shelter rock. The wounded wolf wedges down between the rock and barren ground. Now protected on three sides, he turns and faces all his foes.

The ravens step a few feet closer. The fox slides toward him on his belly. The snowy owl blinks and waits, and on the ridge rim roars the hungry grizzly bear.

Roko growls.

The sun comes up. Far across the Toklat Valley, Roko

Vocabulary Development: **stoic** (stō´ ik) *adj.* showing no reaction to good or bad events; calm and unaffected by hardship

2. **knell** (nel) *n.* mournful sound, like a slowly ringing bell—usually indicating a death.

hears his pack's "hunt's end" song. The music wails and sobs, wilder than the bleating wind. The hunt song ends. Next comes the roll call. Each member of the Toklat pack barks to say that he is home and well.

"Kiglo here," Roko hears his leader bark. There is a pause. It is young Roko's turn. He cannot lift his head to answer. The pack is silent. The leader starts the count once more. "Kiglo here."—A pause. Roko cannot answer.

The wounded wolf whimpers softly. A mindful raven hears. "Kong, kong, kong," he tolls—this is the end. His booming sounds across the valley. The wolf pack hears the raven's message that something is dying. They know it is Roko, who has not answered roll call.

[The hours pass. The wind slams snow on Toklat Ridge. Massive clouds blot out the sun. In their gloom Roko sees the deathwatch move in closer. Suddenly he hears the musk-oxen thundering into their circle. The ice cracks as the grizzly leaves. The ravens burst into the air. The white fox runs. The snowy owl flaps to the top of the shelter rock. And Kiglo rounds the knoll.]

In his mouth he carries meat. He drops it close to Roko's head and wags his tail excitedly. Roko licks Kiglo's chin to honor him. Then Kiglo puts his mouth around Roko's nose. This gesture says "I am your leader." And by mouthing Roko, he binds him and all the wolves together.

The wounded wolf wags his tail. Kiglo trots away.

Already Roko's wound feels better. He gulps the food and feels his strength return. He shatters bone, flesh, and gristle and shakes the scraps out on the snow. The hungry ravens swoop upon them. The white fox snatches up a bone. The snowy owl gulps down flesh and fur. And Roko wags his tail and watches.

For days Kiglo brings young Roko food. He gnashes, gorges, and shatters bits upon the snow.

A purple sandpiper winging north sees ravens, owl, and fox. And he drops in upon the feast. The long-tailed jaeger gull flies down and joins the crowd on Toklat Ridge. Roko wags his tail.

One dawn he moves his wounded leg. He stretches it and pulls himself into the sunlight. He walks—he romps. He runs in circles. He leaps and plays with chunks of ice. Suddenly he stops. The "hunt's end" song rings out. Next comes the roll call.

Vocabulary Development: **gnashes** (nash´ iz) *v.* bites with grinding teeth

◆ Literary Analysis

Mark the Text

The description of the weather in the story helps set a mood of sadness and gloom. Circle details of the weather in the bracketed passage.

◆ Stop to Reflect

Why does Roko shake scraps of food out on the snow?

____

____

____

____

____

◆ Reading Check

What effect does Kiglo's food have on Roko?

____

____

____

____

◆ Stop to Reflect

What do you think would have happened if Kiglo had not found Roko and brought him food?

"Kiglo here."

"Roko here," he barks out strongly.

The pack is silent.

"Kiglo here," the leader repeats.

"Roko here."

Across the distance comes the sound of whoops and yips and barks and howls. They fill the dawn with celebration. And Roko prances down the Ridge.

Reader's Response: Do you admire the wolves in this story? Why or why not?

Thinking About the Skill: What parts of the setting made Roko's problems worse?

The All-American Slurp

Lensey Namioka

Summary

"The All-American Slurp" recalls the Lin family's first few months in the United States. The Lins are a Chinese immigrant family. They want to fit into American society. The daughter befriends an American classmate who introduces her to American customs. The daughter worries about making mistakes. Doing things the Chinese way, like slurping soup, draws attention that she finds embarrassing. Over time, the Lins change many of their habits. They change their clothing style, their speech, and their way of eating. One day they feel comfortable enough to invite their American neighbors for dinner. The daughter is surprised to learn that even Americans slurp.

Visual Summary

Action	Action	Action
As our family of four sat stiffly in a row, my younger brother and I stole glances at our parents for a clue as to what to do next.	I was worried more about making mistakes, and I spoke carefully, making sure I could say everything right before opening my mouth.	The Gleasons were not used to Chinese ways, and they were just coping the best they could.

THEME
Different cultures have different customs, but all people have similar feelings and needs.

◆ Activate Prior Knowledge

Can you think of a time when you were in a situation that seemed to have unwritten rules, or rules that everyone but you seemed to know? Describe the situation.

____

____

____

____

◆ Literary Analysis

The **theme** of a story is its central message or insight. After reading the bracketed passage, what do you think the theme of this story might be?

____

____

____

____

◆ Reading Strategy

You can increase your understanding of a story by **drawing inferences,** or reaching conclusions based on evidence, about things that happen in the story. In the underlined sentence, what inference can you draw from the fact that the Lin family is sitting "stiffly" on the couch?

____

____

____

____

____

The All-American Slurp

Lensey Namioka

In this story, a Chinese family must deal with unfamiliar American eating habits. The following are some Chinese meal-time customs:

1) Tea is usually served during or after meals;
2) food is usually served "family style" on large platters in the center of the table;
3) the only individual dishes used are rice bowls; and
4) food is eaten with slender sticks called chopsticks.

"As any respectable Chinese knows, the correct way to eat your soup is to slurp."

The first time our family was invited out to dinner in America, we disgraced ourselves while eating celery. We had emigrated to this country from China, and during our early days here we had a hard time with American table manners. In China we never ate celery raw, or any other kind of vegetable raw. We always had to disinfect the vegetables in boiling water first. When we were presented with our first relish tray, the raw celery caught us unprepared.

We had been invited to dinner by our neighbors, the Gleasons. After arriving at the house, we shook hands with our hosts and packed ourselves into a sofa. As our family of four sat stiffly in a row, my younger brother and I stole glances at our parents for a clue as to what to do next.

Mrs. Gleason offered the relish tray to Mother. The tray looked pretty, with its tiny red radishes, curly sticks of carrots, and long, slender stalks of pale green celery. "Do try some of the celery, Mrs. Lin," she said. "It's from a local farmer, and it's sweet."

Mother picked up one of the green stalks, and Father followed suit. Then I picked up a stalk, and my brother did too. So there we sat, each with a stalk of celery in our right hand.

Mrs. Gleason kept smiling. "Would you like to try some of the dip, Mrs. Lin? It's my own recipe: sour cream and onion flakes, with a dash of Tabasco sauce."

Most Chinese don't care for dairy products, and in those days I wasn't even ready to drink fresh milk. Sour cream sounded perfectly revolting. Our family shook our heads in unison.

Vocabulary Development: emigrated (em´ i grāt´ id) *v.* left one country to settle in another

Mrs. Gleason went off with the relish tray to the other guests, and we carefully watched to see what they did. Everyone seemed to eat the raw vegetables quite happily. Mother took a bite of her celery. *Crunch.* "It's not bad!" she whispered.

Father took a bite of his celery. *Crunch.* "Yes, it is good," he said, looking surprised.

I took a bite, and then my brother. *Crunch, crunch.* It was more than good; it was delicious. Raw celery has a slight sparkle, a zingy taste that you don't get in cooked celery. When Mrs. Gleason came around with the relish tray, we each took another stalk of celery, except my brother. He took two.

There was only one problem: long strings ran through the length of the stalk, and they got caught in my teeth. When I help my mother in the kitchen, I always pull the string out before slicing celery.

I pulled the strings out of my stalk. *Z-z-zip, z-z-zip.* My brother followed suit. *Z-z-zip, z-z-zip, z-z-zip.* To my left, my parents were taking care of their own stalks. *Z-z-zip, z-z-zip, z-z-zip.*

Suddenly I realized that there was dead silence except for our zipping. Looking up, I saw that the eyes of everyone in the room were on our family. Mr. and Mrs. Gleason, their daughter Meg, who was my friend, and their neighbors the Badels—they were all staring at us as we busily pulled the strings of our celery.

That wasn't the end of it. Mrs. Gleason announced that dinner was served and invited us to the dining table. It was lavishly covered with platters of food, but we couldn't see any chairs around the table. So we helpfully carried over some dining chairs and sat down. All the other guests just stood there.

Mrs. Gleason bent down and whispered to us, "This is a buffet dinner. You help yourselves to some food and eat it in the living room."

Our family beat a retreat back to the sofa as if chased by enemy soldiers. For the rest of the evening, too mortified to go back to the dining table, I nursed a bit of potato salad on my plate.

Next day Meg and I got on the school bus together. I wasn't sure how she would feel about me after the spectacle

Vocabulary Development: **mortified** (môrt′ ə fīd′) *adj.* ashamed; extremely embarrassed

◆ Reading Check

Why do the Lins strip the strings from the celery they have been served?

Mark THE Text

◆ Reading Strategy

What can you **infer** from the reaction of the other guests to the Lin family?

◆ Reading Strategy

The **theme** of a story can be either stated or implied. A **stated theme** is expressed directly by the author. An **implied theme** is suggested, or expressed indirectly, by the actions of the characters. The reader must figure out what it is. From your reading so far, do you think the theme of this story is implied or stated? Explain.

our family made at the party. But she was just the same as usual, and the only reference she made to the party was, "Hope you and your folks got enough to eat last night. You certainly didn't take very much. Mom never tries to figure out how much food to prepare. She just puts everything on the table and hopes for the best."

I began to relax. The Gleasons' dinner party wasn't so different from a Chinese meal after all. My mother also puts everything on the table and hopes for the best.

Meg was the first friend I had made after we came to America. I eventually got acquainted with a few other kids in school, but Meg was still the only real friend I had.

My brother didn't have any problems making friends. He spent all his time with some boys who were teaching him baseball, and in no time he could speak English much faster than I could—not better, but faster.

I worried more about making mistakes, and I spoke carefully, making sure I could say everything right before opening my mouth. At least I had a better accent than my parents, who never really got rid of their Chinese accent, even years later. My parents had both studied English in school before coming to America, but what they had studied was mostly written English, not spoken.

Father's approach to English was a scientific one. Since Chinese verbs have no tense, he was fascinated by the way English verbs changed form according to whether they were in the present, past imperfect, perfect, pluperfect,[1] future, or future perfect tense. He was always making diagrams of verbs and their inflections,[2] and he looked for opportunities to show off his mastery of the pluperfect and future perfect tenses, his two favorites. "I shall have finished my project by Monday," he would say smugly.[3]

Mother's approach was to memorize lists of polite phrases that would cover all possible social situations. She was constantly muttering things like "I'm fine, thank you. And you?" Once she accidentally stepped on someone's foot, and hurriedly blurted, "Oh, that's quite all right!" Embarrassed by her slip, she resolved to do better next time. So when someone stepped on *her* foot, she cried, "You're welcome!"

In our own different ways, we made progress in learning English. But I had another worry, and that was my appearance. My brother didn't have to worry, since Mother bought him blue jeans for school, and he dressed like all the other

---

1. **pluperfect** (plo͞o′ pur′ fikt) *adj.* the past perfect tense of verbs in English.
2. **inflections** (in flek′ shən) *n.* the changes in the forms of words to show different tenses.
3. **smugly** (smug′ lē) *adv.* in a way that shows satisfaction with oneself.

◆ Stop to Reflect

Why might it be difficult for the girl in the story to make friends? Why does it seem easier for her brother?

◆ Reading Check

Describe below Mr. and Mrs. Lin's different approaches to speaking English.

boys. But she insisted that girls had to wear skirts. By the time she saw that Meg and the other girls were wearing jeans, it was too late. My school clothes were bought already, and we didn't have money left to buy new outfits for me. We had too many other things to buy first, like furniture, pots, and pans.

The first time I visited Meg's house, she took me upstairs to her room, and I wound up trying on her clothes. We were pretty much the same size, since Meg was shorter and thinner than average. Maybe that's how we became friends in the first place. Wearing Meg's jeans and T-shirt, I looked at myself in the mirror. I could almost pass for an American—from the back, anyway. At least the kids in school wouldn't stop and stare at me in the hallways, which was what they did when they saw me in my white blouse and navy blue skirt that went a couple of inches below the knees.

When Meg came to my house, I invited her to try on my Chinese dresses, the ones with a high collar and slits up the sides. Meg's eyes were bright as she looked at herself in the mirror. She struck several sultry poses, and we nearly fell over laughing.

The dinner party at the Gleasons' didn't stop my growing friendship with Meg. Things were getting better for me in other ways too. Mother finally bought me some jeans at the end of the month, when Father got his paycheck. She wasn't in any hurry about buying them at first, until I worked on her. This is what I did. Since we didn't have a car in those days, I often ran down to the neighborhood store to pick up things for her. The groceries cost less at a big supermarket, but the closest one was many blocks away. One day, when she ran out of flour, I offered to borrow a bike from our neighbor's son and buy a ten-pound bag of flour at the supermarket. I mounted the boy's bike and waved to Mother. "I'll be back in five minutes!"

Before I started pedaling, I heard her voice behind me. "You can't go out in public like that! People can see all the way up to your thighs!"

"I'm sorry," I said innocently. "I thought you were in a hurry to get the flour." For dinner we were going to have potstickers (fried Chinese dumplings), and we needed a lot of flour.

"Couldn't you borrow a girl's bicycle?" complained Mother. "That way your skirt won't be pushed up."

"There aren't too many of those around," I said. "Almost all the girls wear jeans while riding a bike, so they don't see any point buying a girl's bike."

◆ **Literary Analysis**

In the underlined sentence, what does the girl's statement about almost passing for an American suggest that the **theme** of the story might be?

◆ **Reading Strategy**

What can you **infer** from Meg's reaction to trying on the narrator's Chinese dresses?

◆ **Reading Strategy**

What can you **infer** from the narrator's description of her remarks to her mother as "innocent"?

◆ **Literary Analysis**

How does the narrator's conflict with her mother about clothes reflect the **theme** of the story?

◆ **Reading Check**

At this point in the story, why does the narrator say ,"There was hope that the Lins might become a normal American family"? What is different for the family?

◆ **Reading Check**

Why has Mr. Lin brought his family to a fancy restaurant?

◆ **Reading Strategy**

What does the underlined remark help you **infer** about Mr. Lin's attitude toward new experiences?

We didn't eat pot-stickers that evening, and Mother was thoughtful. Next day we took the bus downtown and she bought me a pair of jeans. In the same week, my brother made the baseball team of his junior high school, Father started taking driving lessons, and Mother discovered rummage sales.

We soon got all the furniture we needed, plus a dart board and a 1,000-piece jigsaw puzzle (fourteen hours later, we discovered that it was a 999-piece jigsaw puzzle). There was hope that the Lins might become a normal American family after all.

Then came our dinner at the Lakeview restaurant.

The Lakeview was an expensive restaurant, one of those places where a headwaiter dressed in tails conducted you to your seat, and the only light came from candles and flaming desserts. In one corner of the room a lady harpist played tinkling melodies.

Father wanted to celebrate, because he had just been promoted. He worked for an electronics company, and after his English started improving, his superiors decided to appoint him to a position more suited to his training. The promotion not only brought a higher salary but was also a tremendous boost to his pride.

Up to then we had eaten only in Chinese restaurants. Although my brother and I were becoming fond of hamburgers, my parents didn't care much for western food, other than chow mein.[4] But this was a special occasion, and Father asked his coworkers to recommend a really elegant restaurant. So there we were at the Lakeview, stumbling after the headwaiter in the murky dining room.

At our table we were handed our menus, and they were so big that to read mine I almost had to stand up again. But why bother? It was mostly in French, anyway.

Father, being an engineer, was always systematic.[5] He took out a pocket French dictionary. "They told me that most of the items would be in French, so I came prepared." He even had a pocket flashlight, the size of a marking pen. While Mother held the flashlight over the menu, he looked up the items that were in French.

"*Pâté en croûte*,"[6] he muttered. "Let's see . . . *pâté* is paste . . . *croûte* is crust . . . hmm . . . a paste in crust."

---

4. **chow mein** (chou′ mān′) *n.* thick stew of meat, celery, and Chinese vegetables.
5. **systematic** (sis′ tə mat′ ik) *adj.* orderly.
6. **pâté en croûte** (pä tā′ än kro͞ot)

The waiter stood looking patient. I squirmed and died at least fifty times.

At long last Father gave up. "Why don't we just order four complete dinners at random?" he suggested.

"Isn't that risky?" asked Mother. "The French eat some rather peculiar things, I've heard."

"A Chinese can eat anything a Frenchman can eat," Father declared.

The soup arrived in a plate. How do you get soup up from a plate? I glanced at the other diners, but the ones at the nearby tables were not on their soup course, while the more distant ones were invisible in the darkness.

Fortunately my parents had studied books on western etiquette before they came to America. "Tilt your plate," whispered my mother. "It's easier to spoon the soup up that way."

She was right. Tilting the plate did the trick. But the etiquette book didn't say anything about what you did after the soup reached your lips. As any respectable Chinese knows, the correct way to eat your soup is to slurp. This helps to cool the liquid and prevent you from burning your lips. It also shows your appreciation.

We showed our appreciation. *Shloop*, went my father. *Shloop* went my mother. *Shloop, shloop*, went my brother, who was the hungriest.

The lady harpist stopped playing to take a rest. And in the silence, our family's consumption of soup suddenly seemed unnaturally loud. You know how it sounds on a rocky beach when the tide goes out and the water drains from all those little pools? They go *shloop, shloop, shloop*. That was the Lin family, eating soup.

At the next table a waiter was pouring wine. When a large *shloop* reached him, he froze. The bottle continued to pour, and red wine flooded the tabletop and into the lap of a customer. Even the customer didn't notice anything at first, being also hypnotized by the *shloop, shloop, shloop*.

It was too much. "I need to go to the toilet," I mumbled, jumping to my feet. A waiter, sensing my urgency, quickly directed me to the ladies' room.

Vocabulary Development: **etiquette** (et´ i ket) *n.* acceptable social manners
consumption (kən sump´ shen) *n.* eating; drinking; using up

◆ Literary Analysis

How does the situation in the bracketed passage relate to the **theme** of the story? Explain.

◆ Literary Analysis

The narrator flees the dinner table at the restaurant. How does this incident fit the **theme** of the story?

◆ Literary Analysis

Underline the sentences in which the narrator tells how she feels about being in this new country.

I splashed cold water on my burning face, and as I dried myself with a paper towel, I stared into the mirror. In this perfumed ladies' room, with its pink-and-silver wallpaper and marbled sinks, I looked completely out of place. What was I doing here? What was our family doing in the Lakeview restaurant? In America?

The door to the ladies' room opened. A woman came in and glanced curiously at me. I retreated into one of the toilet cubicles and latched the door.

◆ Stop to Reflect

Initially, the narrator is terribly embarrassed by this situation at the restaurant. How would you feel if you were she? Why?

Time passed—maybe half an hour, maybe an hour. Then I heard the door open again, and my mother's voice. "Are you in there? You're not sick, are you?"

There was real concern in her voice. A girl can't leave her family just because they slurp their soup. Besides, the toilet cubicle had a few drawbacks as a permanent residence. "I'm all right," I said, undoing the latch.

Mother didn't tell me how the rest of the dinner went, and I didn't want to know. In the weeks following, I managed to push the whole thing into the back of my mind, where it jumped out at me only a few times a day. Even now, I turn hot all over when I think of the Lakeview restaurant.

◆ Reading Check

Underline the sentence that tells one way the narrator's parents try to become Americanized.

But by the time we had been in this country for three months, our family was definitely making progress toward becoming Americanized. I remember my parents' first PTA meeting. Father wore a neat suit and tie, and Mother put on her first pair of high heels. She stumbled only once. They met my homeroom teacher and beamed as she told them that I would make honor roll soon at the rate I was going. Of course Chinese etiquette forced Father to say that I was a very stupid girl and Mother to protest that the teacher was showing favoritism toward me. But I could tell they were both very proud.

◆ Literary Analysis

Why does the narrator's father tell the teacher that his daughter is stupid, and why does her mother say that the teacher must be playing favorites? How do these actions relate to the **theme**?

The day came when my parents announced that they wanted to give a dinner party. We had invited Chinese friends to eat with us before, but this dinner was going to be different. In addition to a Chinese-American family, we were going to invite the Gleasons.

"Gee, I can hardly wait to have dinner at your house," Meg said to me. "I just *love* Chinese food."

That was a relief. Mother was a good cook, but I wasn't sure if people who ate sour cream would also eat chicken gizzards stewed in soy sauce.

Mother decided not to take a chance with chicken gizzards. Since we had western guests, she set the table with large dinner plates, which we never used in Chinese meals. In fact we didn't use individual plates at all, but picked up food from the platters in the middle of the table and brought it directly to our rice bowls. Following the practice of Chinese-American restaurants, Mother also placed large serving spoons on the platters.

The dinner started well. Mrs. Gleason exclaimed at the beautifully arranged dishes of food: the colorful candied fruit in the sweet-and-sour pork dish, the noodle-thin shreds of chicken meat stir-fried with tiny peas, and the glistening pink prawns in a ginger sauce.

At first I was too busy enjoying my food to notice how the guests were doing. But soon I remembered my duties. Sometimes guests were too polite to help themselves and you had to serve them with more food.

I glanced at Meg, to see if she needed more food, and my eyes nearly popped out at the sight of her plate. It was piled with food: the sweet-and-sour meat pushed right against the chicken shreds, and the chicken sauce ran into the prawns. She had been taking food from a second dish before she finished eating her helping from the first!

Horrified, I turned to look at Mrs. Gleason. She was dumping rice out of her bowl and putting it on her dinner plate. Then she ladled prawns and gravy on top of the rice and mixed everything together, the way you mix sand, gravel, and cement to make concrete.

I couldn't bear to look any longer, and I turned to Mr. Gleason. He was chasing a pea around his plate. Several times he got it to the edge, but when he tried to pick it up with his chopsticks, it rolled back toward the center of the plate again. Finally he put down his chopsticks and picked up the pea with his fingers. He really did! A grown man!

All of us, our family and the Chinese guests, stopped eating to watch the activities of the Gleasons. I wanted to giggle. Then I caught my mother's eyes on me. She frowned and shook her head slightly, and I understood the message: the Gleasons were not used to Chinese ways, and they were just coping the best they could. For some reason I thought of celery strings.

When the main courses were finished, Mother brought out a platter of fruit. "I hope you weren't expecting a sweet dessert," she said. "Since the Chinese don't eat dessert, I didn't think to prepare any."

"Oh, I couldn't possibly eat dessert!" cried Mrs. Gleason. "I'm simply stuffed!"

Meg had different ideas. When the table was cleared, she announced that she and I were going for a walk. "I don't know about you, but I feel like dessert," she told me, when we were outside. "Come on, there's a Dairy Queen down the

◆ Reading Strategy

What can you **infer** about Chinese table manners from the narrator's declaration that she was "horrified" and "couldn't bear to look" at the Gleasons as they ate?

◆ Reading Check

What do the Gleason's table manners remind the narrator of? Underline the sentence that tells you she has reminded herself.

Mark THE Text

◆ Literary Analysis

What has the dinner party experience taught the narrator? How does what she has learned fit into the story's theme?

street. I could use a big chocolate milkshake!"

Although I didn't really want anything more to eat, I insisted on paying for the milkshakes. After all, I was still hostess.

Meg got her large chocolate milkshake and I had a small one. Even so, she was finishing hers while I was only half done. Toward the end she pulled hard on her straws and went *shloop, shloop.*

"Do you always slurp when you eat a milkshake?" I asked, before I could stop myself.

Meg grinned. "Sure. All Americans slurp."

◆ **Reading Strategy**

What can you **infer** from what Meg says in the bracketed passage?

How do you think this same question would make the narrator feel?

◆ **Stop to Reflect**

Why might the last sentence in the story be significant to the narrator?

Reader's Response: Imagine being in a totally new culture. Would you care about what people think about you? Explain.

Thinking About the Skill: How does using **inference** help you understand the story?

PREVIEW

The Shutout

Patricia C. McKissack and Fredrick McKissack, Jr.

PITTSBURGH CRAWFORDS BASEBALL CLUB

Summary

This historical essay outlines the early history of baseball and how African American baseball players fit into that history. The authors refer to diaries and other factual sources. They correct some false ideas about the game, such as the belief that Abner Doubleday invented baseball in 1839. For many years, African Americans played baseball in northern cities on teams of black and white players. After the Civil War, baseball became a business and things changed. The National Association of Base Ball Players refused to admit any team with African American members. African American players were "shut out" from playing on major league teams until after World War II. But that did not stop them from playing. African Americans formed their own teams. They started the Negro Leagues and established their own baseball legends.

Visual Summary

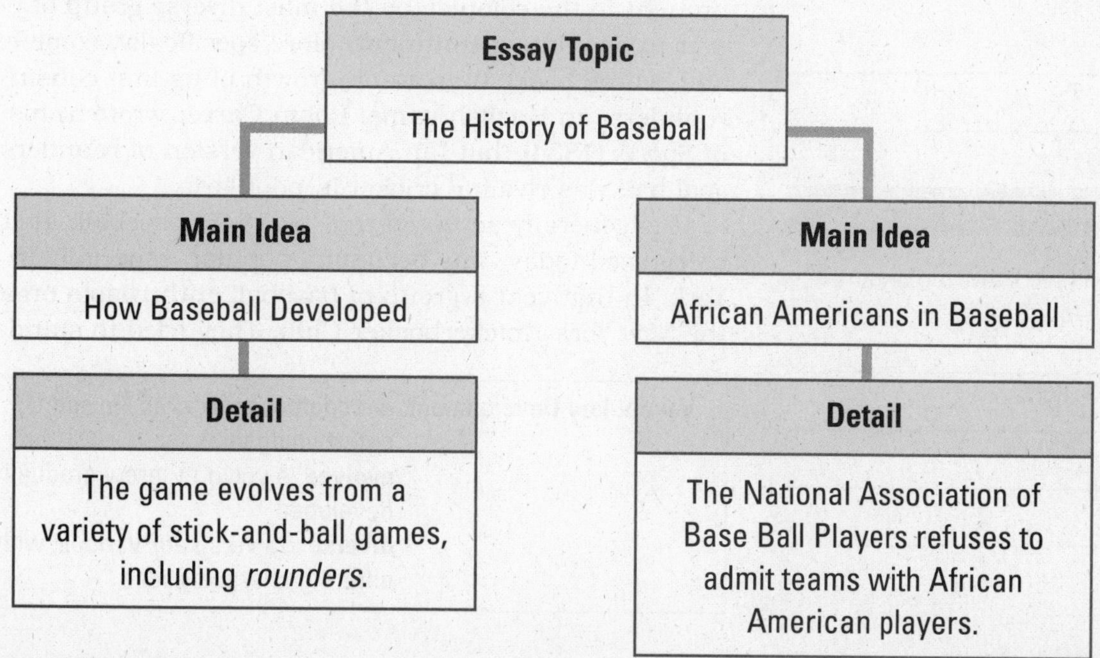
Essay Topic
The History of Baseball
Main Idea
How Baseball Developed
Main Idea
African Americans in Baseball
Detail
The game evolves from a variety of stick-and-ball games, including *rounders*.
Detail
The National Association of Base Ball Players refuses to admit teams with African American players.

◆ Activate Prior Knowledge

Write down two things you know about the history of baseball from books, movies, and television shows.

1. ______________________

____

____

2. ______________________

____

____

◆ Reading Strategy

A **historical essay** is a work that gives facts and explanations about real people and places. What two facts in the bracketed text give evidence that baseball was played before 1839?

1. ______________________

____

2. ______________________

____

How do you know that this is a historical essay?

____

____

◆ Reading Check

Why don't we know the origin of baseball for certain?

____

____

____

____

The Shutout

Patricia C. McKissack and Fredrick McKissack, Jr.

In the earliest days of baseball, African Americans played alongside white players. Eventually, however, baseball was segregated, or separated into teams of "blacks" and teams of "whites." As this essay shows, though, segregation could not shut out African Americans from playing the game and creating baseball legends as amazing as those of their white counterparts.

The history of baseball is difficult to trace because it is embroidered with wonderful anecdotes that are fun but not necessarily supported by fact. There are a lot of myths that persist about baseball—the games, the players, the owners, and the fans—in spite of contemporary research that disproves most of them. For example, the story that West Point cadet Abner Doubleday "invented" baseball in 1839 while at Cooperstown, New York, continues to be widely accepted, even though, according to his diaries, Doubleday never visited Cooperstown. A number of records and documents show that people were playing stick-and-ball games long before the 1839 date.

Albigence Waldo, a surgeon with George Washington's troops at Valley Forge, wrote in his diary that soldiers were "batting balls and running bases" in their free time. Samuel Hopkins Adams (1871–1958), an American historical novelist, stated that his grandfather "played base ball on Mr. Mumford's pasture" in the 1820s.

Although baseball is a uniquely American sport, it was not invented by a single person. Probably the game evolved from a variety of stick-and-ball games that were played in Europe, Asia, Africa, and the Americas for centuries and brought to the colonies by the most diverse group of people ever to populate a continent. More specifically, some historians believe baseball is an outgrowth of its first cousin, rounders, an English game. Robin Carver wrote in his *Book of Sports* (1834) that "an American version of rounders called goal ball was rivaling cricket in popularity."

It is generally accepted that by 1845, baseball, as it is recognized today, was becoming popular, especially in New York. In that year a group of baseball enthusiasts organized the New York Knickerbocker Club. They tried to standardize

Vocabulary Development: **anecdotes** (an´ ik dōts´) *n.* short, entertaining tales
evolved (ē vôlvd´) *v.* grew gradually; developed
diverse (də vurs´) *adj.* various; with differing characteristics

the game by establishing guidelines for "proper play."

The Knickerbockers' rules set the playing field—a diamond-shaped infield with four bases (first, second, third, and home) placed ninety feet apart. At that time, the pitching distance was forty-five feet from home base and the "pitch" was thrown underhanded. The three-strikes-out rule, the three-out inning, and the ways in which a player could be called out were also specified. However, the nine-man team and nine-inning game were not established until later. Over the years, the Knickerbockers' basic rules of play haven't changed much.

In 1857–1858, the newly organized National Association of Base Ball Players was formed, and baseball became a business. Twenty-five clubs—mostly from eastern states—formed the Association for the purpose of setting rules and guidelines for club and team competition. The Association defined a professional player as a person who "played for money, place or emolument [profit]." The Association also authorized an admission fee for one of the first "all-star" games between Brooklyn and New York. Fifteen hundred people paid fifty cents to see that game. Baseball was on its way to becoming the nation's number one sport.

By 1860, the same year South Carolina seceded from the Union, there were about sixty teams in the Association. For obvious reasons none of them were from the South. Baseball's development was slow during the Civil War years, but teams continued to compete, and military records show that, sometimes between battles, Union solders chose up teams and played baseball games. It was during this time that records began mentioning African American players. One war journalist noted that black players were "sought after as teammates because of their skill as ball handlers."

Information about the role of African Americans in the early stages of baseball development is slight. Several West African cultures had stick-and-ball and running games, so at least some blacks were familiar with the concept of baseball. Baseball, however, was not a popular southern sport, never equal to boxing, wrestling, footracing, or horse racing among the privileged landowners.

Slave owners preferred these individual sports because they could enter their slaves in competitions, watch the event from a safe distance, pocket the winnings, and personally never raise a sweat. There are documents to show that slave masters made a great deal of money from the athletic skills of their slaves.

Free blacks, on the other hand, played on and against integrated[1] teams in large eastern cities and in small midwestern hamlets. It is believed that some of the emancipated[2]

1. **integrated** (in´ tə grā tid) *adj.* open to both African Americans and whites.
2. **emancipated** (ē man´ sə pā´ tid) *adj.* freed from slavery.

◆ Stop to Reflect

In 1845, the New York Knickerbockers established rules for playing baseball. Why might people want to make a set of standardized rules for baseball?

______

______

______

______

______

◆ Reading Strategy

To help you understand and **clarify the author's meaning**, look for details, examples, and explanations. In the bracketed paragraph, what two details clarify the authors' main idea that baseball teams still competed during the Civil War?

1. ______

______

2. ______

______

◆ Reading Check

In what parts of the country did African Americans first play baseball? Circle the answer.

Mark THE Text

slaves and runaways who served in the Union Army learned how to play baseball from northern blacks and whites who had been playing together for years.

After the Civil War, returning soldiers helped to inspire a new interest in baseball all over the country. Teams sprung up in northern and midwestern cities, and naturally African Americans were interested in joining some of these clubs. But the National Association of Base Ball Players had other ideas. They voted in December 1867 not to admit any team for membership that "may be composed of one or more colored persons." Their reasoning was as irrational as the racism that shaped it: "If colored clubs were admitted," the Association stated, "there would be in all probability some division of feeling whereas, by excluding them no injury could result to anyone . . . and [we wish] to keep out of the convention the discussion of any subjects having a political bearing as this [admission of blacks on the Association teams] undoubtedly would."

So, from the start, organized baseball tried to limit or exclude African American participation. In the early days a few black ball players managed to play on integrated minor league teams. A few even made it to the majors, but by the turn of the century, black players were shut out of the major leagues until after World War II. That doesn't mean African Americans didn't play the game. They did.

Black people organized their own teams, formed leagues, and competed for championships. The history of the old "Negro Leagues" and the players who barnstormed[3] on black diamonds is one of baseball's most interesting chapters, but the story is a researcher's nightmare. Black baseball was outside the mainstream of the major leagues, so team and player records weren't well kept, and for the most part, the white press ignored black clubs or portrayed them as clowns. And for a long time the Baseball Hall of Fame didn't recognize any of the Negro League players. Because of the lack of documentation, many people thought the Negro Leagues' stories were nothing more than myths and yarns, but that is not the case. The history of the Negro Leagues is a patchwork of human drama and comedy, filled with legendary heroes, infamous owners, triple-headers, low pay, and long bus rides home—not unlike the majors.

Vocabulary Development: composed (kəm pōzd′) *adj.* made up (of)
irrational (ir rash′ ə nəl) *adj.* unreasonable; not making sense

3. **barnstormed** *v.* went from one small town to another, putting on an exhibition.

Reader's Response: How would you feel if you were an African American denied the right to play in the major leagues?

____

◆ **Reading Check**

How did the National Association of Base Ball Players limit the involvement of African Americans in baseball?

____

◆ **Reading Strategy**

Mark the Text

The authors state, "So, from the start, organized baseball tried to limit or exclude African American participation." What details and facts **clarify the authors' meaning?** Circle the sentence that makes the meaning clear.

____

◆ **Literary Analysis**

Why don't the writers include much information about the Negro Leagues in this **historical essay**?

____

PREVIEW

The Drive-In Movies

Gary Soto

Summary

"The Drive-In Movies" is a nonfiction piece in which the author tells a story about his life. He recalls a Saturday when he, his brother, and his sister wanted to go to the drive-in movies. They know that if their mother is happy, she is more likely to take them. To keep her happy, all three children try to be good. The author tries to be extra good. He does his chores without being asked. He weeds the garden and mows the lawn and cleans up the yard. He and his brother even wax the car. Their plan works. That night their mom takes them all to the drive-in movies. However, when they get there, the author is so tired that he falls asleep!

Visual Summary

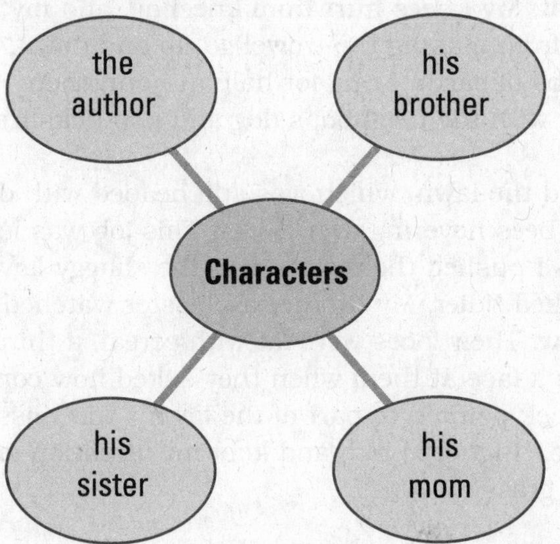

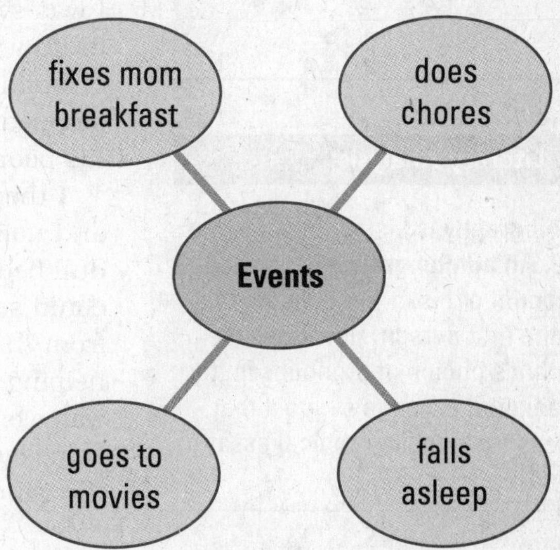

◆ **Activate Prior Knowledge**

Suppose that you want a friend or family member to take you to the movies. Name two strategies you might use to persuade him or her.

1. ____________________

2. ____________________

◆ **Reading Strategy**

When a writer tells the story of someone's life, he or she provides **author's evidence** to support the statements he or she makes. What evidence does the author provide to support his statement that he acted "extra good"?

◆ **Literary Analysis**

A **biography** is a story of someone's life. An **autobiography** is someone's account of his or her own life told in the first person. How does the author's choice of pronouns in the bracketed passage suggest that this is an autobiographical essay?

The Drive-In Movies

Gary Soto

In the 1950s and 1960s, many people saw movies at the "drive-in," where people parked their cars in front of a large, outdoor screen and hooked up to a listening box to enjoy the show. The drive-in movie theater was an inexpensive way for the whole family to see a movie.

For our family, moviegoing was rare. But if our mom, tired from a week of candling eggs,[1] woke up happy on a Saturday morning, there was a chance we might later scramble to our blue Chevy and beat nightfall to the Starlight Drive-In. My brother and sister knew this. I knew this. So on Saturday we tried to be good. We sat in the cool shadows of the TV with the volume low and watched cartoons, a prelude of what was to come.

One Saturday I decided to be extra good. When she came out of the bedroom tying her robe, she yawned a hat-sized yawn and blinked red eyes at the weak brew of coffee I had fixed for her. I made her toast with strawberry jam spread to all the corners and set the three boxes of cereal in front of her. If she didn't care to eat cereal, she could always look at the back of the boxes as she drank her coffee.

I went outside. The lawn was tall but too wet with dew to mow. I picked up a trowel and began to weed the flower bed. The weeds were really bermuda grass, long stringers that ran finger-deep in the ground. I got to work quickly and in no time crescents of earth began rising under my fingernails. I was sweaty hot. My knees hurt from kneeling, and my brain was dull from making the trowel go up and down, dribbling crumbs of earth. I dug for half an hour, then stopped to play with the neighbor's dog and pop ticks from his poor snout.

I then mowed the lawn, which was still beaded with dew and noisy with bees hovering over clover. This job was less dull because as I pushed the mower over the shaggy lawn, I could see it looked tidier. My brother and sister watched from the window. Their faces were fat with cereal, a third helping. I made a face at them when they asked how come I was working. Rick pointed to part of the lawn. "You missed some over there." I ignored him and kept my attention on the windmill of grassy blades.

Vocabulary Development: prelude (prel´ yo͞od´) *n.* an introduction to a main event or action coming later
crescent (kres´ ənt) *n.* anything shaped like the moon in its first or last quarter

1. **candling eggs** examining eggs for freshness by placing them in front of a candle.

While I was emptying the catcher, a bee stung the bottom of my foot. I danced on one leg and was ready to cry when Mother showed her face at the window. I sat down on the grass and examined my foot: the stinger was pulsating. I pulled it out quickly, ran water over the sting and packed it with mud, Grandmother's remedy.

Hobbling, I returned to the flower bed where I pulled more stringers and again played with the dog. More ticks had migrated to his snout. I swept the front steps, took out the garbage, cleaned the lint filter to the dryer (easy), plucked hair from the industrial wash basin in the garage (also easy), hosed off the patio, smashed three snails sucking paint from the house (disgusting but fun), tied a bundle of newspapers, put away toys, and, finally, seeing that almost everything was done and the sun was not too high, started waxing the car.

My brother joined me with an old gym sock, and our sister watched us while sucking on a cherry Kool-Aid ice cube. The liquid wax drooled onto the sock, and we began to swirl the white slop on the chrome. My arms ached from buffing, which though less boring than weeding, was harder. But the beauty was evident. The shine, hurting our eyes and glinting like an armful of dimes, brought Mother out. She looked around the yard and said, "Pretty good." She winced[2] at the grille and returned inside the house.

We began to wax the paint. My brother applied the liquid and I followed him rubbing hard in wide circles as we moved around the car. I began to hurry because my arms were hurting and my stung foot looked like a water balloon. We were working around the trunk when Rick pounded on the bottle of wax. He squeezed the bottle and it sneezed a few more white drops.

We looked at each other. "There's some on the sock," I said. "Let's keep going."

We polished and buffed, sweat weeping on our brows. We got scared when we noticed that the gym sock was now blue. The paint was coming off. Our sister fit ice cubes into our mouths and we worked harder, more intently, more dedicated to the car and our mother. We ran the sock over the chrome, trying to pick up extra wax. But there wasn't enough to cover the entire car. Only half got waxed, but we thought it was better than nothing and went inside for lunch. After lunch, we returned outside with tasty sandwiches.

Vocabulary Development: pulsating (pul′ sāt′ iŋ) *v.* beating or throbbing in rhythm

2. **winced** (winst) *v.* drew back slightly, as if in pain.

◆ **Reading Check**

After getting a painful bee sting, why does Soto rush to return to work?

◆ **Literary Analysis**

List two details in the bracketed text that show this is an **autobiography** because Soto alone would have known about them.

1.

2.

◆ **Reading Check**

Why do the boys wax only one side of the car?

◆ Reading Strategy

What **author's evidence** does Soto give that indicates that he's afraid his mother won't take them to the movies. Circle the sentence.

◆ Stop to Reflect

Why do you think Soto's mother doesn't get angry at the boys for waxing only part of the car?

____

____

____

____

◆ Reading Check

Why doesn't Soto see the last part of the movie?

____

____

____

____

Rick and I nearly jumped. The waxed side of the car was foggy white. We took a rag and began to polish vigorously and nearly in tears, but the fog wouldn't come off. I blamed Rick and he blamed me. Debra stood at the window, not wanting to get involved. Now, not only would we not go to the movies, but Mom would surely snap a branch from the plum tree and chase us around the yard.

Mom came out and looked at us with hands on her aproned hips. Finally, she said, "You boys worked so hard." She turned on the garden hose and washed the car. That night we did go to the drive-in. The first feature was about nothing, and the second feature, starring Jerry Lewis,[3] was *Cinderfella*. I tried to stay awake. I kept a wad of homemade popcorn in my cheek and laughed when Jerry Lewis fit golf tees in his nose. I rubbed my watery eyes. I laughed and looked at my mom. I promised myself I would remember that scene with the golf tees and promised myself not to work so hard the coming Saturday. Twenty minutes into the movie, I fell asleep with one hand in the popcorn.

Vocabulary Development: vigorously (vig′ ər əs lē) *adv.* forcefully; powerfully

3. **Jerry Lewis** comedian who starred in many movies during the 1950s and 1960s.

Reader's Response: What personal experience would you choose to write about in an autobiography?

____

____

____

Thinking About the Skill: How does knowing that this is an autobiographical account help you to better enjoy the story?

____

____

____

PREVIEW

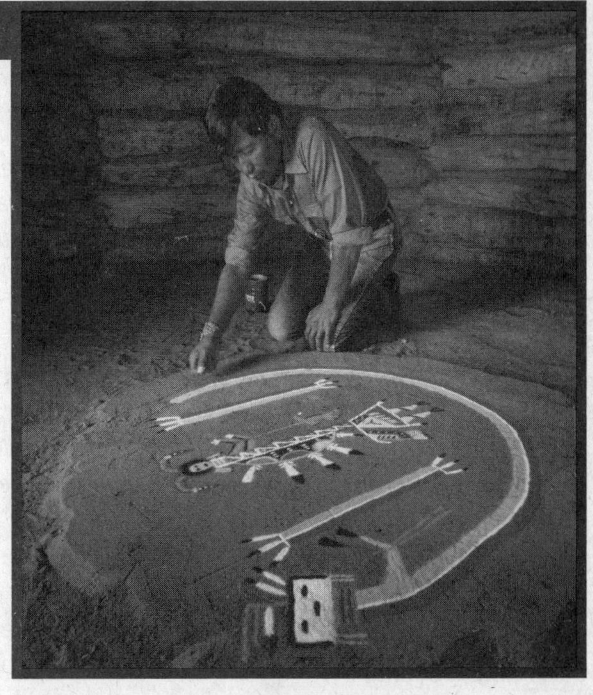

Restoring the Circle

Joseph Bruchac

Summary

"Restoring the Circle" is a persuasive essay that stresses the importance of cultural traditions. In Native American culture, traditions are passed down from generation to generation through stories. The author argues that in order for the culture to survive, the stories children read must be accurate and honest. In the past, many non-Native writers did not understand Native American culture. As a result, their stories contained many false ideas. These ideas caused Native American children to be ashamed of their culture. Today, there are many Native American writers. They understand Native American culture because they have experienced it. Their stories are rich and accurate. Children can read these stories and be proud. Native American cultural traditions can be kept alive.

Visual Summary

Argument
In order for Native American cultural traditions to survive, stories must show Native Americans accurately and honestly.

Support	Support	Support
False information has led to stereotypes of Native Americans.	Native American children have felt ashamed of the stereotypes.	When Native American children feel ashamed, they reject their culture.

◆ Activate Prior Knowledge

List what you know of your own cultural background. Jot down how you know this information.

◆ Reading Strategy

Essays often include unfamiliar words. Use **context to determine meaning** by looking for clues in surrounding words, phrases, and paragraphs. Circle the word *stereotypes*. Write down two clues that help you determine the meaning of *stereotypes* in the underlined passage.

Mark THE Text

1.

2.

◆ Reading Check

Bruchac says, "In many Native American traditions, life is seen as a circle." In your own words, what does this statement mean?

Restoring the Circle

Joseph Bruchac

Joseph Bruchac is part Abenaki, a Native American group in the northeastern United States. Eastern Woodland Indians, of which Abenaki are a part, at first welcomed European settlers. The growing European population, though, decreased the food supply and interfered with Native American traditional lifestyles. By 1800, the Abenaki, who had once ranged over much of the Northeast, found themselves limited to Maine.

In many Native American traditions life is seen as a circle. We enter that circle when we are born and as we travel around that circle we come back, as elders, to the place where we began. The elders, who have spent a lifetime learning their cultural traditions, are the ones who are supposed to be the closest to the children, passing on their traditions through the teaching to be found in stories. As long as that circle remains unbroken, the people will survive.

Imagine what it would be like if someone who never met you and knew nothing about the circle of your life wrote a story about you. Even if that person was a good writer, you probably would not agree with what he wrote. As interesting as imagination may be, it cannot take the place of experience and firsthand knowledge. In a similar way, imaginative portrayals of Native American people and Native American cultures became painful stereotypes and distorted history. Native American men were pictured as savage and dangerous people who were aggressive for no good reason. Yet it is historically true that none of America's so-called "Indian wars" were ever begun by the Indians. Native American women were pictured as nothing more than beasts of burden. Yet in many Native American cultures, such as that of the Iroquois, the women were the heads of families, the owners of the houses, and the ones who chose the chiefs. Details of Native cultures were badly confused. For example, the famous poem Hiawatha by Henry Wadsworth Longfellow actually tells the story of Managozho, a trickster hero of the Chippewa people. The real Hiawatha was a political leader of the Iroquois people. It would be like calling the hero of the Anglo-Saxon epic Beowulf Julius Caesar. More than 400 different languages are spoken by the various Native American nations of North America, but instead of showing the complexity and variety of Native American cultures, much of the literature by non-Native people made all Indians look and sound alike.

Many Native Americans chose to become writers because they wanted to restore the circle through more accurate portrayals of themselves and their people. In many cases, too, they hoped to restore a sense of pride in their own heritage. Because of the inaccurate and unpleasant ways Native

Americans have been portrayed in books by non-Indian authors, Native children have sometimes felt ashamed of themselves and decided that it would be better for them to forget their own cultures and try to be "just like everyone else." Today, because of the writing of such Native American authors as Michael Dorris or Linda Hogan, young Native people can read stories and poems in which Native Americans are presented as fully-rounded characters from accurately described tribal traditions. As portrayed by Native American authors, Indians are sometimes good, sometimes not so good, but no longer one-dimensional stereotypes.

In the period between 1850 and 1950, many Native American children were sent away to Indian boarding schools where they were not allowed to speak their own Native languages. Whether they wanted to or not, they were expected to no longer "be Indian" and, removed completely from the circle of their families, denied contact with their elders. It was felt by many well-meaning people in the United States government that the only way to "help the Indians" was by making them be more like European Americans. Today, of course, we see things differently. In a multicultural world we understand how important cultural traditions are in maintaining a sense of self-worth. It is now believed that whoever you are, whether you are Jewish American, African American, Italian American, or Native American, knowing about your own history and culture can make you a stronger person. Today, many Native American people are discovering that Native American literature can help them find their way back to that old circle of knowledge. In some cases, people who were not taught their tribal languages as children are learning those languages again through literature. In Arizona, a successful project helped Pima and Papago children learn their native O'odham language by reading traditional songs in O'odham and then writing poems in O'odham. Those songs, which had been preserved as literature, and the new poems worked together to help strengthen traditions.

One of the most prominent Native American writers is N. Scott Momaday, who is of Kiowa Indian ancestry. His first novel, *House Made of Dawn*, tells the story of a young Native American man who returns home after fighting as an American soldier in a foreign war. He feels divided between the white world and the Indian world, and that division in himself makes him sick. It is only by understanding his own traditions and returning to them that he is able to restore his health and self-respect. That novel, which won a Pulitzer Prize in 1969, is a good example of the kind of Native American writing which helps preserve cultural traditions. It contains authentic and very well-written descriptions of Native American life around the time of the late 1940s and early 1950s. Many Native Americans who have read this

◆ Reading Check

Why is it valuable to read literature by Native American authors about their culture?

____

____

____

____

◆ Literary Analysis

An **essay** is a work that presents real people, places, and events. This selection is a **persuasive essay** because it attempts to convince the reader to think or act in a certain way.

List two examples in the bracketed text that are meant to persuade you about the value of Native American culture.

1. ______________________

____

____

2. ______________________

____

____

◆ Reading Check

Who is N. Scott Momaday?

____

____

Why is his book a good example of Native American literature?

____

____

◆ Reading Strategy

Circle the word *convictions.* Which **context clues** help you **determine the meaning** of the word?

Mark THE Text

____

____

What is the meaning of *conviction*?

____

____

◆ Stop to Reflect

How do authors who write about their own cultures help build our understanding and acceptance of each other?

____

book have felt deeply inspired by it because its main character, caught between the white and Indian worlds, experiences some of the confusion and pain which they have also felt. It is hard to be a stranger in your own country, but that is the way many Native Americans sometimes feel. By reading Momaday's novel, they gained a better understanding of their own feelings, and it strengthened their convictions about the importance of preserving their own traditions.

Native American literature, like all literatures, is also a way to speak to the world. In some cases, novels by Native American writers are now being used as textbooks in college courses in history and sociology. Writing can become a window into another reality, offering to non-Natives the opportunity to authentically experience something of Native American culture. If you read a book about another culture, you may be more likely to have understanding and tolerance for that culture. When you have respect for another culture, then you are much less likely to do things which will be detrimental to that culture and to the people of that culture. Perhaps, because of the cultural understanding offered through Native American literature, the circle of Native American cultural traditions will be less threatened in the generations to come.

Vocabulary Development: tolerance (täl′ ər əns) *n.* respect for something different
detrimental (de′ trə ment′ əl) *adj.* harmful

Reader's Response: What questions would you ask Bruchac about his cultural heritage?

____

Thinking About the Skill: How did knowing that this is a persuasive essay help you to read with better understanding?

____

PREVIEW

How the Internet Works

Kerry Cochrane

Summary

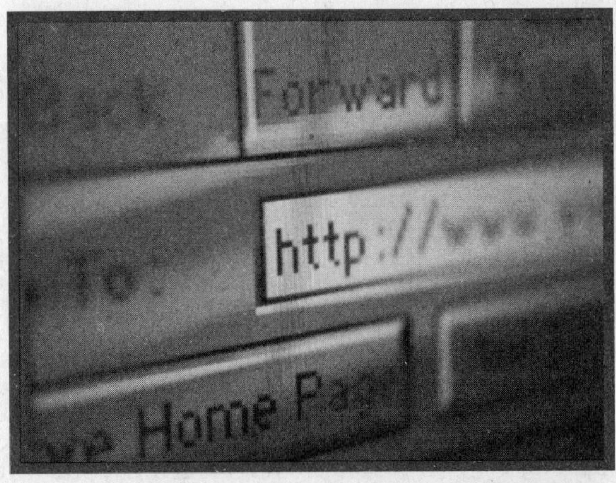

"How the Internet Works" is an informational essay. It explains how the Internet allows computers all over the world to talk to one another. The author gives detailed facts and information, such as what Internet addresses and user IDs are and how they allow e-mail to be sent and received. She supports this information with helpful explanations and examples. Throughout the essay, the author compares the Internet to the postal service. The Internet and the postal service operate in similar ways. The author uses these similarities to give a clearer understanding of how the Internet works. She writes that more and more people want access to the Internet and that this access has become increasingly available.

Visual Summary

THE INTERNET

What is it?

A way for computers to talk to one another

How does it work?

- Uses Internet protocols
- Similar to a post office
- Numerical and alphabetical addresses
- Information travels over phone lines
- More students are connecting
- Ways to connect are improving

◆ Activate Prior Knowledge

Jot down mechanical devices that help you communicate.

◆ Reading Strategy

Use **context to determine meaning** of unfamiliar words. Look at surrounding words, phrases, and paragraphs to give you clues to the meaning of words. What clues in the bracketed text help determine the meaning of *Internet protocols.* Circle the clues.

Mark the Text

What are *Internet protocols*?

◆ Reading Check

To what does the author compare the Internet?

◆ Reading Check

What does *IP* stand for?

How the Internet Works

Kerry Cochrane

The addressing system described in "How the Internet Works" allows Internet users to access hundreds of thousands of sites, or places, on the Internet. Once you arrive at a site, you can navigate through its levels to find the information you are looking for.

The central problem in designing the Internet was finding a way for different kinds of computers all over the country to talk to one another. ARPA solved this problem with Internet protocols. Protocols are sets of rules that standardize how something is done, so that everyone knows what to expect. For example, think of any game you've played and the rules that went with that game. The rules of the game tell you how many players you can have, what order you play in, what's allowed and what's not allowed, and how to keep score. Once you know the rules, you can play with people very different from you. Internet protocols are like game rules: they set up standard procedures for computers to follow so that they can communicate with each other.

The Internet is often compared to the postal service. They both seem to work like one big organization, but are actually made up of smaller parts that work together. There are local post offices in small towns, regional postal systems in big cities, and national postal services for countries. They all use different machinery to handle the mail, and different equipment to deliver it from bicycles to trucks to airplanes. Postal workers all over the world speak hundreds of different languages. But they all manage to work together because of certain rules, or protocols. Postal protocols say that mail must be in envelopes or packages, there must be postage, and every piece of mail must have an address. As long as you know these rules, you can send mail to anyone in the world.

The Internet works in a similar way. As long as everyone knows the protocols, information can travel easily between machines and the people using them worldwide. The basic group of protocols that governs the Internet is the TCP/IP set of protocols. This stands for Transmission Control Protocol (TCP) and Internet Protocol (IP). Internet Protocol says that every computer connected to the Internet must have a unique address. These addresses consist of four sets of numbers separated by periods. For example, the IP address for one of the computers at the University of Illinois at Urbana-Champaign is **128.174.5.49**. Once you have the IP address of a computer, you know where to send messages or other information. Transmission Control Protocol manages the information you send out by computer. TCP breaks each message into manageable chunks and numbers each chunk in order. Then the numbered groups of information are marked with the IP address of the other computer and are sent out to it. When they arrive on the other end, TCP software checks to see that all the pieces are there and puts them back in order, ready to use.

When you drop a letter into a mailbox, it gets collected and sorted with hundreds of other pieces of mail. Your local post office sorts and routes the mail according to its destination and then sends it on to the next post office. Information is sorted and routed on the Internet in the same way. Computers on the Internet called routers, or packet switchers, read the IP addresses on each packet of information, and direct the packets to their destination. The information can be sent from one computer to another on phone lines, by satellite networks, on fiber-optic cables, or even through radio transmissions.

IP addresses are made up of numbers, which can be hard to remember and use. So computers usually have alphabetical addresses as well. Like IP addresses, these alphabetical addresses have several parts separated by periods, although they may have fewer or more than four parts. So a computer at the University of Iowa with the IP address **128.255.40.201** also has the alphabetical address **panda.uiowa.edu,** which is easier to remember. The first part of this address, **panda,** is the name of the host computer. The rest of this address, **uiowa.edu,** is called a domain name, because each part of the name refers to a domain. Each domain gives information about the Internet site, such as where it's located, who's responsible for the computer, and what kind of institution it's connected to. Moving from right to left, the domains give more specific information about the location of the host computer. In the domain name **uiowa.edu,** for example, the domain **edu** tells you that the host computer is run by an educational institution, because **edu** is the domain attached to all United States educational sites. The domain **uiowa** stands for the University of Iowa, which is the specific educational institution where the host computer named panda is located.

In the United States, there are six domains that are used at the end of domain names, and each one refers to the type of site that's running the computer.

Countries outside the United States do not use these domains. Instead, they have two-letter country domains at the end of their names, such as **nz** for New Zealand, **br** for Brazil, or **ca** for Canada.

Every person with an Internet account has a personal address, too. Individual Internet addresses are made up of a unique user ID (sometimes called a user name) for each person, which is attached to an alphabetical address by an "at" symbol (@). User IDs are usually taken from your name. My full Internet address is **kcochra@orion.it.luc.edu.**

◆ Literary Analysis

An **essay** is a work that presents real people, places, and events. This selection is an **informational essay** because it presents facts, information, and explanations about a topic. List two facts about the Internet in the bracketed text.

◆ Reading Check

There are different parts or domains in an Internet address. In the address **panda.uiowa.edu**, what does **edu** stand for? What might **uiowa** stand for? What does **panda** stand for?

1. edu

2. uiowa

3. panda

◆ Reading Strategy

Mark It Text

Circle the **context clues** that help you understand the meaning of the term *user ID*?

What is a *user ID?*

◆ **Stop to Reflect**

How is the Internet different from other forms of communication, such as the telephone, radio, or television?

◆ **Reading Check**

Who are the fastest-growing group of Internet users, according to the author?

Reading this address from left to right, you see that my user ID is **kcochra** (from Kerry Cochrane), and I'm at the address **orion.it.luc.edu. Orion** is the name of the host machine running this account. The office of Information Technologies runs the computer named orion, so the first domain is called **it.** Information Technologies is an office of Loyola University Chicago, so the next domain is **luc.** Because this is an educational institution, the final domain is **edu.** The President of the United States even has an Internet address at the White House: **president@white-house.gov.** Although they may seem complicated at first, Internet addresses make sense when you know how they work.

A few years ago the Internet was not available to the general public. Most people with Internet accounts got them through universities or companies where they were students or employees. As interest in the Internet has grown, however, ways to connect have increased, and they are improving all the time. One of the fastest-growing groups of Internet users is students and teachers in kindergarten through 12th grade. Schools around the world are getting access to the Internet so children can benefit from the immense resources available on-line.

There are several ways for schools to connect to the Internet. Many states or regions have developed their own networks to link schools together and get them on-line. Some universities and colleges provide guest accounts for local schools. Also, companies called Internet providers have begun to market Internet accounts to schools, companies, and private individuals. Your school may already be connected to the Internet, or someone in your family may have an account at work or at home.

Reader's Response: How would your life be different if there were no Internet?

Thinking About the Skill: How did knowing that this is an informational essay help you to understand this selection?

PREVIEW

Turkeys

Bailey White

Summary

"Turkeys" is a narrative essay about the connection between humans and wildlife. The writer remembers when she was six years old. At that time, some ornithologists (people who study birds) had become friendly with her family. The ornithologists were concerned about wild turkeys in the area. They discovered a wild turkey nest and wanted to protect it. One day, the mother turkey left her nest and did not return. The ornithologists became worried. They needed to keep the turkey eggs warm. They remembered that the narrator had a high fever. That night, they placed the eggs in bed beside her. In the morning, the narrator's bed was filled with baby turkeys.

Visual Summary

Characters	the narrator, the ornithologists
Setting	the narrator's house when she was six years old
Problem	Keeping the wild turkey eggs safe and warm.
Events	• Ornithologists find a wild turkey nest. • The mother turkey abandons the nest. • The ornithologists put the eggs in bed with the narrator, who has a high fever. • The baby turkeys hatch.
Resolution (outcome)	With the narrator's help, the ornithologists save a nest of baby turkeys.

◆ Activate Prior Knowledge

Jot down the names of parks that have been set aside for the preservation of wildlife.

____

____

____

____

◆ Reading Strategy

It's helpful to use **context to determine the meaning** of unfamiliar words. Look for clues to meaning in the surrounding words, phrases, and paragraphs. What is the meaning of the word *ornithologist*? Circle the context clues in the first two paragraphs that helped you decide.

Mark THE Text

____

____

____

◆ Reading Check

What has happened to the author?

____

____

____

____

◆ Reading Check

What are the ornithologists doing in the woods near the author's home?

____

____

____

Turkeys

Bailey White

People were not always as aware of the need to care for natural resources as they are today. Conservation became an issue in the United States in the early 1900s. President Theodore Roosevelt established the first federal wildlife refuge at Pelican Island in Florida and set aside more than 140 million acres to be national forest reserves. He also held a national conference on conservation that led leaders in individual states to establish conservation groups.

Something about my mother attracts ornithologists. It all started years ago when a couple of them discovered she had a rare species of woodpecker coming to her bird feeder. They came in the house and sat around the window, exclaiming and taking pictures with big fancy cameras. But long after the red cockaded woodpeckers had gone to roost, the ornithologists were still there. There always seemed to be three or four of them wandering around our place and staying for supper.

In those days, during the 1950s, the big concern of ornithologists in our area was the wild turkey. They were rare, and the pure-strain wild turkeys had begun to interbreed with farmers' domestic stock. The species was being degraded. It was extinction by dilution, and to the ornithologists it was just as tragic as the more dramatic demise of the passenger pigeon or the Carolina parakeet.

One ornithologist had devised a formula to compute the ratio of domestic to pure-strain wild turkey in an individual bird by comparing the angle of flight at takeoff and the rate of acceleration. And in those sad days, the turkeys were flying low and slow.

It was during that time, the spring when I was six years old, that I caught the measles. I had a high fever, and my mother was worried about me. She kept the house quiet and dark and crept around silently, trying different methods of cooling me down.

Even the ornithologists stayed away—but not out of fear of the measles or respect for a household with sickness. The fact was, they had discovered a wild turkey nest. According to the formula, the hen was pure-strain wild—not a taint of the sluggish domestic bird in her blood—and the ornithologists were camping in the woods, protecting her nest from predators and taking pictures.

Vocabulary Development: dilution (di lo͞o′ shən) *n.* process of weakening by mixing with something else
demise (dē mīz′) *n.* death

One night our phone rang. It was one of the ornithologists. "Does your little girl still have measles?" he asked.

"Yes," said my mother. "She's very sick. Her temperature is 102."

"I'll be right over," said the ornithologist.

In five minutes a whole carload of them arrived. They marched solemnly into the house, carrying a cardboard box. "A hundred and two, did you say? Where is she?" they asked my mother.

They crept into my room and set the box down on the bed. I was barely conscious, and when I opened my eyes, their worried faces hovering over me seemed to float out of the darkness like giant, glowing eggs. They snatched the covers off me and felt me all over. They consulted in whispers.

"Feels just right, I'd say."

"A hundred two—can't miss if we tuck them up close and she lies still."

I closed my eyes then, and after a while the ornithologists drifted away, their pale faces bobbing up and down on the black wave of fever.

The next morning I was better. For the first time in days I could think. The memory of the ornithologists with their whispered voices was like a dream from another life. But when I pulled down the covers, there staring up at me with googly eyes and wide mouths were sixteen fuzzy baby turkeys, and the cracked chips and caps of sixteen brown speckled eggs.

I was a sensible child. I gently stretched myself out. The eggshells crackled, and the turkey babies fluttered and cheeped and snuggled against me. I laid my aching head back on the pillow and closed my eyes. "The ornithologists," I whispered. "The ornithologists have been here."

It seems the turkey hen had been so disturbed by the elaborate protective measures that had been undertaken on her behalf that she had abandoned her nest on the night the eggs were due to hatch. It was a cold night. The ornithologists, not having an incubator on hand, used their heads and came up with the next best thing.

The baby turkeys and I gained our strength together. When I was finally able to get out of bed and feebly creep around the house, the turkeys peeped and cheeped around my ankles, scrambling to keep up with me and tripping over their own big spraddle-toed feet. When I went outside for the first time, the turkeys tumbled after me down the steps and scratched around in the yard while I sat in the sun.

Finally, in late summer, the day came when they were ready to fly for the first time as adult birds. The ornithologists gathered. I ran down the hill, and the turkeys ran too. Then, one by one, they took off. They flew high and fast. The

◆ Literary Analysis

An **essay** is a work that presents real people, places, and events. This selection is a **narrative essay** because it tells about a real-life experience, using elements of storytelling. What details in the bracketed text tell you that this is a narrative essay?

◆ Reading Check

What do the ornithologists do to keep the turkey chick eggs warm?

◆ **Reading Check**

Why do the ornithologists measure the angle of the turkeys' flight?

◆ **Stop to Reflect**

How do you think White might have felt when she watched the wild turkeys take off?

ornithologists made Vs with their thumbs and forefingers, measuring angles. They consulted their stopwatches and paced off distances. They scribbled in their tiny notebooks. Finally they looked at each other. They sighed. They smiled. They jumped up and down and hugged each other. "One hundred percent pure wild turkey!" they said.

Nearly forty years have passed since then. Now there's a vaccine for measles. And the woods where I live are full of pure wild turkeys. I like to think they are all descendants of those sixteen birds I saved from the vigilance of the ornithologists.

Vocabulary Development: vigilance (vij´ ə ləns) *n.* watchfulness

Reader's Response: What would your reaction be if you woke up in bed with sixteen turkey chicks?

Thinking About the Skill: How did knowing that this is an narrative essay help you to enjoy the selection?

The Phantom Tollbooth, Act I

Based on the book by Norton Juster

Susan Nanus

Summary

A bored young boy named Milo receives an unexpected package. The package contains a tollbooth. Soon, Milo sets off on an adventure into a fantasy world with a watchdog named Tock. They travel to a place called Dictionopolis, a land of words. During the journey, Tock tells Milo about a terrible argument between the king of Dictionopolis and the king of Digitopolis, a land of numbers. The two kings had argued about what was more important—words or numbers. The Princesses Rhyme and Reason had tried to settle the argument. They said that words and numbers were equally important. However, the kings disagreed. They banished the princesses to the Castle-in-the-Air. After visiting Dictionopolis, Milo, Tock, and a character named Humbug begin a journey to Digitopolis, where they hope to persuade the king to let them rescue the princesses.

Visual Summary

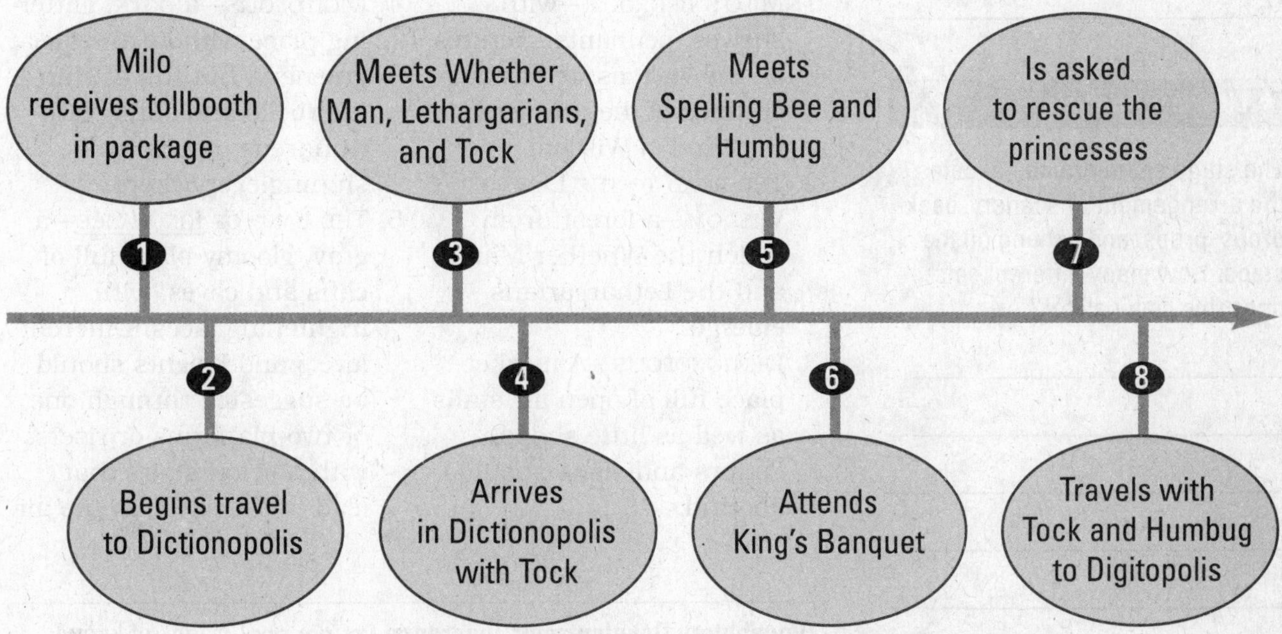

1 Milo receives tollbooth in package
2 Begins travel to Dictionopolis
3 Meets Whether Man, Lethargarians, and Tock
4 Arrives in Dictionopolis with Tock
5 Meets Spelling Bee and Humbug
6 Attends King's Banquet
7 Is asked to rescue the princesses
8 Travels with Tock and Humbug to Digitopolis

◆ Activate Prior Knowledge

Describe the setting of a fantasy world you have encountered in a book or a movie.

____

____

____

____

◆ Literary Analysis

A **drama** is a story written to be performed. Elements of drama include character, setting, and plot. The cast is the list of characters in the drama. What is unusual about the names of the cast in this play?

____

____

____

____

____

◆ Literary Analysis

The stage set in **drama** indicates the arrangement of scenery, backdrops, props, and lighting on the stage. How many different sets does this play call for?

____

____

____

____

____

____

The Phantom Tollbooth
Act I

Based on the book by Norton Juster
Susan Nanus

The names of some of the people and places in The Phantom Tollbooth describe their qualities. For example, Lethargarians is from lethargy, *which means "sluggish; without energy." Digitopolis is from* digit, *which is a number between 1 and 10, and* polis, *which means "city state." Terrible trivium is from* trivia, *which means "an unimportant fact." Check these terms as you read.*

CAST (in order of appearance)

- The Clock
- Milo, a boy
- The Whether Man
- Six Lethargarians
- Tock, the Watchdog (same as the clock)
- Azaz the Unabridged, king of Dictionopolis
- The Mathemagician, king of Digitopolis
- Princess Sweet Rhyme
- Princess Pure Reason
- Gatekeeper of Dictionopolis
- Three Word Merchants
- The Letterman (fourth word merchant)
- Spelling Bee
- The Humbug
- The Duke of Definition
- The Minister of Meaning
- The Earl of Essence
- The Count of Connotation
- The Undersecretary of Understanding

THE SETS

1. Milo's bedroom—with shelves, pennants, pictures on the wall, as well as suggestions of the characters of the Land of Wisdom.
2. The road to the Land of Wisdom—a forest, from which the Whether Man and the Lethargarians emerge.
3. Dictionopolis—A marketplace full of open air stalls as well as little shops. Letters and signs should abound.
4. Digitopolis—a dark, glittering place without trees or greenery, but full of shining rocks and cliffs, with hundreds of numbers shining everywhere.
5. The Land of <u>Ignorance</u>—a gray, gloomy place full of cliffs and caves, with frightening faces. Different levels and heights should be suggested through one or two platforms or risers, with a set of stairs that lead to the castle in the air.

Vocabulary Development: **ignorance** (igʹ ner ens) *n.* lack of knowledge, education, or experience

Scene i

[*The stage is completely dark and silent. Suddenly the sound of someone winding an alarm clock is heard, and after that, the sound of loud ticking is heard.*]

[*LIGHTS UP on the* CLOCK, *a huge alarm clock. The* CLOCK *reads 4:00. The lighting should make it appear that the* CLOCK *is suspended in mid-air (if possible). The* CLOCK *ticks for 30 seconds.*]

CLOCK. See that! Half a minute gone by. Seems like a long time when you're waiting for something to happen, doesn't it? Funny thing is, time can pass very slowly or very fast, and sometimes even both at once. The time now? Oh, a little after four, but what that means should depend on you. Too often, we do something simply because time tells us to. Time for school, time for bed, whoops, 12:00, time to be hungry. It can get a little silly, don't you think? Time is important, but it's what you do with it that makes it so. So my advice to you is to use it. Keep your eyes open and your ears perked. Otherwise it will pass before you know it, and you'll certainly have missed something!

Things have a habit of doing that, you know. Being here one minute and gone the next.
In the twinkling of an eye.

In a jiffy.

In a flash!

I know a girl who yawned and missed a whole summer vacation. And what about that caveman who took a nap one afternoon, and woke up to find himself completely alone. You see, while he was sleeping, someone had invented the wheel and everyone had moved to the suburbs. And then of course, there is Milo. [*LIGHTS UP to reveal* MILO'S *Bedroom. The* CLOCK *appears to be on a shelf in the room of a young boy—a room filled with books, toys, games, maps, papers, pencils, a bed, a desk. There is a dartboard with numbers and the face of the* MATHEMAGICIAN, *a bedspread made from* KING AZAZ'S *cloak, a kite looking like the* SPELLING BEE, *a punching bag with the* HUMBUG'S *face, as well as records, a television, a toy car, and a large box that is wrapped and has an envelope taped to the top. The sound of FOOTSTEPS is heard, and then enter* MILO *dejectedly. He throws down his books and coat, flops into a chair, and sighs loudly.*] Who never knows what to do with himself—not just sometimes, but always. When he's in school, he wants to be out, and when he's out, he wants to be in. [*During the following speech,* MILO *examines the various toys, tools, and other possessions in the room, trying them out and rejecting*

◆ Stop to Reflect

Clock says that "Time is important, but it's what you do with it that makes it so." Do you agree with this statement? Why or why not?

◆ Literary Analysis

Mark the Text

What **setting** do you see when the lights go on in the bracketed text? Circle at least three details in the set.

◆ Reading Check

What is wrong with Milo?

them.] Wherever he is, he wants to be somewhere else—and when he gets there, so what. Everything is too much trouble or a waste of time. Books—he's already read them. Games—boring. T.V.—dumb. So what's left? Another long, boring afternoon. Unless he bothers to notice a very large package that happened to arrive today.

MILO. [*Suddenly notices the package. He drags himself over to it, and disinterestedly reads the label.*] "For Milo, who has plenty of time." Well, that's true. [*Sighs and looks at it.*] No. [*Walks away.*] Well . . . [*Comes back. Rips open envelope and reads.*]

A VOICE. "One genuine turnpike tollbooth, easily assembled at home for use by those who have never traveled in lands beyond."

MILO. Beyond what? [*Continues reading.*]

A VOICE. "This package contains the following items:" [MILO *pulls the items out of the box and sets them up as they are mentioned.*] "One (1) genuine turnpike tollbooth to be erected according to directions. Three (3) precautionary signs to be used in a precautionary fashion. Assorted coins for paying tolls. One (1) map, strictly up to date, showing how to get from here to there. One (1) book of rules and traffic regulations which may not be bent or broken. Warning! Results are not guaranteed. If not perfectly satisfied, your wasted time will be refunded."

MILO. [*Skeptically.*] Come off it, who do you think you're kidding? [*Walks around and examines tollbooth.*] What am I supposed to do with this? [*The ticking of the* CLOCK *grows loud and impatient.*] Well . . . what else do I have to do. [MILO *gets into his toy car and drives up to the first sign.*]

VOICE. "HAVE YOUR DESTINATION IN MIND."

MILO. [*Pulls out the map.*] Now, let's see. That's funny. I never heard of any of these places. Well, it doesn't matter anyway. Dictionopolis. That's a weird name. I might as well go there. [*Begins to move, following map. Drives off.*]

CLOCK. See what I mean? You never know how things are going to get started. But when you're bored, what you need more than anything is a rude awakening.

[*The ALARM goes off very loudly as the stage darkens. The sound of the alarm is transformed into the honking of a car horn, and is then joined by the blasts, bleeps, roars and growls of heavy highway traffic When the lights come up,* MILO'S *bedroom is gone and we see a lonely road in the middle of nowhere.*]

◆ **Reading Check**

What is in the package Milo opens?

____

____

____

____

____

____

____

◆ **Reading Strategy**

To **summarize** is to restate key ideas and events in your own words. Summarize what has happened in this scene so far by listing three key events.

1. ______________________________

____

____

2. ______________________________

____

____

3. ______________________________

____

____

Vocabulary Development: precautionary (prē kô´ shən er´ ē) *adj.* taking care beforehand to prevent danger

Scene ii The Road to Dictionopolis

[*ENTER* MILO *in his car.*]

MILO. This is weird! I don't recognize any of this scenery at all. [*A SIGN is held up before* MILO, *startling him.*] Huh? [*Reads.*] WELCOME TO EXPECTATIONS. INFORMATION, PREDICTIONS AND ADVICE CHEERFULLY OFFERED. PARK HERE AND BLOW HORN. [MILO *blows horn.*]

WHETHER MAN. [*A little man wearing a long coat and carrying an umbrella pops up from behind the sign that he was holding. He speaks very fast and excitedly.*] My, my, my, my, my, welcome, welcome, welcome, welcome to the Land of Expectations, Expectations, Expectations! We don't get many travelers these days; we certainly don't get many travelers. Now what can I do for you? I'm the Whether Man.

MILO. [*Referring to map.*] Uh . . . is this the right road to Dictionopolis?

WHETHER MAN. Well now, well now, well now, I don't know of any *wrong* road to Dictionopolis, so if this road goes to Dictionopolis at all, it must be the right road, and if it doesn't, it must be the right road to somewhere else, because there are no wrong roads to anywhere. Do you think it will rain?

MILO. I thought you were the Weather Man.

WHETHER MAN. Oh, no, I'm the Whether Man, not the weather man. [*Pulls out a SIGN or opens a FLAP of his coat, which reads: "WHETHER."*] After all, it's more important to know whether there will be weather than what the weather will be.

MILO. What kind of place is Expectations?

WHETHER MAN. Good question, good question! Expectations is the place you must always go to before you get to where you are going. Of course, some people never go beyond Expectations, but my job is to hurry them along whether they like it or not. Now what else can I do for you? [*Opens his umbrella.*]

MILO. I think I can find my own way.

WHETHER MAN. Splendid, splendid, splendid! Whether or not you find your own way, you're bound to find some way. If you happen to find my way, please return it. I lost it years ago. I imagine by now it must be quite rusty. You did say it was going to rain, didn't you? [*Escorts* MILO *to the car under the open umbrella.*] I'm glad you made your own decision. I do so hate to make up my mind about anything, whether it's good or bad, up or down, rain or shine. Expect everything, I always say, and the unexpected never happens. Goodbye, goodbye, goodbye, good . . .

◆ Literary Analysis

Why does the **set** change for scene ii?

◆ Literary Analysis

Mark the Text

The word *whether* is used to show that there is a choice between things. Describe the **character** of the Whether Man. Underline dialogue that supports your description.

◆ Reading Check

Expectation is something you look forward to or anticipate. In the bracketed text, what does the Whether Man mean when he says that "some people never go beyond Expectations."

◆ **Literary Analysis**

The word *lethargy* means "a great lack of energy; sluggishness." Based on this definition and on details from the play, why is *Lethargarians* a good name for the **characters** in the Doldrums?

◆ **Reading Check**

What are the doldrums?

◆ **Stop to Reflect**

What suggestions would you have for someone who is stuck in the doldrums?

◆ **Reading Check**

Why does Milo get stuck in the Doldrums?

[A loud CLAP of THUNDER is heard.] Oh dear! *[He looks up at the sky, puts out his hand to feel for rain, and RUNS AWAY.* MILO *watches puzzledly and drives on.]*

MILO. I'd better get out of Expectations, but fast. Talking to a guy like that all day would get me nowhere for sure. *[He tries to speed up, but finds instead that he is moving slower and slower.]* Oh, oh, now what? *[He can barely move. Behind* MILO, *the* LETHARGARIANS *begin to enter from all parts of the stage. They are dressed to blend in with the scenery and carry small pillows that look like rocks. Whenever they fall asleep, they rest on the pillows.]* Now I really am getting nowhere. I hope I didn't take a wrong turn. *[The car stops. He tries to start it. It won't move. He gets out and begins to tinker with it.]* I wonder where I am.

LETHARGARIAN 1. You're . . . in . . . the . . . Dol . . . drums . . . [MILO *looks around.]*

LETHARGARIAN 2. Yes . . . the . . . Dol . . . drums . . . *[A YAWN is heard.]*

MILO. *[Yelling.]* WHAT ARE THE DOLDRUMS?

LETHARGARIAN 3. The Doldrums, my friend, are where nothing ever happens and nothing ever changes. *[Parts of the Scenery stand up or Six People come out of the scenery colored in the same colors of the trees or the road. They move very slowly and as soon as they move, they stop to rest again.]* Allow me to introduce all of us. We are the Lethargarians at your service.

MILO. *[Uncertainly.]* Very pleased to meet you. I think I'm lost. Can you help me?

LETHARGARIAN 4. Don't say think. *[He yawns.]* It's against the law.

LETHARGARIAN 1. No one's allowed to think in the Doldrums. *[He falls asleep.]*

LETHARGARIAN 2. Don't you have a rule book? It's local ordinance 175389-J. *[He falls asleep.]*

MILO. *[Pulls out rule book and reads.]* Ordinance 175389-J: "It shall be unlawful, illegal and unethical to think, think of thinking, surmise, presume, reason, meditate or speculate while in the Doldrums. Anyone breaking this law shall be severely punished." That's a ridiculous law! Everybody thinks.

ALL THE LETHARGARIANS. We don't!

LETHARGARIAN 2. And most of the time, you don't, that's why you're here. You weren't thinking and you weren't paying attention either. People who don't pay attention often get stuck in the Doldrums. Face it, most of the time, you're just like us. *[Falls, snoring, to the ground.* MILO *laughs.]*

LETHARGARIAN 5. Stop that at once. Laughing is against the law. Don't you have a rule book? It's local ordinance 574381-W.

MILO. [*Opens rule book and reads.*] "In the Doldrums, laughter is frowned upon and smiling is permitted only on alternate Thursdays." Well, if you can't laugh or think, what can you do?

LETHARGARIAN 6. Anything as long as it's nothing, and everything as long as it isn't anything. There's lots to do. We have a very busy schedule . . .

LETHARGARIAN 1. At 8:00 we get up and then we spend from 8 to 9 daydreaming.

LETHARGARIAN 2. From 9:00 to 9:30 we take our early mid-morning nap . . .

LETHARGARIAN 3. From 9:30 to 10:30 we dawdle and delay . . .

LETHARGARIAN 4. From 10:30 to 11:30 we take our late early morning nap . . .

LETHARGARIAN 5. From 11:30 to 12:00 we bide our time and then we eat our lunch.

LETHARGARIAN 6. From 1:00 to 2:00 we linger and loiter . . .

LETHARGARIAN 1. From 2:00 to 2:30 we take our early afternoon nap . . .

LETHARGARIAN 2. From 2:30 to 3:30 we put off for tomorrow what we could have done today . . .

LETHARGARIAN 3. From 3:30 to 4:00 we take our early late afternoon nap . . .

LETHARGARIAN 4. From 4:00 to 5:00 we loaf and lounge until dinner . . .

LETHARGARIAN 5. From 6:00 to 7:00 we dillydally . . .

LETHARGARIAN 6. From 7:00 to 8:00 we take our early evening nap and then for an hour before we go to bed, we waste time.

LETHARGARIAN 1. [*Yawning.*] You see, it's really quite strenuous doing nothing all day long, and so once a week, we take a holiday and go nowhere.

LETHARGARIAN 5. Which is just where we were going when you came along. Would you care to join us?

MILO. [*Yawning.*] That's where I seem to be going, anyway. [*Stretching.*] Tell me, does everyone here do nothing?

LETHARGARIAN 3. Everyone but the terrible watchdog. He's always sniffing around to see that nobody wastes time. A most unpleasant character.

MILO. The Watchdog?

LETHARGARIAN 6. THE WATCHDOG!

ALL THE LETHARGARIANS. [*Yelling at once.*] RUN! WAKE UP!

◆ **Reading Strategy**

Summarize what is not allowed in the Doldrums? Include at least two rules.

1. ______________________

____

____

2. ______________________

____

____

◆ **Reading Strategy**

In one sentence, **summarize** what Lethargarians do each day.

____

____

____

____

____

____

◆ **Reading Check**

What does Watchdog do?

____

____

____

Why do the Lethargarians not like Watchdog?

____

____

____

◆ Reading Check

Why won't Watchdog help Milo get out of the Doldrums?

◆ Stop to Reflect

How do you feel when you are concentrating on something that you are really interested in?

Does time pass slowly or quickly when you are concentrating? Explain.

◆ Reading Check

How does Milo get out of the Doldrums?

RUN! HERE HE COMES! THE WATCHDOG! [*They all run off and ENTER a large dog with the head, feet, and tail of a dog, and the body of a clock, having the same face as the character* THE CLOCK.]

WATCHDOG. What are you doing here?

MILO. Nothing much. Just killing time. You see . . .

WATCHDOG. KILLING TIME! [*His ALARM RINGS in fury.*] It's bad enough wasting time without killing it. What are you doing in the Doldrums, anyway? Don't you have anywhere to go?

MILO. I think I was on my way to Dictionopolis when I got stuck here. Can you help me?

WATCHDOG. Help you! You've got to help yourself. I suppose you know why you got stuck.

MILO. I guess I just wasn't thinking.

WATCHDOG. Precisely. Now you're on your way.

MILO. I am?

WATCHDOG. Of course. Since you got here by not thinking, it seems reasonable that in order to get out, you must *start* thinking. Do you mind if I get in? I love automobile rides. [*He gets in. They wait.*] Well?

MILO. All right. I'll try. [*Screws up his face and thinks.*] Are we moving?

WATCHDOG. Not yet. Think harder.

MILO. I'm thinking as hard as I can.

WATCHDOG. Well, think just a little harder than that. Come on, you can do it.

MILO. All right, all right. . . . I'm thinking of all the planets in the solar system, and why water expands when it turns to ice, and all the words that begin with "q," and . . . [*The wheels begin to move.*] We're moving! We're moving!

WATCHDOG. Keep thinking.

MILO. [*Thinking.*] How a steam engine works and how to bake a pie and the difference between Fahrenheit and Centigrade . . .

WATCHDOG. Dictionopolis, here we come.

MILO. Hey, Watchdog, are you coming along?

TOCK. You can call me Tock, and keep your eyes on the road.

MILO. What kind of place is Dictionopolis, anyway?

TOCK. It's where all the words in the world come from. It used to be a marvelous place, but ever since Rhyme and Reason left, it hasn't been the same.

MILO. Rhyme and Reason?

TOCK. The two princesses. They used to settle all the arguments between their two brothers who rule over the Land of Wisdom. You see, Azaz is the king of Dictionopolis and the Mathemagician is the king of Digitopolis and they almost never see eye to eye on anything. It was the job of the Princesses Sweet Rhyme and Pure Reason to solve the differences between the two kings, and they always did so well that both sides usually went home feeling very satisfied. But then, one day, the kings had an argument to end all arguments. . . .

[*The LIGHTS DIM on* TOCK *and* MILO, *and come up on* KING AZAZ OF DICTIONOPOLIS *on another part of the stage.* AZAZ *has a great stomach, a gray beard reaching to his waist, a small crown and a long robe with the letters of the alphabet written all over it.*]

AZAZ. Of course, I'll abide by the decision of Rhyme and Reason, though I have no doubt as to what it will be. They will choose *words*, of course. Everyone knows that words are more important than numbers any day of the week.

[*The* MATHEMAGICIAN *appears opposite* AZAZ. *The* MATHEMAGICIAN *wears a long flowing robe covered entirely with complex mathematical equations, and a tall pointed hat. He carries a long staff with a pencil point at one end and a large rubber eraser at the other.*]

MATHEMAGICIAN. That's what you think, Azaz. People wouldn't even know what day of the week it is without *numbers*. Haven't you ever looked at a calendar? Face it, Azaz. It's numbers that count.

AZAZ. Don't be ridiculous. [*To audience, as if leading a cheer.*] Let's hear it for WORDS!

MATHEMAGICIAN. [*To audience, in the same manner.*] Cast your vote for NUMBERS!

AZAZ. A, B, C's!

MATHEMAGICIAN. 1, 2, 3's! [*A FANFARE is heard.*]

AZAZ AND MATHEMAGICIAN. [*To each other.*] Quiet! Rhyme and Reason are about to announce their decision.

[RHYME *and* REASON *appear.*]

RHYME. Ladies and gentlemen, letters and numerals, fractions and punctuation marks—may we have your attention, please. After careful consideration of the problem set before us by King Azaz of Dictionopolis [AZAZ *bows.*] and the Mathemagician of Digitopolis [MATHEMAGICIAN *raises his hands in a victory salute.*] we have come to the following conclusion:

REASON. Words and numbers are of equal value, for in the cloak of knowledge, one is the warp and the other is the woof.

RHYME. It is no more important to count the sands than it is to name the stars.

◆ **Reading Strategy**

Summarize the role of the princesses Rhyme and Reason.

◆ **Literary Analysis**

What do the **stage directions** in the bracketed text tell you about lights?

◆ **Reading Check**

Mark the Text

Circle the words that are in italics in the underlined passages. Why do you think the writer put these words in italics?

◆ **Literary Analysis**

What is the argument between the **characters** Azaz and Mathemagician?

◆ Reading Check

Why do Azaz and Mathemagician banish Rhyme and Reason rather than accepting their ruling?

◆ Reading Strategy

The scene with the dim lights was a flashback, or an interruption in the action in order to portray an earlier episode. **Summarize** the main events in the flashback.

◆ Reading Check

Explain why it would be difficult to rescue Rhyme and Reason.

RHYME AND REASON. Therefore, let both kingdoms, Dictionopolis and Digitopolis, live in peace.

[The sound of CHEERING is heard.]

AZAZ. Boo! is what I say. Boo and Bah and Hiss!

MATHEMAGICIAN. What good are these girls if they can't even settle an argument in anyone's favor? I think I have come to a decision of my own.

AZAZ. So have I.

AZAZ AND MATHEMAGICIAN. [*To the* PRINCESSES.] You are hereby banished from this land to the Castle-in-the-Air. [*To each other.*] And as for you, KEEP OUT OF MY WAY! [*They stalk off in opposite directions.*]

[During this time, the set has been changed to the Market Square of Dictionopolis. LIGHTS come UP on the deserted square.]

TOCK. And ever since then, there has been neither Rhyme nor Reason in this kingdom. Words are misused and numbers are mismanaged. The argument between the two kings has divided everyone and the real value of both words and numbers has been forgotten. What a waste!

MILO. Why doesn't somebody rescue the Princesses and set everything straight again?

TOCK. That is easier said than done. The Castle-in-the-Air is very far from here, and the one path which leads to it is guarded by ferocious demons. But hold on, here we are. [*A Man appears, carrying a Gate and a small Tollbooth.*]

GATEKEEPER. AHHHHREMMMM! This is Dictionopolis, a happy kingdom, advantageously located in the foothills of Confusion and caressed by gentle breezes from the Sea of Knowledge. Today, by royal proclamation, is Market Day. Have you come to buy or sell?

MILO. I beg your pardon?

GATEKEEPER. Buy or sell, buy or sell. Which is it? You must have come here for a reason.

MILO. Well, I . . .

GATEKEEPER. Come now, if you don't have a reason, you must at least have an explanation or certainly an excuse.

MILO. [*Meekly.*] Uh . . . no.

GATEKEEPER. [*Shaking his head.*] Very serious. You can't get in without a reason. [*Thoughtfully.*] Wait a minute. Maybe I have an old one you can use. [*Pulls out an old suitcase from the tollbooth and rummages through it.*] No . . . no . . . no . . . this won't do . . . hmmm . . .

MILO. [*To* TOCK.] What's he looking for? [TOCK *shrugs.*]

GATEKEEPER. Ah! This is fine. [*Pulls out a Medallion on a chain. Engraved in the Medallion is: "WHY NOT?"*] Why not. That's a good reason for almost anything . . . a bit used, perhaps, but still quite serviceable. There you are, sir. Now I can truly say: Welcome to Dictionopolis.

[*He opens the Gate and walks off.* CITIZENS *and* MERCHANTS *appear on all levels of the stage, and* MILO *and* TOCK *find themselves in the middle of a noisy marketplace. As some people buy and sell their wares, others hang a banner which reads: WELCOME TO THE WORD MARKET.*]

MILO. Tock! Look!

MERCHANT 1. Hey-ya, hey-ya, hey-ya, step right up and take your pick. Juicy tempting words for sale. Get your fresh-picked "ifs" "and's" and "but's!" Just take a look at these nice ripe "where's" and "when's."

MERCHANT 2. Step right up, step right up, fancy, best-quality words here for sale. Enrich your vocabulary and expand your speech with such elegant items as "quagmire," "flabbergast," or "upholstery."

MERCHANT 3. Words by the bag, buy them over here. Words by the bag for the more talkative customer. A pound of "happy's" at a very reasonable price . . . very useful for "Happy Birthday," "Happy New Year," "happy days," or "happy-go-lucky." Or how about a package of "good's," always handy for "good morning," "good afternoon," "good evening," and "goodbye."

MILO. I can't believe it. Did you ever see so many words?

TOCK. They're fine if you have something to say. [*They come to a Do-It-Yourself Bin.*]

MILO. [*To* MERCHANT 4 *at the bin.*] Excuse me, but what are these?

MERCHANT 4. These are for people who like to make up their own words. You can pick any assortment you like or buy a special box complete with all the letters and a book of instructions. Here, taste an "A." They're very good. [*He pops one into* MILO*'s mouth.*]

MILO. [*Tastes it hesitantly.*] It's sweet! [*He eats it.*]

MERCHANT 4. I knew you'd like it. "A" is one of our best-sellers. All of them aren't that good, you know. The "Z," for instance—very dry and sawdusty. And the "X"? Tastes like a trunkful of stale air. But most of the others aren't bad at all. Here, try the "I."

MILO. [*Tasting.*] Cool! It tastes icy.

MERCHANT 4. [*To* TOCK.] How about the "C" for you? It's as crunchy as a bone. Most people are just too lazy to make their own words, but take it from me, not only is it more

◆ Literary Analysis

List two details that you learn about setting from the **stage directions** in the bracketed text.

1. ______________________________

____

2. ______________________________

____

◆ Reading Strategy

Summarize what happens at the Word Market.

____

____

____

____

____

Mark the Text

Underline at least three examples of things the merchants sell.

◆ Stop to Reflect

Choose a letter that has not been mentioned, and describe how you think it would taste.

____

____

____

____

◆ Reading Check

In what way is Spelling Bee like his name?

◆ Literary Analysis

The stage directions suggest that Milo asks the audience for assistance. What might be the purpose of including the audience in the **drama**?

◆ Literary Analysis

Why is *Humbug* a good name for the **character** Humbug? For a hint, look up *humbug* in a dictionary.

fun, but it's also *de*-lightful, [*Holds up a "D."*] *e*-lating, [*Holds up an "E."*] and extremely *u*seful! [*Holds up a "U."*]

MILO. But isn't it difficult? I'm not very good at making words.

[*The* SPELLING BEE, *a large colorful bee, comes up from behind.*]

SPELLING BEE. Perhaps I can be of some assistance . . . a-s-s-i-s-t-a-n-c-e. [*The Three turn around and see him.*] Don't be alarmed . . . a-l-a-r-m-e-d. I am the Spelling Bee. I can spell anything. Anything. A-n-y-t-h-i-n-g. Try me. Try me.

MILO. [*Backing off,* TOCK *on his guard.*] Can you spell goodbye?

SPELLING BEE. Perhaps you are under the misapprehension . . . m-i-s-a-p-p-r-e-h-e-n-s-i-o-n that I am dangerous. Let me assure you that I am quite peaceful. Now, think of the most difficult word you can, and I'll spell it.

MILO. Uh . . . o.k. [*At this point,* MILO *may turn to the audience and ask them to help him choose a word or he may think of one on his own.*] How about . . . "Curiosity"?

SPELLING BEE. [*Winking.*] Let's see now . . . uh . . . how much time do I have?

MILO. Just ten seconds. Count them off, Tock.

SPELLING BEE. [*As* TOCK *counts.*] Oh dear, oh dear. [*Just at the last moment, quickly.*] C-u-r-i-o-s-i-t-y.

MERCHANT 4. Correct! [ALL *Cheer.*]

MILO. Can you spell anything?

SPELLING BEE. [*Proudly.*] Just about. You see, years ago, I was an ordinary bee minding my own business, smelling flowers all day, occasionally picking up part-time work in people's bonnets. Then one day, I realized that I'd never amount to anything without an education, so I decided that . . .

HUMBUG. [*Coming up in a booming voice.*] BALDERDASH! [*He wears a lavish coat, striped pants, checked vest, spats and a derby hat.*] Let me repeat . . . BALDERDASH! [*Swings his cane and clicks his heels in the air.*] Well, well, what have we here? Isn't someone going to introduce me to the little boy?

SPELLING BEE. [*Disdainfully.*] This is the Humbug. You can't trust a word he says.

HUMBUG. NONSENSE! Everyone can trust a Humbug. As I was saying to the king just the other day . . .

SPELLING BEE. You've never met the king. [*To* MILO.] Don't believe a thing he tells you.

Vocabulary Development: misapprehension (mis′ ap rē hen′ shən) *n.* misunderstanding

HUMBUG. Bosh, my boy, pure bosh. The Humbugs are an old and noble family, honorable to the core. Why, we fought in the Crusades with Richard the Lionhearted, crossed the Atlantic with Columbus, blazed trails with the pioneers. History is full of Humbugs.

SPELLING BEE. A very pretty speech . . . s-p-e-e-c-h. Now, why don't you go away? I was just advising the lad of the importance of proper spelling.

HUMBUG. BAH! As soon as you learn to spell one word, they ask you to spell another. You can never catch up, so why bother? [*Puts his arm around* MILO.] Take my advice, boy, and forget about it. As my great-great-great-grandfather George Washington Humbug used to say. . .

SPELLING BEE. You, sir, are an impostor i-m-p-o-s-t-o-r who can't even spell his own name!

HUMBUG. What? You dare to doubt my word? The word of a Humbug? The word of a Humbug who has direct access to the ear of a King? And the king shall hear of this, I promise you . . .

VOICE 1. Did someone call for the King?

VOICE 2. Did you mention the monarch?

VOICE 3. Speak of the sovereign?

VOICE 4. Entreat the Emperor?

VOICE 5. Hail his highness?

[*Five tall, thin gentlemen regally dressed in silks and satins, plumed hats and buckled shoes appear as they speak.*]

MILO. Who are they?

SPELLING BEE. The King's advisors. Or in more formal terms, his cabinet.

MINISTER 1. Greetings!

MINISTER 2. Salutations!

MINISTER 3. Welcome!

MINISTER 4. Good Afternoon!

MINISTER 5. Hello!

MILO. Uh . . . Hi.

[*All the* MINISTERS, *from here on called by their numbers, unfold their scrolls and read in order.*]

MINISTER 1. By the order of Azaz the Unabridged . . .

MINISTER 2. King of Dictionopolis . . .

MINISTER 3. Monarch of letters . . .

MINISTER 4. Emperor of phrases, sentences, and miscellaneous figures of speech . . .

MINISTER 5. We offer you the hospitality of our kingdom . . .

MINISTER 1. Country

◆ Literary Analysis

What does the **dialogue,** "or conversation," among the ministers tell you about the importance of words in Dictionopolis?

____

____

____

____

____

◆ Stop to Reflect

What do the words spoken by the five ministers in the bracketed text have in common?

____

____

____

____

____

MINISTER 2. Nation

MINISTER 3. State

MINISTER 4. Commonwealth

MINISTER 5. Realm

MINISTER 1. Empire

MINISTER 2. Palatinate

MINISTER 3. Principality.

MILO. Do all those words mean the same thing?

MINISTER 1. Of course.

MINISTER 2. Certainly.

MINISTER 3. Precisely.

MINISTER 4. Exactly.

MINISTER 5. Yes.

MILO. Then why don't you use just one? Wouldn't that make a lot more sense?

MINISTER 1. Nonsense!

MINISTER 2. Ridiculous!

MINISTER 3. Fantastic!

MINISTER 4. Absurd!

MINISTER 5. Bosh!

MINISTER 1. We're not interested in making sense. It's not our job.

MINISTER 2. Besides, one word is as good as another, so why not use them all?

MINISTER 3. Then you don't have to choose which one is right.

MINISTER 4. Besides, if one is right, then ten are ten times as right.

MINISTER 5. Obviously, you don't know who we are. [*Each presents himself and* MILO *acknowledges the introduction.*]

MINISTER 1. The Duke of Definition.

MINISTER 2. The Minister of Meaning.

MINISTER 3. The Earl of Essence.

MINISTER 4. The Count of Connotation.

MINISTER 5. The Undersecretary of Understanding.

ALL FIVE. And we have come to invite you to the Royal Banquet.

SPELLING BEE. The banquet! That's quite an honor, my boy. A real h-o-n-o-r.

HUMBUG. DON'T BE RIDICULOUS! Everybody goes to the Royal Banquet these days.

SPELLING BEE. [*To the* HUMBUG.] True, everybody does go. But some people are invited and others simply push their way in where they aren't wanted.

◆ Reading Check

What characters has Milo met so far in Dictionopolis?

____

____

____

____

____

____

____

____

____

____

____

____

____

____

____

◆ Reading Strategy

Summarize what the ministers have said to Milo so far.

____

____

____

____

____

HUMBUG. HOW DARE YOU? You buzzing little upstart, I'll show you who's not wanted . . . [*Raises his cane threateningly.*]

SPELLING BEE. You just watch it! I'm warning w-a-r-n-i-n-g you! [*At that moment, an ear-shattering blast of TRUMPETS, entirely off-key, is heard, and a* PAGE *appears.*]

PAGE. King Azaz the Unabridged is about to begin the Royal Banquet. All guests who do not appear promptly at the table will automatically lose their place. [*A huge Table is carried out with* KING AZAZ *sitting in a large chair, carried out at the head of the table.*]

AZAZ. Places. Everyone take your places. [*All the characters, including the* HUMBUG *and the* SPELLING BEE, *who forget their quarrel, rush to take their places at the table.* MILO *and* TOCK *sit near the* KING. AZAZ *looks at* MILO.] And just who is this?

MILO. Your Highness, my name is Milo and this is Tock. Thank you very much for inviting us to your banquet, and I think your palace is beautiful!

MINISTER 1. Exquisite.

MINISTER 2. Lovely.

MINISTER 3. Handsome.

MINISTER 4. Pretty.

MINISTER 5. Charming.

AZAZ. SILENCE! Now tell me, young man, what can you do to entertain us? Sing songs? Tell stories? Juggle plates? Do tumbling tricks? Which is it?

MILO. I can't do any of those things.

AZAZ. What an ordinary little boy. Can't you do anything at all?

MILO. Well . . . I can count to a thousand.

AZAZ. AARGH, numbers! Never mention numbers here. Only use them when we absolutely have to. Now, why don't we change the subject and have some dinner? Since you are the guest of honor, you may pick the menu.

MILO. Me? Well, uh . . . I'm not very hungry. Can we just have a light snack?

AZAZ. A light snack it shall be!

[AZAZ *claps his hands. Waiters rush in with covered trays. When they are uncovered, Shafts of Light pour out. The light may be created through the use of battery-operated flashlights which are secured in the trays and covered with a false bottom. The Guests help themselves.*]

HUMBUG. Not a very substantial meal. Maybe you can suggest something a little more filling.

MILO. Well, in that case, I think we ought to have a square meal . . .

◆ **Literary Analysis**

What do you learn in the underlined stage directions? How do the directions establish the next **setting** for the drama?

◆ **Reading Check**

What does King Azaz forbid Milo to talk about? Why?

◆ **Literary Analysis**

In the bracketed **stage directions,** how do you know that the light snack will be something special?

◆ Reading Strategy

Summarize what has happened at the banquet so far.

____

____

____

____

____

____

____

____

____

____

◆ Reading Check

The common expression "eat my words" means "to admit I was wrong." How is this meaning different from Milo's meaning in the underlined passage?

____

____

____

____

____

◆ Reading Check

What is the meaning of a "half-baked idea"? Use the two underlined examples to help you figure it out.

____

____

____

____

AZAZ. [*Claps his hands.*] A square meal it is! [*Waiters serve trays of Colored Squares of all sizes. People serve themselves.*]

SPELLING BEE. These are awful. [HUMBUG *coughs and all the Guests do not care for the food.*]

AZAZ. [*Claps his hands and the trays are removed.*] Time for speeches. [*To* MILO.] You first.

MILO. [*Hesitantly.*] Your Majesty, ladies and gentlemen, I would like to take this opportunity to say that . . .

AZAZ. That's quite enough. Mustn't talk all day.

MILO. But I just started to . . .

AZAZ. NEXT!

HUMBUG. [*Quickly.*] Roast turkey, mashed potatoes, vanilla ice cream.

SPELLING BEE. Hamburgers, corn on the cob, chocolate pudding p-u-d-d-i-n-g. [*Each Guest names two dishes and a dessert.*]

AZAZ. [*The last.*] Pâté de fois gras, soupe a l'oignon, salade endives, fromage et fruits et demi-tasse. [*He claps his hands. Waiters serve each Guest his Words.*] Dig on. [*To* MILO.] Though I can't say I think much of your choice.

MILO. I didn't know I was going to have to eat my words.

AZAZ. Of course, of course, everybody here does. Your speech should have been in better taste.

MINISTER 1. Here, try some somersault. It improves the flavor.

MINISTER 2. Have a rigamarole. [*Offers bread-basket.*]

MINISTER 3. Or a ragamuffin.

MINISTER 4. Perhaps you'd care for a synonym bun.

MINISTER 5. Why not wait for your just desserts?

AZAZ. Ah yes, the dessert. We're having a special treat today . . . freshly made at the half-bakery.

MILO. The half-bakery?

AZAZ. Of course, the half-bakery! Where do you think half-baked ideas come from? Now, please don't interrupt. By royal command, the pastry chefs have . . .

MILO. What's a half-baked idea?

[AZAZ *gives up the idea of speaking as a cart is wheeled in and the Guests help themselves.*]

HUMBUG. They're very tasty, but they don't always agree with you. Here's a good one. [HUMBUG *hands one to* MILO.]

MILO. [*Reads.*] "The earth is flat."

SPELLING BEE. People swallowed that one for years. [*Picks up one and reads.*] "The moon is made of green cheese." Now, there's a half-baked idea.

[*Everyone chooses one and eats. They include: "It Never Rains But Pours," "Night Air Is Bad Air," "Everything Happens for the Best," "Coffee Stunts Your Growth."*]

AZAZ. And now for a few closing words. Attention! Let me have your attention! [*Everyone leaps up and Exits, except for* MILO, TOCK, *and the* HUMBUG.] Loyal subjects and friends, once again on this gala occasion, we have . . .

MILO. Excuse me, but everybody left.

AZAZ. [*Sadly.*] I was hoping no one would notice. It happens every time.

HUMBUG. They're gone to dinner, and as soon as I finish this last bite, I shall join them.

MILO. That's ridiculous. How can they eat dinner right after a banquet?

AZAZ. SCANDALOUS! We'll put a stop to it at once. From now on, by royal command, everyone must eat dinner before the banquet.

MILO. But that's just as bad.

HUMBUG. Or just as good. Things which are equally bad are also equally good. Try to look at the bright side of things.

MILO. I don't know which side of anything to look at. Everything is so confusing, and all your words only make things worse.

AZAZ. How true. There must be something we can do about it.

HUMBUG. Pass a law.

AZAZ. We have almost as many laws as words.

HUMBUG. Offer a reward. [AZAZ *shakes his head and looks madder at each suggestion.*] Send for help? Drive a bargain? Pull the switch? Lower the boom? Toe the line?

[*As* AZAZ *continues to scowl, the* HUMBUG *loses confidence and finally gives up.*]

MILO. Maybe you should let Rhyme and Reason return.

AZAZ. How nice that would be. Even if they were a bother at times, things always went so well when they were here. But I'm afraid it can't be done.

HUMBUG. Certainly not. Can't be done.

MILO. Why not?

HUMBUG. [*Now siding with* MILO.] Why not, indeed?

AZAZ. Much too difficult.

HUMBUG. Of course, much too difficult.

MILO. You could, if you really wanted to.

HUMBUG. By all means, if you really wanted to, you could.

AZAZ. [*To* HUMBUG.] How?

MILO. [*Also to* HUMBUG.] Yeah, how?

◆ Reading Check

Where do all the guests go after the banquet?

____

____

____

____

____

◆ Literary Analysis

What is the problem that must be solved in the **plot**—the sequence of events—in the drama?

____

____

____

◆ Reading Check

What does Milo suggest to Azaz to solve the problem in Dictionopolis?

____

____

____

____

____

Reading Strategy

Summarize the difficulties in the bracketed text that must be overcome to rescue the princesses. List at least two main ones in your summary.

Reading Check

What gift does King Azaz give Milo for protection on his journey?

HUMBUG. Why . . . uh, it's a simple task for a brave boy with a stout heart, a steadfast dog and a serviceable small automobile.

AZAZ. Go on.

HUMBUG. Well, all that he would have to do is cross the dangerous, unknown countryside between here and Digitopolis, where he would have to persuade the Mathemagician to release the Princesses, which we know to be impossible because the Mathemagician will never agree with Azaz about anything. Once achieving that, it's a simple matter of entering the Mountains of Ignorance from where no one has ever returned alive, an effortless climb up a two thousand foot stairway without railings in a high wind at night to the Castle-in-the-Air. After a pleasant chat with the Princesses, all that remains is a leisurely ride back through those chaotic crags where the frightening fiends have sworn to tear any intruder from limb to limb and devour him down to his belt buckle. And finally after doing all that, a triumphal parade! If, of course, there is anything left to parade . . . followed by hot chocolate and cookies for everyone.

AZAZ. I never realized it would be so simple.

MILO. It sounds dangerous to me.

TOCK. And just who is supposed to make that journey?

AZAZ. A very good question. But there is one far more serious problem.

MILO. What's that?

AZAZ. I'm afraid I can't tell you that until you return.

MILO. But wait a minute, I didn't . . .

AZAZ. Dictionopolis will always be grateful to you, my boy, and your dog. [AZAZ *pats* TOCK *and* MILO.]

TOCK. Now, just one moment, sire . . .

AZAZ. You will face many dangers on your journey, but fear not, for I can give you something for your protection. [AZAZ *gives* MILO *a box.*] In this box are the letters of the alphabet. With them you can form all the words you will ever need to help you overcome the obstacles that may stand in your path. All you must do is use them well and in the right places.

MILO. [*Miserably.*] Thanks a lot.

AZAZ. You will need a guide, of course, and since he knows the obstacles so well, the Humbug has cheerfully volunteered to accompany you.

HUMBUG. Now, see here . . . !

AZAZ. You will find him dependable, brave, resourceful and loyal.

HUMBUG. [*Flattered.*] Oh, your Majesty.

MILO. I'm sure he'll be a great help. [*They approach the car.*]

TOCK. I hope so. It looks like we're going to need it.

[*The lights darken and the* KING *fades from view.*]

AZAZ. Good luck! Drive carefully! [*The three get into the car and begin to move. Suddenly a thunderously loud NOISE is heard. They slow down the car.*]

MILO. What was that?

TOCK. It came from up ahead.

HUMBUG. It's something terrible, I just know it. Oh, no. Something dreadful is going to happen to us. I can feel it in my bones. [*The NOISE is repeated. They all look at each other fearfully as the lights fade.*]

◆ Reading Strategy

Summarize what has happened so far to Milo in Act I. Include the main characters Milo, Tock, Azaz, the Mathemagician, Rhyme, and Reason in your summary. Mention at least three main events.

____

____

____

____

____

____

____

____

____

____

____

____

____

____

____

____

Reader's Response: Which character in this drama would you most like to meet?

____

____

____

Thinking About the Skill: How did identifying the elements of drama help you better understand the play?

____

____

____

Grandpa and the Statue

Arthur Miller

Summary

A soldier is in an army hospital, recovering from his injuries. He stares out of a hospital window and sees the Statue of Liberty. The statue was put up in New York Harbor when he was a boy. He remembers a funny story about his grandfather and the statue. He tells the story to another patient. When the soldier was a boy, people in his grandfather's neighborhood collected money to help build a base for the statue. His grandfather refused to donate a dime. He was sure that the statue would soon be blown over by strong winds. Finally, the boy convinces his grandfather to visit the statue. There, Grandpa reads a welcome poem on a tablet. He is very moved by the words. He feels ashamed that he did not donate the dime, so he places a half-dollar in a crack of the statue's base.

Visual Summary

Monaghan's Story	
Characters	Grandpa Monaghan, Child Monaghan, Sheean, neighborhood friends
Setting	Butler Street, Statue of Liberty
Events	• Grandpa refuses to give a dime. • He convinces others the statue will fall. • He takes his grandson to see the statue. • He realizes the importance of the statue.
Conclusion	• Places a half-dollar in base of the statue.

Grandpa and the Statue

Arthur Miller

In 1865, a French politician suggested building a shared French-American monument celebrating the idea of liberty. A famous newspaper publisher launched a huge campaign in the United States to raise money for the pedestal. Within five months, enough money was collected to build the pedestal.

CHARACTERS

Characters in the present time of the play:

ANNOUNCER

AUGUST

MONAGHAN (*Young Monaghan, a soldier*)

Characters from the past, heard in the flashback scenes which Young Monaghan remembers:

SHEEAN

MONAGHAN (*Grandfather of Young Monaghan*)

CHILD MONAGHAN (*Young Monaghan himself, as a child*)

GEORGE, **CHARLEY**, **JACK**, **MIKE**, **JOE** (*Neighborhood children, Child Monaghan's friends*)

ALF, **GIRL**, **YOUNG MAN** (*Passengers on the Statue of Liberty boat*)

MEGAPHONE VOICE

VETERAN (*Visitor to the statue*)

[*Music: Theme*]

ANNOUNCER. The scene is the fourth floor of a giant army hospital overlooking New York Harbor. A young man sitting in a wheel chair is looking out a window—just looking. After a while another young man in another wheel chair rolls over to him and they both look.

[*Music out*]

AUGUST. You want to play some checkers with me, Monaghan?

MONAGHAN. Not right now.

AUGUST. Okay. [*Slight pause*] You don't want to go feeling blue, Monaghan.

◆ **Reading Warm-up**

What feelings and ideas come to mind as you think of the Statue of Liberty? Consider movies, books, and television.

◆ **Literary Analysis**

Drama takes place through **dialogue**—conversation among characters. *Grandpa and the Statue* was written as a radio play so much of the plot, setting, and characters' thoughts are revealed in the dialogue. How does the announcer in the bracketed text prepare you for the dialogue among the characters?

◆ **Literary Analysis**

In the bracketed text, what does the **dialogue** tell you about the time and setting of the beginning of the play?

Time: ______________________

____

____

Setting: ______________________

____

____

◆ **Reading Strategy**

Some drama includes both **fact and fantasy**. Facts can be proved. Fantasy is made-up. What part of the underlined text is fact? What part is fantasy?

Fact: ______________________

____

____

Fantasy: ______________________

____

____

◆ **Reading Check**

Why was Grandpa called "Mercyless" Monaghan?

____

____

____

____

____

____

MONAGHAN. I'm not blue.

AUGUST. All you do most days is sit here looking out this window.

MONAGHAN. What do you want me to do, jump rope?

AUGUST. No, but what do you get out of it?

MONAGHAN. It's a beautiful view. Some companies make millions of dollars just printing that view on postcards.

AUGUST. Yeh, but nobody keeps looking at a postcard six, seven hours a day.

MONAGHAN. I come from around here, it reminds me of things. My young days.

AUGUST. That's right, you're Brooklyn, aren't you?

MONAGHAN. My house is only about a mile away.

AUGUST. That so. Tell me, are you looking at just the water all the time? I'm curious. I don't get a kick out of this view.

MONAGHAN. There's the Statue of Liberty out there. Don't you see it?

AUGUST. Oh, that's it. Yeh, that's nice to look at.

MONAGHAN. I like it. Reminds me of a lot of laughs.

AUGUST. Laughs? The Statue of Liberty?

MONAGHAN. Yeh, my grandfather. He got all twisted up with the Statue of Liberty.

AUGUST. [*Laughs a little*] That so? What happened?

MONAGHAN. Well. My grandfather was the stingiest man in Brooklyn. "Mercyless" Monaghan, they used to call him. He even used to save umbrella handles.

AUGUST. What for?

MONAGHAN. Just couldn't stand seeing anything go to waste. After a big windstorm there'd be a lot of broken umbrellas laying around in the streets.

AUGUST. Yeh?

MONAGHAN. He'd go around picking them up. In our house the closets were always full of umbrella handles. My grandma used to say that he would go across the Brooklyn Bridge on the trolley just because he could come back on the same nickel. See, if you stayed on the trolley they'd let you come back for the same nickel.

AUGUST. What'd he do, just go over and come back?

MONAGHAN. Yeh, it made him feel good. Savin' money. Two and a half cents.

Vocabulary Development: stingiest (stin′ jē est) *adj.* most unwilling to spend any money

AUGUST. So how'd he get twisted up with the Statue of Liberty?

MONAGHAN. Well, way back in 1887 around there they were living on Butler Street. Butler Street, Brooklyn, practically runs right down to the river. One day he's sitting on the front porch, reading a paper he borrowed from the neighbors, when along comes this man Jack Sheean who lived up the block.

[*Music: Sneak into above speech, then bridge, then out*]

SHEEAN. [*Slight brogue*[1]] A good afternoon to you, Monaghan.

MONAGHAN. [*Grandfather*] How're you, Sheean, how're ya?

SHEEAN. Fair, fair. And how's Mrs. Monaghan these days?

MONAGHAN. Warm. Same as everybody else in summer.

SHEEAN. I've come to talk to you about the fund, Monaghan.

MONAGHAN. What fund is that?

SHEEAN. The Statue of Liberty fund.

MONAGHAN. Oh, that.

SHEEAN. It's time we come to grips with the subject, Monaghan.

MONAGHAN. I'm not interested, Sheean.

SHEEAN. Now hold up on that a minute. Let me tell you the facts. This here Frenchman has gone and built a fine statue of Liberty. It costs who knows how many millions to build. All they're askin' us to do is contribute enough to put up a base for the statue to stand on.

MONAGHAN. I'm not . . . !

SHEEAN. Before you answer me. People all over the whole United States are puttin' in for it. Butler Street is doin' the same. We'd like to hang up a flag on the corner saying—"Butler Street, Brooklyn, is one hundred per cent behind the Statue of Liberty." And Butler Street *is* a hundred per cent subscribed except for you. Now will you give us a dime, Monaghan? One dime and we can put up the flag. Now what do you say to that?

MONAGHAN. I'm not throwin' me good money away for somethin' I don't even know exists.

SHEEAN. Now what do you mean by that?

MONAGHAN. Have you seen this statue?

SHEEAN. No, but it's in a warehouse. And as soon as we get the money to build the pedestal they'll take it and put it

Vocabulary Development: subscribed (səb skrībd′) *adj.* signed up to give money

1. **brogue** (brōg) *n.* Irish accent.

◆ Literary Analysis

What does the **dialogue** tell you about the change in time and setting in the drama?

Time: ______

Setting: ______

◆ Reading Strategy

Identify two **facts** that you learn from the bracketed paragraph.

1. ______

2. ______

◆ Reading Check

For what is Sheean asking Monaghan to contribute money?

______

◆ Literary Analysis

What does the **dialogue** in the bracketed text reveal about Grandpa Monaghan's personality?

◆ Reading Check

Why does Grandpa Monaghan think the Statue of Liberty is broken?

up on that island in the river, and all the boats comin' in from the old country will see it there and it'll raise the hearts of the poor immigrants to see such a fine sight on their first look at this country.

MONAGHAN. And how do I know it's in this here warehouse at all?

SHEEAN. You read your paper, don't you? It's been in all the papers for the past year.

MONAGHAN. Ha, the papers! Last year I read in the paper that they were about to pave Butler Street and take out all the holes. Turn around and look at Butler Street, Mr. Sheean.

SHEEAN. All right. I'll do this: I'll take you to the warehouse and show you the statue. Will you give me a dime then?

MONAGHAN. Well . . . I'm not sayin' I would, and I'm not sayin' I wouldn't. But I'd be more *likely* if I saw the thing large as life, I would.

SHEEAN. [*Peeved*] All right, then. Come along.

[*Music up and down and out*]

[*Footsteps, in a warehouse . . . echo . . . they come to a halt.*]

Now then. Do you see the Statue of Liberty or don't you see it?

MONAGHAN. I see it all right, but it's all broke!

SHEEAN. *Broke!* They brought it from France on a boat. They had to take it apart, didn't they?

MONAGHAN. You got a secondhand statue, that's what you got, and I'm not payin' for new when they've shipped us something that's all smashed to pieces.

SHEEAN. Now just a minute, just a minute. Visualize what I'm about to tell you, Monaghan, get the picture of it. When this statue is put together it's going to stand ten stories high. Could they get a thing ten stories high into a four-story building such as this is? Use your good sense, now Monaghan.

MONAGHAN. What's that over there?

SHEEAN. Where?

MONAGHAN. That tablet there in her hand. What's it say? July Eye Vee (IV) MDCCLXXVI . . . what . . . what's all that?

SHEEAN. That means July 4, 1776. It's in Roman numbers. Very high class.

MONAGHAN. What's the good of it? If they're going to put a sign on her they ought to put it: Welcome All. That's it. Welcome All.

Vocabulary Development: peeved (pēvd) *adj.* bad-tempered or annoyed

SHEEAN. They decided July 4, 1776, and July 4, 1776, it's going to be!

MONAGHAN. All right, then let them get their dime from somebody else!

SHEEAN. Monaghan!

MONAGHAN. No, sir! I'll tell you something. I didn't think there was a statue but there is. She's all broke, it's true, but she's here and maybe they can get her together. But even if they do, will you tell me what sort of a welcome to immigrants it'll be, to have a gigantic thing like that in the middle of the river and in her hand is July Eye Vee MCDVC . . . whatever it is?

SHEEAN. That's the date the country was made!

MONAGHAN. The divil with the date! A man comin' in from the sea wants a place to stay, not a date. When I come from the old country I git off at the dock and there's a feller says to me, "Would you care for a room for the night?" "I would that," I sez, and he sez, "All right then, follow me." He takes me to a rooming house. I no sooner sign me name on the register—which I was able to do even at that time—when I look around and the feller is gone clear away and took my valise[2] in the bargain. A statue anyway can't move off so fast, but if she's going to welcome let her say welcome, not this MCDC. . . .

SHEEAN. All right, then, Monaghan. But all I can say is, you've laid a disgrace on the name of Butler Street. I'll put the dime in for ya.

MONAGHAN. Don't connect me with it! It's a swindle, is all it is. In the first place, it's broke; in the second place, if they do put it up it'll come down with the first high wind that strikes it.

SHEEAN. The engineers say it'll last forever!

MONAGHAN. And I say it'll topple into the river in a high wind! Look at the inside of her. She's all hollow!

SHEEAN. I've heard everything now, Monaghan. Just about everything. Good-bye.

MONAGHAN. What do you mean, good-bye? How am I to get back to Butler Street from here?

SHEEAN. You've got legs to walk.

MONAGHAN. I'll remind you that I come on the trolley.

SHEEAN. And I'll remind you that I paid your fare and I'm not repeating the kindness.

MONAGHAN. Sheean? You've stranded me!

[*Music up and down*]

---

2. **valise** (və lēs′) *n.* small suitcase.

◆ Stop to Reflect

According to Grandpa, what is wrong with the message on the Statue of Liberty?

____

____

____

What message would you put on the Statue of Liberty for newly-arriving immigrants?

____

____

____

____

____

____

◆ Reading Check

Why does Grandpa Monaghan have to walk home to Butler Street?

____

____

____

____

____

____

____

◆ **Literary Analysis**

How does the **dialogue** in the bracketed text bring you back to the present time?

◆ **Reading Check**

What does Grandpa predict will happen to the statue?

◆ **Literary Analysis**

What does the **dialogue** in the bracketed text tell you about the relationship between the boy and his grandfather?

YOUNG MONAGHAN. That was Grandpa. That's why I have to laugh every time I look at the statue now.

AUGUST. Did he ever put the dime in?

YOUNG MONAGHAN. Well—in a way. What happened was this: His daughters got married and finally my mom . . . put *me* out on Butler Street. I got to be pretty attached to Grandpa. He'd even give me an umbrella handle and make a sword out of it for me. Naturally, I wasn't very old before he began working on me about the statue.

[*High wind*]

CHILD MONAGHAN. [*Softly, as though* GRANDPA *is in bed*] Grampa?

MONAGHAN. [*Awakened*] Heh? What are you doin' up?

CHILD MONAGHAN. Ssssh! Listen!

[*Wind rising up and fading. Rising higher and fading*]

MONAGHAN. [*Gleefully*] Aaaaaaaah! Yes, yes. This'll do it, boy. This'll do it! First thing in the morning we'll go down to the docks and I'll bet you me life that Mr. Sheean's statue is smashed down and layin' on the bottom of the bay. Go to sleep now, we'll have a look first thing.

[*Music up and down*]

[*Footsteps*]

CHILD MONAGHAN. If it fell down, all the people will get their dimes back, won't they, Grampa? Slow down, I can't walk so fast.

MONAGHAN. Not only will they get their dimes back, but Mr. Sheean and the whole crew that engineered the collection are going to rot in jail. Now mark my words. Here, now, we'll take a short cut around this shed . . .

[*Footsteps continue a moment, then gradually. . . disappointedly they come to a halt.*]

CHILD MONAGHAN. She's . . . she's still standing, Grampa.

MONAGHAN. She is that. [*Uncomprehending*] I don't understand it. That was a terrible wind last night. Terrible.

CHILD MONAGHAN. Maybe she's weaker though. Heh?

MONAGHAN. Why . . . sure, that must be it. I'll wager she's hangin' by a thread. [*Realizing*] Of course! That's why they put her out there in the water so when she falls down she won't be flattening out a lot of poor innocent people. Hey—feel that?

CHILD MONAGHAN. The wind! It's starting to blow again!

MONAGHAN. Sure, and look at the sky blackening over!

Vocabulary Development: uncomprehending (ən cäm prē hend´ iŋ) *adj.* not understanding

[*Wind rising*]

Feel it comin' up! Take your last look at the statue, boy. If I don't mistake me eyes she's takin' a small list[3] to Jersey already!

[*Music up and down*]

YOUNG MONAGHAN. It was getting embarrassing for me on the block. I kept promising the other kids that when the next wind came the statue would come down. We even had a game. Four or five kids would stand in a semicircle around one kid who was the statue. The statue kid had to stand on his heels and look right in our eyes. Then we'd all take a deep breath and blow in his face. He'd fall down like a stick of wood. They all believed me and Grampa . . . until one day. We were standing around throwing rocks at an old milk can . . .

[*Banging of rocks against milk can*]

GEORGE. [*Kid*] What're you doin'?

CHILD MONAGHAN. What do we look like we're doin'?

GEORGE. I'm going someplace tomorrow.

CHARLEY. [*Kid*] I know, church. Watch out, I'm throwin'.

[*Can being hit*]

GEORGE. I mean after church.

JACK. Where?

GEORGE. My old man's going to take me out on the Statue of Liberty boat.

[*Banging against can abruptly stops.*]

CHILD MONAGHAN. You're not going out on the statue, though, are you?

GEORGE. Sure, that's where we're going.

CHILD MONAGHAN. But you're liable to get killed. Supposing there's a high wind tomorrow?

GEORGE. My old man says that statue couldn't fall down if all the wind in the world and John L. Sullivan[4] hit it at the same time.

CHILD MONAGHAN. Is that so?

GEORGE. Yeh, that's so. My old man says that the only reason your grandfather's saying that it's going to fall down is that he's ashamed he didn't put a dime in for the pedestal.

CHILD MONAGHAN. Is that so?

GEORGE. Yeh, that's so.

CHILD MONAGHAN. Well, you tell your old man that if he gets

---

3. **list** (list) *n.* lean; tilt.
4. **John L. Sullivan** American prizefighter at the time of the play's action.

◆ Stop to Reflect

In 1865, why might people have believed, as Grandpa did, that the Statue of Liberty would fall?

◆ Reading Strategy

Is John L. Sullivan a real person or a made-up character?

◆ Literary Analysis

How does the **dialogue** here show that things between Child Monaghan and his friends have changed?

◆ Literary Analysis

In Child Monaghan's **dialogue** in the bracketed passage, what is he trying to tell Grandpa Monaghan?

killed tomorrow not to come around to my grandfather and say he didn't warn him!

JACK. Hey, George, would your father take me along?

GEORGE. I'll ask him, maybe he—

CHILD MONAGHAN. What, are you crazy, Jack?

MIKE. Ask him if he'd take me too, will ya, George?

CHILD MONAGHAN. Mike, what's the matter with you?

JOE. Me too, George, I'll ask my mother for money.

CHILD MONAGHAN. Joe! Didn't you hear what my grampa said?

JOE. Well . . . I don't really believe that any more.

CHILD MONAGHAN. You don't be . . .

MIKE. Me neither.

JACK. I don't really think your grampa knows what he's talkin' about.

CHILD MONAGHAN. He don't, heh? [*Ready to weep*] Okay . . . Okay. [*Bursting out*] I just hope that wind blows tomorrow, boy! I just hope that wind blows!

[*Music up and down*]

[*Creaking of a rocking chair*]

Grampa . . . ?

MONAGHAN. Huh?

CHILD MONAGHAN. Can you stop rocking for a minute?

[*Rocking stops*]

Can you put down your paper?

[*Rustle of paper*]

I—I read the weather report for tomorrow.

MONAGHAN. The weather report . . .

CHILD MONAGHAN. Yeh. It says fair and cool.

MONAGHAN. What of it?

CHILD MONAGHAN. I was wondering. Supposing you and me we went on a boat tomorrow. You know, I see the water every day when I go down to the docks to play, but I never sat on it. I mean in a boat.

MONAGHAN. Oh. Well, we might take the ferry on the Jersey side. We might do that.

CHILD MONAGHAN. Yeh, but there's nothing to see in Jersey.

MONAGHAN. You can't go to Europe tomorrow.

CHILD MONAGHAN. No, but couldn't we go toward the ocean? Just . . . *toward* it?

MONAGHAN. Toward it. What—what is it on your mind, boy? What is it now?

CHILD MONAGHAN. Well, I . . .

MONAGHAN. Oh, you want to take the Staten Island ferry.

Sure, that's in the direction of the sea.

CHILD MONAGHAN. No, Grampa, not the Staten Island ferry.

MONAGHAN. You don't mean—[*Breaks off*] Boy!

CHILD MONAGHAN. All the kids are going tomorrow with Georgie's old man.

MONAGHAN. You don't believe me any more.

CHILD MONAGHAN. I do, Grampa, but . . .

MONAGHAN. You don't. If you did you'd stay clear of the Statue of Liberty for love of your life!

CHILD MONAGHAN. But, Grampa, when is it going to fall down? All I do is wait and wait.

MONAGHAN. [*With some uncertainty*] You've got to have faith.

CHILD MONAGHAN. But every kid in my class went to see it and now the ones that didn't are going tomorrow. And they all keep talking about it and all I do . . . Well, I can't keep telling them it's a swindle. I—I wish we could see it, Grampa. It don't cost so much to go.

MONAGHAN. As long as you put it that way I'll have to admit I'm a bit curious meself as to how it's managed to stand upright so long. Tell you what I'll do. Barrin' wind, we'll chance it tomorrow!

CHILD MONAGHAN. Oh, Gramp!

MONAGHAN. But! if anyone should ask you where we went you'll say—Staten Island. Are y' on?

CHILD MONAGHAN. Okay, sure. Staten Island.

MONAGHAN. [*Secretively*] We'll take the early boat, then. Mum's the word, now. For if old man Sheean hears that I went out there I'll have no peace from the thief the rest of m' life.

[*Music up and down*]

[*Boat whistles*]

CHILD MONAGHAN. Gee, it's nice ridin' on a boat, ain't it, Grampa?

MONAGHAN. Never said there was anything wrong with the boat. Boat's all right. You're sure now that Georgie's father is takin' the kids in the afternoon.

CHILD MONAGHAN. Yeh, that's when they're going. Gee, look at those two sea gulls. Wee!—look at them swoop! They caught a fish!

MONAGHAN. What I can't understand is what all these people see in that statue that they'll keep a boat like this full makin' the trip, year in year out. To hear the newspapers talk, if the statue was gone we'd be at war with the nation that stole her the followin' mornin' early. All it is is a big high pile of French copper.

◆ **Reading Check**

Why is Grandpa disappointed in Child Monaghan?

◆ **Literary Analysis**

Mark the Text

What words and expressions in the **dialogue** in the bracketed text indicate that people's speech then was different from today's speech? Underline these expressions.

◆ **Reading Check**

Why is Grandpa concerned about meeting George's father?

◆ Stop to Reflect

Grandpa says that if you are free and have liberty, you don't need a statue as a symbol to remind you that you are free. Do you agree with Grandpa or not? Explain.

◆ Literary Analysis

How does the playwright use **dialogue** in the bracketed text to tell you about actions and speeches of characters you cannot see?

◆ Reading Check

What reasons do people give for visiting the statue? List two.

1.

2.

CHILD MONAGHAN. The teacher says it shows us that we got liberty.

MONAGHAN. Bah! If you've got liberty you don't need a statue to tell you you got it; and if you haven't got liberty no statue's going to do you any good tellin' you you got it. It was a criminal waste of the people's money. [*Quietly*] And just to prove it to you I'll ask this feller sitting right over there what he sees in it. You'll see what a madness the whole thing was. Say, mister?

ALF. Hey?

MONAGHAN. I beg your pardon. I'm a little strange here, and curious. Could you tell me why you're going to the Statue of Liberty?

ALF. Me? Well, I tell ya. I always wanted to take an ocean voyage. This is a pretty big boat—bigger than the ferries—so on Sundays, sometimes, I take the trip. It's better than nothing.

MONAGHAN. Thank you. [*To the kid*] So much for the great meaning of that statue, me boy. We'll talk to this lady standing at the rail. I just want you to understand why I didn't give Sheean me dime. Madam, would you be good enough to . . . Oh pardon me. [*To the kid*] Better pass her by, she don't look so good. We'll ask that girl there. Young lady, if you'll pardon the curiosity of an old man . . . could you tell me in a few good words what it is about that statue that brings you out here?

GIRL. What statue?

MONAGHAN. Why, the Statue of Liberty up 'head. We're coming up to it.

GIRL. Statue of Liberty! Is this the Statue of Liberty boat?

MONAGHAN. Well, what'd you think it was?

GIRL. Oh, my! I'm supposed to be on the Staten Island ferry! Where's the ticket man? [*Going away*] Ticket man! Where's the ticket man?

CHILD MONAGHAN. Gee whiz, nobody seems to want to see the statue.

MONAGHAN. Just to prove it, let's see this fellow sitting on this bench here. Young man, say . . .

YOUNG MAN. I can tell you in one word. For four days I haven't had a minute's peace. My kids are screaming, my wife is yelling, upstairs they play the piano all day long. The only place I can find that's quiet is a statue. That statue is my sweetheart. Every Sunday I beat it out to the island and sit next to her, and she don't talk.

CHILD MONAGHAN. I guess you were right, Grampa. Nobody seems to think it means anything.

MONAGHAN. Not only doesn't mean anything, but if they'd used the money to build an honest roomin' house on that island, the immigrants would have a place to spend the night, their valises wouldn't get robbed, and they—

MEGAPHONE VOICE. *Please keep your seats while the boat is docking. Statue of Liberty—all out in five minutes!*

CHILD MONAGHAN. Look down there, Gramp! There's a peanut stand! Could I have some?

MONAGHAN. I feel the wind comin' up. I don't think we dare take the time.

[*Music up and down*]

CHILD MONAGHAN. Ssssseuuuuuww! Look how far you can see! Look at that ship way out in the ocean!

MONAGHAN. It is, it's quite a view. Don't let go of me hand now.

CHILD MONAGHAN. I betcha we could almost see California.

MONAGHAN. It's probably that grove of trees way out over there. They do say it's beyond Jersey.

CHILD MONAGHAN. Feels funny. We're standing right inside her head. Is that what you meant . . . July IV, MCD . . . ?

MONAGHAN. That's it. That tablet in her hand. Now shouldn't they have put Welcome All on it instead of that foreign language? Say! Do you feel her rockin'?

CHILD MONAGHAN. Yeah, she's moving a little bit. Listen, the wind!

[*Whistling of wind*]

MONAGHAN. We better get down, come on! This way!

CHILD MONAGHAN. No, the stairs are this way! Come on!

[*Running in echo. Then quick stop*]

MONAGHAN. No, I told you they're the other way! Come!

VETERAN. [*Calm, quiet voice*] Don't get excited, pop. She'll stand.

MONAGHAN. She's swayin' awful.

VETERAN. That's all right. I been up here thirty, forty times. She gives with the wind, flexible. Enjoy the view, go on.

MONAGHAN. Did you say you've been up here forty times?

VETERAN. About that many.

MONAGHAN. What do you find here that's so interesting?

VETERAN. It calms my nerves.

MONAGHAN. Ah. It seems to me it would make you more nervous than you were.

VETERAN. No, not me. It kinda means something to me.

MONAGHAN. Might I ask what?

◆ **Reading Check**

Why do Grandpa and Child Monaghan run for the stairs?

◆ **Reading Strategy**

Do you think the detail that the Philippine War occurred in 1898 is **fact** or **fantasy**? Explain.

Do you think that the veteran is a real person or a made-up character?

◆ **Reading Check**

Why does Grandpa Monaghan say the statue "had Welcome All on it all the time"?

VETERAN. Well . . . I was in the Philippine War . . . back in '98.[5] Left my brother back there.

MONAGHAN. Oh, yes. Sorry I am to hear it. Young man, I suppose, eh?

VETERAN. Yeh. We were both young. This is his birthday today.

MONAGHAN. Oh, I understand.

VETERAN. Yeh, this statue is about the only stone he's got. In my mind I feel it is anyway. This statue kinda looks like what we believe. You know what I mean?

MONAGHAN. Looks like what we believe . . . I . . . I never thought of it that way. I . . . I see what you mean. It does look that way. [*Angrily*] See now, boy? If Sheean had put it that way I'd a give him me dime. [*Hurt*] Now, why do you suppose he didn't tell me that! Come down now. I'm sorry, sir, we've got to get out of here.

[*Music up and down*]

[*Footsteps under*]

Hurry now, I want to get out of here. I feel terrible. I do, boy. That Sheean, that fool. Why didn't he tell me that? You'd think . . .

CHILD MONAGHAN. What does this say?

[*Footsteps halt*]

MONAGHAN. Why, it's just a tablet, I suppose. I'll try it with me spectacles, just a minute. Why, it's a poem, I believe. . . "Give me your tired, your poor, your huddled masses yearning to breathe free, the wretched refuse of your teeming[6] shore. Send these, the homeless, tempest-tost to me, I lift . . . my lamp beside . . . the golden door!" Oh, dear. [*Ready to weep*] It had Welcome All on it all the time. Why didn't Sheean tell me? I'd a given him a quarter! Boy . . . go over there and here's a nickel and buy yourself a bag of them peanuts.

CHILD MONAGHAN. [*Astonished*] Gramp!

MONAGHAN. Go on now, I want to study this a minute. And be sure the man gives you full count.

CHILD MONAGHAN. I'll be right back.

[*Footsteps running away*]

MONAGHAN. [*To himself*] "Give me your tired, your poor, your huddled masses . . ."

Vocabulary Development: tempest (tem´ pist) *n.* violent storm with high winds

5. **back in '98** 1898.
6. **teeming** (tēm´ iŋ) *adj.* swarming with life.

[*Music swells from a sneak to full, then under to background*]

YOUNG MONAGHAN. [*Soldier*] I ran over and got my peanuts and stood there cracking them open, looking around. And I happened to glance over to Grampa. He had his nose right up to that bronze tablet, reading it. And then he reached into his pocket and kinda spied around over his eyeglasses to see if anybody was looking, and then he took out a coin and stuck it in a crack of cement over the tablet.

[*Coin falling onto concrete*]

It fell out and before he could pick it up I got a look at it. It was a half a buck. He picked it up and pressed it into the crack so it stuck. And then he came over to me and we went home.

[*Music: Change to stronger, more forceful theme*]

That's why, when I look at her now through this window, I remember that time and that poem, and she really seems to say, Whoever you are, wherever you come from, Welcome All. Welcome Home.

[*Music: Flare up to finish*]

Reader's Response: Does Grandpa remind you of anyone that you know? Explain why or why not.

____

____

Thinking About the Skill: How did distinguishing between fact and fantasy help you to better appreciate the play?

____

____

◆ Literary Focus

What does the **dialogue** in the bracketed text reveal about Grandpa's character?

____

____

____

____

____

◆ Stop to Reflect

What do the words that Grandpa reads at the base of the statue mean to you?

____

____

____

____

____

____

____

____

____

PREVIEW

The Walrus and the Carpenter

Lewis Carroll

Summary

"The Walrus and the Carpenter" is a funny poem about a walrus and a carpenter walking along the beach. They invite some young Oysters to walk with them. The Oysters are eager to go along. They consider it a treat to walk with the Walrus and the Carpenter. But soon the Oysters realize that the Walrus and the Carpenter want to eat them! The Oysters beg the Walrus and the Carpenter to leave them alone. But the Walrus and the Carpenter eat them anyway.

Visual Summary

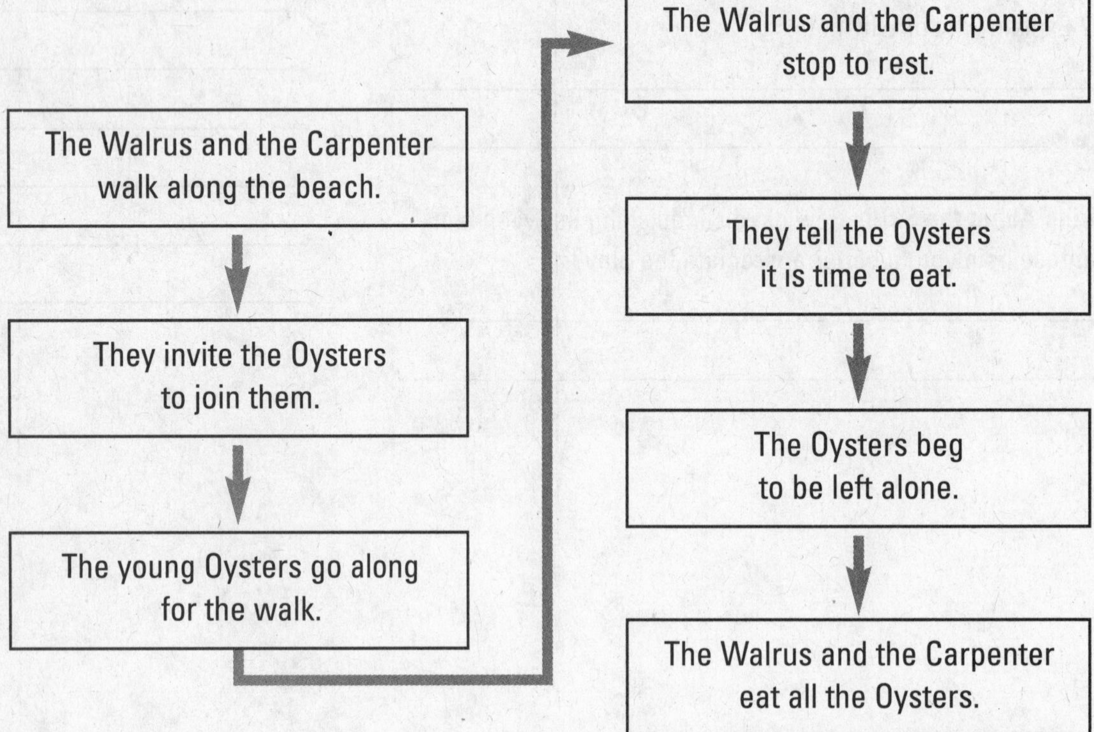
The Walrus and the Carpenter walk along the beach.
They invite the Oysters to join them.
The young Oysters go along for the walk.
The Walrus and the Carpenter stop to rest.
They tell the Oysters it is time to eat.
The Oysters beg to be left alone.
The Walrus and the Carpenter eat all the Oysters.

The Walrus and the Carpenter

Lewis Carroll

Lewis Carroll is the pen name for an Englishman Charles Ludwidge Dodgson. Sometimes an author chooses to use a pen name in place of his or her real name. Dodgson was a professor of mathematics and a photographer, as well as a poet and novelist. Among his best known works are Alice's Adventures in Wonderland *and* Through the Looking-Glass, *which contains "The Walrus and the Carpenter."*

The sun was shining on the sea,
Shining with all his might:
He did his very best to make
The billows smooth and bright—
And this was odd, because it was
The middle of the night.

The moon was shining sulkily,
Because she thought the sun
Had got no business to be there
After the day was done—
"It's very rude of him," she said,
"To come and spoil the fun!"

The sea was wet as wet could be,
The sands were dry as dry.
You could not see a cloud, because
No cloud was in the sky:
No birds were flying overhead—
There were no birds to fly.

The Walrus and the Carpenter
Were walking close at hand:
They wept like anything to see
Such quantities of sand:
"If this were only cleared away,"
They said, "it would be grand!"

"If seven maids with seven mops
Swept it for half a year,
Do you suppose," the Walrus said,
"That they could get it clear?"
"I doubt it," said the Carpenter,
And shed a bitter tear.

◆ Activate Prior Knowledge

Jot down songs or poems that tell a story.

◆ Reading Strategy

The **speaker** is the imaginary voice that the poet uses. The speaker can be, but is not always, the same person as the poet. Sometimes the speaker is outside the action of the poem. Other times the speaker is inside the action of the poem. In the bracketed text, who is the speaker?

◆ Literary Analysis

Narrative poetry tells a story in verse. It often uses character, plot, setting, and dialogue.

Mark the Text

Circle three details that describe the poem's setting. In your own words, where is the poem set?

◆ Literary Analysis

This **narrative poem** contains dialogue or conversation. What characters are having the conversation in the underlined text?

◆ Reading Check

Who do the Walrus and the Carpenter ask to walk with them?

◆ Stop to Reflect

Why does the eldest Oyster refuse to leave his oyster bed? Circle the details in the bracketed text that helped you decide.

Mark the Text

◆ Literary Analysis

Identify the main characters in this **narrative poem.**

"O Oysters, come and walk with us!"
The Walrus did beseech.
"A pleasant walk, a pleasant talk,
Along the briny beach:
We cannot do with more than four,
To give a hand to each."

The eldest Oyster looked at him,
But never a word he said:
The eldest Oyster winked his eye,
And shook his heavy head—
Meaning to say he did not choose
To leave the oyster-bed.

But four young Oysters hurried up,
All eager for this treat:
Their coats were brushed, their faces
washed,
Their shoes were clean and neat—
And this was odd, because, you know,
They hadn't any feet.

Four other Oysters followed them,
And yet another four;
And thick and fast they came at last,
And more, and more, and more—
All hopping through the frothy waves,
And scrambling to the shore.

The Walrus and the Carpenter
Walked on a mile or so,
And then they rested on a rock
Conveniently low:
And all the little Oysters stood
And waited in a row.

"The time has come," the Walrus said,
"To talk of many things:
Of shoes—and ships—and sealing wax—
Of cabbages—and kings—
And why the sea is boiling hot—
And whether pigs have wings."

Vocabulary Development: beseech (bi sēch′) *v.* beg

"But wait a bit," the Oysters cried,
"Before we have our chat;
For some of us are out of breath,
And all of us are fat!"
"No hurry!" said the Carpenter.
They thanked him much for that.

"A loaf of bread," the Walrus said,
"Is what we chiefly need:
Pepper and vinegar besides
Are very good indeed—
Now, if you're ready, Oysters dear,
We can begin to feed."

"But not on us!" the Oysters cried,
Turning a little blue.
"After such kindness, that would be
A dismal thing to do!"
"The night is fine," the Walrus said.
"Do you admire the view?"

"It was so kind of you to come!
And you are very nice!"
The Carpenter said nothing but
"Cut us another slice.
I wish you were not quite so deaf—
I've had to ask you twice!"

"It seems a shame," the Walrus said,
"To play them such a trick.
After we've brought them out so far,
And made them trot so quick!"
The Carpenter said nothing but
"The butter's spread too thick!"

"I weep for you," the Walrus said:
"I deeply sympathize."
With sobs and tears he sorted out
Those of the largest size,
Holding his pocket-handkerchief
Before his streaming eyes.

◆ Stop to Reflect

What do you think the Walrus and the Carpenter are going to do with the Oysters?

____

____

____

◆ Literary Analysis

Reread the bracketed lines. Then, describe one difference between the **character** of the Walrus and that of the Carpenter.

____

____

____

____

____

____

____

____

◆ Reading Check

Why can't the Oysters answer the Carpenter's question in the last stanza?

◆ Stop to Reflect

In what way is this poem both funny and sad?

"O Oysters," said the Carpenter,
"You've had a pleasant run!
Shall we be trotting home again?"
But answer came there none—
And this was scarcely odd, because
They'd eaten every one.

Reader's Response: What passage in the poem do you most enjoy?

Thinking About the Skill: How does knowing that this is a narrative poem help you better understand it?

PREVIEW

The Fairies' Lullaby *from* A Midsummer Night's Dream

William Shakespeare

Summary

A group of forest fairies is singing a lullaby to their Queen. In their song they warn snakes, hedgehogs, lizards, spiders, and other creatures to stay away from the Queen. A chorus invites a Philomel, or Nightingale, to join them as they sing the Queen to sleep.

Visual Summary

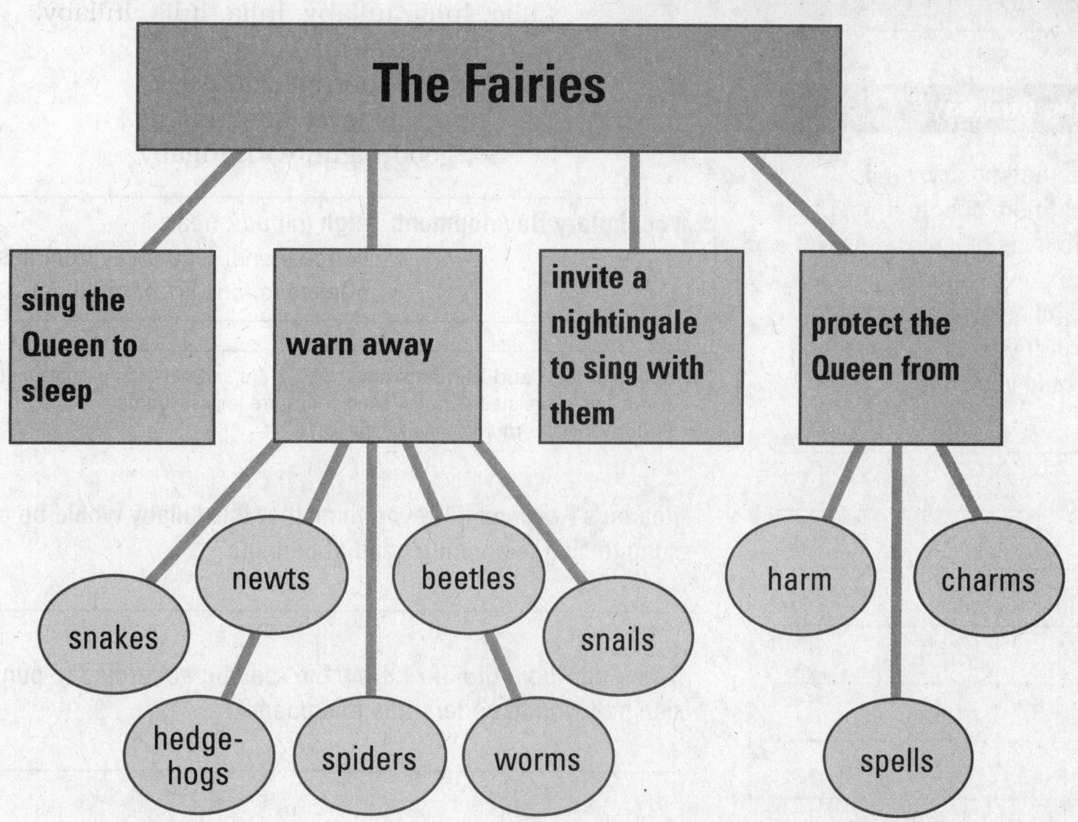

The Fairies' Lullaby *from* A Midsummer Night's Dream

William Shakespeare

Fairies, elves, and spirits are a part of legends and myths in many cultures. In the stories about them, fairies often act as spirits of lakes and streams or as the guardians of trees, animals, and crops. These beings are usually believed to be small and to have special magical powers. Although basically good, fairies are often portrayed as mischief makers.

Fairies. You spotted snakes with double tongue,
Thorny hedgehogs, be not seen.
Newts and blindworms,[1] do no wrong,
Come not near our fairy Queen.
Chorus. Philomel,[2] with melody
Sing in our sweet lullaby;
Lulla, lulla, lullaby, lulla, lulla, lullaby.
Never harm,
Nor spell, nor charm,
Come our lovely lady nigh.
So, good night, with lullaby.

Fairies. Weaving spiders, come not here.
Hence, you long-legged spinners, hence!
Beetles black, approach not near.
Worm nor snail do no offense
Chorus. Philomel, with melody
Sing in our sweet lullaby;
Lulla, lulla, lullaby, lulla, lulla, lullaby.
Never harm
Nor spell nor charm,
Come our lovely lady nigh.
So, good night, with lullaby.

Vocabulary Development: **nigh** (nī) *adv.* near
hence (hens) *v.* go away from this place
offense (ə fens′) *n.* harmful act

1. **newts** (no͞ots) **and blindworms** *n.* newts are salamanders, animals that look like lizards but are related to frogs. Blindworms are legless lizards.
2. **Philomel** (fil′ o mel′) *n.* nightingale.

Reader's Response: Do you think that this lullaby would be a good song to sing to a young child at bedtime?

___

Thinking About the Skill: How did reading according to punctuation help you to understand this poem?

___

◆ Activate Prior Knowledge

Jot down what you know about creatures of the forest, such as hedgehogs, newts, salamanders, beetles, and snails.

___

___

___

◆ Literary Analysis

Poets use the **sound** of words—the musical quality of words—to convey meaning and feelings in poetry. In addition to rhymes, poets use other sound devices, such as repetition of a word or phrase. A **refrain** is a line or group of lines that are repeated. Circle the refrains in the poem.

Mark THE Text

What effect do the refrains have?

___

___

___

◆ Reading Strategy

When you read poetry, **read according to the punctuation.** Don't stop at the ends of lines where there is no punctuation. Pause for commas and semicolons; stop for periods. After which words in the chorus would you stop?

___

___

___

___

___

___

___

PREVIEW

Parade

Rachel Field

Summary

In "Parade," the speaker describes the excitement of a circus parade coming into town. The circus band fills the air with festive sounds. Horses with riders dressed in red and blue march by. Silly clowns and decorated floats add fun and color. Camels and elephants pass slowly by. Everything is clean and shiny.

Visual Summary

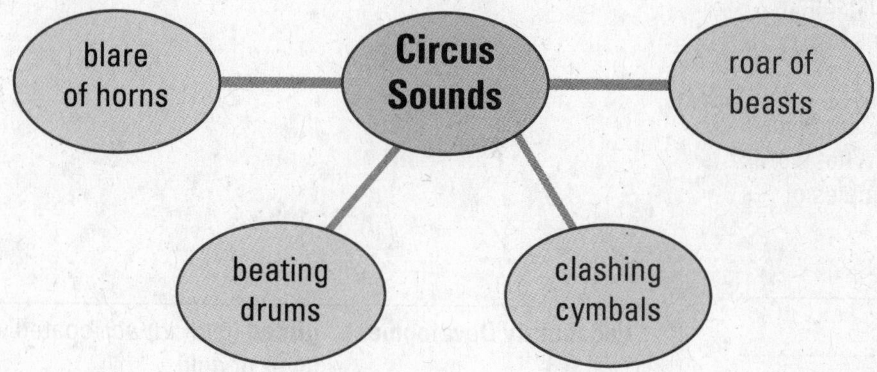

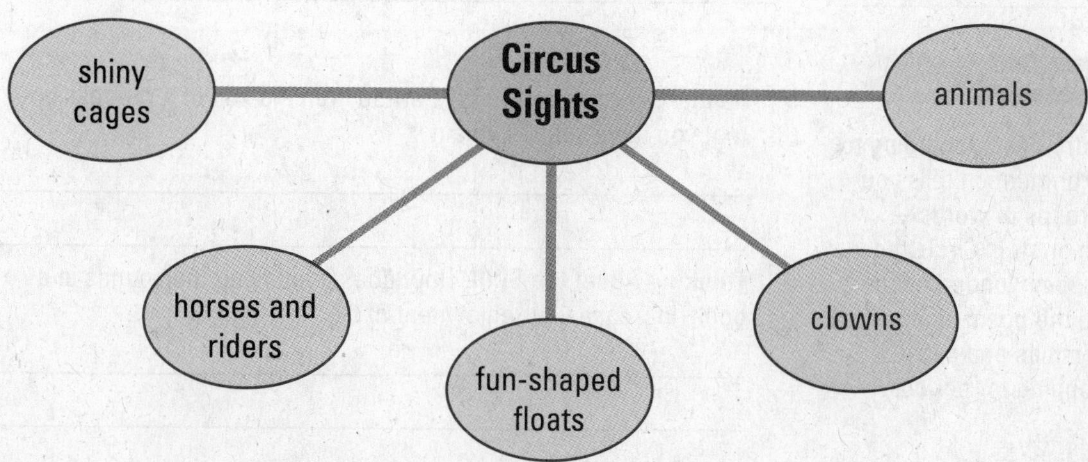

◆ Activate Prior Knowledge

List parades or marches that you have watched or participated in. What sounds, sights, and smells do you remember?

______

______

______

______

______

◆ Literary Analysis

Poets use the **sound** of words—the musical quality of words—to express images and feelings in poetry. **Rhyme**, repetition of sounds at the ends of lines, is the most obvious sound device. Circle the rhymes in the poem.

Mark the Text

Alliteration is the repetition of initial consonant sounds. What words in lines 2 and 5 are examples of alliteration?

Line 2: ______

______

Line 5: ______

______

◆ Reading Strategy

In reading poetry, read according to **punctuation**. Punctuation tells you how to read groups of words—when to pause or stop. Circle the periods in the poem; underline the commas. Read the poem aloud, pausing for commas and semicolons and stopping for periods.

Parade

Rachel Field

"Parade" describes a circus tradition that is more than 100 years old—the circus parade. In the days before television and radio, a circus poster was the best way to announce the performance to come. The poster might advertise beautiful women on horses, clowns on stilts, cages of wild animals, or a musical instrument called a calliope.

This is the day the circus comes
With blare of brass, with beating drums,
And clashing cymbals, and with roar
Of wild beasts never heard before
Within town limits. Spick and span
Will shine each gilded cage and van;
Cockades at every horse's head
Will nod, and riders dressed in red
Or blue trot by. There will be floats
In shapes like dragons, thrones and boats,
And clowns on stilts; freaks big and small,
Till leisurely and last of all
Camels and elephants will pass
Beneath our elms, along our grass.

Vocabulary Development: **gilded** (gild′ id) *adj.* coated with a thin layer of gold
leisurely (lē′ zhər lē) *adv.* in an unhurried way

Reader's Response: Does "Parade" remind you of a procession that you have seen? Explain.

______

______

Thinking About the Skill: How does identifying the sounds in a poem increase your enjoyment of it?

______

______

April Rain Song

Langston Hughes

Summary

"April Rain Song" is a poem that describes a rain shower on an early spring day. Its vivid images make the water come alive. Readers feel the rain on their heads. They hear it singing to them. They see it on sidewalks and in gutters. They can tell, before reading the final line, that the writer loves the rain.

Visual Summary

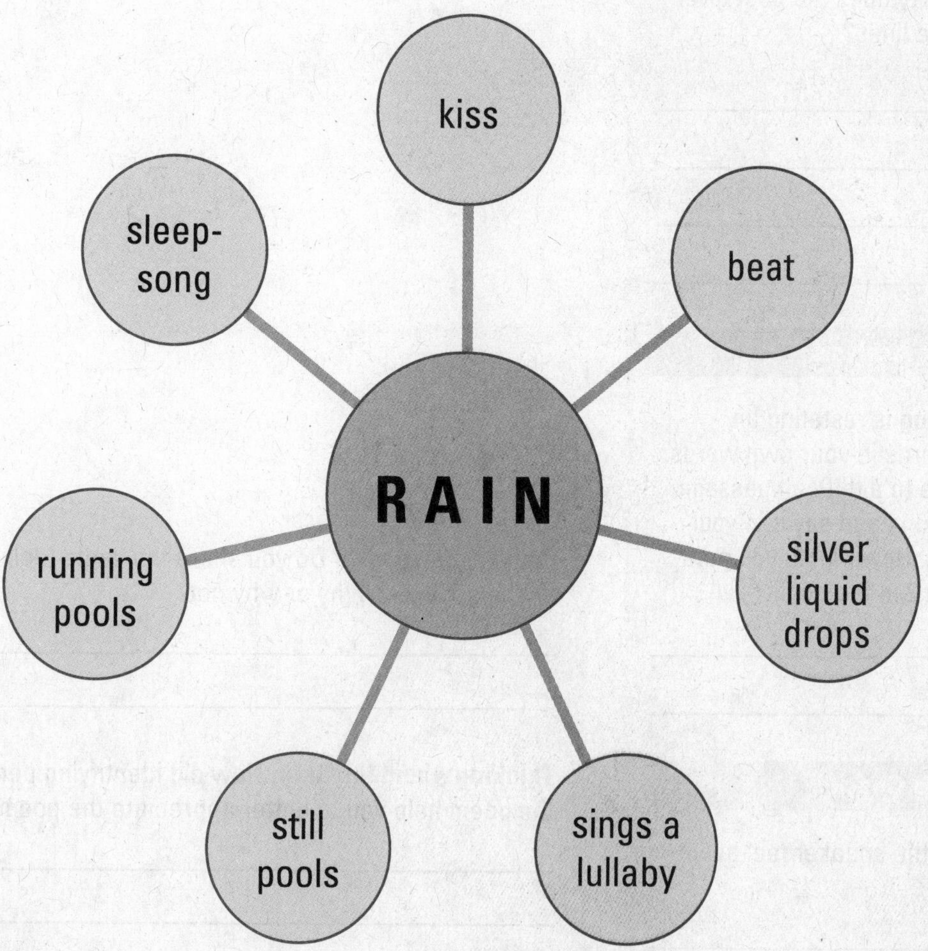

◆ **Activate Prior Knowledge**

List times when you have seen ordinary subjects in a new way, such as sun on a rain drop.

____

____

____

◆ **Literary Analysis**

Figurative language is language that uses comparisons to help you see things in a new way. One type of figurative language is **personification**—language that gives human characteristics to a non-human subject, such as "the tree sang in the wind." Circle lines 3 and 6. What human quality does the poet give rain in these lines?

Line 3: ______________________________

____

Line 6: ______________________________

____

◆ **Literary Analysis**

Paraphrasing is restating an author's words in your own words. If you come to a difficult passage, stop, reread it, and say it in your own words. How would you paraphrase line 2 in the poem?

____

____

◆ **Reading Check**

How does the speaker feel about the rain?

____

____

April Rain Song

Langston Hughes

Langston Hughes was a major figure in the Harlem Renaissance, a creative movement that took place in the 1920s in the New York City community of Harlem. Hughes and other writers, poets, musicians, and artists used their talents to celebrate their African American heritage.

Let the rain kiss you.
Let the rain beat upon your head with silver liquid drops.
Let the rain sing you a lullaby.

The rain makes still pools on the sidewalk.
The rain makes running pools in the gutter.
The rain plays a little sleep-song on our roof at night—

And I love the rain.

Reader's Response: Do you share the same feeling about the rain as the speaker? Why or why not?

____

____

Thinking About the Skill: How did identifying personification in the poem help you to better appreciate the poem?

____

____

PREVIEW

He Lion, Bruh Bear, and Bruh Rabbit

Virginia Hamilton

Summary

He Lion is scaring the other animals in the forest. His roar is so loud that the animals are afraid to hunt for their food. The animals ask Bruh Bear and Bruh Rabbit for help. Bruh Bear and Bruh Rabbit find he Lion. They tell him that Man is the real king of the forest, not him. He Lion does not believe them, so they take him to find Man. He Lion roars at Man. Man roars back by firing his gun. He Lion runs away because he is scared. He realizes that there is someone even more powerful than himself. He Lion learns what it feels like to be afraid. He stops scaring the other animals.

Visual Summary

Conflict		
He Lion is roaring too loudly and scaring the smaller forest animals.	↔	The forest animals want he Lion to stop. They are afraid to hunt.

Events

- The small animals ask Bruh Bear and Bruh Rabbit for help.
- Bruh Bear and Bruh Rabbit ask he Lion to stop roaring.
- He Lion refuses to stop.
- Bruh Bear and Bruh Rabbit take he Lion to see Man.
- Man scares he Lion with his gun.

Resolution (outcome)
He Lion realizes Man is the king of the forest. He stops roaring so loudly.

◆ Activate Prior Knowledge

Think of a story or a movie you know in which the characters are all animals. How would the story be different if the characters were human beings, not animals?

◆ Literary Analysis

Folk tales, stories composed orally and passed from generation to generation, often have plots featuring animal characters who talk. They are often told in the everyday language and usually teach a lesson or explain something about nature.

What two elements of a folk tale do you find in the first paragraph?

1.

2.

◆ Literary Analysis

The characters in **folk tales** often represent personality traits or qualities. What quality do you think he Lion represents?

He Lion, Bruh Bear, and Bruh Rabbit

African American Folk Tale

Virginia Hamilton

Cartoons you see on television often make you laugh at animal characters acting like humans. Like cartoons, the folk tale "He Lion, Bruh Bear, and Bruh Rabbit" includes animal characters that seem like people. Rather than coming from a single author, a folk tale is a story shared by "the folk." At some point, a specific author might write the tale down for all to enjoy, as is the case with this tale.

Say that he Lion would get up each and every mornin. Stretch and walk around. He'd roar, "ME AND MYSELF, ME AND MYSELF," like that. Scare all the little animals so they were afraid to come outside in the sunshine. Afraid to go huntin or fishin or whatever the little animals wanted to do.

"What we gone do about it?" they asked one another. Squirrel leapin from branch to branch, just scared. Possum[1] playin dead, couldn't hardly move him.

He Lion just went on, stickin out his chest and roarin, "ME AND MYSELF, ME AND MYSELF."

The little animals held a sit-down talk, and one by one and two by two and all by all, they decide to go see Bruh[2] Bear and Bruh Rabbit. For they know that Bruh Bear been around. And Bruh Rabbit say he has, too.

So they went to Bruh Bear and Bruh Rabbit. Said, "We have some trouble. Old he Lion, him scarin everybody, roarin every mornin and all day, 'ME AND MYSELF, ME AND MYSELF,' like that."

"Why he Lion want to do that?" Bruh Bear said.

"Is that all he Lion have to say?" Bruh Rabbit asked.

"We don't know why, but that's all he Lion can tell us and we didn't ask him to tell us that," said the little animals. "And him scarin the children with it. And we wish him to stop it."

"Well, I'll go see him, talk to him. I've known he Lion a long kind of time," Bruh Bear said.

"I'll go with you," said Bruh Rabbit. "I've known he Lion most long as you."

That bear and that rabbit went off through the forest. They kept hearin somethin. Mumble, mumble. Couldn't make it out. They got farther in the forest. They heard it plain now. "ME AND MYSELF. ME AND MYSELF."

"Well, well, well," said Bruh Bear. He wasn't scared. He'd been around the whole forest, seen a lot.

1. **Possum** (päs´ əm) colloquial for "opossum," a small tree-dwelling mammal that pretends to be dead when it is trapped.
2. **Bruh** (bru) early African American dialect for "brother."

"My, my, my," said Bruh Rabbit. He'd seen enough to know not to be afraid of an old he lion. Now old he lions could be dangerous, but you had to know how to handle them.

The bear and the rabbit climbed up and up the cliff where he Lion had his lair. They found him. Kept their distance. He watchin them and they watchin him. Everybody actin cordial.

"Hear tell you are scarin everybody, all the little animals, with your roarin all the time," Bruh Rabbit said.

"I roars when I pleases," he Lion said.

"Well, might could you leave off the noise first thing in the mornin, so the little animals can get what they want to eat and drink?" asked Bruh Bear.

"Listen," said he Lion, and then he roared: "ME AND MYSELF. ME AND MYSELF. Nobody tell me what not to do," he said. "I'm the king of the forest, *me and myself*."

"Better had let me tell you something," Bruh Rabbit said, "for I've seen Man, and I know him the real king of the forest."

He Lion was quiet awhile. He looked straight through that scrawny lil Rabbit like he was nothin atall. He looked at Bruh Bear and figured he'd talk to him.

"You, Bear, you been around," he Lion said.

"That's true," said old Bruh Bear. "I been about everywhere. I've been around the whole forest."

"Then you must know something," he Lion said.

"I know lots," said Bruh Bear, slow and quiet-like.

"Tell me what you know about Man," he Lion said. "He think him the king of the forest?"

"Well, now, I'll tell you," said Bruh Bear, "I been around, but I haven't ever come across Man that I know of. Couldn't tell you nothin about him."

So he Lion had to turn back to Bruh Rabbit. He didn't want to but he had to. "So what?" he said to that lil scrawny hare.

"Well, you got to come down from there if you want to see Man," Bruh Rabbit said. "Come down from there and I'll show you him."

He Lion thought a minute, an hour, and a whole day. Then, the next day, he came on down.

He roared just once, "ME AND MYSELF. ME AND MYSELF. Now," he said, "come show me Man."

So they set out. He Lion, Bruh Bear, and Bruh Rabbit.

Vocabulary Development: lair (lār) *n.* cave or den
cordial (kôr′ jəl) *adj.* warm and friendly

◆ **Literary Analysis**

In the bracketed passage, underline two things that he Lion tells Bruh Rabbit and Bruh Bear when they ask him not to roar in the morning. What qualities do his answers point out?

Mark THE Text

______

◆ **Stop to Reflect**

Why do you think Bruh Rabbit tells he Lion that Man is king of the forest?

______

◆ **Reading Strategy**

If you are able to recognize the **storyteller's purpose,** you can better understand a folk tale. A storyteller might wish to entertain, to explain something, to teach a lesson, or he/she may have a combination of these purposes in mind. From your reading so far, what do you think this storyteller's purpose might be?

______

◆ Literary Analysis

Name one quality that Bruh Bear shows in the first bracketed passage. Then, name a quality that Bruh Rabbit shows.

1. ______________________

____

2. ______________________

____

◆ Stop to Reflect

Why do you think Bruh Rabbit tells he Lion to go meet Man?

____

____

◆ Literary Analysis

In the second bracketed passage, what two qualities does he Lion say Man has?

1. ______________________

____

2. ______________________

____

◆ Reading Check

Underline three things that happen in he Lion's encounter with Man. What really happens?

Mark THE Text

____

____

They go along and they go along, rangin the forest. Pretty soon, they come to a clearin. And playin in it is a little fellow about nine years old.

"Is that there Man?" asked he Lion.

"Why no, that one is called Will Be, but it sure is not Man," said Bruh Rabbit.

So they went along and they went along. Pretty soon, they come upon a shade tree. And sleepin under it is an old, olden fellow, about ninety years olden.

"There must lie Man," spoke he Lion. "I knew him wasn't gone be much."

"That's not Man," said Bruh Rabbit. "That fellow is Was Once. You'll know it when you see Man."

So they went on along. He Lion is gettin tired of strollin. So he roars, "ME AND MYSELF. ME AND MYSELF." Upsets Bear so that Bear doubles over and runs and climbs a tree.

"Come down from there," Bruh Rabbit tellin him. So after a while Bear comes down. He keepin his distance from he Lion, anyhow. And they set out some more. Goin along quiet and slow.

In a little while they come to a road. And comin on way down the road, Bruh Rabbit sees Man comin. Man about twenty-one years old. Big and strong, with a big gun over his shoulder.

"There!" Bruh Rabbit says. "See there, he Lion? There's Man. You better go meet him."

"I will," says he Lion. And he sticks out his chest and he roars, "ME AND MYSELF. ME AND MYSELF." All the way to Man he's roarin proud, "ME AND MYSELF. ME AND MYSELF!"

"Come on, Bruh Bear, let's go!" Bruh Rabbit says.

"What for?" Bruh Bear wants to know.

"You better come on!" And Bruh Rabbit takes ahold of Bruh Bear and half drags him to a thicket. And there he makin the Bear hide with him.

For here comes Man. He sees old he Lion real good now. He drops to one knee and he takes aim with his big gun.

Old he Lion is roarin his head off: "ME AND MYSELF. ME AND MYSELF!"

The big gun goes off: PA-LOOOM!

He Lion falls back hard on his tail.

The gun goes off again. PA-LOOOM!

He Lion is flyin through the air. He lands in the thicket.

"Well, did you see Man?" asked Bruh Bear.

"I seen him," said he Lion. "Man spoken to me unkind, and got a great long stick him keepin on his shoulder. Then Man taken that stick down and him speakin real mean. Thunderin at me and lightnin comin from that stick, awful bad. Made me sick. I had to turn around. And Man pointin that stick again and thunderin at me some more. So I come in here, cause it seem like him throwed some stickers at me each time it thunder, too."

"So you've met Man, and you know zactly what that kind of him is," says Bruh Rabbit.

"I surely do know that," he Lion said back.

Awhile after he Lion met Man, things were some better in the forest. Bruh Bear knew what Man looked like so he could keep out of his way. That rabbit always did know to keep out of Man's way. The little animals could go out in the mornin because he Lion was more peaceable. He didn't walk around roarin at the top of his voice all the time. And when he Lion did lift that voice of his, it was like, "Me and Myself and Man. Me and Myself and Man." Like that.

Wasn't too loud atall.

Reader's Response: Which of the four main characters in the story would you have chosen for a friend? Why?

____

____

____

____

Thinking About the Skill: How does recognizing the characteristics of the different animals help you to **recognize the author's purpose?**

____

____

____

____

◆ Stop to Reflect

Why is he Lion more peaceable after his encounter with Man?

____

____

____

____

◆ Literary Analysis

What lesson has he Lion learned in this **folk tale**?

____

____

____

Does he Lion change because of this lesson? Explain.

____

____

____

◆ Reading Strategy

Was your guess on p. 249 about the **storyteller's purpose** correct? Explain.

____

____

____

____

Arachne

Olivia E. Coolidge

Summary

A young Greek woman named Arachne weaves cloth faster than anyone else. People come to watch her weave her beautiful work. But Arachne becomes too proud of herself. She says that she can weave better than anyone, even the goddess Athene. One day Athene appears and the two have a contest. Both weave well, but Athene is faster. When Arachne realizes that Athene is faster, she insults her by weaving an insulting picture in her cloth. Athene becomes furious and turns Arachne into a spider. Whenever Greeks saw spiders weaving webs, they were reminded of Arachne and her dangerous pride.

Visual Summary

What Arachne does	What Happens to Her
• She shows off her talent to onlookers from near and far. • She boasts that she is a better spinner than the goddess Athene. • She competes against Athene in a weaving contest. • She loses the contest and insults Athene.	• Athene punishes her by changing her into a spider. • Whenever Greeks saw spiders, they remembered Arachne and were reminded that it is not wise to challenge the gods.

Arachne

Greek Myth

Olivia E. Coolidge

Like other ancient people, the Greeks created myths to help them understand occurrences in nature. They also built into their myths their beliefs about right and wrong. One of their main beliefs was that humans should be careful about having too much pride and especially about claiming to have powers that only the gods could have.

Arachne[1] was a maiden who became famous throughout Greece, though she was neither wellborn nor beautiful and came from no great city. She lived in an obscure little village, and her father was a humble dyer of wool. In this he was very skillful, producing many varied shades, while above all he was famous for the clear, bright scarlet which is made from shellfish, and which was the most glorious of all the colors used in ancient Greece. Even more skillful than her father was Arachne. It was her task to spin the fleecy wool into a fine, soft thread and to weave it into cloth on the high, standing loom within the cottage. Arachne was small and pale from much working. Her eyes were light and her hair was a dusty brown, yet she was quick and graceful, and her fingers, roughened as they were, went so fast that it was hard to follow their flickering movements. So soft and even was her thread, so fine her cloth, so gorgeous her embroidery, that soon her products were known all over Greece. No one had ever seen the like of them before.

At last Arachne's fame became so great that people used to come from far and wide to watch her working. Even the graceful nymphs[2] would steal in from stream or forest and peep shyly through the dark doorway, watching in wonder the white arms of Arachne as she stood at the loom and threw the shuttle from hand to hand between the hanging threads, or drew out the long wool, fine as a hair, from the distaff[3] as she sat spinning. "Surely Athene[4] herself must have taught her," people would murmur to one another. "Who else could know the secret of such marvelous skill?"

Arachne was used to being wondered at, and she was immensely proud of the skill that had brought so many to

Vocabulary Development: obscure (əb skyoor′) *adj.* not well known

1. **Arachne** (ä räk′ nē)
2. **nymphs** (nimfz) *n.* minor nature goddesses thought of as beautiful maidens living in rivers, trees, and so forth.
3. **distaff** (dis′ taf) *n.* a stick on which flax or wool is wound for use in spinning.
4. **Athene** (ə thē′ nə) Greek goddess of wisdom, skills, and warfare.

◆ Activate Prior Knowledge

Think of two bits of information that you know about weaving. For example, which animals or plants provide materials to spin thread or what are spinning wheels and looms used for?

1. ______________________

____

____

2. ______________________

____

____

◆ Literary Analysis

Mark the Text

Folk tales, legends, and myths handed down from generation to generation by word of mouth are said to come from the **oral tradition.** Myths were often used as teaching tools. Greek myths usually revolve around the interactions of the gods and goddesses with humans.

In the second paragraph, underline two references that tell that this story is a myth.

◆ **Literary Analysis**

The Greeks believed that one of the worst things humans could do was to take excessive pride in their abilities and to think that they were better than the gods. This **theme,** or central message, of a story, was common in Greek myths. Underline the sentence in the first bracketed passage that shows this theme.

Mark THE Text

◆ **Reading Strategy**

Make a **prediction,** or an educated guess, about a story's future events by using what you already know from your experiences. In the second bracketed passage, predict who the old woman might be. Explain.

____

____

____

____

____

◆ **Stop to Reflect**

How would you feel if, like Arachne, you had spoken negatively to someone so much more powerful than you? How does Arachne react? Why does she react in this way?

____

____

____

____

____

____

look on her. Praise was all she lived for, and it displeased her greatly that people should think anyone, even a goddess, could teach her anything. Therefore when she heard them murmur, she would stop her work and turn round indignantly to say, "With my own ten fingers I gained this skill, and by hard practice from early morning till night. I never had time to stand looking as you people do while another maiden worked. Nor if I had, would I give Athene credit because the girl was more skillful than I. As for Athene's weaving, how could there be finer cloth or more beautiful embroidery than mine? If Athene herself were to come down and compete with me, she could do no better than I."

One day when Arachne turned round with such words, an old woman answered her, a gray old woman, bent and very poor, who stood leaning on a staff and peering at Arachne amid the crowd of onlookers. "Reckless girl," she said, "how dare you claim to be equal to the immortal gods themselves? I am an old woman and have seen much. Take my advice and ask pardon of Athene for your words. Rest content with your fame of being the best spinner and weaver that mortal eyes have ever beheld."

"Stupid old woman," said Arachne indignantly, "who gave you a right to speak in this way to me? It is easy to see that you were never good for anything in your day, or you would not come here in poverty and rags to gaze at my skill. If Athene resents my words, let her answer them herself. I have challenged her to a contest, but she, of course, will not come. It is easy for the gods to avoid matching their skill with that of men."

At these words the old woman threw down her staff and stood erect. The wondering onlookers saw her grow tall and fair and stand clad in long robes of dazzling white. They were terribly afraid as they realized that they stood in the presence of Athene. Arachne herself flushed red for a moment, for she had never really believed that the goddess would hear her. Before the group that was gathered there she would not give in; so pressing her pale lips together in obstinacy and pride, she led the goddess to one of the great looms and set herself before the other. Without a word both began to thread the long woolen strands that hang from the rollers, and between which the shuttle[5] moves back and

Vocabulary Development: **immortal** (i môr´ təl) *adj.* living forever
mortal (môr´ təl) *adj.* referring to humans, who are subject to death
obstinacy (äb´ stə nə sē) *n.* stubbornness

5. **shuttle** (shut´ əl) *n.* an instrument used in weaving to carry the thread back and forth.

forth. Many skeins lay heaped beside them to use, bleached white, and gold, and scarlet, and other shades, varied as the rainbow. Arachne had never thought of giving credit for her success to her father's skill in dyeing, though in actual truth the colors were as remarkable as the cloth itself.

Soon there was no sound in the room but the breathing of the onlookers, the whirring of the shuttles, and the creaking of the wooden frames as each pressed the thread up into place or tightened the pegs by which the whole was held straight. The excited crowd in the doorway began to see that the skill of both in truth was very nearly equal, but that, however the cloth might turn out, the goddess was the quicker of the two. A pattern of many pictures was growing on her loom. There was a border of twined branches of the olive, Athene's favorite tree, while in the middle, figures began to appear. As they looked at the glowing colors, the spectators realized that Athene was weaving into her pattern a last warning to Arachne. The central figure was the goddess herself competing with Poseidon[6] for possession of the city of Athens; but in the four corners were mortals who had tried to strive with gods and pictures of the awful fate that had overtaken them. The goddess ended a little before Arachne and stood back from her marvelous work to see what the maiden was doing.

Never before had Arachne been matched against anyone whose skill was equal, or even nearly equal to her own. As she stole glances from time to time at Athene and saw the goddess working swiftly, calmly, and always a little faster than herself, she became angry instead of frightened, and an evil thought came into her head. Thus as Athene stepped back a pace to watch Arachne finishing her work, she saw that the maiden had taken for her design a pattern of scenes which showed evil or unworthy actions of the gods, how they had deceived fair maidens, resorted to trickery, and appeared on earth from time to time in the form of poor and humble people. When the goddess saw this insult glowing in bright colors on Arachne's loom, she did not wait while the cloth was judged, but stepped forward, her gray eyes blazing with anger, and tore Arachne's work across. Then she struck Arachne across the face. Arachne stood there a moment, struggling with anger, fear, and pride. "I will not live under this insult," she cried, and seizing a rope from the wall, she made a noose and would have hanged herself.

The goddess touched the rope and touched the maiden. "Live on, wicked girl," she said. "Live on and spin, both you and your descendants. When men look at you they may remember that it is not wise to strive with Athene." At that the body of Arachne shriveled up, and her legs grew tiny,

6. Poseidon (pō sī́ dən) Greek god of the seas and of horses.

◆ Literary Analysis

How is the underlined sentence an example of Arachne's pride?

◆ Reading Strategy

In the bracketed passage, how does the warning that Athene weaves into her pattern help you **predict** what might happen after the contest?

◆ Reading Check

How does Arachne react when she sees that Athene is working quickly and calmly and weaving beautifully? What plan does she devise?

◆ Reading Strategy

What do you **predict** Athene might do when she sees Arachne's design?

spindly, and distorted. There before the eyes of the spectators hung a little dusty brown spider on a slender thread.

All spiders descend from Arachne, and as the Greeks watched them spinning their thread wonderfully fine, they remembered the contest with Athene and thought that it was not right for even the best of men to claim equality with the gods.

◆ Reading Strategy

Was your **prediction** correct about what would happen to Arachne? What is her punishment?

◆ Literary Analysis

What lesson is taught by this myth? How is it related to the **theme**?

◆ Literary Analysis

What occurrence in nature does this myth explain?

Reader's Response: If you were a Greek living two or three thousand years ago and you believed in gods and goddesses, how would you feel if you were told this myth?

Thinking About the Skill: How does trying to **predict** what is going to happen help your understanding of this story?

PREVIEW

The Three Wishes

Puerto Rican Folk Tale

Ricardo E. Alegría

Summary

A loving woodsman and his wife live together in the forest. They are poor but they always share what they have with others. One day the woman shares her food with a stranger. The stranger grants her three wishes to show his thanks. The wishes are granted, but greediness begins to change the couple. The farmer and his wife discover that happiness comes from love, not from riches.

Visual Summary

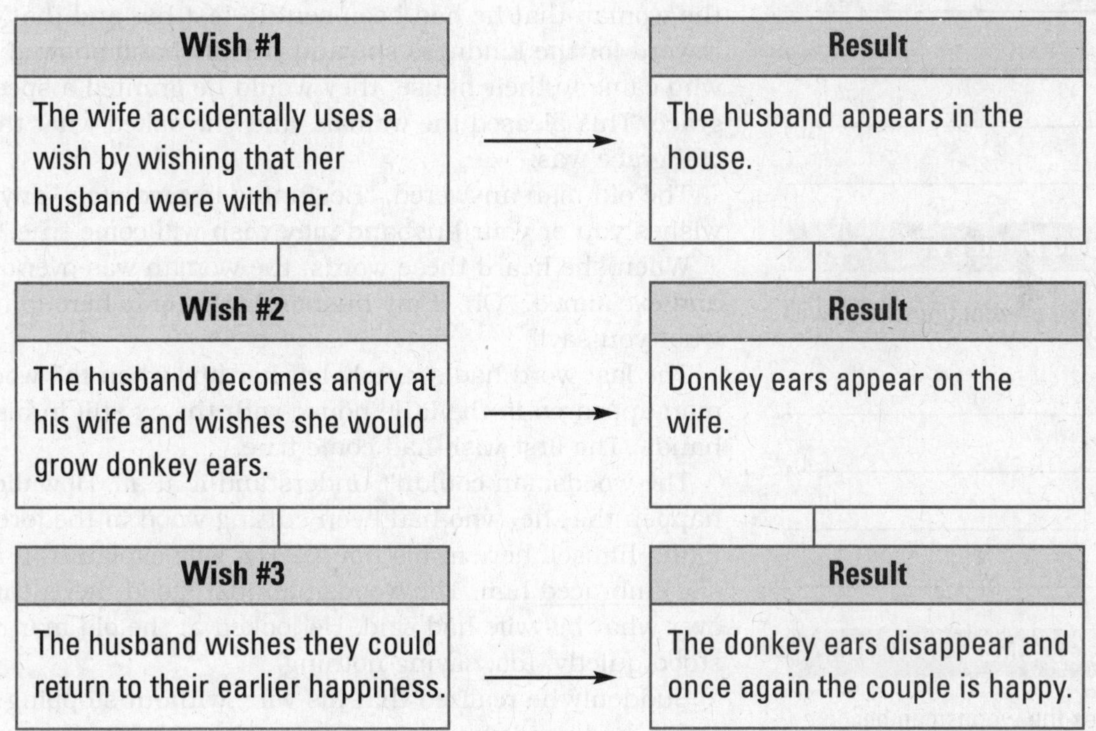

Wish #1
The wife accidentally uses a wish by wishing that her husband were with her.
Result
The husband appears in the house.
Wish #2
The husband becomes angry at his wife and wishes she would grow donkey ears.
Result
Donkey ears appear on the wife.
Wish #3
The husband wishes they could return to their earlier happiness.
Result
The donkey ears disappear and once again the couple is happy.

◆ **Activate Prior Knowledge**

Think about another story where a mysterious visitor announces that the characters in the story could have any wish they asked for fulfilled. Name or describe the story.

◆ **Literary Analysis**

A story's **theme** is its central insight into life or human nature. How do you think the feeding of the stranger by the woman might be connected to the theme?

◆ **Reading Strategy**

How do you **predict** the wishes will turn out?

◆ **Reading Check**

Why does the woodsman become angry with his wife?

The Three Wishes

Puerto Rican Folk Tale

Ricardo E. Alegría

Different versions of "The Three Wishes" exist in cultures around the world. Because folk tales are passed on orally, they can "migrate" from one place to another. Each storyteller adds details based on personal experience or their culture. After a number of tellings, a new version of the tale emerges.

Many years ago, there lived a woodsman and his wife. They were very poor but very happy in their little house in the forest. Poor as they were, they were always ready to share what little they had with anyone who came to their door. They loved each other very much and were quite content with their life together. Each evening, before eating, they gave thanks to God for their happiness.

One day, while the husband was working far off in the woods, an old man came to the little house and said that he had lost his way in the forest and had eaten nothing for many days. The woodsman's wife had little to eat herself, but, as was her custom, she gave a large portion of it to the old man. After he had eaten everything she gave him, he told the woman that he had been sent to test her and that, as a reward for the kindness she and her husband showed to all who came to their house, they would be granted a special grace. This pleased the woman, and she asked what the special grace was.

The old man answered, "Beginning immediately, any three wishes you or your husband may wish will come true."

When she heard these words, the woman was overjoyed and exclaimed, "Oh, if my husband were only here to hear what you say!"

The last word had scarcely left her lips when the woodsman appeared in the little house with the ax still in his hands. The first wish had come true.

The woodsman couldn't understand it at all. How did it happen that he, who had been cutting wood in the forest, found himself here in his house? His wife explained it all as she embraced him. The woodsman just stood there, thinking over what his wife had said. He looked at the old man who stood quietly, too, saying nothing.

Suddenly he realized that his wife, without stopping to think, had used one of the three wishes, and he became very annoyed when he remembered all of the useful things she might have asked for with the first wish. For the first time,

Vocabulary Development: embraced (em brāsd′) *v.* clasped in the arms, usually as an expression of affection

he became angry with his wife. The desire for riches had turned his head, and he scolded his wife, shouting at her, among other things, "It doesn't seem possible that you could be so stupid! You've wasted one of our wishes, and now we have only two left! May you grow ears of a donkey!"

He had no sooner said the words than his wife's ears began to grow, and they continued to grow until they changed into the pointed, furry ears of a donkey.

When the woman put her hand up and felt them, she knew what had happened and began to cry. Her husband was very ashamed and sorry, indeed, for what he had done in his temper, and he went to his wife to comfort her.

The old man, who had stood by silently, now came to them and said, "Until now, you have known happiness together and have never quarreled with each other. Nevertheless, the mere knowledge that you could have riches and power has changed you both. Remember, you have only one wish left. What do you want? Riches? Beautiful clothes? Servants? Power?"

The woodsman tightened his arm about his wife, looked at the old man, and said, "We want only the happiness and joy we knew before my wife grew donkey's ears."

No sooner had he said these words than the donkey ears disappeared. The woodsman and his wife fell upon their knees to ask forgiveness for having acted, if only for a moment, out of covetousness and greed. Then they gave thanks for all their happiness.

The old man left, but before going, he told them that they had undergone this test in order to learn that there can be happiness in poverty just as there can be unhappiness in riches. As a reward for their repentance, the old man said that he would bestow upon them the greatest happiness a married couple could know. Months later, a son was born to them. The family lived happily all the rest of their lives.

Vocabulary Development: covetousness (kuv′ ət əs nəs) *n.* envy; wanting what another person has

Reader's Response: If you were given three wishes, how would you avoid the problems the woodsman and his wife had?

____

____

Thinking About the Skill: How does identifying the story's theme help you understand the story?

____

____

____

◆ Reading Strategy

What do you **predict** will happen after the wife's ears turn into donkey ears?

____

____

◆ Reading Check

Mark the Text

Underline the passage in which the old man tells the couple how the wishes have affected them. What does the couple choose to do with their last wish?

____

____

____

◆ Literary Analysis

What is the old man "testing" in the couple?

____

____

What behavior is rewarded?

____

____

How does the reward relate to the **theme** of the story?

____

____

◆ Literary Analysis

What is the couple's real reward?

____

How does it connect to the **theme** of the story?

____

____

A Crippled Boy

Tran My-Van

Summary

Theo is a poor and lonely disabled boy who cannot work for his food. He survives by begging for handouts from kind neighbors. To keep busy, he learns to throw pebbles at targets. He even creates animal shapes out of bushes by throwing the pebbles at them. One day the King passes by and admires Theo's ability. He takes Theo home to toss pebbles into the mouths of the King's advisors who always talk and never listen. The king rewards the boy by keeping him at the palace.

Visual Summary

Theo's Life Improves

Theo pleases the King and stays at the palace. He is no longer poor and lonely.

The King invites Theo to help him with a task at the palace.

Theo's skill attracts the attention of the King.

Theo shapes bushes into animals by throwing pebbles at the leaves.

Theo is poor and lonely. He cannot work and must beg for food.

A Crippled Boy
Vietnamese Folk Tale
Tran My-Van

Many cultures have folk tales, stories told by ordinary people and passed from person to person by word of mouth in the oral tradition. Just like myths, folk tales communicate the ideas and values that are important to people in a culture. You can learn a lot about a particular culture by studying its folk tales.

Long, long ago there was a boy called Theo. He was crippled in both legs and could hardly walk. Since he could not work, he had no choice but to live on rice and vegetables which kind people gave him.

Often he sat watching other children play and run about. Unable to join them, he felt very miserable. To amuse himself Theo practiced throwing pebbles at targets. Hour after hour he would spend practicing his aim. Having nothing else to do he soon learned to hit all his targets. Other children took pity on him and gave him more pebbles to throw. Besides this, Theo could also make all sorts of shapes with stones on the ground.

One hot day Theo sat under a big banyan tree[1] which provided him with a delightful, cool shade under its thick leaves. He aimed stones at the thick foliage and managed to cut it into the outlines of animal forms. He was very pleased at what he could do and soon forgot his loneliness.

One day Theo was under his favorite banyan tree. To his surprise, he heard a drumbeat. Soon he saw many men in official clothes. It happened that the King was out for a country walk with some of his officials and was passing by Theo's tree.

The King's attention was caught by the unusual shadow of the tree. He stopped and was very surprised to see little crippled Theo sitting there all alone.

Theo was very frightened and tried to get away; but he could not crawl very far. The King asked Theo what he had been doing. Theo told the King his story.

Then the King asked Theo to demonstrate his skill at pebble throwing. Theo was happy to do so. The King was impressed and asked Theo to return with him to the palace where the King said:

Vocabulary Development: foliage (fō´ lē ij) *n.* leaves of trees and bushes

1. **banyan tree** a tropical fig tree.

◆ Activate Prior Knowledge

Think of some special talents you might have. Write about one of these talents and tell why it is important to you.

◆ Reading Strategy

After reading the bracketed passage, **predict** how Theo's special skill will help him.

◆ Reading Strategy

Predict what you think the king will want Theo to do.

◆ **Reading Check**

Why does the king want Theo to throw pebbles in the mandarins' mouths?

◆ **Literary Analysis**

Tales from the **oral tradition** are often used as teaching tools. The **theme** of a tale is what is intended to be taught. What do you think the theme of this tale is?

"I have a little job for you to do."

The following day, before the King had a meeting with his mandarins,[2] he ordered Theo to sit quietly behind a curtain. The King had ordered a few holes to be made in the curtain so that Theo could see what was going on.

"Most of my mandarins talk too much," the King explained. "They never bother to listen to me or let me finish my sentence. So if anybody opens his mouth to speak while I am talking, just throw a pebble into his mouth. This will teach him to shut up."

Sure enough, just as the meeting was about to start one mandarin opened his big mouth, ready to speak.

Oops! Something got into his mouth and he quickly closed it.

Another mandarin opened his mouth to speak but strangely enough he, too, shut his mouth without saying a word.

A miracle had happened. Throughout the whole meeting all the mandarins kept their silence.

For once the King could speak as much as he wanted without being interrupted. The King was extremely pleased with his success and the help that Theo had given him.

After that he always treasured Theo's presence and service. So Theo remained happily at the palace, no longer needing to beg for food and no longer always sitting alone under the banyan tree.

2. **mandarins** (man´ də rinz) *n.* high-ranking officials and counselors.

Reader's Response: What lesson does this tale from the oral tradition have for people today?

Thinking About the Skill: How did making predictions and thinking about the oral tradition help you understand this tale?

Part 2

Reading Informational Materials

Part 2 contains the Reading Informational Materials features from *Prentice Hall Literature: Timeless Voices, Timeless Themes* with reading support and practice.

- Review the **Reading Informational Materials** page. You will use the information and skills on this page as you read the selection.
- Read the selection and respond to the questions. Look for the **Mark the Text** logo for special help with interactive reading.
- Use the **Reading Informational Materials** questions at the end of each selection to build your understanding of various types of informational materials.

NEWSPAPER ARTICLES

About Newspaper Articles

Newspapers keep people informed about local, national, and world events. Daily newspapers in large cities focus on world and national news and events. Local, or hometown, newspapers mainly focus on regional news such as a fire or an election. Most newspapers have one or two pages dedicated to editorials and readers' opinions on current events. Newspaper articles provide information and facts, while editorials express opinions.

Reading Strategy

Using Newspapers to Find Information

Most newspapers are divided into sections that cover specific subjects—for example, news, sports, business, and entertainment. However, few people read newspapers from beginning to end. Instead, most people read only those sections that interest them. This chart shows some of the features of a newspaper that can help you **find information.**

Feature	Function
Section heads, such as *News, Editorials,* or *Home.*	Tell the focus of the articles within the section
Article titles are set on their own line in larger, heavier type than the article text.	Indicate topic of article
Run-in heads are printed in heavier type than the article but are not set on a separate line.	Call out the key points in the article. The text that follows a run-in head gives more detail.
Pull quotes	Highlight an important or interesting statement made by someone in the article
Photos and captions	Add visual information to the text

BUILD UNDERSTANDING

Knowing these words will help you read this newspaper article.

editorial (ed′ i tôr′ ē əl) *n.* a statement of opinion by an editor, publisher, or owner of a newspaper, magazine, or other media

criteria (krī tir′ ē ə) *n.* a standard by which something can be judged

portfolio (pôrt fō′ lē ō′) *n.* a selection of works, such as the works of an artist

Summer Hats

Amy Lindgren

If you're looking for work, different work, or more work, summertime is a great time to try a variety of jobs.

Summer's back! And our worker shortage prevails. These look like good conditions for a little experimenting with new jobs.

Of course, if you are a parent with school-age children, you may feel your summer "job" already has been chosen for you. Just arranging the kids' schedules for three months gives you training to be a high-level events planner.

Some of those kids are probably the right age for summer employment. Other people who might benefit from a short-term job include retirees; students; "winter workers," such as teachers and snowplow drivers; and, of course, the unemployed.

Summer employment is also a good option for the underemployed and dissatisfied workers who wonder what else they could do for a living. And, if you are struggling with a debt load, you might find relief by working to pay off a specific bill.

Some common summer jobs—for adults or kids—include farm work, lawn care, tourism work, anything in retail or food service, day-care/camp work, construction and some kinds of food production. Positions are available at all levels in most of these fields, although the short-term jobs tend to be at the entry level.

Be careful. As many of my readers have reminded me, it's possible to choose poorly. Indeed, bad summer jobs are almost a rite of passage[1] in this country. To increase your chances of success, take these two simple steps:

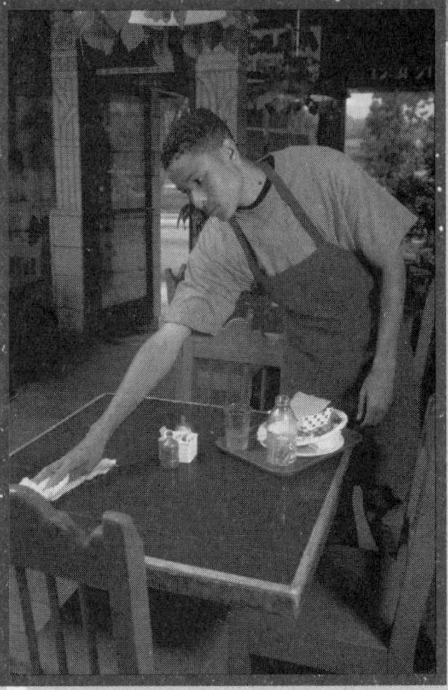

◆ Reading Newspaper Articles

This **newspaper article** contains information about summer jobs. What do you think is meant by the headline "Summer Hats"?

Does the headline grab your interest? Why or why not?

◆ Reading Check

Based on the information in the bracketed paragraph above, what five groups of people might benefit from reading this article? Circle the answers in the text.

1. **rite of passage** n. an event or achievement in a person's life that has great significance.

◆ **Reading Check**

In the bracketed paragraphs, identify two ways to be successful at a summer job. Circle the answers in the text.

Mark the Text

First, define success. If you are taking a job purely for the money, figure out how much money you want to clear and establish a savings plan to safeguard the funds. If you are trying something new just for fun, how many hours a week can you spare? Perhaps you are trying to get experience in a new field so you can impress an employer later in your career; what kind of work would fit that bill?

Second, choose a job that meets the criteria you just established. You may have to approach employers instead of waiting for ads in the paper, but you'll be glad you took the initiative.

For example, if you would like to work at a garden center because you love plants and want to learn more about them (maybe you just want the discount!), don't hesitate to ask the manager of the center nearest you if the store needs help for the summer. If you can only work certain days, stick as close to that plan as possible. Otherwise, what started out to be fun will become a strain on your schedule.

Whatever your reasons for choosing a summer job, use these tips to make the experience a good one for you and your employer:

- **Take it seriously.** This may be just a summer fling for you, but it means everything to the employer. Your boss is counting on you to be dependable and to help keep the operation running.
- **Learn a new skill.** From corn detasseling to computer tutoring, every job has something to teach you. Perhaps you'll pick up some supervisory skills, or learn how to teach somebody else how to do what you're doing.
- **Learn about the business.** So you're delivering phone books? Why not ask a few questions about how the routes are created. Someday you may use that knowledge when you're setting up your own business as a product distributor. Working at an amusement park? How do they create promotions to attract visitors

◆ **Reading Strategy**

In what way do these bold, run-in heads help you to **find information?**

____

____

____

____

____

to the slow days? Ask questions and keep learning. If nothing else, it makes the time pass faster.

• **Get along with your co-workers and customers.** Whatever you do, make this a priority. After all, this is just a summer job. If you can't deal with difficult people for a few months, how will you ever manage it over the long haul?

• **Don't overwork.** Keep a balance between time off and your job so you don't collapse in September.

• **Leave on a good note.** There are several steps to take when leaving a short-term job. First, give plenty of notice. Ask for letters of recommendation and select a few samples of your work for your portfolio. For example, photos of you helping kids onto a carnival ride can work well later to demonstrate patience and responsibility. Give your contact information to anyone who might be able to connect you to more work later, and take down their names and numbers as well. Finally, thank your boss for the opportunity. Even if you hated the job, it's a classy touch.

Of course, don't forget to put your experiences on your resume. If you already have a career, you might include this job as a single line in an "Other" category. Workers just starting out will want to give this job higher billing and include more detail.

Have a good summer!

Reading Informational Materials

Newspapers often contain photographs and other art that illustrate the articles. Does the photograph in "Summer Hats" help you understand the article? Explain.

READING INFORMATIONAL MATERIALS

INTERVIEWS

About Interviews

In an **interview,** questions are asked by an interviewer for the person being interviewed to answer. To identify the kinds of information you will find in an interview, read the questions. (Questions are usually set off in a separate color or font.) The questions in "An Astronaut's Answers" show that the interview contains the following information:

- Details about John Glenn's first space mission
- Glenn's reasons for becoming an astronaut
- Glenn's reflections on space exploration

Reading Strategy

Using Prior Knowledge

To help you understand the main ideas in an interview, use your **prior knowledge.** Your prior knowledge is the information and experiences you already have. For example, you might already know that John Glenn was the first American to orbit the Earth.

As you read, use a graphic organizer like the one shown to record what you know about astronauts and space travel. When you have finished reading, write down what you learned from the interview.

My Prior Knowledge
astronauts:
John Glenn:
space travel:

What I Learned
astronauts:
John Glenn:
space travel:
Other:

BUILD UNDERSTANDING

Knowing these words will help you read this interview.

NASA (nas' ə) *n.* the **N**ational **A**eronautics and **S**pace **A**dministration. This government agency, established in 1958, provides for research into the problems of flight within and outside Earth's atmosphere.

capsule (kap' səl) *n.* space capsule. A detachable, closed compartment designed to hold and protect people and instruments in a rocket

retrorocket (re' trō räk it) *n.* small rocket that reduces the speed of a spacecraft by pushing in a direction opposite from the direction of flight

An Astronaut's Answers

John Glenn

This interview was conducted shortly before Glenn returned to space at the age of seventy-seven on board the shuttle *Discovery*.

The first time you went into space, how did it feel to be all alone except for communication through radio?

In 1962, I looked down from an orbit high above our planet and saw our beautiful Earth and its curved horizon against the vastness of space. I have never forgotten that sight nor the sense of wonder it engendered. Although I was alone in *Friendship 7*, I did not feel alone in space. I knew that I was supported by my family, my six fellow astronauts, thousands of NASA engineers and employees, and millions of people around the world.

Why did you want to be an astronaut? How did you fly around the Earth three times? Was it hard?

I served as a fighter pilot in World War II and the Korean conflict. After Korea, I graduated from the Naval Test Pilot School and worked as a fighter test pilot. I applied for the astronaut program because I thought it was a logical career step, a challenging opportunity and one in which I could help start a new area of research that would be very valuable to everyone here on Earth. I have always considered myself very fortunate to be selected in the first group of seven astronauts.

◆ Reading Interviews

Why do you think the **interview** questions are set in boldface?

____

____

____

◆ Stop to Reflect

Why did John Glenn become an astronaut?

____

____

____

Would you consider becoming an astronaut? Why or why not?

____

____

____

____

◆ Reading Check

What was the name of Glenn's space capsule? Circle the answer in the text.

Mark the Text

An Atlas rocket boosted me into space and I orbited the Earth in my space capsule, the *Friendship 7*. It certainly was a challenge but one for which I was well prepared. The National Aeronautics and Space Administration (NASA) wanted people who were test pilots and accustomed to working under very unusual conditions, including emergencies. During my first orbit I experienced some troubles with the automatic control system and so I had to take control of the capsule's movements by hand for the rest of the trip. Another problem developed when the signals showed that the heat shield was loose. To keep it secured during re-entry, I kept the retrorocket pack in place to steady the shield. When the *Friendship 7* entered the atmosphere, the retrorocket pack burned off and flew by my window, but the heat shield stayed in place. These were problems we could not have foreseen prior to the flight.

How long was your trip around the Earth?

My trip around the Earth lasted 4 hours and 55 minutes, and I flew about 81,000 miles.

◆ Reading Strategy

Read the bracketed paragraph. Why do you think the food is packaged in tubes? Use your **prior knowledge** about gravity in space to answer this question.

What did you eat while you were in outer space?

I took along a number of different kinds of food, such as applesauce and a mixture of meat and vegetables, all emulsified like baby food. It was packaged in containers much like toothpaste tubes so I could squeeze food into my mouth. I had no trouble eating any of it, and it tasted fine.

Why do astronauts go to the moon?

As adventurers of earlier eras crossed oceans and scaled mountains, astronauts in our time have flown to the moon and explored the heavens. The crucial hands-on experience of my flight in the Mercury program helped make the Gemini flights possible. The Gemini flights then helped make the Apollo missions to the moon a reality. Apollo gave us valuable information for the Shuttle missions, and the Shuttle/Mir program prepares us for the International Space Station. This is the nature of progress. Each of these missions has built on the knowledge gained from previous flights.

We are curious, questing people and our research in this new laboratory of space represents an opportunity to benefit people right here on Earth and to increase our understanding of the universe. The potential scientific, medical, and economic benefits from space are beyond our wildest dreams. That's why astronauts went to the moon, and that's why we continue to pursue our dreams of space exploration.

◆ Reading Check

List three space programs that Glenn mentions in the bracketed paragraph.

1. ____________________
2. ____________________
3. ____________________

Reading Informational Materials

Write two **interview** questions that you would like to ask John Glenn about his first trip in space.

1. ____________________
____
____
2. ____________________
____
____

READING INFORMATIONAL MATERIALS

INTERVIEWS

About Interviews

An **interview** is a formal conversation in which one person (the interviewer) asks questions, and another person (the subject) answers them. Interviews with writers, actors, sports figures, and other celebrities can be found in newspapers and magazines. You can tell the words of the interviewer from those of the subject because they are usually labeled with a name or initials. They may also be in a different typeface.

Reading Strategy

Connecting and Clarifying Main Ideas

In an interview, the questions and answers can help you identify a few **main ideas** about the subject. Clarify these ideas by connecting them to what you already know about the subject. You can also clarify main ideas by making connections to related topics. For example, you can read books about the subject or review other interviews. The chart provides ideas for sources you can consult to clarify ideas in interviews.

	Actors	Writers	Athletes
Other Sources	His or her performances	Themes in his or her written works	The athlete's performance in the sport
	Talk show appearances	Reviews of his or her works	Articles about the athlete
	Comments from other actors or directors	Biography or autobiography of the writer	Comments from coaches and teammates
Related Topics	Style of acting	Other writers' treatment of similar themes	The athlete's particular sport

BUILD UNDERSTANDING

Knowing these words will help you read this interview.

Flash Gordon *n.* fictional spaceman who was the subject of three movie serials

graduate (graj´ oo wit) **school** *n.* school for advanced study; a university or university division for advanced students who have obtained a bachelor's degree

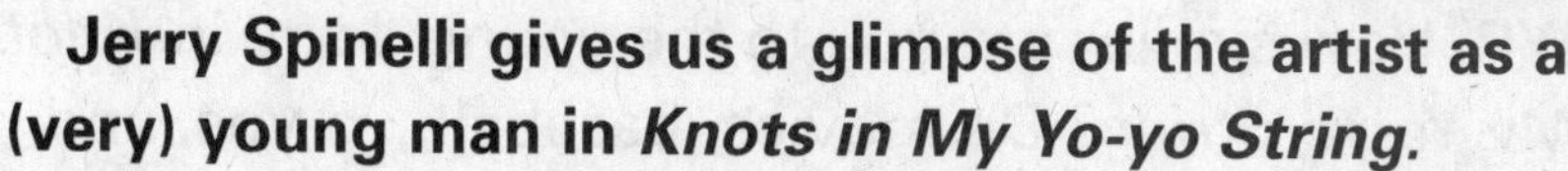

Interview with Jerry Spinelli

from
The Borzoi Young Reader 1998

Jerry Spinelli gives us a glimpse of the artist as a (very) young man in *Knots in My Yo-yo String.*

Borzoi Young Reader: You have an incredible memory of your early childhood. Has this always been the case—or did you do a lot of research and conduct interviews to fill in the gaps?

JS: Memories of childhood seem to come naturally to me. Until I started writing books for kids, I thought that was the case with everybody. I did consult my mother and brother at length, and the family scrapbooks. Others I spoke with are listed in the "Acknowledgments."

BYR: Readers who know your books can find many seeds and details from your novels in your own childhood. Is there a character in one of your novels who's the most like you as a boy?

JS: No one character in any book is all me. I guess the one who comes closest is Jason in *Space Station Seventh Grade*. Others include Maniac Magee and Eddie Mott in the School Daze series.

BYR: We learn from your memoir that you weren't much of a reader (of books) all through your childhood. When did this change?

◆ Stop to Reflect

Read the text in the first bracket. What type of publication might *The Borzoi Young Reader* be?

____

____

◆ Reading Strategy

Mark the Text

A **main idea** of this interview is that Jerry Spinelli draws on his own childhood when he creates characters. In the second bracketed passage, underline three characters Spinelli mentions who are somewhat like he was as a boy. According to Spinelli, which character is most like him?

____

◆ Reading Check

When did Jerry Spinelli become an enthusiastic reader?

____

____

◆ Stop to Reflect

Does reading this interview make you want to read some of Jerry Spinelli's books? ________ Why or why not?

____

____

____

____

Reading Informational Materials

What are two things you learned from reading this **interview** with Jerry Spinelli?

1. ______________________

____

2. ______________________

____

What questions do you have based on the information in the interview?

____

____

____

____

JS: I finally became a willing, enthusiastic reader during my year in graduate school at the Writing Seminars, Johns Hopkins University. Because I regret that it took me so long, I put a book in Maniac Magee's hand everywhere he goes.

BYR: What are you reading right now?

JS: A book about tuning into your life called *Callings* by Gregg Lavoy and a murder mystery, *Nocturne*, by Ed McBain.

BYR: How similar are you to the young Jerry in *Knots in My Yo-yo String*? Do movies, baseball, yo-yos, and fanatical neatness still have a place in your life?

JS: The game I play now is tennis rather than baseball; I haven't spun a yo-yo in years; and no father of six kids is fanatically neat. But I recently watched a bunch of Flash Gordon episodes on the AMC channel, and I still hate war and love cowboys and sports, and I still feel bad for not visiting Garfield Shainline, and I still swoon when I look at the night sky and try to imagine eternity. I finally learned to swim (a little) and eat hot peppers (a little), but I still can't blast an earsplitting, two-fingered whistle.

READING INFORMATIONAL MATERIALS

REVIEWS

About Reviews

A **review** describes and evaluates a product or performance. Reviews are one source of information you can use to find out about the following topics:

- a book
- a movie or television program
- a stage performance
- a music disc, collection, or performance
- a restaurant

A review gives the reader information that can be used to make a decision. If a reviewer likes something, he or she can influence readers positively. A negative review, however, can discourage people from buying, visiting, reading, or viewing.

The following selection is a music review about the *Smithsonian Folkways' Anthology of American Folk Music.* As you read, think about whether you would or would not purchase the collection, based on the review.

Reading Strategy

Reading Accurately

To **read accurately** means to read each word correctly and to understand the meaning of each word. When you are reading informational texts, follow these steps:

- Scan the text—run your eyes quickly over the words—before you read it closely.
- Identify unfamiliar words and terms.
- Look them up in a dictionary or other resource.
- Learn their pronunciations.

BUILD UNDERSTANDING

Knowing these words will help you read this review.

Smithsonian (smith sō´ nē ən) *n.* institution and museum in Washington, D.C. Its branches cover a wide range of fields in the arts and sciences.

Mason-Dixon (mā´ s'n dik´ s'n) **Line** *n.* boundary line between Pennsylvania and Maryland regarded as separating the North from the South

As Close As We Can Get

Carl Zebrowski

Listening to the recordings in *Smithsonian Folkways' Anthology of American Folk Music* is like looking at a photo of a Civil War soldier dressed in a crumpled uniform. Beneath the medium's[1] time-worn surface you can sense the presence of a vibrant living person.

What cuts through the mild surface noise of the anthology's 70-year-old recordings is people in all their joy and sorrow. These are plain folk, mostly from south of the Mason-Dixon Line. They have no pretensions. They are not self-conscious. Their music is earthy yet at the same time other-worldly.

◆ Reading Strategy

To **read accurately**, scan the text and circle two words you do not know. Write the words on the lines below. Look up the words in a dictionary and write the meaning that fits the usage in this text.

Mark THE Text

1. ____________________

____

2. ____________________

____

◆ Reading Check

From where do most of the people who made the recordings come?

____

____

1. **medium** (mē´ dē əm) *n.* material holding information (in this case musical information).

There's plenty of sloppy string plucking and bowing[2] here, and warbling voices, too, but surely that's what folk music sounded like in the 1860s (and often still does). It was a time when entertainment for a social gathering often meant a friend playing his banjo. He probably wasn't an accomplished musician by traditional standards, but his confident rhythm and enthusiasm made the music come alive in ways sheer virtuosity[3] can't. This anthology is about as close as we can get to the music of that era.

Although the recordings here were, of course, not made during the war, the performances are timeless. The songs are even more so. Indeed, many of them have been around for hundreds of years. They were played in the 1860s and are still played today. As everything in history does, these simple tunes have picked up a little bit of all the generations they've passed through. That historical gold dust shows up on these recordings.

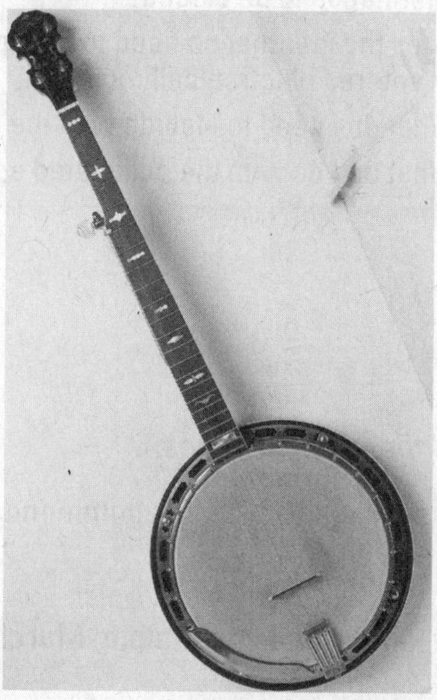

◆ Reading Check

Mark the Text

The reviewer mentions strengths and weakness of the collection. In the bracketed paragraph, circle two weaknesses. Underline two strengths.

Reading Informational Materials

Based on this **review**, would you buy this collection of music? ______ Why or why not?

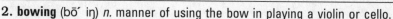

2. **bowing** (bō´ iŋ) *n.* manner of using the bow in playing a violin or cello.

3. **virtuosity** (vur´ cho͞o wäs´ ə tē) *n.* great skill in some fine art, especially in the performance of music.

READING INFORMATIONAL MATERIALS

APPLICATIONS

About Applications

An **application** is a form people fill out to be considered for certain privileges. At one time or another, you will probably fill out an application for some of the following reasons:

- to get a library card
- to get a job
- to be admitted to a school
- to open a savings account
- to join a club or sports league
- to get a driver's license

Reading Strategy

Following Multiple-Step Directions

Applications often have **multiple-step directions**—instructions that have several steps or parts that must be done before the application is complete. Before you begin filling out an application, make sure you can answer the questions listed in the chart. After you have filled out the application, check that you have completed all the necessary sections and that the information is legible, or readable.

Previewing an Application

1. What information is being asked for?
2. On which line or in which space is the information to be placed?
3. Does the information need to be typed, printed, or entered electronically?
4. What do I need to include with the application?
5. What do I do with the completed application?

BUILD UNDERSTANDING

Knowing these words will help you read these applications.

reference (ref′ ər əns) *n.* a person who is willing to give a recommendation or statement of character, qualification, or ability.

mm/dd/yy *n.* abbreviation for month, day, and year. For example, March 5, 2003 would be written 03/05/03.

DOB *n.* abbreviation for Date of Birth

VILLA PARK PUBLIC LIBRARY

Library Card Application

To obtain a Villa Park Public Library card, you will need to bring the following to the Library:

- Two forms of identification with your Villa Park address (one of which includes a photograph).
- An application form, which must be signed at the Library's circulation desk.
- If you are under the age of 18, you will also need a parent to sign the form at the Library's circulation desk.
- For Oakbrook Terrace residents, a certificate of residence from the City of Oakbrook Terrace (available at the City Clerk's office).
- Other non-residents must pay a fee for a library card.

STAFF USE **Expiration**

Date: ____________ **Spec Designation** ____________
OBT—1/4ly—Family Fee

Name typed ______________________
Last, First, MI

New - Renew - Ex Rew

REGISTRATION WORKSHEET

Today's Date ____________

Name ______________________
Please Print First, Middle Initial, Last

Address ______________________
Street City, State, Zip Code

Phone Number ____________ Social Security Number____________

Reference ____________ Phone Number ____________

Address ______________________
Street City, State, Zip Code

Business Name ____________ Phone Number ____________

Business Address ______________________
Street City, State, Zip Code

Date of Birth (if under 18) ____________

The lines below must be signed in person at the Library's circulation desk:
I agree to be responsible for all materials checked out on my library card and fines and fees accrued.

Signed____________

If person signing this application is under 18, a parent's signature is needed.

I am responsible for all materials checked out on my child's library card and fines and fees accrued.

____________ ____________
Please Print Parent's Name Parent's Signature

◆ Reading Applications

List two things that you should bring with you when you apply for a library card.

1. ____________

2. ____________

◆ Stop to Reflect

Why do you think you need references to get a library card?

____

◆ Reading Check

Mark the Text

Circle the word or phrase that indicates where the applicant should sign.

◆ **Stop to Reflect**

The first question asks the applicant to make a choice. Who might you ask if you do not understand the choices?

____

____

____

◆ **Reading Strategy**

Circle the **instructions** that indicate how information is to be entered on the form.

Mark the Text

◆ **Stop to Reflect**

Why is it important to write clearly and neatly on an application?

____

____

____

◆ **Reading Applications**

On the **application**, write today's date in the mm/dd/yy format.

Mark the Text

SAVINGS ACCOUNT APPLICATION

Simply complete this short form to start your application process.

1. What type of account would you like to open?

    ❑ Young Investors' Club

    ❑ Statement Savings

    ❑ Holiday Savings

2. Would you like Internet banking?

    ❑ Yes ❑ No

3. Provide the following information. (Please print.)

    Name ______________________

    E-Mail ______________________

    Street Address ______________________

    Address (cont.) ______________________

    City ____________ State ____ Zip code ______

    Work Phone ______________________

    Home Phone ______________________

4. Today's Date ☐☐☐☐☐☐ mm/dd/yy

5. Initial Deposit Amount ______________________

    You must make an initial deposit as required by the type of savings account you are opening.

6. Date of Birth ☐☐☐☐☐☐ mm/dd/yy

Social Security Number ______________________

Signature ______________________

PASADENA YOUTH ROLLER HOCKEY REGISTRATION FORM

REGISTRATION DEADLINE APRIL 6, 2002

COST $75.00 ($65.00 IF YOU REGISTER BY APRIL 6, 2002)

Player Tryout & Draft: Saturday, April 6, 2002
League Starts: Thursday, April 18, 2002

EQUIPMENT NEEDED:

Skates—In-line or Regular Quad
Helmet—MANDATORY[1] with full face mask or shield. No Goalie Helmet
Stick—Regulation hockey stick, preferred to be no higher than nose
Gloves—Regulation hockey gloves
Elbow Pads/Shin Guards—Recommended, but not Mandatory

ALL EQUIPMENT NEEDS ARE AVAILABLE AT THE PASADENA ROLLER RINK, USUALLY CHEAPER THAN OR EQUAL TO ATHLETIC STORE PRICES.

TO REGISTER—MAIL YOUR FORM(S) TO 4100 JANA LN, PASADENA, TX 77505 OR COME BY THE PASADENA ROLLER RINK AT 2602 CHERRYBROOK, PASADENA, TX.

PASADENA YOUTH ROLLER HOCKEY LEAGUE
Registration Form, 4100 Jana Ln, Pasadena, TX 77505
REGISTRATION DEADLINE APRIL 6, 2002

PLAYER'S NAME______________ AGE ______ DOB _____

ADDRESS______________ CITY ________ ZIP _____

PARENTS' NAMES (Mom)______________(Dad)______________

PHONE NUMBER (____)____________ SHIRT SIZE ________

The player listed above has my permission to participate in this activity. I understand that the Pasadena Roller Rink and the Pasadena Youth Hockey League do not provide insurance and are not responsible for accident coverage.

PARENT'S SIGNATURE______________ DATE __/__/__

◆ **Stop to Reflect**

Why do you think a registration deadline is necessary for a sports program?

____
____
____
____

◆ **Reading Check**

Circle two ways in which you can submit your application.

Reading Informational Materials

Choose one of the **applications** and list the multiple steps that you must follow to complete the application process. Reading the application form should be your first step in each case.

____
____
____
____
____
____

1. **mandatory** (man´ də tôr´ ē) *adj.* required.

READING INFORMATIONAL MATERIALS

CAUSE-AND-EFFECT ARTICLES

About Cause-and-Effect Articles

A **cause-and-effect article** explains the circumstances leading to an event or a situation. To get the most information from a cause-and-effect article, look for the following:

- a clear explanation of one or more causes or one or more effects
- a presentation of facts and details that support each explanation
- transitions that clearly show the connections among the details

Cause-and-effect articles may be found in many newspapers and magazines and in your textbooks.

Reading Strategy

Analyze Causes and Effects

Ancient peoples used fables, myths, and legends to explain events. Today, however, we look for **causes**—the reasons behind events—and **effects**—the results produced by causes. As you read a cause-and-effect essay, follow these steps. First, identify the topic event or effect—such as the decrease in the population of manatees. Then identify the causes and effects presented by the writer. Note the causes and effects in the chart before you read "Gentle Giants in Trouble." As you read, notice how the author presents the causes and effects to the reader.

Manatee Cause-and-Effect Chart

Causes	Effects
Construction	Manatees' feeding grounds disappeared
Pollution	Manatees injured or killed
Power boats	Manatees injured or killed

BUILD UNDERSTANDING

Knowing this word will help you read this cause-and-effect article.

manatee (man′ ə tē′) *n.* large water mammal that lives in shallow tropical waters; also called a sea cow

Gentle Giants in Trouble

Ross Bankson

They have no natural enemies, but they are in trouble anyway. West Indian manatees—large, gentle marine mammals—are in danger because of people...

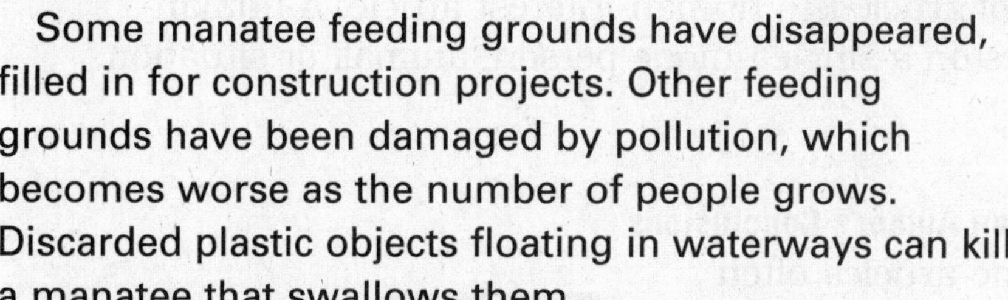

Some manatee feeding grounds have disappeared, filled in for construction projects. Other feeding grounds have been damaged by pollution, which becomes worse as the number of people grows. Discarded plastic objects floating in waterways can kill a manatee that swallows them.

Boaters create the greatest hazard for West Indian manatees in the shallow water that the animals prefer. The slow-moving manatees often cannot get away from speeding boats. In a collision with a boat, a manatee may be killed or injured by the force of the hit or by cuts from the propeller. Of some 1,500 manatees in Florida today, nearly all adults bear scars from run-ins with propellers.

The good news for the West Indian manatee is this: People can help as well as harm. Many in fact are working to save manatees. Some Florida car owners pay extra money for a "Save the Manatee" license plate. By doing so they help fund the state's manatee protection program and other programs for environmental education. Florida laws regulate boating in areas where manatees live. Other laws protect the animal as an endangered species.

Still, the experts say, even more safeguards[1] are needed. The manatee population is shrinking. "With public support," says Judith Valee, "we can bring the species back from the brink of extinction."

◆ Reading Strategy

What problem, or **effect**, is introduced in the first paragraph?

______

______

______

◆ Reading Strategy

Mark the Text

In the bracketed paragraph, underline the words that describe the main **cause** of danger to the manatee. Circle words that name the effect.

Reading Informational Materials

In what other classes might you read a **cause-and-effect article**?

______

Explain your answer.

______

______

______

1. **safeguards** (sāf′ gardz′) *n.* protective arrangements.

READING INFORMATIONAL MATERIALS

MAGAZINE ARTICLES

About Magazine Articles

Magazine articles can be found on almost any subject you can name. Although each magazine article has unique characteristics, articles do share some common qualities.

- Articles give facts about a subject.
- Articles often include a comment by the writer on the subject.
- Articles are usually short enough to be read in one sitting.

One common type of article is a human-interest article. A human-interest article focuses on a single unique person, animal, or situation.

Reading Strategy

Evaluating Evidence for an Author's Conclusions

Authors of magazine articles often draw conclusions based on the information they present. When you read a magazine article, decide for yourself if you accept the **author's conclusions.** Evaluate the evidence. Then, evaluate whether the evidence actually supports the writer's claims.

Use an organizer like the one shown to record the information presented in this article. Put a star next to any facts or details you would like to check.

Conclusion
Facts
Quotes
Details
Examples
Citations
Supporting evidence

BUILD UNDERSTANDING

Knowing these words will help you read this magazine article.

major leagues (mā´jər lēg) *n.* the two main leagues of professional baseball clubs in the Unites States, the National League and the American League

rookie (ro͝ok´ē) *n.* a new player in a professional sport

scout (skout) *n.* a person sent out to find people with talent

THROW AND TELL

Gifted with a 98-mph fastball, teacher Jim Morris goes from a Texas classroom to baseball's big leagues.

The Reagan County High School baseball team had a beef. Not about their field in Big Lake, Texas—where dust from a nearby rodeo arena sometimes stops games—but about batting practice. According to the kids, coach Jim Morris, a former minor leaguer forced out of the game a decade earlier by arm problems, was making pitches that they just couldn't hit. "The team used to tell me I was throwing too hard," says Morris, 35, who also taught science. "I thought they were complaining because they didn't want to take batting

◆ Reading Strategy

Is the photograph of Jim Morris a form of **evidence** that supports a main point of this article? ________

Explain. ________

____

____

____

◆ Stop to Reflect

Do you think "Throw and Tell" is a good title for this magazine article?

____

Why or why not?

____

____

____

◆ Reading Check

What led Jim Morris to try out for the major leagues? Circle your answer in the article.

Mark the Text

◆ Stop to Reflect

How do you think Morris must have felt as he tried out for the major leagues? Explain.

Reading Informational Materials

Some **magazines** print the title and issue date on their pages. Why might the title and publishing date be important to readers?

practice." Finally, he proposed a deal: If the team made the state play-offs, he would try out for the major leagues.

The kids did their part, and in mid-June, Morris did his, dazzling scouts with his 98-mph fastball. Within a week Morris had signed with the Tampa Bay Devil Rays and, with the blessing of wife Lorri, was launched on one of the most improbable baseball adventures this side of Kevin Costner. After posting a 3-1 record at the Devil Rays' Durham, N.C., farm club, the big lefthander got his call to the majors last month. On Sept. 18, against the Texas Rangers, Morris entered the game in the eighth inning, becoming the oldest big league rookie in nearly three decades. As Lorri, a college admissions officer, and the couple's three children looked on, Morris struck out Royce Clayton on four pitches. "My 8-year-old is ecstatic—he took that ball to school," says Morris. "My 5-year-old just wants me to come home."

Unfortunately for little Jessica, Daddy still has work to do. He's headed to the Arizona Fall League, where teams send their most promising prospects. "It's been an unbelievable journey," says Morris. "It's strange to go from signing report cards to signing autographs almost overnight."

READING INFORMATIONAL MATERIALS

PERSUASIVE SPEECHES

About Persuasive Speeches

A **persuasive speech** argues for or against a particular position. Most persuasive speeches have the following characteristics:

- An issue with two sides
- A clear statement of the speaker's purpose and position
- Powerful language intended to persuade

Reading Strategy

Understanding a Writer's Purpose

The basic **purpose** of a persuasive speech is to persuade you to accept the writer's position. This position can usually be learned by reading the opening paragraphs of the speech. The rest of the speech should support the position with facts and arguments.

As you read the speech, think about the writer's purpose. Ask whether the speech achieves this purpose.

Writer's Purpose	Was it achieved?
The writer was trying to persuade me to believe that ______________ ______________ ______________ ______________	Did the writer present accurate facts? Did the writer support a position with convincing arguments? Were the arguments presented clearly, in a logical order? Did the writer convince me to accept that position?

BUILD UNDERSTANDING

Knowing these words will help you read this speech.

designated (dez´ ig nāt´ əd) **hitter** *n.* player who bats in place of the pitcher and does not play any other position. The position was created in 1973 in the American League. Some fans argue it has changed the game for the worse.

Wrigley (rig´ lē) **Field** *n.* historic baseball field in Chicago. It did not have lights for night games until 1988. Some fans regretted the change.

Preserving a Great American Symbol

Richard Durbin

◆ Stop to Reflect

Why might a speaker use humor in a speech?

Congressman Richard Durbin gave the following humorous speech in the House of Representatives on July 26, 1989. While most speeches to Congress are serious, Durbin's is humorous yet persuasive and "drives home" the point that wooden baseball bats should not be replaced with metal ones.

◆ Reading a Speech

What is the topic of Durbin's **speech**? Circle the answer in the first paragraph of the speech.

Mr. Speaker, I rise to condemn the desecration[1] of a great American symbol. No, I am not referring to flag-burning; I am referring to the baseball bat.

Several experts tell us that the wooden baseball bat is doomed to extinction, that major league baseball players will soon be standing at home plate with aluminum bats in their hands.

1. **desecration** (des´ i krā´ shən) *n.* the act of insulting something sacred.

Baseball fans have been forced to endure countless indignities by those who just cannot leave well enough alone: designated hitters, plastic grass, uniforms that look like pajamas, chicken clowns dancing on the baselines, and, of course, the most heinous[2] sacrilege, lights in Wrigley Field.

Are we willing to hear the crack of a bat replaced by the dinky ping? Are we ready to see the Louisville Slugger replaced by the aluminum ping dinger? Is nothing sacred?

Please do not tell me that wooden bats are too expensive, when players who cannot hit their weight are being paid more money than the President of the United States.

Please do not try to sell me on the notion that these metal clubs will make better hitters.

What will be next? Teflon baseballs? Radar-enhanced gloves? I ask you.

I do not want to hear about saving trees. Any tree in America would gladly give its life for the glory of a day at home plate.

I do not know if it will take a constitutional amendment to keep our baseball traditions alive, but if we forsake the great Americana of broken-bat singles and pine tar,[3] we will have certainly lost our way as a nation.

◆ Reading Check

In the bracketed paragraph, circle the word Durbin uses to describe the sound made when an aluminum bat hits the ball.

◆ Reading Strategy

What is Durbin's **purpose** in giving this speech?

____

____

____

Reading Informational Materials

Do you find Durbin's **speech** convincing? ____

Why or why not?

____

____

____

____

2. **heinous** (hā´ nəs) *adj.* very wicked or evil.

3. **broken-bat singles . . . pine tar** When a batter breaks a wooden bat while hitting the ball and makes it to first base, it is a notable event in a baseball game. Pine tar is a substance used to improve the batter's grip on a wooden bat.

READING INFORMATIONAL MATERIALS

WEB SITES AND WEB PAGES

About Web Sites

Web sites are specific locations on the Internet. If you think of the Internet as a giant library, Web sites are individual books within that library. As you explore a Web site on a computer, what you see on the screen is a part of the site called a Web page. A Web site can have many Web pages, just as a book has many pages. You can move from one Web page to another by using the mouse to click on the following items, which are known as *links*:

- a picture
- a "button"
- a highlighted or underlined word or phrase

Reading Strategy

Using Structural Features of Web Sites

Use the special features of a Web site to move quickly around the site and find the information you need. Web sites and Web pages have some of the same **structural features** as textbooks and magazines, such as headings and graphics. They also have some special features unique to electronic texts. Learn to navigate, or find your way around, a Web site by using the special features shown in the chart.

Web Site Features	
Link	A connection to another spot on the same Web page or to a different Web page or Web site. A link can be underlined or highlighted text, or an image or photograph.
Icon	An image or small drawing that may appear by itself or with accompanying text. Icons are often links as well.
Graphics	Pictures, maps, tables, and other graphic sources are often featured on a Web site. These graphics are often sources of information in themselves, but they may also be links to other Web pages.

BUILD UNDERSTANDING

Knowing this word will help you understand the information on this Web site.

Tyrannosaurus rex (tə ran′ ə sôr′əs reks) *n.* a huge, flesh-eating dinosaur that walked upright on its hind legs

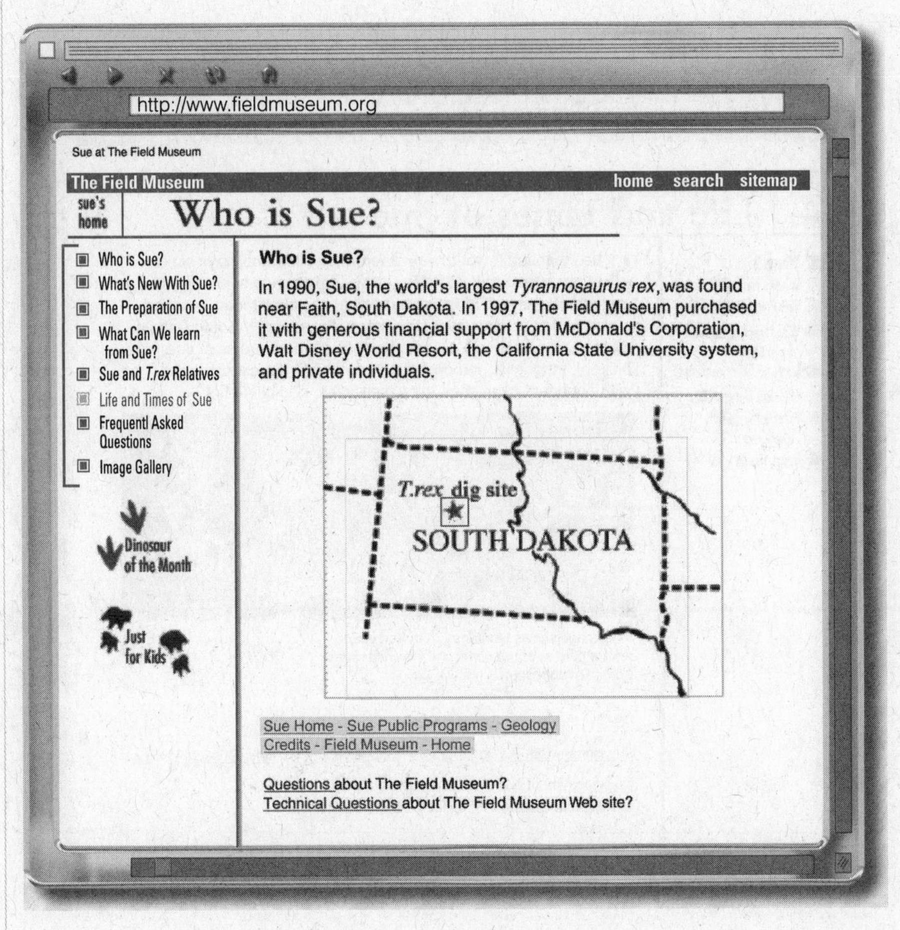

◆ Reading Web Pages

Museums, libraries, and other nonprofit organizations usually have the letters *org* at the end of their **Web** addresses. What types of organizations do you think use the letters *gov* at the end of their Web addresses?

____

____

◆ Reading Strategy

Links to other sites are a common **structural feature** of many Web sites. These lists often appear in a side column, as shown in the bracketed text. Why do you think Web designers use this format to display links?

____

____

____

____

◆ Reading Strategy

Compare this Web page with the one on the previous page. Circle the **structural features** that are the same. Why do you think the pages repeat this information?

Mark THE Text

____

____

____

____

◆ Reading Check

Describe the environment in which Sue lived.

____

____

____

Reading Informational Materials

Today, people use the Internet for a wide variety of reasons. List two ways that the creation of **Web sites** has changed the way people get information.

1. ________________________

____

2. ________________________

____

Life and Times of Sue

- Who is Sue?
- What's New With Sue?
- The Preparation of Sue
- What Can We Learn from Sue?
- Sue and *T.rex* Relatives
- Life and Times of Sue
- Frequently Asked Questions
- Image Gallery

Sue inhabited a world very different, yet in some ways similar to our own. Snakes, turtles, frogs, salamanders, shore birds, and opossums—all of which have relatives alive today—walked, swam and flew across the landscape. Present-day South Dakota, where Sue was found, was home to hardwood forests of oak, hickory, magnolia, and cycads. Swamps were present as well, with abundant cypresses, giant sequoias, and china firs.

http://www.fieldmuseum.org

This image shows Montana, 75 million years ago--a herd of *Parasaurolophus* is under attack from a *Tyrannosaurus rex*.

next

Sue Home - Sue Public Programs - Geology Credits - Field Museum - Home

Questions about The Field Museum?
Technical Questions about The Field Museum Web site?

READING INFORMATIONAL MATERIALS

SOCIAL STUDIES TEXTS

About Social Studies Texts

Social Studies deals with a wide variety of people, places, and cultures. Information about social studies topics can be found in a variety of texts. You might consult social studies texts other than your **social studies textbook** for several reasons, including the following:

- **General interest**—to find out more about a topic.
- **Background**—to improve your understanding of a topic.
- **Perspective**—to look at an event or topic from several different viewpoints to get a clear picture of it.
- **Research**—to find facts and details that support an idea.

Reading Strategy

Watch for Unknown Words

When you read an article on a specialized topic, **watch for unknown words.** Decide which ones to look up immediately, which to check later, and which to take notes on.

- Knowing the pronunciation of a name will not affect your understanding of the text, so you can wait to look it up.
- Knowing the meaning of a specialized term may help you understand your reading, so you might want to look it up right away.
- Take notes on unfamiliar words. You may run into them again in related texts.

March 26, 20__
"Human Footprints at Chauvet Cave"
by Spencer Harrington
Summary:
Scientists discover oldest human footprints and more than 447 paintings in a cave in France.
Names:
* Aldene, Montespan, Niaux, Pech Merle = other caves
* Jean-Marie Chauvet = He discovered the cave
New Words:
* upper paleolithic— 40,000–10,000 BC
* "ca." = "circa" = about; approximately

BUILD UNDERSTANDING

Knowing these words will help you read this social studies text.

Homo sapiens (hō′mō sā′pē enz′) *n.* human being; the scientific name for the only living species of human

species (spē′shēz) *n.* a group of plants or animals that are alike in certain ways

Human Footprints at Chauvet Cave

Spencer P.M. Harrington

Recent exploration of the Chauvet [shō vā´] Cave near Vallon-Pont-d'Arc [valoŋ´ poŋ dark] in southern France has yielded the oldest footprints of *Homo sapiens* and a cavern with a dozen new animal figures. The footprints appear to be those of an eight-year-old boy, according to prehistorian Michel-Alain Garcia [mē shel´ a lan´ gär sē´ ä] of the Centre National de la Recherche Scientifique, Nanterre.[1] They are between 20 and 30 thousand years old, perhaps twice as old as those discovered previously at Aldene, Montespan [mon tə span], Niaux [nē o´], Pech Merle [pesh merl], and other Upper Palaeolithic sites.[2]

Garcia estimates that the boy was about four-and-a-half feet tall, his feet more than eight inches long and three-and-a-half inches wide. First spotted in 1994 by Jean-Marie [zhäŋ mä rē´] Chauvet, the cave's discoverer, the footsteps stretch perhaps 150 feet and at times cross those of bears and wolves. The steps lead to the so-called room of skulls, where a number of bear skulls have been found. In a few places, there is evidence that the boy slipped on the soft clay floor, though Garcia says the prints show the boy was not running, but walking normally. The boy appears at one point to have stopped to clean his torch, charcoal from which has been dated to ca. 26,000 years ago. The prints from the Chauvet Cave, like nearly all footprints thus far discov-

◆ **Reading Strategy**

Some **unknown words** will not affect your immediate understanding of a text. You can look them up after you have finished reading. Circle two examples of this type of unknown word in the first paragraph.

Mark the Text

◆ **Reading Check**

How much older are the footprints in the Chauvet Cave compared to ones previously found?

____

1. **Centre National de la Recherche Scientifique, Nanterre** French for "National Center for Scientific Research [at] Nanterre."

2. **Upper Palaeolithic sites** places believed to have artifacts from the period of time between approximately 40,000 and 10,000 B.C.

ered in Palaeolithic caves, are from bare feet, which has led scholars to speculate that people of the time either left footwear at cave entrances or carried them.

Meanwhile, a team of 15 specialists directed by French prehistorian Jean Clottes recently investigated an uninventoried room originally discovered by Chauvet. There they found a dozen new paintings of mammoth, bison, and horses, among other animals. Clottes' team has so far documented 447 animals of 14 different species. By comparison, Niaux Cave in the French Pyrenees, cited by the French Palaeolithic specialist Abbé Breuil [ä bā´ brool] as one of the half-dozen great caves containing prehistoric art, has 110 images of six species.

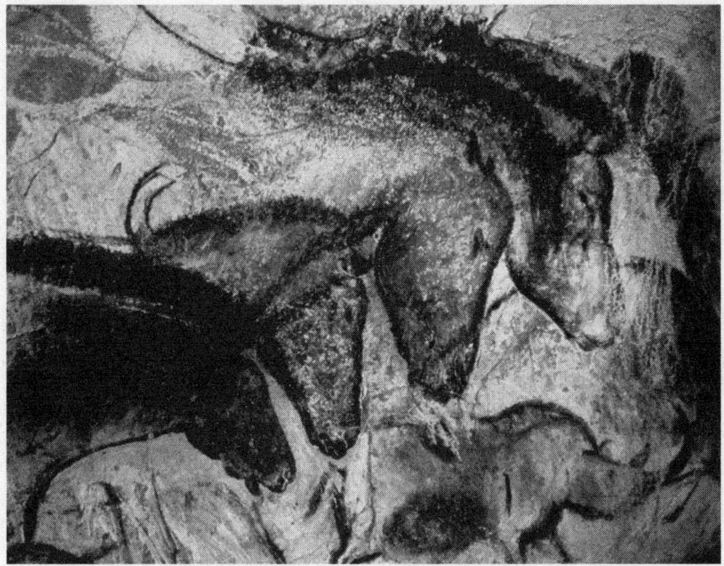

◆ Stop to Reflect

Why might you read this article in an art class?

____

____

Reading Informational Materials

Social studies articles can be found in a wide variety of magazines. Where else might you find a social studies article like this one?

____

____

____

____

MAGAZINE ARTICLES

About Magazine Articles

Magazine articles are nonfiction texts written for different reasons, such as the following:

- to inform readers about a person or topic
- to state a viewpoint
- to convince readers to take a specific action

Reading Strategy

Recognizing Supported and Unsupported Claims

As you read magazine articles, ask yourself these questions about the claims or statements presented:

- Does the writer **support his or her claims** with facts (information that can be proved to be true) or with opinions (the writer's or someone else's viewpoint)?
- Are quotes and sources of information accurate? Are they related to the claims?
- Does the writer's reasoning make sense?

As you read the article, use a chart like the one shown to identify and analyze the writer's statements. Write the statement and its supporting text. If there is no supporting text, explain the support that is needed.

Analyzing Support

Statement	Support	Support Needed
Rehabilitation techniques have come a long way in the past quarter century.	None	The writer needs to tell *how* techniques have improved.

BUILD UNDERSTANDING

Knowing these words will help you read this magazine article.

plumage (plo͞om′ij) *n.* a bird's feathers

rehabilitated birds (rē′hə bil′ə tā′təd bʉrdz) *n.* birds that have been rescued and brought back to a normal or good condition

Can Oiled Seabirds Be Rescued, Or Are We Just Fooling Ourselves?

Sharon Levy

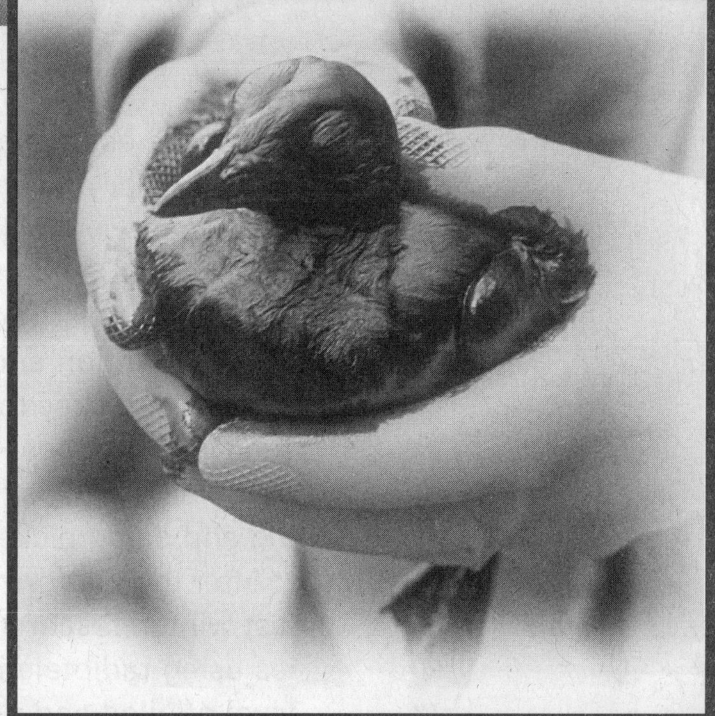

Like dozens of other volunteers, I felt compelled to help when a cargo ship spilled 5,000 gallons of fuel oil in Humboldt Bay, near my home on California's north coast. When we released rehabilitated birds, we all felt great. Later, I learned that what we had done was controversial. Many biologists believe that rescuing oiled birds serves more to soothe human feelings than to help wildlife and some studies show that many cleaned birds survive for only a few days. But there are a number of encouraging success stories.

Plumage normally keeps a seabird warm and dry even as it dives far below the surface. When oil coats feathers, the plumage loses its ability to insulate, leaving a bird susceptible to hypothermia.[1] Beached birds also suffer from dehydration, anemia and pneumonia.

Rehabilitation techniques have come a long way in the past quarter century. But critics contend that the surviving birds represent an insignificant proportion of the bird populations affected in most spills. "Future oil company support for bird rescue should be considered a public relations effort to counteract negative public opinion," wrote Oregon biologist Brian Sharp in a 1995

◆ Stop to Reflect

Based on the title and the picture, what do you think is the writer's opinion about oiled seabirds?

____

____

____

◆ Reading Check

Mark the Text

In the first paragraph, underline the claim that the writer makes about the success of rescuing oiled seabirds.

◆ Reading Strategy

Read the underlined sentence. Then, evaluate the writer's **claim** by answering the following question: Is this statement a fact or an opinion? Explain.

____

____

1. **"the plumage loses . . . susceptible to hypothermia"** the feathers are no longer able to keep the bird warm. It is now possible that the bird's body temperature could drop dangerously below normal.

report. He estimates that only 4 percent of cleaned birds live for a year in the wild.

"Bird survival will be quite different from spill to spill," says David Jessup, a veterinarian with the California Department of Fish and Game's Office of Spill Prevention and Response, which has established regional facilities to provide rapid response during such catastrophes. "The species involved, the toxicity of the oil, the weather and length of time between oiling and being picked up, all influence survival."

After the Platform Irene oil spill near Santa Barbara last winter, researchers conducted one of the first studies using radiotelemetry to directly compare the survival of oiled and unoiled western gulls. "It was a sticky, nasty crude oil that pasted the birds' feathers, wings and legs to their bodies," recalls veterinarian Jonna Mazet, director of the state's Oiled Wildlife Care Network. <u>"Following release, all of the rehabilitated gulls survived for the life of their radio transmitters [more than eight months] and did as well or better than a control group of unoiled birds."</u>

The most successful cases of oiled-bird rescue have occurred at the tip of South Africa, where African penguin colonies have suffered from several serious oil spills over the last decade. Penguins have a better chance of surviving oiling and rehabilitation than most other seabirds. They have a layer of blubber to keep them warm. And their normal life cycle involves periods of fasting. Following a spill in 1994, more than 65 percent of the 4,076 penguins that were cleaned were later resighted in good health.

Dee Boersma, a University of Washington biologist who works with Magellanic penguins in Argentina, hasn't experienced the same success. "The reason South Africa worked is they had a huge aquarium and fire department that delivered water free so that they could really wash the birds. In Argentina, it's a desert.

◆ Reading Strategy

Does the underlined sentence **support the claim** the writer made in the first paragraph? ____________

Explain. ____________

____

____

◆ Reading Check

What type of bird has the best chance of surviving an oil spill? Circle the answer in the text. Then, explain why this is true.

Mark the Text

____

____

____

The nearest town is many miles from the large penguin colonies and there's no water."

During a major spill off Argentina in 1991, Boersma estimates 17,000 birds were oiled. "Perhaps 360 birds were recovered, giving a false impression that the population was being rescued," she says.

At the Humboldt spill, I experienced the joy of seeing birds recover as well as the sorrow of seeing them suffer. If an oil spill does hit here again, chances are I'll go back to the wildlife care center to help out. I'll do this for some good reasons and for some bad ones. I'll do it because I know action is an effective antidote to the grief I'll feel. I'll do it in the hope that a majority of the birds that go through rehabilitation will survive. That's a goal that seems far more attainable here than on the remote beaches of Argentina.

Yes, I'd work at the center again. But I'd know as I started up my car engine to go there that I was applying a Band-Aid, not solving the problem of oil pollution. Like everyone else in our oil-addicted society, I am still part of that dilemma.

Californian Sharon Levy specializes in topics relating to science and nature.

Reading Informational Materials

Magazines are often published by organizations that have a specific purpose. For example, this article appeared in a wildlife magazine. How might the article have been different if it had appeared in an oil industry publication?

READING INFORMATIONAL MATERIALS

BOOK REVIEWS

About Book Reviews

If you want to learn about a book before you decide to read it, you can find useful information in a **book review**. Most book reviews include the following:

- a brief summary of the book
- a description of the background of the author or authors
- an opinion about the quality of the book
- an excerpt from the book

Reading Strategy

Reading to Take Action

When you **read to take action**, you look for specific information that will help you do something. To guide your reading, begin by asking one or two questions. Then, look for answers as you read. For example, if you were planning a snorkeling trip, you might ask, "How can I protect the wildlife I see?" As you read to take action, take notes on the information that answers your question. Then organize the information in a graphic organizer like the one shown.

Read to Take Action

Questions	Facts That Answer Questions
1.	a.
	b.
	c.
2.	a.
	b.

BUILD UNDERSTANDING

Knowing these words will help you read this book review.

snorkeling (snôr′ kəl iŋ) *n.* swimming while using a snorkel, a short tube for breathing underwater

coral reef (kôr′ əl rēf) *n.* a ridge of coral, a hard stony substance made up of the skeletons of tiny sea animals

scuba (sko͞o′ bə) *n.* equipment worn by divers for breathing underwater. The letters stand for **s**elf-**c**ontained **u**nderwater **b**reathing **a**pparatus

Snorkeling Tips

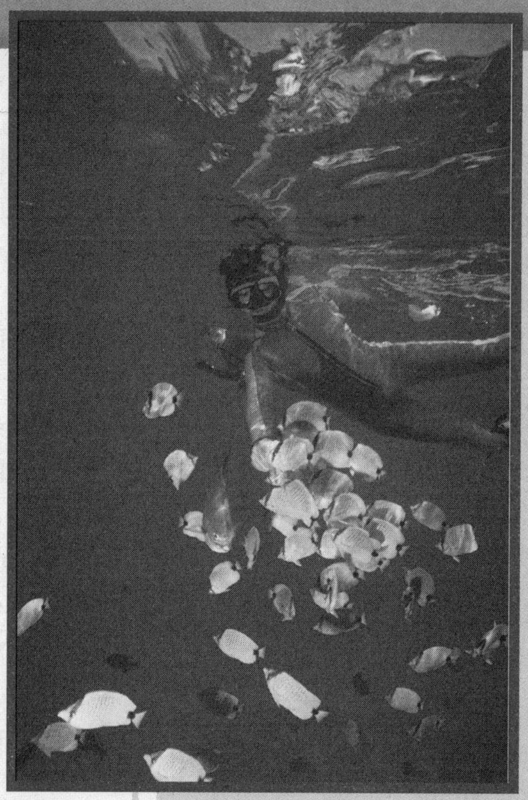

Daniel Lenihan and John D. Brooks

Underwater Wonders of the National Parks, published last year, is an indispensable resource for anyone considering a snorkeling trip. Written by Daniel Lenihan, director of the NPS Submerged Cultural Resource Unit, and John D. Brooks, an underwater photographer with the unit, the book details the watery wonders of the park system, from the coral reefs of the Caribbean to the icebergs in Alaska.

The two have gone snorkeling and scuba diving at every park mentioned in the book and include detailed suggestions on where to go, how to get there, and what you might find. They also have some sound advice for making your snorkeling excursion more enjoyable and helping to protect the fragile reef environment, including these tips:

- Do not touch the animals. Even a gentle caress can disturb the mucous coating that helps protect fish from disease.
- Do not feed the fish. If fed by humans, after a while they become dependent on handouts and lose the ability to forage. Also, they lose their natural wariness, which makes them easy prey for poachers. Even though harvesting fish for tropical collectors is illegal in the national parks, it still goes on.
- Do not touch the coral. The tiny jelly-like polyps that live inside the hard calcium casing are fragile. One swipe of the hand can kill hundreds of them. Many popular shallow reefs have been decimated by careless swimmers who stand on them when they get tired.
- Swim gently and avoid kicking up a lot of sand when near a reef. The sediment can eventually smother the coral and block vital sunlight.

◆ Reading Book Reviews

Why do you think the title, authors, and a brief summary of the book are included in the opening paragraph of this **book review**?

____

____

____

____

◆ Stop to Reflect

Read the bulleted items. Then, list three dangers to wildlife that can be caused by humans.

1. ________________________

____

2. ________________________

____

3. ________________________

____

◆ **Reading Strategy**

If you were **reading to take action** to protect your skin while snorkeling, what information would help you? Circle two useful tips.

Mark the Text

◆ **Reading Book Reviews**

This **book review** contains two different types of tips from the book. What are the first four tips about?

____

____

What are the last eight tips about?

____

____

Reading Informational Materials

This **book review** includes tips from the book *Underwater Wonders of the National Parks.* Do you think it is useful to include an excerpt from the actual book in a review? _____ Explain.

____

____

____

____

- Wear a liberal coating of waterproof sunscreen on your back and the backs of your legs. The thin film of water over you acts as a magnifier, and because the water keeps your skin cool, you may not realize your skin is burning until it is too late. People who are especially sun-sensitive should wear a covering.
- Keep an eye out for stinging organisms like jellyfish and fire coral.
- Do not reach into holes or crevices in the reef. They could turn out to be the lair of a moray eel.
- Take off your jewelry. While barracuda attacks are almost unheard of, the toothy fish are attracted to shiny objects.
- Shark spottings are rare on the shallow reefs that snorkelers frequent, but if you see a shark, do not panic. Most reef sharks are passive types, not man-eaters, and they usually ignore swimmers. If one acts aggressively or pays undue attention to you, calmly and slowly leave the water.
- Do not walk in shallow water near the reef; sea urchin spines can cause nasty puncture wounds to the bottom of your feet.
- Shuffle your feet across the bottom as you wade through the shallow sandy areas on your way to and from the reef. Stingrays lying on the bottom will swim off if you bump into them, but sometimes sting when they are stepped on.
- Be aware of currents. Unless you plan to do a "drift dive" where you start in one spot and let the current carry you to an exit point, it's usually best to swim into the current first and then let it carry you back at the end of your dive when you are most tired.

READING INFORMATIONAL MATERIALS

TEXTBOOKS

About Textbooks

Since you first started school, you have read and used many **textbooks**. Though they covered different topics, they were alike in these ways:

- The purpose of a textbook is to help students learn new material.
- A textbook gives information about a particular subject.
- The material is divided into units, chapters, and sections, usually by topic. Within the text, boldface heads and other graphics highlight important ideas. Questions at the end of a unit or section help you review what you have read.
- Textbooks also include visual aids such as photos, graphs, charts, and fine art. Visual aids help students understand the material.

Reading Strategy

Making an Outline

An **outline** is a list of main ideas and details. Its organization shows the relationship between ideas and information.

Outlines usually follow a form like the one shown here. Each main heading is listed under a Roman numeral: I, II, III, and so on. Each subhead is identified by a capital letter: A, B, C. Supporting details are numbered: 1, 2, 3.

In a textbook, the organization of the material itself helps shape your outline. Boldface heads and subheads point out the main ideas.

Model: Outline

I. First main topic or idea
- **A.** Subheading #1
- **B.** Subheading #2
  - **1.** Supporting detail 1
    - (a) smaller detail
    - (b) smaller detail
  - **2.** Supporting detail 2
  - **3.** Supporting detail 3

II. Second main topic or idea
- **A.** Subheading #1
- **B.** Subheading #2
- **C.** Subheading #3

BUILD UNDERSTANDING

Knowing these words will help you read this textbook section.

prairie (prer´ ē) *n.* large area of flat or slightly rolling grasslands

prairie dog *n.* small, burrowing rodent of North America

SECTION 1

Populations and Communities

◆ **Reading Textbooks**

Circle the topic of this section of the **textbook**.

◆ **Stop to Reflect**

Why do you think some words in the text appear in boldface type?

____

____

____

____

◆ **Reading Check**

What is one example of a population?

____

____

Populations

In 1900, travelers saw a prairie dog town in Texas covering an area twice the size of the city of Dallas. The sprawling town contained more than 400 million prairie dogs! These prairie dogs were all members of one species, or single kind, of organism.[1] A **species** (SPEE sheez) is a group of organisms that are physically similar and can reproduce with each other to produce fertile offspring.

All the members of one species in a particular area are referred to as a **population**. The 400 million prairie dogs in the Texas town are one example of a population. All the pigeons in New York City make up a population, as do all the daisies in a field. In contrast, all the trees in a forest do not make up a population, because they do not all belong to the same species. There may be pines, maples, birches, and many other tree species in the forest.

The area in which a population lives can be as small as a single blade of grass or as large as the whole planet.

Figure 1
A single organism

Figure 2
A population

1. **organism** (ôr´ gə niz´ əm) *n.* living thing.

Scientists studying a type of organism usually limit their study to a population in a defined area. For example, they might study the population of bluegill fish in a pond, or the population of alligators in the Florida Everglades.

Some populations, however, do not stay in a contained area. For example, to study the population of finback whales, a scientist might need to use the entire ocean.

☑ **CHECKPOINT** ***What is the difference between a species and a population?***

Communities

Of course, most ecosystems contain more than one type of organism. The prairie, for instance, includes prairie dogs, hawks, grasses, badgers, and snakes, along with many other organisms. All the different populations that live together in an area make up a **community**.

The smallest unit of organization is a single **organism** *(figure 1)*. The organism belongs to a **population** of other members of its species *(figure 2)*. The population belongs to a **community** of different species *(figure 3)*. The community and abiotic[2] factors together form an **ecosystem** *(figure 4)*.

To be considered a community, the different populations must live close enough together to interact. One way the populations in a community may interact is by

Figure 3
A community

◆ Stop to Reflect

What is the purpose of the Checkpoint question?

____

____

____

____

◆ Reading Strategy

If you were **outlining** this textbook section, what would your two main headings be?

1. ______________________

____

2. ______________________

____

2. **abiotic** (ā′ bī ăt′ ik) *adj.* nonliving.

Reading Informational Materials

Many **textbooks** contain photographs, charts, or illustrations. What four important concepts are illustrated by the drawings on these pages?

1. ______________

2. ______________

3. ______________

4. ______________

How do the drawings help you as a reader?

____

____

____

____

____

____

using the same resources, such as food and shelter. For example, the tunnels dug by the prairie dogs also serve as homes for burrowing owls and black-footed ferrets. The prairie dogs share the grass with other animals. Meanwhile, prairie dogs themselves serve as food for many species.

☑ **CHECKPOINT** ***What is a community? How is it different from an ecosystem?***

Figure 4
An ecosystem

RESEARCH REPORTS

About Research Reports

A **research report** presents facts about a subject. People use research reports for many reasons. A new parent might turn to research to learn about raising children. As a student, you might use a research report to learn about an interesting subject. Most research reports have the following characteristics:

- a well-defined topic
- a clear organization
- information from a variety of sources
- facts and details supporting each main point

Reading Strategy

Asking Questions

To understand a research report better, **ask questions** *before*, *while*, and *after* you read:

Before you read, you may not know much about the subject. Ask general questions, such as, "What types of sharks are there?"

While you read, ask questions about the information the author is presenting. If the author has just claimed that sharks should fear people, you might reasonably ask, "Why is that?" These questions can usually be answered by reading further.

After you read, ask, "What did I just learn?" and "What more do I still want to know?" For the first question, go back to the reading material. For the second question, choose another book or article on the subject to find out more. Use the Works Cited list or the Bibliography to find additional resources.

Research Phase	General Questions You Can Ask
Before you read . . .	What do I already know about the subject? What would I like to learn?
While you read . . .	What is the author's main point? How does the author support the main point?
After you read . . .	What new information did I learn? Do I agree with the author's conclusions? Do I have additional questions?

BUILD UNDERSTANDING

Knowing these words will help you read this research report.

predator (pred´ ə tər) *n.* an animal that kills and eats other animals

fin (fin) *n.* winglike part of the body of a fish used for swimming, turning, and balancing

SHARKS

Susan McGrath

They're big, they're ugly, they're vicious, and the only good one is a dead one. That's what some people say about sharks. Is their bad reputation based on truth? "No!" say the experts. But is time running out for sharks?

The blue shark looks like any typical shark: streamlined, powerful, bluish gray—more fighter jet than fish. But shark experts are quick to tell you that, among the 370 species of sharks, there simply *isn't* a "typical" shark (Springer 52–53).

A whale shark is as long as a school bus, while a cigar shark would fit neatly in a pencil case. A frilled shark looks like an eel with a lacy collar. A Pacific angel shark is as flat as a pancake. And the megamouth shark's gums glow in the dark.

Not mindless monsters, sharks are more intelligent than once thought (Allen, *Shadows* 24). They possess highly developed senses, also (Parker 90–91). And a chemical compound that seems to help sharks fight off infections may someday help doctors treat humans (Springer 90).

As for their killer reputation, very few shark species attack humans, and then only under certain conditions (Taylor 50–51). Sharks have more reason to be afraid of people than the reverse. Surprised? Just look at the numbers. Sharks kill between five and ten people a year (Allen, *Almanac* 44–46). People kill more than 100 *million* sharks a year (Perrine 17). Placed snout-to-tail-fins, that many sharks would circle the Earth five times. So many sharks have been killed that scientists fear some species may be wiped out.

Why are sharks on the hit list? They are fished for food—shark steak has taken the place of more expensive tuna and swordfish on many menus (Perrine

◆ Reading Strategy

Circle two **questions** that the author asks in the opening paragraph. Look for answers to these questions as you read.

◆ Reading Check

How many species of sharks are there?

____

Name two species that the author mentions.

1. ______________________
2. ______________________

◆ Reading Strategy

Read the bracketed paragraph. In your own words, answer the two **questions** the author asks at the beginning of the article.

1. ______________________

____

2. ______________________

____

144–148). Also, in a cruel practice called "finning," sharks are hooked; their fins are sliced off; and the animals are tossed back into the sea to die. The sail-shaped fins are used to make shark-fin soup (Allen 240). Other sharks are killed after being trapped in nets intended for other fish (*Reader's* 133–134).

When you figure that many sharks don't breed until they are more than 12 years old and that only about half of all sharks born survive (Allen, *Shadows* 17–23), you can see how overfishing could eventually threaten sharks with extinction.

The oceans would be a very different place without sharks. As predators at the top of the oceans' food chain, large sharks play an important role in keeping the population of other species in check. Part of their job is to weed out weak and injured animals, leaving the healthiest to reproduce.

Concerned scientists are working with government officials to put reasonable limits on shark fishing (Taylor 35). If they succeed, sharks will survive and maintain a useful place in the oceans of the world.

Works Cited

Allen, Thomas B. *Shadows in the Sea.* New York: Lyons & Burford Publishers, 1996.

The Shark Almanac. New York: The Lyons Press, 1999.

Parker, Steve and Jane. *The Encyclopedia of Sharks.* Buffalo, NY: Firefly Books, 1999.

Perrine, Doug. *Sharks.* Stillwater, MN: Voyageur Press, Inc., 1995.

Reader's Digest Explores Sharks. Pleasantville, NY: Reader's Digest, 1998.

Sharks, Silent Hunters of the Deep. Pleasantville, NY: Reader's Digest, 1986-1995.

Springer, Victor G., and Joy P. Gold. *Sharks in Question: The Smithsonian Answer Book.* Washington, DC: Smithsonian Institution Press, 1989.

Taylor, Leighton, ed. *Sharks and Rays: The Nature Company Guides.* New York: Time-Life Books. 1997.

◆ Stop to Reflect

Have your feelings about sharks changed since you began reading this article? ____________

Explain.

____

____

____

____

Reading Informational Materials

Mark the Text

At the end of a **research report**, the author lists his or her sources of information. These sources are also cited, or referred to, in the body of the report. Circle three places where the author cites a source.

Why do you think page numbers are included in the citations?

____

____

____

READING INFORMATIONAL MATERIALS

NEWSPAPER FEATURE ARTICLES

About Newspaper Feature Articles

Most newspaper articles are about very recent events. However, articles about issues of current *interest* may or may not be on current *events*. These are called **feature articles**. The list shows a few types of feature articles you will find in newspapers.

At the time this article was written, Angel Island had recently been declared a National Landmark. This event stirred public interest in the topic of the article.

A Few Types of Feature Articles

- Historical articles on the anniversary of an event
- Articles on education at the beginning of a school year
- Biographical articles on a famous person's birthday

Reading Strategy

Making Assertions About the Text

An **assertion** is a statement of opinion. When you make an assertion about a text, you give an opinion. For example, when you say "The article was interesting," you are making an assertion. However, the statement "The article contains details, statistics, and quotations" is a statement of fact. It is not an assertion. When you make an assertion about a text, you should be prepared to support it with evidence from the text.

BUILD UNDERSTANDING

Knowing these words will help you read this feature article.

immigrant (im´ ə grənt) *n.* person who comes into a new country to settle there

Ellis (el´ is) **Island** *n.* small island in New York Bay on which an immigration station was located

barracks (bar´ əks) *n.* usually, buildings for housing soldiers. Here, temporary housing for groups of people

from Chinese Immigrants Remember Detention at Angel Island

By Esther Wu
The Dallas Morning News,
May 19, 2000

ANGEL ISLAND, Calif. Dale Ching was a teenager in 1937 when he rode on a steamer bound for America from China. For 22 days, he dreamed about San Francisco, fortified by the knowledge that his father was waiting for him there.

But when his boat docked in San Francisco's bay, he didn't see his father. Instead, his welcoming committee was a group of armed guards who ordered him and other Chinese immigrants to board a boat bound for Angel Island, where he was detained.

Ching was one of 175,000 Chinese immigrants who entered this country between 1910 and 1940 through the Angel Island Immigration Station, often called the Ellis Island of the West. They came to escape war and famine in their homeland. But once in America, they were subjected to interrogations,[1] and some were held for as long as three to four years.

"Life here was harsh," Ching said recently during a tour of the immigration station.

"When we landed at Angel Island, the guards took away our suitcases. We were allowed the clothes we had on and one change of underwear."

Days after he arrived on the island, Ching learned that he could not leave because his description of his family's house in China did not match what his uncle had told immigration authorities. Officials, suspicious of

◆ **Reading Feature Articles**

What is the subject of this **feature article**?

How can you tell?

◆ **Reading Check**

In which newspaper was this article originally printed?

When was it published?

◆ **Stop to Reflect**

Why do you think Angel Island is often called "the Ellis Island of the West"?

◆ **Reading Strategy**

Mark the Text In the bracketed paragraphs, circle one **assertion** and underline one fact.

1. **interrogations** (in ter´ ə gā´ shənz) *n.* questioning sessions.

immigrants entering the United States using false identity papers, detained Ching for three months before his father successfully petitioned officials for his release.

While immigrants coming to America through Ellis Island were welcomed by the Statue of Liberty, Chinese immigrants here had no such symbol, and many felt the sting of scorn and discrimination.

"The stories of Angel Island are not as welcoming, obviously, as it is on the East Coast," said Nick Franco, Angel Island park superintendent. "But it is still a symbolic place, and the stories need to be preserved. It's uncomfortable, but that's all the more why they need to be told."

Today, visitors to the island can experience the immigrants' despair in poems written and carved on barracks walls. More than 135 poems from the barracks have been recorded, most undated and unsigned.

Some voice resentment at being confined and bitterness over the political process that imprisoned the immigrants on the island. Most simply record a writer's anguish. Others reflect on being homesick and longing for freedom.

Some of the immigrants' despair can be traced to the early history of Chinese immigration to this country.

Long before the Angel Island Immigration Station was opened in 1910, officials tried to stem the flow of Chinese immigration to America.

The Chinese Exclusion Act of 1882 barred immigration of Chinese laborers to the United States and prohibited Chinese immigrants from becoming naturalized U.S. citizens. The National Origins Act of 1924 banned all Chinese from coming to America but was later amended to allow a small number, determined by the number of immigrants already in the United States.

The Exclusion Act was the first and only time the United States restricted immigration by ethnicity.[2] It was not repealed[3] until 1943, when China was a U.S.

2. **ethnicity** (eth nis´ ə tē) *n.* cultural background.
3. **repealed** (ri pēld´) *v.* cancelled.

◆ **Reading Feature Articles**

Feature articles often contain quotations that give individual viewpoints or expert opinions. Read the bracketed paragraph. Does this quotation express an individual viewpoint, an expert opinion, or both?

____

Explain.

____

____

____

____

◆ **Reading Check**

What was the purpose of the Chinese Exclusion Act of 1882?

____

____

____

____

ally in World War II, and Congress established a set quota of 105 Chinese immigrants into the country annually. The quota system was banned in 1965.

Outcry for Preservation

Angel Island, in the western part of San Francisco Bay a few miles beyond the Golden Gate Bridge and Alcatraz, served as a military base as early as the Civil War. The base was active during World War II, when the threat of a West Coast invasion by the Japanese was a possibility. After the war, however, the hilly island was deserted and became covered with lush vegetation.

U.S. officials closed the island's immigration station in 1940 after a fire destroyed the administration building. And in 1962, the abandoned island was given to California's state park system. The barracks were about to be demolished in 1970 when a park ranger discovered the poems on the walls.

Public outcry persuaded state officials to preserve what was left of the immigration station, and it became a National Historic Landmark in 1997. Last year, the National Trust named it one of 11 endangered historic sites.

In March, Californians approved a $15 million bond issue that will help restore some of the buildings and preserve the writings. Preliminary renovation studies are being done, and work may start as early as 2001 and take as long as eight years to complete.

What's left of the immigration station is basically the hospital and barracks. What remained of a two-story administration building, kitchen and dining hall has been demolished.

A few small houses that were once used as officers' private quarters have been refurbished as offices for park officials.

Public tours have been conducted since 1982, and schoolchildren take field trips here. Groups often come to boat, hike or camp overnight. An estimated 200,000 people visit the island each year.

◆ Reading a Feature Article

Why is "Outcry for Preservation" set in bolder type than the rest of the **article**?

____

____

◆ Stop to Reflect

Why is Angel Island being preserved?

____

____

____

Reading Informational Materials

This **feature article** begins with the story of a real person. What do you think the writer accomplishes by taking this approach?

____

____

____

____

READING INFORMATIONAL MATERIALS

HOW-TO ESSAYS

About How-to Essays

A **how-to essay** describes a step-by-step process for completing a task. How-to essays teach you how to do or make something new, how to improve a skill, or how to achieve a desired result.

Most how-to-essays include the following:

- a result that the reader can accomplish by following the directions
- a list of the materials needed
- a series of steps explained in logical order
- details that tell when, how much, how often, or to what extent

Reading Strategy

Identifying Cause-and-Effect Relationships

When a baseball hits a glass window, the glass breaks. This is an example of a simple **cause-and-effect relationship**. The ball hitting the window is the cause, or reason. The glass breaking is the effect, or result.

In a how-to essay, each step is a cause that results in an effect. In the following example, the fold is the cause, the legs are the effect.

Example: Fold the long bubble over again and twist against the two new bubbles (another locking twist). Now you have two front legs.

As you read, identify the cause-and-effect relationships in "Twist and Shout."

BUILD UNDERSTANDING

Knowing these words will help you read this how-to essay.

uninflated (un in flāt´ əd) *adj.* not filled with air

critter (krit´ ər) *n.* creature

hind (hīnd) *adj.* back, rear

Twist and Shout

K. Wayne Wincey

A pinch here, a twist there, and you've made a balloon animal! Creating balloon animals is easy. All you need is a bag of balloons and the desire to have some fun. You can usually master the basics in about a week.

The best part of balloon twisting is that most animal sculptures follow the same 10-step order: nose, ear, ear, neck, leg, leg, body, leg, leg, and tail. What varies is the size of the bubbles and the amount of uninflated balloon (tail) that you start with.

Supplies are cheap. A gross of animal balloons, that's 144 of 'em, costs about $10. Find the balloons (also called 260's, twisties, or pencil balloons) at party supply stores or magic shops. While there, consider paying about $4 for a palm pump that helps blow up the balloons. (It'll save time and heavy breathing.)

Start with an easy balloon animal, like a dog. Experiment a little, and you'll soon have a whole zoo of critters!

1. Blow up a balloon, leaving about three inches uninflated. This is called the tail; the open end is the nozzle. Tie off the nozzle in an overhand knot. Note: The more twists in your sculpture, the more uninflated the balloon must be.

◆ Reading How-to Essays

What task can you complete by following the instructions in this **how-to essay**?

____

____

◆ Reading Check

What materials are necessary if you want to make balloon animals?

____

What equipment is useful but not necessary?

____

◆ Stop to Reflect

Why does the author divide the essay into numbered steps instead of using paragraphs?

____

____

2. Using your thumb and forefinger, pinch or squeeze off three inches of the balloon from the nozzle for the dog's nose. Twist the body of the balloon around at least three times. Don't worry about pops—they happen, but not often with this type of balloon.
3. Pinch off another three inches of balloon and twist. This will be one ear of your dog.
4. Fold the first two bubbles against the rest of the balloon. Squeeze the long segment against the twist of the two shorter segments. Keep a firm grip on all the bubbles at this point or they'll come undone. Twist the long bubble and the two short bubbles together. Now your critter has two ears and a nose.
5. Pinch off and twist three more inches for the neck, followed by three additional inches for one front leg.
6. Fold the long bubble over again and twist against the two new bubbles (another locking twist). Now you have two front legs.
7. Another three inches and a twist gives your dog a body. Squeeze and twist off three more.
8. Now give your canine[1] one last locking twist with the rest of the balloon. You've got two hind legs, a tail, and finally, a dog!

◆ Reading Strategy

The writer tells you what the **effect** will be if you don't complete Step 4 correctly. Circle the effect.

Mark the Text

Reading Informational Materials

Explain why it is important to complete the steps in the order in which they are presented in a **how-to essay**.

1. **canine** (kā′ nīn) *n.* dog.

READING INFORMATIONAL MATERIALS

LITERARY BACKGROUNDS

About Literary Backgrounds

A **literary background** sometimes appears in the introduction to a book. It gives information about the author, the setting, or the time when the book was written.

Reading Strategy

Taking Notes

Taking notes is one of the best ways to remember what you have read. There are many note-taking methods:

- To create an **outline**, break down the information into main points. Then list supporting details. The outline shown gives you the basic structure you can use to take notes on almost any topic.
- **Highlighting a photocopy** is also an effective note-taking tool. After highlighting sentences that state main ideas, you can underline or circle supporting details.
- Another way to take notes is to summarize. **Summaries** are created by stating in your own words the main ideas and major details of what you have read.

Outline

1. Sentence about first main idea
- Sentence or phrase about major detail
  Words and phrases related to supporting details
- Sentence or phrase about major detail
  Words and phrases related to supporting details

2. Sentence about second main idea
- Sentence or phrase about major detail
- Sentence or phrase about major detail

BUILD UNDERSTANDING

Knowing these words will help you read this literary background.

Shakespeare (shāk´spir), William (1564–1616). English poet and writer of plays such as *The Tragedy of Romeo and Juliet*

Elizabethan (ē liz´ə bē´thən) *adj.* having to do with the time when Elizabeth I was queen of England (1558–1603)

Shakespeare's London

Anna Claibourne and Rebecca Treays

Shakespeare's poem "The Fairies' Lullaby" comes from his play A Midsummer Night's Dream. *In Shakespeare's time, most people believed that fairies and goblins lived among the humans. The following background gives more information about the times in which Shakespeare lived.*

"All the World's a Stage"

The world Shakespeare knew was full of danger, excitement and change. Elizabethan London was filthy, crowded, crime-ridden, hazardous, thrilling and inspiring. The theatres, situated in the seedier parts of town, were among the most popular places of entertainment, and the best plays to see were Shakespeare's. . . .

By the early 1590s, Shakespeare had arrived in London, England's capital city. It was a thriving port with an expanding population. His first impressions would have been of teeming crowds, the squalor of poverty, and

◆ **Reading Literary Backgrounds**

Literary backgrounds sometimes include photos or pictures. How can a picture, like this one, help to improve your understanding of a work?

____

____

____

◆ **Reading Strategy**

Take notes on the first paragraph by using the outline form. First, write the main idea of the paragraph.

____

____

Then, list two major details in the paragraph.

1. __________________

____

2. __________________

____

the extravagance of the wealthy. Although none of Shakespeare's plays is set wholly in London, the city must have had a great influence on him. He would have attended lectures on new scientific discoveries, discussed the latest trends in playwriting, listened to tales of foreign lands from merchants and enjoyed the lively night life.

"From Tower to Temple"

The City of London was said to stretch "from Tower to Temple"—from the Tower of London in the east, to the Temple Bar (the buildings where young men trained to be lawyers) about a mile away in the west. It was bordered to the north by a wall about two miles long, and to the south by the River Thames. Beyond these boundaries were London's suburbs, areas outside the strict control of the City authorities.

There was no shortage of entertainment in London. Apart from the attractions of inns and taverns, cock-fighting and bear-baiting were popular sports, and many people enjoyed watching public beatings and executions.

Plague

Crowded conditions and poor sanitation made London an ideal breeding ground for plague, a fatal disease carried by fleas on rats. In 1592-4, 1603-4 and 1623 London was devastated by the disease. Over 100,000 people died.

◆ Reading Literary Backgrounds

The subheadings in a **literary background** give clues about the information that will appear in the paragraphs that follow. What information do you think you will find under the subheading "Plague"?

____

____

____

Reading Informational Materials

Why is it helpful to read a **literary background** before reading a work of literature?

____

____

____

____

READING INFORMATIONAL MATERIALS

COMPARISON-AND-CONTRAST ARTICLES

About Comparison-and-Contrast Articles

In a **comparison-and-contrast article,** a writer looks at ways in which two things are the same and ways in which they are different. For example, a comparison-and-contrast article in a newspaper might feature the similarities or differences in the policies of two presidential candidates. Comparison-and-contrast articles include

- two or more items that are similar or different in some ways
- organized presentations that show the similarities and differences

Reading Strategy

Identifying Main Points

The **main points** of a comparison-and-contrast article are the similarities and differences of two or more things. Identifying the main points helps you to understand the information in the article. In "More Than a Pinch: Two Salt Lakes," the first main point is a similarity—the Dead Sea and the Great Salt Lake both have very high percentages of salt. Identify each main point as you read, and record the similarities and differences in a Venn diagram.

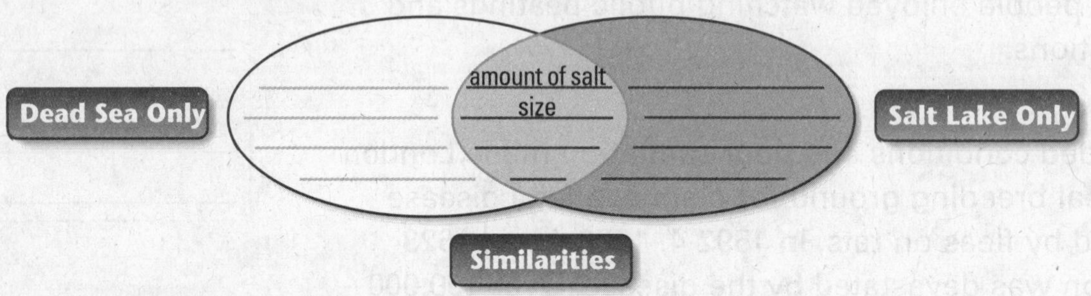

BUILD UNDERSTANDING

Knowing these words will help you read this comparison-and-contrast article.

seabed (sē´ bed) *n.* ocean floor, especially areas with rich mineral or oil deposits

upheaval (up hē´ vəl) *n.* a sudden or violent uplifting, as of part of the earth's crust by an earthquake

More Than a Pinch: Two Salt Lakes

Douglas Armine

At 1300 feet below sea level, the Dead Sea is the lowest body of water on Earth.

Holidaymakers on a first visit to the Dead Sea are invariably in for a surprise: those who enjoy swimming underwater in town pools at home have great difficulty in just staying below the surface. This is because the Dead Sea contains 25 to 30 percent salt, compared to 4 to 6 percent in ocean water. Similar readings have been recorded at Utah's Great Salt Lake in the United States, where it is equally difficult to sink.

The two salt lakes have very different histories. The spectacular trench occupied by the Dead Sea and the Jordan River, which flows into it, was created some 26 million years ago by an upheaval on the seabed at a time when the Mediterranean covered the Holy Land. At 1300 feet below sea level, the Dead Sea is the lowest body of water on Earth.

◆ Reading Comparison-and-Contrast Articles

Many **articles** feature photographs that illustrate the topic. What do you notice about the woman in this picture that is unusual?

◆ Reading Check

Why do swimmers in the Dead Sea have difficulty staying below the surface?

◆ Reading Strategy

In the first paragraph, **identify a main point** about the two bodies of water, and underline it in the text. Then, explain the similarity or difference.

The Great Salt Lake is of more recent origin, being the remnant of the glacial Lake Bonneville which came into existence 18,000 to 25,000 years ago. Having shrunk, through evaporation, to one-twentieth of its original size, it now, like the Dead Sea, has no outlet. But rivers still feed the lake, bearing minerals dissolved from surrounding rocks. As the water evaporates, the minerals remain—66 million tons of them, including magnesium, lithium, boron, and potash.

Salt lakes are conventionally seen as barren, because they support no fish, but the Dead Sea is not completely dead: certain algae and bacteria are adapted to its salt-rich environment. The Great Salt Lake, too, has its single-cell organisms, most noticeably the algae that color the northern part of the lake pink. There are also larger life forms: brine shrimps and flies, whose larvae develop in the water. The shrimps are eaten by gulls, and shrimp eggs are harvested for sale as tropical fish food.

This business is miniscule compared to trade in the lake's great mineral wealth, such as the valuable potash used for fertilizer. The Dead Sea also yields potash, and the Israelis run health spas where tourists can coat themselves in rich, black mineral mud.

◆ **Stop to Reflect**

Based on the information in the bracketed paragraph, how do you think the Dead Sea earned its name?

____

____

Reading Informational Materials

In this **comparison-and-contrast** article the writer applies each main point to both of his subjects. Do you think this point-by-point organization is a good way to show similarities and differences?

____

Explain.

____

____

____

About Comparison-and-Contrast Articles

In a **comparison-and-contrast article,** the writer points out similarities and differences. There are two common organizations for such writing.

- In the **block** method, all the details about one subject are presented. Then, all the details about the next subject are presented.
- In the **point-by-point** method, one point about all the subjects is presented. Then, another point about all the subjects is presented.

Reading Strategy

Analyzing Compare-and-Contrast Text

In the following magazine article, the writer uses comparison and contrast to describe two men who raced each other to the South Pole. When reading materials that make comparisons and contrasts, read critically. **Analyze** the information by breaking it down into categories. Then, ask yourself the following questions:

1. Are the same categories covered for each half of the comparison?
2. Is the same number of details in each category supplied for each half of the comparison?

Finally, decide if the writer supports statements that compare and contrast with examples and facts.

BUILD UNDERSTANDING

Knowing these words will help you read this article.

South Pole *n.* the southernmost point on Earth

expedition (eks´ pə dish´ ən) *n.* a journey for some definite purpose

Race to the End of the Earth

William G. Scheller

Two explorers competed against each other and a brutal environment to reach the South Pole.

The drifts were so deep and the snow was falling so heavily that the team of five Norwegian explorers could hardly see their sled dogs a few feet ahead of them. Behind rose a monstrous mountain barrier. The men had been the first to cross it. But now they and their dogs were stumbling toward a stark[1] and desolate[2] plateau continually blasted by blizzards. The landscape was broken only by the towering peaks of mountains that lay buried beneath a mile of ancient ice. Led by Roald Amundsen, the men were still 300 miles from their goal: the South Pole.

On that same day, a party of 14 British explorers was also struggling across a similarly terrifying landscape toward the same destination. But they were almost twice as far from success. Their commander was Capt. Robert Falcon Scott, a naval officer. Amundsen was Scott's rival.

Exploration Preparation Both expedition leaders had long been preparing for their race to the South Pole. Amundsen came from a family of hardy sailors, and he had decided at the age of 15 to become a polar explorer. He conditioned himself by taking long ski trips across the Norwegian countryside and by sleeping with his windows open in winter.

By the time of his South Pole attempt, Amundsen was an experienced explorer. He had sailed as a naval officer on an expedition in 1897 that charted sections of the Antarctic coast. Between 1903 and 1906 he

1. **stark** (stärk) *adj.* harsh and empty.
2. **desolate** (des´ ə lit) *adj.* lonely.

◆ **Reading Strategy**

What will the author **compare and contrast** in this article?

____

____

◆ **Reading an Article**

Information in this **article** is organized under four headings. How does this organization help readers?

____

____

____

commanded the ship that made the first voyage through the Northwest Passage, the icy route that threads its way through the Canadian islands separating the Atlantic and Pacific Oceans. During that long journey Amundsen learned how the native people of the Arctic dress and eat to survive in extreme cold. He also learned that the dogsled was the most efficient method of polar transportation. These lessons would serve him well at Earth's frozen southern end.

Robert Scott was an officer in the British Navy. He had decided that leading a daring expedition of discovery would be an immediate route to higher rank. He heard that Great Britain's Royal Geographical Society was organizing such an exploration, and he volunteered in 1899 to be its commander. Now he was in command again.

The two expedition leaders had different styles. Scott followed a British tradition of brave sacrifice. He felt that he and his men should be able to reach the South Pole with as little help as possible from sled dogs and special equipment. He did bring dogs to Antarctica, as well as 19 ponies and three gasoline-powered sledges, or sturdy sleds. But his plan was for his team to "man-haul," or carry, all of their own supplies along the final portion of the route.

Scott's ill-fated team

◆ Reading Check

Mark the Text What did Amundsen learn on his voyage through the Northwest Passage? Circle the sentences that contain the answer.

◆ Reading Strategy

Compare and contrast the two men. Why did Amundsen become an explorer?

____

____

____

Why did Scott become an explorer?

____

____

____

Roald Amundsen had spent much time in the far north, and he was a practical man. He'd seen how useful dogs were to Arctic inhabitants. He would be traveling in one of the most dangerous places on Earth, and he knew that sled dogs would be able to get his party all the way to the South Pole and make a safe return. Amundsen also placed great faith in skis, which he and his Norwegian team members had used since childhood. The British explorers had rarely used skis before this expedition and did not understand their great value.

The two leaders even had different ideas about diet. Scott's men would rely on canned meat. But Amundsen's plan made more sense. He and his men would eat plenty of fresh seal meat. Amundsen may not have fully understood the importance of vitamins, but fresh meat is a better source of vitamin C, which prevents scurvy, a painful and sometimes deadly disease.

The Race Is On! After making long sea voyages from Europe, Scott and Amundsen set up base camps in January on opposite edges of the Ross Ice Shelf. Each team spent the dark winter months making preparations to push on to the Pole when spring would arrive in Antarctica. Amundsen left base camp on October 20, 1911, with a party of four. Scott, accompanied by nine men, set off from his camp 11 days later. Four others had already gone ahead on the motorized sledges.

Scott's Final Diary Entry Things went wrong for Scott from the beginning. The sledges broke down and had to be abandoned. Scott and his men soon met up with the drivers, who were traveling on foot. Blizzards then struck and lasted several weeks into December. Scott's ponies were proving to be a poor choice for Antarctic travel as well. Their hooves sank deep into the snow, and their perspiration froze on their bodies, forming sheets of ice. (Dogs do not perspire; they pant.) On December 9, the men shot the last of the surviving

◆ Stop to Reflect

Think about what you have learned about each man's background and plans for the trip. Which man do you think was better prepared to lead an expedition to the South Pole?

Explain.

◆ Reading Strategy

Compare and contrast Amundsen's departure from base camp with Scott's. Who left first?

Who traveled with a greater number of men?

◆ Reading an Article

What clue does the **article's** underlined heading give you about the outcome of Scott's expedition?